Advance Praise for

Constructing Motherhood and Daughterhood Across the Lifespan

"In this volume, editors Allison M. Alford and Michelle Miller-Day and the chapter authors explore communication and negotiation of mother-daughter dyads in a breadth of family types and across all points in the lifespan. This insightful array of chapters points to the centrality of daughters and mothers in the network of primary and external family relationships and the different challenges of family identity and enactment from parenting, to navigating change, to later years as families, and often daughters, provide care for family members. Editors Alford and Miller-Day share a goal of stimulating courses focused on the topic and end the volume with practical resources as a starting point. Whether adopting the book for a whole course or a specialization within a family course, this collection will be a treasure for students, scholars, and practitioners."

Dawn O. Braithewaite, Ph.D., Willa Cather Professor of Communication Studies and Chair, University of Nebraska-Lincoln

"This trailblazing book is unparalleled on the current market. This highly accessible compilation deftly translates cutting-edge research on mother-daughter communication for the undergraduate and graduate classroom. The inquiry-based format of the imminently readable chapters invites students into researchers' processes of discovery and meaning-making. Moreover, this volume pedagogically advances the communication discipline. Based on fifteen years of teaching experience, the final chapter provides an invaluable guide for instructors interested in developing their own courses on mother-daughter communication. I heartily recommend this text!"

Elizabeth A. Suter, Director of Graduate Teaching Instructors, University of Denver

"This book offers important insights that illustrate the significance of how mothers and daughters interface with each other. Often, books either emphasize the mothers' points of view or concentrate on the daughters' perspectives in relation to the mothers. This book, crafted by Allison M. Alford and Michelle Miller-Day, gives the reader a different vantage point to understand a complicated relationship between mothers and daughters. The authors advocate for examining motherhood and daughterhood as socially constructed.

"The perspective Alford and Miller-Day ascribe allows fluidity in the way relationships between and among mothers and daughters are defined. Through the element of communication, the authors illustrate the meaning of motherhood and daughterhood across the lifespan.

"To accomplish these goals, the book presents a number of contexts that reflect multiple aspects of change and recalibration of mother-daughter relationships in everyday life. For example, this book helps readers consider outside influences such as the significance of media representation of mothers and daughters and new technologies. Contributors identify life issues such as coping with pregnancy and disabilities, as well as navigating difficult conversations such as sexuality and stages of life.

"Overall, this book is rich with insights that are easily accessible and clear about the way communication functions to yield a better understanding of the mother-daughter relationship. This is a must-read for the general public and for researchers interested in this area of inquiry."

Sandra Petronio, Director, Communication Privacy Management Center;
Senior Affiliate Faculty, Charles Warren Fairbanks Center for Medical Ethics;
Professor, Department of Communication Studies, School of Liberal Arts,
Indiana University – Purdue University, Indianapolis;
National Communication Association Distinguished Scholar

Constructing
Motherhood
AND Daughterhood
Across THE Lifespan

LIFESPAN
COMMUNICATION
Children, Families, and Aging

Thomas J. Socha
GENERAL EDITOR

Vol. 14

The Lifespan Communication series
is part of the Peter Lang Media and Communication list.
Every volume is peer reviewed and meets
the highest quality standards for content and production.

PETER LANG
New York • Bern • Berlin
Brussels • Vienna • Oxford • Warsaw

Constructing
Motherhood
AND Daughterhood
Across THE Lifespan

Allison M. Alford AND
Michelle Miller-Day, EDITORS

PETER LANG
New York • Bern • Berlin
Brussels • Vienna • Oxford • Warsaw

Library of Congress Cataloging-in-Publication Data

Names: Alford, Allison M., editor. | Miller-Day, Michelle, editor.
Title: Constructing motherhood and daughterhood across the lifespan /
edited by Allison M. Alford and Michelle Miller-Day.
Description: New York: Peter Lang, 2019.
Series: Lifespan communication: children, families, and aging; vol. 14
ISSN 2166-6466 (print) | ISSN 2166-6474 (online)
Includes bibliographical references and index.
Identifiers: LCCN 2018055021 | ISBN 978-1-4331-6571-9 (hardback: alk. paper)
ISBN 978-1-4331-4119-5 (paperback: alk. paper) | ISBN 978-1-4331-4120-1 (ebook pdf)
ISBN 978-1-4331-6569-6 (epub) | ISBN 978-1-4331-6570-2 (mobi)
Subjects: LCSH: Parent and child. | Mothers and daughters. | Intergenerational relations.
Classification: LCC HQ755.85 .C6575 2019 | DDC 306.874/3—dc 23
LC record available at https://lccn.loc.gov/2018055021
DOI 10.3726/b10841

Bibliographic information published by **Die Deutsche Nationalbibliothek.**
Die Deutsche Nationalbibliothek lists this publication in the "Deutsche
Nationalbibliografie"; detailed bibliographic data are available
on the Internet at http://dnb.d-nb.de/.

The paper in this book meets the guidelines for permanence and durability
of the Committee on Production Guidelines for Book Longevity
of the Council of Library Resources.

© 2019 Peter Lang Publishing, Inc., New York
29 Broadway, 18th floor, New York, NY 10006
www.peterlang.com

Printed in the United States of America

We dedicate this book to amazing women everywhere:
May we know them,
May we be them,
May we raise them,
May we care for them.

In honor of Allison's mom, Pamela Sparkman McGuire, who showed us that,
In all seasons, her love for us will flourish.

In memory of Michelle's late mother, Donna Miller Hodan,
She left fingerprints of grace on her daughters' lives.

Probably there is nothing in human nature more resonant with charges than the flow of energy between two biologically alike bodies, one of which has lain in amniotic bliss inside the other, one of which has labored to give birth to the other. The materials are here for the deepest mutuality and the most painful estrangement.

—Rich (1976, p. 226)

REFERENCE

Rich, A. (1976). Of woman born: Motherhood as experience and institution. New York, NY: Norton.

Table of Contents

Tables AND Figure

TABLES

FIGURE

Preface from THE Series Editor

THOMAS J. SOCHA
Old Dominion University

In *Constructing Motherhood and Daughterhood Across the Lifespan*, Allison M. Alford and Michelle Miller-Day elegantly remind us that all communication is developmental and unfolds across the entire human lifespan. As a developmental and lifespan phenomenon, each and every communication transaction builds upon what has come before in order to create what is to come. In the unfolding narratives of mothers and daughters, like all family relationships, the heart and soul of "family" lives, literally, in the stories of our lives. In particular, Alford and Miller-Day's volume sends a clarion call that in the course of human history mother-daughter narratives are a primary, central, and powerful force in human development. They and their team of accomplished authors have assembled a most excellent overview of the various aspects of this important genre of family discourse. Peter Lang's *Lifespan Communication: Children, Families and Aging* series seeks to illuminate significant aspects of human communication development, and certainly mother-daughter communication is among life's most significant aspects of communication. To understand human development and to empower families, the discourses of all of society's primary forces is needed. The volume is a must-read for those in family communication, family studies, women's studies, gender studies, as well as human psychological, sociological, and communicative development. Like all volumes in this series, and indeed all the volumes published by Peter Lang Publishing, this volume showcases world-class scholars sharing cutting-edge scholarly work for the benefit of us all.

Acknowledgments

We would like to acknowledge the carefully cultivated contributions from our many authors and the participants in their research that made this manuscript possible.

Thanks to our respective departments for generously supporting the time and travel allocated to this project.

Thank you to Tom Socha for believing in this work and graciously allowing us to join his growing anthology. We are honored that our work is available alongside the many terrific texts in the *Lifespan* series which highlight the essential features of communication in families.

Thank you to our reviewers who gave critical feedback that surely made this manuscript better.

And thank you to our partners, whose unconditional support provides the platform from which we take big leaps.

The Social Construction OF Motherhood AND Daughterhood

Clever men create themselves, but clever women are created by their mothers. Women can never quite escape their mothers' cosmic pull, not their lip-biting expectations or their faulty love. We want to please our mothers, emulate them, disgrace them, outrage them, and bury ourselves in the mysteries and consolations of their presence. When my mother and I are in the same room we work magic on each other ... It's my belief that between mothers and daughters there is a kind of blood-hyphen that is, finally, indissoluble.

—SHIELDS (1987, P. 127)

REFERENCE

Shields, C. (1987). *Swann*. New York, NY: Viking Press.

CHAPTER ONE

Introduction

ALLISON M. ALFORD* AND MICHELLE MILLER-DAY†

OVERVIEW

The social construction of motherhood has been well-documented for years (e.g., Heisler & Ellis, 2008; Ruddick & Daniels, 1977; Tardy, 2000). Media representations of maternal relationships have constructed an array of complex and contradictory messages about mothering girls, promoting archetypes of "best friends" or "sacrificial mothers" while creating social norms and expectations for how women should enact these roles and perform their relationships (Walters, 1992). Tardy (2000) argues that over time, the construction of motherhood in public and private spheres has led women to feel an exorbitant amount of guilt and blame that can ultimately affect their opportunities and choices. The ideology of motherhood is powerful in shaping the lives of women over the lifespan (Cowdery & Knudson-Martin, 2005).

In contrast to motherhood, there is less research on the social construction of daughterhood (Baruch & Barnett, 1983; Hampton, 1997; Korolczuk, 2010). Daughters are often relegated to a passive, backseat role, while mothers are "semantically overburdened" in their role (Walters, 1992, p. 10), or as van Mens-Verhulst

* Allison M. Alford, clinical assistant professor, Baylor University, allison_alford@baylor.edu.
† Michelle Miller-Day, professor, Chapman University, millerda@chapman.edu.

(1995) describes it, our language is missing a verb: "to daughter" (p. 531). What it means to be a mother or daughter is cobbled together "not only through the exigencies of family life, economic survival, and social policies, but through the systems of representation and cultural production that help give shape and meaning to that relationship" (Walters, 1992, p. 10).

As communication scholars, we believe that mother and daughter identities and roles are socially and communicatively constructed over the life course (Braithwaite, Foster, & Bergen, 2017). Relational connection between mothers and daughters is characterized, above all, by communication (Jordan, 1993). Women describe communication as the prime source of establishing their relational identity with their mother or daughter (Mann, 1998) and it is through "mutually responsive communication that mothers and daughters establish patterns of relational communication that link them to one another, shaping each woman's sense of self" (Miller-Day, 2004, p. 10). Indeed, mothers, daughters, daughters who become mothers, and mothers who become grandmothers are women co-authoring their lives across the life course, co-authoring personal stories within the context of the mother-daughter relationship.

This book will explore what it means to be a mother and daughter across the lifespan in Western society and how both parties navigate, respond to, and negotiate cultural and familial discourses defining motherhood and daughterhood. The book will address the following questions:

- How is motherhood and/or daughterhood socially constructed at different points in the lifespan?
- What master narratives, counter narratives, assumptions, and myths surround talk about motherhood and daughterhood?
- What communication processes are central to the construction of the mother and/or daughter identity and enactment of the mother-daughter relationship?
- What language do mothers and daughters use to describe their identities/roles?
- What are the turning points that mothers and/or daughters experience across the lifespan?
- What is the impact of relational storytelling on mother-adult daughter relationships?
- How can mothers and daughters communicate about health issues?
- What are salient issues surrounding pregnancy, caregiving, and end-of-life experiences for mothers and daughters?
- What are the future directions for conducting lifespan research on motherhood and daughterhood?

BACKGROUND OF THE BOOK

The idea for this book was born out of discussions with a group of mother-daughter communication scholars who recognized the need to answer the above questions. In early 2015, on a whim, Allison reached out to the very best mother-daughter communication scholars whose work she admired, and the group agreed to present a panel on mother-daughter communication scholarship at the 2015 National Communication Association conference in Las Vegas, Nevada. That is where Allison and Michelle finally met in person. We both agreed that the best way to promote this important work and to encourage other educators to lead courses on mother-daughter communication would be to create a compilation of the emerging mother-daughter communication scholarship. Our backgrounds, though different, have led us both to pursue this area of study.

I (Allison) was raised by a mother who became a marriage and family therapist during my adolescence. I like to say that I was raised talking about talking. Indeed, my conversations with my mother have always been about more than facts; we discuss the tone of what was said, the intentions of saying it, and the ramifications of the communication. It took well into my adult years to realize that other mothers and daughters don't dissect their talk in this way. And while my mother and I have an undeniable connection, and in general I tend to focus on the positives, I cannot help but notice that there are days (sometimes months) where we have a B+ relationship at best. That garden won't tend itself; I must work diligently to keep it growing. As a mother of a son and daughter, my studies on relationships have transformed the way I raise my little people. Learning more about social construction, I quickly realized that I must plant messages before the world does, and I must carefully tend to the ideas that I want to take root. Spurred by my love of talk and fascination with relationships, I returned to graduate school with the goal of learning more about these complexities and the desire to share that knowledge in an accessible way. The result is this book.

I (Michelle) am both a mother and a daughter; I have been a stepmother to a stepdaughter; and I am currently the mother of two biological sons. These multiple roles have colored how I view the world and have influenced my scholarship. I first became interested in studying mother-daughter communication when I wrote a play on the topic. To write the play I interviewed more than 100 women about their mother-daughter relationships and the stories that emerged from those interviews provided insight into broader relational processes, highlighting the centrality of communication in managing, maintaining, and repairing relationships across the lifespan. In 2004, I published a book titled *Communication among Grandmothers, Mothers and Adult Daughters: A Qualitative Study of Maternal Relationships* (Miller-Day). I soon discovered that people were hungry for this information. While research on mother-daughter relationships existed in the disciplines of psychology and women's studies, it was virtually non-existent in the discipline of communication. Since that time, I have continued my scholarly interest in the topic of mother-daughter communication; but, it was not until recently that felt—in a visceral way—the importance of the topic. In 2017 my mother passed away and I am now a motherless daughter. I look at what I have written in the past and what I write in this current volume and I can see clearly how much my communication with my mother over the years has created who I am as a person now.

These backgrounds are part of what shaped and molded us into the mothers, daughters, and researchers we are today. The topic is important to mothers, daughters, and anyone who has a female in their life. We are excited to bring you a book that provides insights for readers into salient topics central to understanding mother-daughter communication across the lifespan.

FEATURES OF THIS BOOK

For ease of reading, you will find that all chapters in the book have been organized similarly. Toward the end of every chapter you will find the heading *What does all this mean?* Here the authors have synthesized the materials from the chapter into reader-friendly concepts. Following this, you will see a bulleted list labeled *What do we still need to know?* This section describes future directions that scholars indicate we need to explore. You will also see the bulleted list *How does this work in real life?* which describes application of the ideas in the chapter to relationships in real life. Each chapter ends with a section recommending ideas for *Classroom Activities*, suggesting discussion questions, class activities, and projects to reinforce learning from the chapter. The intention of this volume is to make information accessible and allow readers to put results of scientific research into practice in their everyday lives.

INSIDE THIS BOOK

This book is organized into three parts. The first part, introduces readers to the concept of social constructionism and the social construction of social roles, reviewing literature on the social construction of motherhood, daughterhood, and cultural constructions through media. The second part is the majority of the book and it addresses a number of topics that scholars are currently studying in the area of mother-daughter communication, from pregnancy and maternal identity to end-of-life communication. Finally, the third part of the book is comprised of a single chapter that is intended to equip a course instructor to design and teach a course focusing on mother-daughter communication.

Part One: The Social Construction of Motherhood and Daughterhood

Chapter 2 explores the role of adult daughters in relationship with their mothers. Alford looks at social construction as daughter's work and asks us to think about the value of daughtering to a mother and to society. While motherhood has received the lion's share of attention in our scholarly literature, she asks us to consider where ideas about daughtering come from and explores the nature of daughterhood, or shared daughtering experience. Of note is a discussion of role performance as labor; for example, the emotional, love, mental, and kinkeeping effort that goes into daughter work.

In Chapter 3 motherhood and mothering are discussed from a social constructionist perspective. Frameworks and definitions are provided for motherhood and mothering, questioning the origins of these concepts. Alford describes how roles are communicatively constructed and points us to consider our views on birth mothers, social mothers, and caregiving mothers. In addition, she calls attention to the concept of mothering as valuable work product (labor) and explores how our valuation of mothers' work lays a foundation for the labels we use to discuss it. Mothering styles such as tiger mother, bad mom, and free-range parent are explored, along with a discussion of good enough mothering. As you read, consider if daughtering is parallel to mothering? Can we distinguish between the characteristics of each and is it necessary to do so?

In Chapter 4, you will find a discussion of media representations of mothers and daughters from the 1950's to 2017. Miller-Day, Tukachinsky, and Jacobs explore how media representations help give shape and meaning to the mother-daughter relationship. Media such as television and film provide societal cues for performing the roles of mother and daughter, while also socially constructing ideals. The authors point out that motherhood, daughterhood, mothering, daughtering and their meanings are not fixed nor inevitable. They convince us that seeing a woman outside her role of mother is an important stepping stone in making progress for women who may embrace several identities in their lifetime.

Chapter 5 is the final chapter in this section and it uncovers a variety of relational turning points in the mother-daughter relationship. Miller-Day discusses how memorable events between mothers and daughters over the life course can trigger an increase or decrease of intimacy in the relationship. These memorable moments, or turning points, signal a change in the status quo of the mother-daughter relationship. This chapter takes us through the most common types of relational turning points and provides an in-depth discussion of the role of social support as a turning point. Miller-Day found that both emotional and tangible forms of social support were most likely to serve as a relational turning point for daughters. It is important for both mothers and daughters to remember that social support communication is key to maintaining strong bonds. Daughters feel closer to their mothers when mothers talk with them, listen to them, and are present for them during hardship. Equally, daughters feel closer to mothers when they can reciprocate and provide emotional and tangible support to their mothers.

Part Two: Enacting the Mother-Daughter Relationship over the Lifespan

In Chapter 6, Lawler describes the intersection of pregnancy and disability. She reveals how women with disabilities have constructed a view of self since childhood, particularly incorporating messages from their mothers. Through their support, women with disabilities may create positive disability identities, which incorporate their disability but do not view it as a hindrance to a good life. Later, when she becomes a mother, a woman's view of self can enhance her experience of pregnancy. Though there are many hurdles and communication challenges from those who see her as incapable, a woman with a disability can advocate for herself to be seen as independent and capable, rather than being seen as secondary to her disability. Lawler calls for us to question how we see ourselves and others related to our abilities, especially in relation to mothering.

In Chapter 7, Colaner, Horstman, and Butauski apply critical feminist theory to the topic of adoptive mothers' ritual communication. They describe how family rituals honor past, present, and future, creating a valuable base for families to communicate about events, create family identity, and generate a sense of home. These rituals are particularly valuable for keeping a birth family connected to the life of their biological child who was adopted into another family. The work of rituals serves as relational maintenance, and can often be invisible, so is therefore undervalued for the effort it takes. Done primarily by adoptive mothers, this work, on behalf of an adopted child, is a unique aspect of mothering labor.

Chapter 8 dives deep into the topics of sex and sexuality, describing how these are communicated between mothers and daughters over a life course. Both conversations and silence are key forms of communication in family talk patterns, which is the primary site for sex education. Faulkner and Watson reveal the use of "metaphoric boundaries" in sexual discussions to mitigate risk and embarrassment. Additionally, they urge families to communicate both positive and negative information about sex and sexuality for the best outcomes related to health and healthy relationships. Daughters engaged in open conversations, the authors found, when their mothers offered reciprocal relationships, but remained quiet when there was a family pattern of ignorance, fear, or silence. Additionally, the authors explore how communication about sex may change as both mothers and daughters age. The unique relationship between mothers and daughters makes this an important space for disclosing personal details.

Continuing this discussion of health, Chapter 9 explores how mothers and adolescent daughters communicate about HPV, sexual health, and HPV vaccination.

Human papillomavirus (HPV) is the most common sexually transmitted infection in the U.S. affecting approximately one in four Americans throughout their lifetime. In this chapter Hopfer, Duong, and Garcia provide a thorough review of the research literature and discuss how mother-daughter conversations play an important role in the decision to vaccinate adolescents against this disease. Valuable insights for providers and mothers of adolescents are offered.

Chapter 10 begins the discussion of later adolescence and emerging adulthood. Emerging adults are those entering adulthood and often move away from home for college, a job, or a relationship. If you are a student, we ask you to grab your cell phone and look at your recent calls. When's the last time you phoned mom? Or maybe you texted instead. Meadows and Harrigan discuss the various technological methods daughters use to communicate with their moms. Especially in situations where daughters are geographically distant from their mothers, technology becomes increasingly important. Coupling the many changes occurring in a daughter's life during emerging adulthood with the increased geographic separation requires a renegotiation of communication methods. In order to explore how daughters use technology to communicate with their mothers and share (or conceal) private information, the authors report the results of their study investigating adult daughters' choices when conveying information to their moms. They found that daughters who reported less everyday talk with their mothers had a greater perception of positivity about the mother-daughter relationship and reported less conflict.

Chapter 11 explores the mother-daughter relationship once the daughter is married. As daughters age and experience many changes in life, many will marry and thus experience changes in the relationship with their mother. This chapter examines closeness and distance in the mother-married adult daughter relationship. As daughters age, they experience a tension between having both a friendship and a parent-child relationship with mothers. Miller-Ott discusses the negotiation needed to manage that tension. She found that when mothers try to cross into the "friend zone" with daughters, and share information daughters feel is inappropriate or too friend-like, daughters report more distance. Additionally, after marriage, adult daughters in this study reported concern with mothers' reactions to any shared information about their marriage or family life. Daughters reported being afraid of mothers' unhelpful feedback and the possibility of promoting negative perceptions of their spouse. The chapter addresses the slippery slope of calling our mothers our friends.

Speaking of calling your mom, Miller-Ott and Kelly in Chapter 12 examine the preferred technology for communication between mothers and daughters. Not surprisingly, use of technology can be frustrating and cause some conflict. However, it is also a useful tool to maintain connection. With technological advances, there are many media for mothers and daughters to choose from. In their study, Miller-Ott and Kelly asked both daughters and mothers to report on preferred method of communication and describe the best and worst aspects of communicating via technology. They found that mothers and daughters seem to have a love-hate relationship with using technology to communicate with one other, and these opposing feelings seem to relate to autonomy and connection. Tension arose around perceptions of the benefits of constant contact versus uninhibited access.

In Chapter 13, Kellas, Holman, and Flood detail the many ways storytelling is at the heart of families and the mother-daughter relationship. Families tell stories to socialize one another to the beliefs, values, and norms that come to guide daily life, creating meaning-making maps of their shared relationship terrain. The authors conducted a study exploring meanings, values, and beliefs mothers pass onto their daughters about relationships and love in the stories they tell. Using the backdrop of mother-daughter shared connection and talk, the authors revealed the importance of mothers' messages about love in the lives of their adult daughters.

Continuing along the life course, Chapter 14 explores daughters' perceptions of their full-time working mothers in the United States and South Korea. Harrigan, Hosek, and Yang argue that ideas about motherhood in general and about effective mothering, in particular, are socially constructed through discourse. How daughters make sense of and evaluate their mothers could affect how the daughters enact the role of a mother, when they become mothers. The authors examine the identity construction of working mothers through the talk of their daughters and the role of culture in discussions of mothering. Through original research, the authors show how daughters' talk about their mothers may impact how mothers see themselves. Whether daughters realize it or not, the things they say have an impact on their mothers. Talk about mothering may also impact how daughters behave in the future when they themselves become mothers. Notably, the authors report a great deal of positivity and pride when daughters' talk about their working mothers.

In Chapter 15, Rittenour and Odenweller explore the underbelly of mothering, enumerating the challenges and complexities of this role. Social expectations can sometimes crush mothers in their paths. Many women combat these tensions by cultivating a feminist identity in themselves and their daughters. With this in mind, it is possible to fight against the Mommy Wars that divide mothers and see the underlying causes of the divisiveness. The authors review previous research and discuss how generativity and support networks enhance the experience of mothering.

Chapter 16 explores mother-daughter communication and health, specifically within the experience of breast cancer. Fisher and Wolf discuss a script of responsible womanhood that represents a blend of social discourses that inform family members' expectations of the "right" way for mothers to cope with a breast cancer diagnosis. The authors show that the ways women react to—and fight—breast cancer are tied to greater social expectations of womanhood. Though it may surprise you to learn that even illnesses are subject to gendered ideologies, it is at the heart of breast cancer battles because this disease is so inherently feminine. The authors thoughtfully provide lessons learned from their research and offer potential responses for each.

In Chapter 17, Seurer explores the complexities and subtleties of communicating about mental health within the mother-daughter dyad. The chapter reveals how daughters of mothers with depression come to understand the meaning of depression and subsequently the meaning of motherhood. Through a discussion of struggles found in her study, the author takes a nuanced look at how notions of motherhood intertwine with embedded social ideologies. The author takes a look at ways the problem and the person can be disentangled, creating more supportive family relationships.

Even for those who have lost mothers, the identity of a daughter still beats inside her. In Chapter 18, Miller-Day and Grainger explore what it means to be a motherless daughter. Maternal loss is something experienced by most women as they age and out-live their parents. The authors examine digital messages shared by motherless daughters on Mother's Day. Findings of this study suggest that while daughters post several different kinds of messages to help cope with a difficult holiday for them, the ties that bind mother and daughter are enduring, even past a mother's death.

Though death is a challenging topic to explore, in Chapter 19 the authors allow us a personal view inside the difficult, but necessary, conversations mothers and daughters may have leading up to death. Whereas, in Chapter 20, Keeley, Lee, and Generous take us to the end of a mother's life and explore final conversations (FCs) at the end of life (EOL). In their interviews with adult daughters' who had these FCs with their mothers, the authors found six themes of FCs revealing that, while challenges exist, FCs leave adult daughters with lasting gifts from their departed mothers.

Part Three: Moving Forward to Develop Mother-Daughter Communication Courses

The third part of this book is a single chapter providing a guide for developing a mother-daughter communication course. With course instructors in mind, Miller-Day provides a sample course description, objectives, sample course outlines, weekly topics with accompanying readings from this text, and suggested course assignments.

FUTURE DIRECTIONS

Each of the following chapters has a section titled *What do we still need to know?* These sections point out future directions for research and ideas for future scholars to pursue. These recommendations mirror our own suggestions for future research directions including the need to examine the role of culture and diversity in motherhood and daughterhood, additional attention to the dark side of mother-daughter communication, increased attention to different developmental periods of the mother-daughter relationship across the lifespan, and the need for communication theory and clearly defined measures in mother-daughter communication research.

In soliciting chapters for this book, we approached male and female scholars from a variety of cultural backgrounds, inside the United States and outside, able bodied and disabled, and who study various family forms such as foster families, single-parent families, and blended families. Yet, the chapters in this volume are by and large not highly diverse. Happily, there are several exceptions including Lawler's chapter on disability and pregnancy, and Harrigan, Hosek, and Yang's chapter on discursive constructions of full-time working mothers from both American and South Korean daughters. Yet these authors also point out the need for more multicultural and multinational research attention to examine the role of culture in motherhood and daughterhood. Additionally, diverse perspectives are needed on the variety of family forms that exist, including but not restricted to multigenerational grandmother-mother-daughter relationships, mother-daughter communication in single, blended, and foster family forms.

Much of the mother-daughter communication research that exists tends to presume relational positivity and relational satisfaction between mothers and daughters. Scholars are encouraged to continue these investigations on communication to develop and maintain high levels of mother-daughter relational quality; yet, additional work is sorely needed on the darkside of mother-daughter communication. The research in many of these chapters point out that emotional distance, maternal criticism, conflict, familial obligations and expectations negatively impact relational quality. More research is needed to further examine imbalanced family systems, estranged mother-daughter relationships, and mother-daughter communication as a potential risk factor for negative physical and mental health outcomes. This also requires scholars to examine the darkside of mother-daughter communication across the life course.

There is still a great need to examine mother-daughter communication over the lifespan. As pointed out elsewhere in Socha and Punyanunt-Carter (in press), Miller-Day, Pezalla, and Chesnut (2013), Socha and Yingling (2010), children have occupied a marginal status in the field of human communication studies. We believe that truly taking a lifespan approach involves investigating the communicative experiences of children and adolescents along with emerging adults, mid-life adults, and older adults. This, of course, introduces complications with research ethics but we encourage communication scholars to join our colleagues in psychology, family studies and other disciplines who regularly include children's development in their areas of inquiry. Communication is central to mother-daughter bonding, nurturing, discipline, and socialization, investigating emotional neglect and physical punishment are all issues that can be addressed by communication scholars. While there is growing research on mother-emerging and young adult daughters, research on newly married daughters such as that conducted in the chapter by Miller-Ott is still needed. What is the role mother-daughter communication plays in fertility and pregnancy decisions, decisions to divorce, family system adaptation once a daughter starts her own family, and relational maintenance using technology? Mid-life is a time when daughters and mothers may experience emotional distance and unexpected stress (Miller-Day, 2004). Research efforts are needed to examine how the relationship is recalibrated in mid-life to withstand this stress, especially if mothers are "sandwiched" between the needs of her daughter and her own mother. Lastly, as Faulkner and Watson point out in their chapter, there is a necessity to know more about women's sexuality and sexual health in later life and the role that daughters play in that sphere of her mother's world.

Finally, all future research endeavors would be well served to closely consider the theories guiding mother-daughter communication research and the clarity of definitions used when conducting that research. As Alford points out in her chapter on daughterhood, we have not had the language to describe the relational work conducted by daughters in the mother-daughter relationship until now. Our eyes have previously been focused on motherhood and mothering. It may require formative, qualitative research to explore daughtering more fully before operationalizing this as a construct. Yet, we believe that scholars should look closely at the theories being used to guide mother-daughter communication research or test hypotheses. Are those theories being borrowed from other disciplines? Are family communication and interpersonal communication theories sufficient to explain and predict what occurs in mother-daughter communication or should new theories be developed to extend our knowledge? These are all ideas, recommendations, and hopes for scholars conducting future research in the area of mother-daughter communication. We are excited to see what you can accomplish!

SUMMARY

All told, *Constructing Motherhood and Daughterhood Across the Lifespan* is designed to build upon the publications of a range of scholars doing work in this area. This book takes up where these authors' current published manuscripts leave off, synthesizing this body of work and moving in new directions, and linking this work to theories and concepts central to the understanding of relationships across the lifespan. Moreover, in addition to its focus on the mother-daughter relationship, we are hopeful that this book contributes substantially to an understanding of broad relationship processes. For theorists, therapists, and the rest of us, this theme is of immense significance.

REFERENCES

Baruch, G., & Barnett, R. C. (1983). Adult daughters' relationships with their mothers. *Journal of Marriage and Family, 45*(3), 601–606. Retrieved from http://www.jstor.org/stable/351664

Braithwaite, D. O., Foster, E., & Bergen, K. M. (2017). Social construction theory: Communication co-creating families. In D. O. Braithwaite & L. A. Baxter's (Eds.), *Engaging theories in family communication: Multiple perspectives* (pp. 267–278). Thousand Oaks, CA: Sage.

Cowdery, R. S., & Knudson-Martin, C. (2005). The construction of motherhood: Tasks, relational connection, and gender equality. *Family Relations, 54*(3), 335–345. https://doi.org/10.1111/j.1741-3729.2005. 00321.x

Hampton, M. R. (1997). Adopted women give birth: Connection between women and matrilineal continuity. *Feminism & Psychology, 7*(1), 83–106. https://doi.org/10.1177/0959353597071011

Heisler, J. M., & Ellis, J. B. (2008). Motherhood and the construction of "mommy identity":
Messages about motherhood and face negotiation. *Communication Quarterly, 56*(4), 445–467. doi: 10.1080/01463370802448246

Jordan, J. (1993). The relational self: A model of women's development. In J. van Mens-Verhulst, K. Schreurs, & L. Woertman (Eds.), *Daughtering and mothering: Female subjectivity reanalysed* (pp. 135–144). New York, NY: Routledge.

Korolczuk, E. (2010). The social construction of motherhood and daughterhood in contemporary Poland—a trans-generational perspective. *Polish Sociological Review, 172*(4), 467–485. Retrieved from http://www.jstor.org/stable/41275175

Mann, C. (1998). The impact of working-class mothers on the educational success of their adolescent daughters at a time of social change. *British Journal of Sociology Education, 19*(2), 211–226.

Miller-Day, M. (2004). *Communication among grandmothers, mothers, and adult daughters: A qualitative study of maternal relationships.* Mahwah, NJ: Lawrence Erlbaum.

Miller-Day, M., Pezalla, A., & Chesnut, R. (2013). Children are in families too! The presence of children in communication research. *Journal of Family Communication, 13*(2), 150–165.

Ruddick, S., & Daniels, P. (1977). *Working it out.* New York, NY: Pantheon.

Socha, T. J., & Punyanunt-Carter, N. (Eds.). (in press). *Children's communication sourcebook: Managing legacy and potential.* New York, NY: Peter Lang.

Socha, T. J., & Yingling, J. (2010). *Families communicating with children.* Cambridge, MA: Polity Press.

Tardy, R. W. (2000). "But I am a good mom": The social construction of motherhood through health-care conversations. *Journal of Contemporary Ethnography, 29*(4), 433–473. https://doi.org/10.1177/089124100129023963

van Mens-Verhulst, J. (1995). Reinventing the mother-daughter relationship. *American Journal of Psychotherapy, 49*(4), 526–538. https://doi.org/10.1176/appi.psychotherapy.1995.49.4.526

Walters, S. D. (1992). *Lives together, worlds apart: Mothers and daughters in popular culture.* Berkeley, CA: University of California Press.

CHAPTER TWO

Daughtering AND Daughterhood

Adult Daughters in Communication with Their Mothers

ALLISON M. ALFORD[*]

I recently met my mom for lunch at a favorite spot where we routinely split a burger and the check. We laugh with each other, catch up on happenings in our lives, discuss various family members (such as my kids or my dad) and reconnect. Doesn't that sound idyllic? In addition to these lovely things, I usually fix some settings on her phone, bite my tongue about a strange recommendation she has for my career, probe for medical updates and suggest healthy substitutions, respectfully listen to advice about parenting (it's 50/50 whether I put it into practice), and one or both of us says, "It is so frustrating when you do that to me" or "Let's not get into this today." Sound familiar? Adult daughters have relationships with their mothers that are complex, beautiful, and frustrating; like other close relationships, this one is not immune to difficulties. Despite these convoluted issues, by and large, adult daughters find the relationship with their mothers to be valuable, imbuing it with meaning and sometimes angst. Whether or not you, reader, are an adult daughter, I bet this sounds familiar if you've seen mothers and their adult daughters in action.

The most enjoyable people in our lives require an investment of our time and energy and often require that we make sacrifices to keep the relationship going. Whether it's our romantic partner, friend, child, or boss, we get out of a relationship what we put into it. However, for too long the mother-daughter relationship has

* Allison M. Alford, clinical assistant professor, Baylor University, allison_alford@baylor.edu.

been thought of in two categorically different ways—imagined as either a perfect pair who never argue or as bitter opponents. Do either of these characterizations describe the mother-daughter pairs in your life? It's more likely that the mothers and daughters you're picturing fall somewhere along a continuum between the two extremes of bliss and brokenness. Why don't we see more examples of mother-daughter relationships that fall between the two extremes in contemporary media and scholarship? Although more attention has been paid in recent decades to the mother-adult daughter relationship across a variety of disciplines (e.g., Fingerman, 2001; Fischer, 1986; Fisher, 2010; Miller-Day, 2004; Scharlach, 1987; Schwarz, 2006), it remains an area ripe for further inquiry (Shrier, Tompsett, & Shrier, 2004).

As investigations of the mother-daughter relationship grow in number, our knowledge base expands, and we gather a complete picture of the intricacies of communication between mothers and daughters in adulthood. However, despite the increased attention to this family dyad, there remains a lack of attention paid specifically to the adult daughter's role—not as one-half of a dyad—but as an individual. Relatively few studies foreground adult daughters' experiences over mothers' experiences. Rather, studies sampling adult daughter populations tend to solicit data on dyadic relational interactions, with this commonly resulting in more discussion dedicated to mothers' past experiences and future outcomes than daughters'. The findings of these studies tend to provide us with information about the mother or about interactions between mother and daughter, rather than a sharp focus on daughters' thoughts, feelings, and behaviors. Contemporary scholarship about mother-daughter communication is still lacking investigation of daughters' communication and their lived experiences in the mother-daughter relationships. I propose that it is time for a shift in the way scholars investigate daughters within families.

Consider the many investigations of mothers' experiences of mothering which have resulted in data and recommendations for improved experiences of mothering, wellbeing, and role satisfaction (See for example, Arendell, 2000; Chodorow, 1999; O'Reilly, 2010; Ruddick, 1995). If daughters' experiences are as salient as mothers', scholars must first match the template for investigating daughters to the same employed for investigating mothers. Then we can begin to offer the best, most practical solutions to improve adult daughters' everyday lives.

To be clear, the robust and ongoing investigations of mothers and daughters contribute a wealth of information about mother-daughter dyads, as you will read in the following chapters. However, when scholarship focuses primarily on the mother's value-add, we miss a crucial component in our understanding of family roles when we deny daughters leading-lady status as an agentic member of the relationship. Much of what you may hear, see, or read (in scholarly or popular works) present daughters as vessels ready to be filled by their mothers; we think of daughters as waiting around, reacting to mothering when it crops up. Likewise, many portrayals of daughters nurturing their mothers rely on caricatures of the perfect daughter or the disgruntled daughter, leaving little room for common, humdrum daughtering. In this chapter, I offer some alternative ways to consider the daughter role and suggest preliminary definitions for the communicative behaviors that daughters demonstrate. Because these are nascent ideas, I solicit feedback to add, shape, change, and test these definitions to ameliorate and expand existing notions of daughtering.

DAUGHTERING

Imagine a 30-year-old daughter's cell phone rings, she looks down and sees that it is her mother. In your mind's eye, how does she react? Personally, when I see my mom's name I might be curious (Oh, what's up with her today?), concerned (Uh oh, what's wrong?), dismissive (Well she can wait until I call her back later), or happy (Aww, it's so nice of her to reach out to me)—Yes, these are all MY reactions to MY mom at various times. When I answer that call, I am prepared to contribute to an interaction, but first I think about ME. What am I willing to give to this person today? I imagine that, when receiving calls, you do that too. Whether it be a call from your mom or your friend, you must assess what you're willing to give of yourself to that conversation before you pick up the phone (or ignore the call). When a friend is on the line, these giving behaviors are called "friendship." If a child, partner, or boss is calling, you might be performing "parenting," "loving," or "working." Thus far, there's no adequate word for what a daughter is doing when interacting with her mother.

The first to state the need for new verbiage was van Mens-Verhulst (1995), who said that the language we use is missing the verb: "to daughter" (p. 531). Over the past two decades, some scholars have begun to take up her request and use descriptors like "to daughter" or its accompanying form of "daughtering" when describing behaviors daughters enact. But, what is that? The current go-to word for those who are caretaking others is "mothering" (whether male or female, older or younger relational partner)! Lucy Rose Fischer, who was in the vanguard of mother-daughter scholars (1986) said that behaviors enacted by daughters and mothers toward each other that showed reciprocal responsibility were "mutual mothering" (p. 58). This term has proliferated and leads a frustrating neglect toward daughters' role participation.

Co-opting the behavioral term associated with the mothering role continues the cycle of subordinating daughters' experiences to mothers'. Daughters, then, have no label for the behaviors they enact or the ways they put effort toward relationships with their mothers. Daughters have been relegated to a passive, backseat role, while mothers are "semantically overburdened" in their role (Walters, 1992, p. 10). What's more, when we use the word "mothering" for other role descriptors, we oversaturate and therefore devalue, this descriptive as well.

Toward the goal of agreement on the nature of adult daughter behaviors, I propose the following description for the term *daughtering*, which highlights the many behaviors an adult daughter employs in the relationship with her mother.

> Daughtering is shown through the many behaviors done by a daughter in relation to her mother to fulfill the social requirements a daughter understands as ascribed or inherent to the role of adult daughter, including the management and avoidance of conflict necessary to maintain a positive—or at least bearable—relationship; protecting herself from possible adverse outcomes; considering and managing her mother's emotions (including emotion work and emotional labor); giving respect to her mother and demanding it for her from others; deciding to fulfill or ignore obligations, whether implied or stated; management of closeness or distance within the relationship with her mother inclusive of decisions to include the mother into the daughter's daily activities; the mental work of thinking about her mother's well-being and future care; carrying out kin work including visits, phone calls, social media communication and assisting the maintenance of extended family relationships; teaching and training her mother in contemporary ideas and methodologies; and eliciting mothering for herself or her family of creation.

This description illustrates the many ways daughters perform their roles and portrays the active enactment of the adult daughter role. Daughtering, used as a verb to describe the behaviors enacted by a woman in the adult daughter role, is a crucial element that we have been missing in descriptions of the adult daughter role and which ties together the various behaviors and labors of this role. The true value of this description will be revealed through future testing and evaluation of it in research studies. The advantage of outlining daughtering—naming, labeling, and outlining the role—adds to our overall understanding of the place of an adult daughter within a social system (Galvin, 2006). This term provides a way for us to discuss the many ways women can daughter their mothers.

As individuals, there are many roles that we play in our families and relationships and we do not often take the time to consider and evaluate these roles carefully. We occasionally spend some time thinking about our contributions to our relationships and imagine how we can do more or do better. For example, we sometimes think of ourselves as friends and ponder what it means to be a friend and subsequently attempt to be a good friend to others. We evaluate ourselves as romantic partners and put thought into bettering ourselves for our partners. We may have also thought about the ways we want to be good parents (now or in the future). When relationships are important to us, we put energy into them. However, do you know any women who talk to their friends about their efforts *to daughter* their mothers? Do you know of a daughter who asks her mother if she is *daughtering* her well enough or do you know of a mother who gives unsolicited kudos to her daughter for her excellent *daughtering* efforts? If these questions leave you scratching your head, you're not alone. It's clear that we are leaving a topic out of our conversations and have forgotten to notice a vital role that women play: daughter.

The description of daughtering I present above emerged from my qualitative investigations of mothers and daughters (Alford, 2016). After obtaining permission from the Internal Review Board (IRB), I interviewed women aged 25–45, with a living and healthy mother aged 70 or younger, where daughters were asked to talk about themselves and their role as an adult daughter. Participants completed both an information sheet and IRB study agreement form at the outset of the study. For confidentiality, all names and identifying information for participants has been changed in this discussion. Exploratory objectives of this study included discovering what daughters say about the adult daughter role and identifying the everyday role behaviors that constitute *daughtering* in the mother-daughter relationship once they reached adulthood. To better understand the role of adult daughter in these interviews, women were asked not only to discuss the nature of their relationships with their mothers and how they communicate but to discuss the nature of the role itself.

The questions and topics that arose in these discussions surprised many of the daughters interviewed. While they anticipated discussing their mothers, when asked to think about *themselves* and *their* communication in the relationship, many women began thinking about the relationship in a whole new light. For most of us, a social label we identify with is "daughter"; but we often fail to consider how "daughter" is also a role that we play. Thanks to the insightfulness of those interviewed, together we co-constructed a preliminary description of the essence of daughtering, including emotions associated with daughtering, and assumptions about what it means to be an adult daughter. The experience of *daughtering* has some commonalities.

Building on those early interviews, I have continued to ask women about daughtering. At first, an interviewee may experience some awkwardness or confusion, thinking about what actions she performs and realizing that I am asking her to be vulnerable and open up to talk about herself. As daughters become accustomed to this shift in the thinking, they also experience a frustrating inability to precisely describe their daughtering actions; instead of demonstrating their points, daughters often resort to borrowed language from other relationship depictions.

These discussions often take some time for the cognizance of identifiable adult daughter role behaviors to emerge, yet eventually, daughters moved from uncertainty toward growing awareness and, eventually, to an eagerness to discuss their lived experiences. Daughtering, it turns out, is being enacted every day in social situations, but because it is not usually pinpointed as a role, the idea of daughtering stays somewhat invisible. Though daughters report that their mother-daughter relationships have unique, distinguishing features—taken collectively, daughtering is a socially embedded performance.

How is it that daughters can easily report that they "do things" for their mothers, but cannot find the exact words to express what they do or how much it means? Why is it that women can productively work on being better at their roles as Wife, Girlfriend, Friend, and Mother, but don't notice the ways they evaluate and produce the Daughter role? Strangely, our social notions of daughtering exist as a backdrop in the lives of most women and in their relationships. This occurs to such a degree that daughtering efforts go unnoticed, uncategorized, and undervalued. These queries led me to a burgeoning awareness that in order to enable scholars to accurately study family roles, there must be preliminary work done to collectively clarify terms related to daughters. Clarifying terminology around "daughter" as a construct as well as her role in "daughtering" will enhance our accuracy in studying similar phenomenon and allow scholars to more deeply understand a daughter's role in a family system.

The Daughtering Construct

For a rich understanding of the social construction of daughtering, we must first consider daughters as independent agents of change. The prevailing cultural representations of "daughter" allow only for understanding daughters referentially as either their mother's peer or their adult mini-me (see chapter 11, this volume, for a discussion of mothers as best friends). The social construct of mothering as an empowered and skilled performance has traction, but daughters have come to be considered an artifact of their mothers' production. It is an unfortunate reality that roles of women are differentially constructed, but those constructs are linked (Glenn, 1994), creating a dichotomy between mother as an agent of control and daughter as an object of control. This stance allows us to consider daughters only as objects rather than agentic beings. This point of view is often reflected in the language of the women with whom I speak. They frequently consider "daughter" as a label rather than a job with job functions. Additionally, daughters tend to borrow language from other relationships when describing their role, including words like *friends*, *mothering*, and *caregiving*. The result of this borrowed language is daughters fall back on terminology that describes a similar kind of role, but not exactly the daughter role. In turn, the use of somewhat imprecise language to talk about daughtering continues the misperceptions associated with daughters' contributions.

If we understand that "A rich vocabulary on a given subject reveals an area of concern of the society whose language is being studied" (Schulz, 1975, p. 64), then it becomes clear that lack of communal language for describing the vital family job of daughtering means daughters remain in a marginalized status in family units and our greater social system. Daughters reveal that the available vocabulary for nurturing one's mother is not only inadequate but contradictory. This may be due to different connotations of language describing women and may be because this language is nestled within a patriarchal system that favors men and derogates women (Schulz, 1975). Words in the English language most likely to escape this trap are related to motherhood. I argue that it is time now to pursue language creation that depicts the unique qualities of daughtering but resists the urge to equate daughterhood with womanhood, and womanhood with motherhood.

It is not uncommon for adult daughters to describe themselves as now "mothering" their mothers, or "mutual mothering" (Fischer, 1986). In fact, Glenn (1994) describes *mothering* as "a historically and culturally variable relationship in which one individual nurtures and cares for another" (p. 3). Indeed, the word mothering carries quite a bit of cultural baggage, functioning as a substitute in popular verbiage for any caregiving. Mothering, Glenn asserts, is a *social construct* created "through men's and women's actions within specific historical circumstances. Thus, agency is central to an understanding of mothering as a social, rather than biological, construct" (p. 3). Glenn stresses that the construction of mothering takes shape not only in ideas and beliefs, but within social interactions, identities, and social institutions. This position challenges the biological notions of mothering, and I, similarly, challenge existing notions of daughtering. Just as Glenn (1994) asserts there are many ways to mother that look dissimilar to prevailing cultural representations of the mothering construct (middle-class, White, and biologically related), I argue that a daughter interacting with her mother is a crucial part of the mother-daughter relationship and scholars must take a closer look at what daughters are doing to sustain this bond; and as we see it, we must label it accordingly.

Daughters tell me time and again that their mother-daughter relationship falls somewhere in between the extremes of "perfect" and "terrible" and can even change on a day-to-day basis. Everyday, even banal, interactions between mother and daughter are the basis for the relationship, as events and memories are layered on top of one another over the course of many years. In these moments, the mother-daughter relationship is changed and molded based on communication behaviors between the two. If we fail to explore daughters' agency in mother-daughter relationships, we ignore the lived experiences of the younger, subordinate, obligated relational partner in this crucial family construct. To remedy this, we begin to consider the social construction of daughtering and daughters' place in the architecture of families.

Many elements inform our understanding of mother-daughter relationships. Socially, daughters are linked to their mothers through a history of kinship obligation. Rossi and Rossi (1990) investigated the links between family members and presented data from their study of obligation in families. They asked participants to rate vignettes about specific family members based on the level of obligation, including crisis events and celebratory events, which the researchers theorized would activate kin obligation. Their findings were that daughters showed greater obligation to and offered more comfort to their mothers than to any other kin relation. In return, mothers offered greater financial support to daughters, and even to sons-in-law, which the authors believed was due to "the greater affective closeness of the mother-daughter relationship than any other parent-child dyad that ripples out into more distant kin relations, and provides the asymmetrical tilt to the maternal side in the American kinship system" (Rossi & Rossi, 1990, p. 189). While it was no surprise that parental obligation topped the list of greatest kin obligation, the patterns found in Rossi and Rossi's data reinforce the importance of "the especially close bond between mothers and daughters, a closeness that begins in childhood and continues throughout life" (p. 207). Daughters, as we well know, do a lot of caring for their mothers, in early, mid, and late life.

Likewise, Buhl (2008) noted distinctive qualities of the relationship between mothers and daughters in her German study. Her study included 156 daughters and 202 mothers as well as sons and fathers. Buhl analyzed the data by gender and role. Buhl measured *individuation* (the process where children pull away from their parents and become individuals) assessing the *connectedness* and *individuality* of participants. Connectedness consists of a "desire to please them, self-disclosure, a sense of obligation to the family and a feeling of attachment to the parents," whereas individuality, sometimes called separateness or separation, consists of "independence from parental authority, the construction of a self that is separate from parental influence, a change from unilateral authority to cooperation and a change in perceptions—from 'parents as figures' to 'parents as persons'—combined with de-idealization" (Buhl, 2008, p. 381). The results of Buhl's study, as it relates to women, showed that individuation is a process between daughters and their mothers that continues as both age. Within that process, connectedness to mother decreases with age from the daughter's point of view, but individuality, assessed as relative power, stays symmetrical, with daughters reporting less power overall than do mothers. In effect, daughters see themselves growing away from their mothers and becoming individuals, but their mothers continue to hold greater power in the relationship; though different, daughters maintain a subordinate place.

Daughtering is performed in many styles, much like how people clean their houses differently or exercise in their unique ways. Daughters choose how to interact with their mothers, based partly on social expectations and partly on their unique mother-daughter relationship. A study by Harrigan and Miller-Ott (2013) found that the interconnectedness of mothers and daughters can be tricky to navigate because "on one hand daughters value the opportunity to be independent of their mothers, yet too much independence makes them feel disconnected from their mothers" (Harrigan & Miller-Ott, 2013, p. 27). Boundaries, they also reported, were essential to mother-daughter communication. While adult daughters in their study sought guidance from their mothers, they believed there was a fine line between helping and intervening. Additionally, daughters in their study said they valued their independence, but too much distance could lead to a feeling of disconnection from their mothers. We know that daughters tend to value the mother-daughter relationship, but like all interpersonal connections, there is a lot of work to do to set up parameters for how the relationship operates. This means an outlay of time and energy to nurture the relationship if adult daughters want the connection with their mothers to thrive.

Daughter Work

Chatting on the phone with my mom recently, I found myself again having a quarrel with her about her health. I did not want to have this argument, not now nor the ten times we had previously discussed it. Yet, because I care deeply about my mother, I believe that it is my job to look out for her, even if that means saying things she does not want to hear, may wound her feelings, or leave her feeling judged. That is an unpleasant part of my *daughter work*, or the labor I perform as an adult daughter. I must carefully choose my words, tone, and the timing for health discussions with my mother because I know that she receives those messages differently from me than she does from her doctor, a friend, or my father. In my experience, mothers can be quite sensitive to things their daughters say and do. Would you agree?

When talking with one woman, Celeste, about her relationship with her mother, she summed it up like this, "I care because I have to, but also because I am her daughter" (Alford, 2016). While feelings of obligation are common to daughters (I must because no one else will), on the flip side, we enjoy reaping the rewards of daughtering done well (I feel needed and that is valuable).

Although daughters revert to borrowed language to discuss themselves and their mothers, at the core of their examples are *tending behaviors*, which involve caring for someone's needs versus caring about someone (O'Connor, 1990). For instance, daughters have told me that they care for their mothers by avoiding conflict, defending her honor, and carrying the mental load. Daughters are expending energy on the mother-daughter relationship, conducting kin work, emotion work, emotional labor, care labor, mental labor, and love labor (Alford, 2016). According to O'Connor (1990), unintended consequences of linking "tending activities" to explanations of the mother/daughter relationship are legitimating traditional notions of women as caretakers and reinforcing unequal division of labor within family systems. Further problematizing this issue is lack of acknowledgment for daughters' efforts within family systems.

Daughters understand that the adult daughter role includes emotion work and emotional labor. Hochschild (1979) first described *emotion work*, saying that "it is the act of trying to change, in degree or quality, an emotion or feeling" (p. 561). This work is done when a daughter feels a pinch between what she *is feeling* and what she *"should" be feeling*. She knows what she "should" feel in a situation based on, often latent, socially shared rules appropriate for a role and situation (Hochschild, 1979). But, what she "is" feeling may be inappropriate to express to her mother, based on power differences or social expectations for how daughters behave. So, she makes a decision to manage her emotions in a socially appropriate way. It is hard work that takes plenty of practice and self-talk. This emotion work is linked to a daughter's understanding of social expectations for adult daughters. *Emotional labor*, on the other hand, is the public face one puts on emotion work, either because she chooses to or because it is a requirement of a position, such as in employment scenarios. Emotional labor is a visible display complying with the requirements of a given position. For daughters, emotional labor is the "deep acting" of playing the part of a good daughter based upon the social requirements she understands that accompany this role. She does the emotion work in her head and wears the emotional labor on her face.

Labor is, by definition, hard work or toil, even if one enjoys or receives a benefit from doing it. *Love labor*, according to Lynch (2007), is a form of care labor that brings about the realization of love, not just the declaration of it. "Love laboring is affectively-driven and involves at different times and to different degrees, emotion work, mental work, cognitive skills, and physical work" (p. 550). Love labor is that which we provide to our primary relations, those with whom we have a mutuality, inherited understanding, dependency or deep respect. For an adult daughter, love labor means showing her love and not just saying it. Specifically, adult daughters love labor through hugs, questions about mothers' interests, or thoughtful gift-giving to demonstrate how they "get" their mothers. Though love labor is not exclusively performed with our biological relations, the mother-daughter relationship is a likely site for it:

> [Love labor] is undertaken through affection, commitment, attentiveness and the material investment of time, energy and resources. It is visible in its purest form in relations of obligation that are inherited or derived from the deep dependencies that are integral to our existence as relational beings. (Lynch, 2007, p. 557)

Love labor, like emotional labor, may be driven by obligation, which is often a motivating force for daughters to interact with their mothers (Rossi & Rossi, 1990). As such, labor is an aspect of role management, learned and organized over time, then used to guide behavior. This labor, however, may go uncredited, even by the daughters who are doing it. Add up the hugs, energy given to "paying attention" during phone calls and visits, and the time spent searching for a meaningful gift—you start to see how the labor can total a large a cost for one's time and energy. Those investments in her mother mean an adult daughter likely shorts another area of her work. What area of a woman's life must give for her to love labor for her mother?

Not only in the case of daughters but among all women, everyday kinds of work are often undervalued. Micaela Di Leonardo (1987) defined the term *kin work* to describe a new category of labor separate from household work or marketplace labor:

> By kin work I refer to the conception, maintenance, and ritual celebration of cross-household kin ties, including visits, letters, telephone calls, presents, and cards to kin; the organization of holiday gatherings; the creation and maintenance of quasi-kin relations; decisions to neglect or to intensify particular ties; the mental work of reflection about all these activities; and the creation and communication of altering images of family and kin vis-a-vis the images of others, both folk and mass media. (Di Leonardo, 1987, p. 442)

Di Leonardo's description of kin work shows how everyday activities of women can often be taken for granted or undervalued due to the low profile of the activity, or due to the low value placed on gendered work. Altering the value of the work performed by women, Di Leonardo says, changes the conversation about how gendered work makes power accessible for women in non-market activities (p. 452). This means that women do not get acknowledgment for unpaid work like organizing family gatherings or solving family crises.

Notably, Di Leonardo also includes "*mental work*" in her definition. While mental work (Di Leonardo, 1987) (such as thinking about a mother's future care) may be motivated by obligation, or multiple goals, it is valuable to consider carrying the mental load as a form of labor a daughter enacts for her mother. *Mental load* describes the burden perceived from juggling tasks, some quite complex, and often in a limited time; it is the amount of remembering and processing of information that one's mind can balance seamlessly. And, as you may have guessed, the heavier mental load is usually carried by women, whether as mothers to their children or as daughters to their mothers.

James (1989) noted that society believes some forms of labor to be "natural" for females to undertake (p. 22). Therefore, "unskilled women's work, because it is unpaid and because it is obscured by the privacy of the domestic domain where much of it takes place, the significance of its contribution and value in social reproduction is ignored" (James, 1989, p. 22). We can all agree that what seems "natural" for women is a social construct based on thousands of years of women's unpaid labor (why would men want to do it if it's uncredited and unpaid?). But, her point can also help us understand a specific female role. Though James's point addresses the labor performed in many female roles, daughtering particularly is obfuscated by observations of other roles or dominance of those roles in everyday life (i.e., mothering), rendering the daughtering experience mostly uncredited. Likely, the lack of language specific to the daughter role makes it difficult for others to describe the daughtering experience, leaving daughtering deleted from many observations of family dynamics.

Daughtering efforts are not only vital to the mother-daughter dyad but contribute to our greater social structure through *social reproductive labor* which include routine activities—for people of any age—that "feed, clothe, shelter and care for" others (Coltrane, 2000, p. 1209). Social reproductive labor, according to Coltrane (2000) is a type of work that occurs within families and "is just as important to the maintenance of society as the productive work that occurs in the formal market economy" (p. 1209). Located not only in cultural spaces and within role prescriptions, the work of daughtering is often overlooked as labor, and the cost of that labor for daughters is little understood.

In an investigation of middle-aged adult daughters' role with elderly mothers, Scharlach (1987) examined how role strain for adult daughters is related to both the affectual quality of daughters' relationships with her mother and to her mother's well-being. Forty middle-aged daughters and 24 elderly mothers were given questionnaires to report on their filial behavior, role strain, relationship quality, conflict and affectual solidarity. Scharlach found that daughters experienced role strain, from role demand overload and perceived role inadequacy and that this role strain created decreased relationship satisfaction for daughters as well as lower psychological well-being for mothers.

In addition to filial responsibilities, a middle-aged woman typically has a variety of vocational, parental, marital, and social obligations, as prescribed by societal and personal values. To the extent that a daughter's relationship with her mother is perceived as interfering with her ability to fulfill these other role demands and meet her own needs, a woman is apt to experience a sense of "role strain" (Scharlach, 1987, p. 627).

Furthermore Scharlach (1987) describes a daughter's role as one of commitment and responsibility to her family while also managing many other commitments in her life. The requisite balancing act to adequately fulfill these obligations can lead to role strain. Findings from this study indicated that role strain could impact the quality of the elderly mother-mid-life daughter relationship, leading to reduced emotional well-being for the elderly mother. It is important to note that the role of a daughter as described by Scharlach is not only the fulfillment of obligation toward her mother, but also *balancing* her many responsibilities.

Similarly, a study by Phoenix and Seu (2013) provides evidence that adult daughters being reunited with birth mothers after a long separation consciously evaluated what role she would play with a new mothering figure. The daughters experienced a process of actively consenting to be mothered and/or providing daughtering to the birth mother. These daughters made a conscious choice to do the work of daughtering in this new mother-daughter relationship. "They, therefore, exercised agency in daughterhood" (Phoenix & Seu, 2013, p. 312). In a setting like this, it is a bit easier to see the choice that a daughter can make—to accept mothering, to initiate daughtering—and when we apply that same lens to the mother-daughter relationships we see in our everyday lives, it still rings true. Daughters, as this study illustrates, must actively participate in daughtering and choose to labor in this role; it is not a passive interaction between daughter and mother.

Daughtering can also function in voluntary or non-biological relationships. Hampton (1997) explored the meaning-making of daughters who were adopted, reporting on both their biological and adoptive mothers. She interviewed pregnant adult daughters about their upcoming role transition to mother, asking about the influence of both their adoptive and biological mothers on the daughters' identities. As the adopted daughters transitioned into motherhood, meeting their biological mothers became essential but did not overpower their desire to include their adoptive mothers in their transition, including the birth experience. Daughters indicated that it was important to foster a connection with their biological mothers before they gave birth to destroy negative messages, such as believing a biological mother did "not want" her daughter or she "gave me away." Adopted daughters did not exclude adoptive mothers from their process of embracing the new identity of "mother," but continued the ongoing dance of intimacy and ambivalence typical of long-term mother-daughter relationships. Hampton (1997) supports the argument that daughtering can be enacted in a variety of ways and it requires an investment of effort; that is, it requires relational work.

Depictions of relational work as labor are not a new idea. It was Sara Ruddick (1995) who pioneered the discussion of mothering as effort, or work, and not merely a biological tie between mother and child. Instead, she said that mothering develops from the *practice* of the discipline of mothering—meaning that as mothers *do* mothering, the iterative dual process of doing and understanding emerges organically. Daughters, considered in the same light as mothers learning and practicing a role, must be understood through their practice and discipline of daughtering; it is a parallel construct to mothering. It must be noted that consideration of the effort a woman undertakes to daughter her mother places emphasis on *what she does for mother*, not only how she feels about her mother. Like Nelson's (2006), analysis of daughters' interviews revealed that the act of *doing* daughter work kept adult daughters connected to their mothers. Nelson classified *"doing family"* as actively fostering the connections through which family is created and rehearsed. Additionally, doing family means creating attachments, building boundaries, and defining limits. In sum, *doing daughtering* takes effort, and the payoff is the maintenance of family ties.

Roles, according to Bourdieu (1977), are not just existing structures that cause meaning, but a *social space* that helps people map possible behaviors. Think about that: Roles are a space in our social lives where we perform, interact, and practice our thoughts about ourselves and others. The outcome of these role behaviors: Meaning. As we participate in the social sport of roles, inside the social space that we allow for ourselves and others, we form meanings about ourselves and who we are in society. As women, we learn what it means to be a daughter by observing other daughters, watching how they daughter their mothers, listening to the social discourse about daughtering, and internalizing social meanings on daughterhood. The following section further explores how daughters learn how to daughter their mothers in a socially constructed world.

Daughterhood

Many friends commented on my relationship with my mother throughout my adolescence and early adulthood. "Yes, I've got a good one," I thought to myself, while also congratulating myself for working hard to maintain that mother-daughter tie. My friends' appraisals also pushed me to think about their mother-daughter interactions, comparing those things that made me believe that the grass looked greener from the other side. Building on this experience, I now ask adult daughters to talk with me about how and from whom they learned about daughterhood expectations. In one interview, Clara told me:

> Yeah, I think I am a good daughter. I think that if the world had more daughters like me then it would be …, well, what are the expectations for a daughter? That's strange, but I think that I am a good model for a daughter. I try to be. (Alford, 2016)

Like many other daughters I spoke to, Clara struggled to place her role as a daughter in the mother-daughter relationship within a broader social system. As discussed earlier, it is comfortable for women to think of being a daughter as a label rather than a role which functions within a more extensive social system; we are more comfortable talking about what our mothers do than what daughters do. However, adult daughters can evaluate their role through a broader social lens. Daughters and mothers may come to understand their roles, according to Walters (1992), "not only through the exigencies of family life, economic survival, and social policies, but through the systems of representation and cultural production that help give shape and meaning to that relationship" (p. 10). Daughters are raised learning how to daughter from childhood, whether it be from their mothers and grandmothers or other family members, from community members sharing the same ethnicity and culture, from religious training, and other social messages like media portrayals (for more information on daughtering and media portrayals see chapter 4, this volume).

Daughters' perceived expectations for themselves and others continue to be shaped and reified through interactions with other daughters. Daughters, thus, function within the greater social structure as maintainers and promoters of a system for how and when to employ daughtering. This is a kind of collective competence prescribing expected behaviors of women who are members of a daughterhood. Korolczuk (2010) was the first to use the term *daughterhood* and said that "the role of daughter is fluid, flexible, culturally and historically diverse" (p. 470). She concluded that while there exists a general narrative about a daughterhood of women enacting the daughter roles collectively, the notion of a daughterhood is abstract in its definition but prevalent in the discussions of the women she talked to. Describing daughterhood, Korolczuk (2010) said that it is the "entirety of the emotional, intellectual and physical effort which the daughter's role involves" (p. 470). While naming and describing this phenomenon is undoubtedly valuable, defining the term daughterhood is imperative for scholars to further investigations of the role of daughters in society.

When we imagine a collective competence that daughters have for the role of adult daughter, enacting these role behaviors at the same time and for a similar purpose, the architecture of a daughterhood emerges. *Daughterhood* is like "brotherhood" or "sisterhood," connoting a fellowship not achieved simply through status or role transition (as in "motherhood") but as a collective of people doing the same tasks and functioning within the same role. I propose the following definition for *daughterhood:*

> By daughterhood, I mean the performance of the collective competence of the role of adult daughters, wherein a daughter's participation requirement is as simple as having a mother and maintaining any relationship with her or as complex as meeting the understood demands associated with daughtering, garnered from a variety of sources, while assessing how others are doing it and reifying the role through relational labor; this experience is lived by daughters doing the work of daughtering side-by-side, whether or not they realize their participation in a systemic experience of daughtering.

Understanding how adult daughters function within a daughterhood means that researchers can better explore the ways roles are socially constructed and linked. Moreover, as we allow the idea of a daughterhood of women to take root, we learn something about communication in society in a broader sense. The common characteristics of the members of a social system are its cultural attributes. When, during our interviews, daughters described expectations from various sources including larger social platforms like peers, media, and religious structure, they were sensemaking about daughtering, contributing to their understanding of their role as well as adding to the culture of a daughterhood through the publication of this research. These are valuable additions to our understanding of how communication works in everyday settings and close relationships, but also inform us about the prevailing cultural discourses of today.

Daughters use this social knowledge reflected in the daughterhood to make decisions about how to behave in their roles based on these shared social conceptions, acting in parallel with other adult daughters performing their roles. As they share the practice of enacting the adult daughter role, daughters are creating a community experience, a daughterhood, even though daughters may not realize they are community members. We know that roles are learned and constructed through practice and observation of one's community and communicating with one's reference groups, creating a collective experience for adult daughters. When we think about this system of daughters shaping each other through their performance of daughtering, the notion of a daughterhood reveals a complex social system in which all adult daughters are members. Social construction means that there are communication processes at work on many levels, as understood through daughters doing identity work, individual family role performance, and reacting to cultural norms for daughters.

Embedded within the social system, the adult daughter role also works dyadically in partnership with the role of aging mother. As a daughter plays her role, she examines how mother plays her role. Daughters have been watching for many years how their mothers (and others around them) play their familial roles. They have also seen their mothers played the role of adult daughter to *her* mother in the past. The behaviors they witness inform their own typification schemes for the role of adult daughter (Berger & Luckmann, 1966). It is through repeated interactions that mothers and daughters internalize these guidelines, perform the routinized behaviors, and learn the role. Each time an interaction with her mother is begun, whether in a new context or timeworn, a daughter leans on her existing typification schemes to determine how to appropriately behave. If she is lacking experience in that context, she cobbles together ideas based on her knowledge of a broad social system, tests out her hunch, and forms a new schema for future use. Through these practices, she blazes a trail that is just <*this much*> like her peers and her mother, while just <*this much*> hers alone.

Some communication scholars refer to this social space—where one can absorb her role through interaction—as a community of practice (Lave & Wenger, 1991). Learning about one's place in the world is not only a cognitive endeavor but situated within a community wherein it is formed and organized. We can think of daughters learning their role within a community of practice; thus, daughters are absorbing messages through continued interaction with role peers, absorbing the essence of daughtering over a lifespan while living among community members. "Such a view sees mind, culture, history, and the interrelated social processes that constitute each other" (Lave, 1991, p. 63). Daughterhood membership begins at birth and continues even if one's mother leaves or has died (see chapter 18, this volume, on motherless daughters).

Collective daughtering experiences are influenced by time and cultural influences (Glenn, 1994). Cultural discourses inform daughters' communication and the mother-daughter relationship (Korolczuk, 2010; Rastogi & Wampler, 1999). So, while daughters may observe other daughters to form a community (or daughter-hood) these communities are situated in various cultures, time periods, and other contexts. As many authors in this book show, influences such as mental health, tech-nology, and age—to name a few—impact women's performance of the daughter role.

WHAT DOES ALL THIS MEAN?

Considering the many influences and factors that intermix to create a daughter-hood of women daughtering their mothers, and a lack of vocabulary to discuss these instances, we have much to learn about what it means to be a daughter. I urge other researchers to consider how to better foreground the activity of daugh-tering in future studies. Using the perspective of daughtering as a valuable role—conceptualizing women with agency who are putting effort into the mother-daughter relationship—we imbue the daughter role with a deserving sense of importance; we are participating in the social construction of the daughtering role by reading this chapter and using these ideas in our own lives (so meta!). In sum, when we write about daughters as strong, purposeful women embedded in a social system, who work hard on their relationships, putting thought into action, putting pen to paper, we reinforce that it is so. Can you imagine if adult daughters were not performing these essential functions that bridge a lifespan? Within the hidden community of adult daughters, fulfilling their roles through a variety of role per-formances, women are working to create loving and interactive relationships that impact family systems. Daughtering is more than being filled up by mothering; daughtering is an active role performance by a valuable community of women practiced in an exclusive social space, benefitting an entire society.

WHAT DO WE STILL NEED TO KNOW?

- Does daughtering apply to non-biological mothers, such as step-mothers or mothers-in-law? What are the similarities/differences in daughtering one's father versus mother?
- Can son-ing be conceptualized in the same way as daughtering? (See Sotirin & Ellingson, 2007 for a discussion of "aunting.")
- Are there differences in daughtering based on socioeconomic status or other demographic features? Does available time and ability to perform daugh-tering, access to a daughtering community, or proximity to one's mother influence the likelihood or quality of daughtering behaviors?
- How does one's satisfaction with daughtering and the relationship with one's mother contribute to overall life satisfaction?

HOW DOES THIS WORK IN REAL LIFE?

- Daughters contribute efforts like kin work, emotion work, emotional labor, care labor, mental labor, and love labor toward their relationships with their mother. This energy contributes to a productive relationship but is given little credit, by daughters, mothers, or society in general. Different from mothering, daughtering is invisible labor. To change this, mothers can tell their daughters how much they value these labors. This may mean that daughters need to introduce the concept of daughtering to their loved ones to shine a light on their valuable relationship contributions.
- Women are looking at our peers to see how they are daughtering their mothers and incorporating that information into our daughtering styles. Reach out to a friend and ask her about daughtering without any judgment on her performance or yours. When you're going through something new with your mother, ask your peers if they have gone through it and learn from their daughtering wisdom.
- Recognize that mother/daughter relationships are all unique and none of them are perfect. Some daughters have terrible relations with their mothers or, worse yet, have a terrible mother. First, you always have the option to take a step away from this mother and choose not to be in a relationship with her. No one deserves abuse or pain, and the mother/daughter tie is, like all relationships, optional. It is important to know that the mother/daughter bond is not predetermined but is a result of two people working to create a mutually satisfying relationship. Second, if you want to be in a relationship with your mother, then value every contribution you are making, even if the relationship is not currently meeting your needs. All attempts at daughtering are important contributions that move you closer to the goal of a satisfying relationship with one's mother. Also, these attempts to daughter are the vehicle toward those #relationshipgoals.

CLASSROOM ACTIVITIES

- As a class, discuss the concept of daughtering as a recognized contribution to a relationship between mothers and daughters. What does it mean to explore the idea that daughters are not only receivers of mothering, but are also generators of daughtering and fully participate in the creation of the mother/daughter relationship? By a show of hands, how many of you have had your mother verbally recognized your daughtering efforts?
- Name one type of "work" that you enact toward your mother and describe why you would characterize it as labor. Then analyze whether your mother

recognizes this as work on your behalf and discuss why/why not. Does recognition of your work change the satisfaction you gain from doing this work?

- Just like mothering is often considered a non-biological behavior (which may alternatively be called caregiving or social support), can you imagine any scenarios or non-familial relationships where daughtering behaviors are enacted? What are the similarities/differences between a daughter/mother relationship and a business mentee/mentor? Does the name of the behavior change the nature of the work?

- Determine three things that you do for your mother that are significant contributions to your relationship. Brainstorm how to discuss these "daughtering" behaviors with your mother and ask for her recognition of these contributions.

REFERENCES

Alford, A. M. (2016). *Daughtering and daughterhood: An exploratory study of the role of adult daughters in relation to mothers* (Doctoral dissertation). The University of Texas, Texas ScholarWorks, Austin. Retrieved from https://doi.org/10.15781/t2bg2hc0w

Arendell, T. (2000). Conceiving and investigating motherhood: The decade's scholarship. *Journal of Marriage and Family, 62*(4), 1192–1207. https://doi.org/10.1111/j.1741-3737.2000.01192.x

Berger, P., & Luckmann, T. (1966). *The social construction of reality: A treatise on the sociology of knowledge.* New York, NY: Anchor Books.

Bourdieu, P. (1977). *Outline of a theory of practice.* Cambridge, UK: Cambridge University Press.

Buhl, H. M. (2008). Development of a model describing individuated adult child–parent relationships. *International Journal of Behavioral Development, 32*(5), 381–389. https://doi.org/10.1177/0165025408093656

Chodorow, N. (1999). *The reproduction of mothering* (2nd ed.). Los Angeles, CA: University of California Press.

Coltrane, S. (2000). Research on household labor: Modeling and measuring the social embeddedness of routine family work. *Journal of Marriage and Family, 62*(4), 1208–1233. Retrieved from http://www.jstor.org/stable/1566732

Di Leonardo, M. (1987). The female world of cards and holidays: Women, families, and the work of kinship. *Signs, 12*(3), 440–453. Retrieved from http://www.jstor.org/stable/3174331

Fingerman, K. L. (2001). *Aging mothers and their adult daughters: A study in mixed emotions.* New York, NY: Springer Publishing.

Fischer, L. R. (1986). *Linked lives: Adult daughters and their mothers.* New York, NY: Harper & Row.

Fisher, C. L. (2010). Coping with breast cancer across adulthood: Emotional support communication in the mother–daughter bond. *Journal of Applied Communication Research, 38*(4), 386–411. https://doi.org/10.1080/00909882.2010.513996

Galvin, K. M. (2006). Diversity's impact on defining the family: Discourse dependence and identity. In L. H. Turner & R. West (Eds.), *The family communication sourcebook* (pp. 3–19). Thousand Oaks, CA: Sage.

Glenn, E. N. (1994). Social constructions of mothering: A thematic overview. In E. N. Glenn, G. Chang, & L. R. Forcey (Eds.), *Mothering: Ideology, experience, and agency* (pp. 1–32). New York, NY: Routledge.

Hampton, M. R. (1997). Adopted women give birth: Connection between women and matrilineal continuity. *Feminism & Psychology, 7*(1), 83–106. https://doi.org/10.1177/0959353597071011

Harrigan, M. M., & Miller-Ott, A. E. (2013). The multivocality of meaning making: An exploration of the discourses college-aged daughters voice in talk about their mothers. *Journal of Family Communication, 13*(2), 114–131. https://doi.org/10.1080/15267431.2013.768249

Hochschild, A. R. (1979). Emotion work, feeling rules, and social structure. *American Journal of Sociology, 85*(3), 551–557. Retrieved from http://www.jstor.org/stable/2778583

James, N. (1989). Emotional labour: Skill and work in the social regulation of feeling. *The Sociological Review, 37*(1), 15–42. https://doi.org/10.1111/j.1467-954X.1989.tb00019.x

Korolczuk, E. (2010). The social construction of motherhood and daughterhood in contemporary Poland—a trans-generational perspective. *Polish Sociological Review,* (172), 467–485. Retrieved from http://www.jstor.org/stable/41275175

Lave, J. (1991). Situating learning in communities of practice. In L. B. Resnick, J. M. Levine, & S. D. Teasley (Eds.), *Perspectives on socially shared cognition* (pp. 63–82). Washington, D.C.: American Psychological Association.

Lave, J., & Wenger, E. (1991). *Situated learning: Legitimate peripheral participation.* Cambridge, UK: Cambridge University Press.

Lynch, K. (2007). Love labour as a distinct and non-commodifiable form of care labour. *The Sociological Review, 55*(3), 550–570. https://doi.org/10.1111/j.1467-954X.2007.00714.x

Miller-Day, M. (2004). *Communication among grandmothers, mothers, and adult daughters: A qualitative study of maternal relationships.* Mahwah, NJ: Lawrence Erlbaum Associates.

Nelson, M. K. (2006). Single mothers "do" family. *Journal of Marriage and Family, 68*(4), 781–795. https://doi.org/10.1111/j.1741-3737.2006.00292.x

O'Connor, P. (1990). The adult mother/daughter relationship: A uniquely and universally close relationship? *The Sociological Review, 38*(2), 293–323. https://doi.org/10.1111/j.1467-954X.1990.tb00913.x

O'Reilly, A. (2010). *Twenty-first century motherhood: Experience, identity, policy, agency.* New York, NY: Columbia University Press.

Phoenix, A., & Seu, B. (2013). Negotiating daughterhood and strangerhood: Retrospective accounts of serial migration. *Feminism & Psychology, 23*(3), 299–316. https://doi.org/10.1177/0959353512473954

Rastogi, M., & Wampler, K. S. (1999). Adult daughters' perceptions of the mother-daughter relationship: A cross-cultural comparison. *Family Relations, 48*(3), 327–336. https://doi.org/10.2307/585643

Rossi, A. S., & Rossi, P. H. (1990). *Of human bonding: Parent–child relationships across the life course.* Hawthorne, NY: Aldine de Gruyter.

Ruddick, S. (1995). *Maternal thinking: Towards a politics of peace* (2nd ed.). Boston, MA: Beacon Press.

Scharlach, A. E. (1987). Role strain in mother-daughter relationships in later life. *The Gerontologist, 27*(5), 627–631. https://doi.org/10.1093/geront/27.5.627

Schulz, M. (1975). The semantic derogation of woman. In B. Thorne & N. Henley (Eds.), *Language and sex: Difference and dominance* (pp. 64–75). Rowley, MA: Newbury House.

Schwarz, B. (2006). Adult daughters' family structure and the association between reciprocity and relationship quality. *Journal of Family Issues, 27*(2), 208–228. https://doi.org/10.1177/0192513X05282186

Shrier, D. K., Tompsett, M., & Shrier, L. A. (2004). Adult mother–daughter relationships: A review of the theoretical and research literature. *Journal of the American Academy of Psychoanalysis and Dynamic Psychiatry, 32*, 91–115. https://doi.org/10.1521/jaap.32.1.91.28332

Sotirin, P., & Ellingson, L. L. (2007). Rearticulating the aunt: Feminist alternatives of family, care, and kinship in popular performances of aunting. *Cultural Studies↔Critical Methodologies, 7*(4), 442–459. https://doi.org/10.1177/1532708607304538

van Mens-Verhulst, J. (1995). Reinventing the mother-daughter relationship. *American Journal of Psychotherapy, 49*(4), 526–539. https://doi.org/10.1176/appi.psychotherapy.1995.49.4.526

Walters, S. D. (1992). *Lives together, worlds apart: Mothers and daughters in popular culture.* Berkeley, CA: University of California Press.

CHAPTER THREE

Mothering AND Motherhood

Socially Constructing the Role of Mothers

ALLISON M. ALFORD*

Life doesn't come with a manual. It comes with a mother.

—ANONYMOUS

Like many little girls, I remember playing with my baby dolls—holding them, putting them to bed, feeding with a tiny spoon—as I pretended to be a mommy. These daydreams eventually came true, but the role of mother holds so much more meaning and responsibility than I ever could have imagined. For a girl, her nascent conception of all things maternal forms in childhood as she watches her own mother, her grandmother, mothers on television, and the mothers of her friends. Little girls are sponges for messages about adulthood, soaking up every drop of meaning in storybooks, community events, and commentary on motherhood that circulate throughout their childhood (Berger & Luckmann, 1966; Stryker & Burke, 2000; Walters, 1992). For instance, I was amused when I recently visited my sister's family and spent some time with my three-year-old niece. She picked up a toy cell phone and said, "Cheese, Aunt Alli!"—so I posed for the faux pic. To my amusement, she then looked down at the "screen" and said, "I'm going to text it to Grammy." How many times has she seen her mom (my sister) take a cute picture on the cell phone and then immediately text it to our mom? I'm still chuckling from that one, but the heart of the matter is

* Allison M. Alford, clinical assistant professor, Baylor University, allison_alford@baylor.edu.

that this three-year-old girl is learning how to be a 21st century mom, sharing pictures of the grandkids via text or social media in order to please mom's mom (i.e., Grammy).

If you have been around small children, you may have some funny stories of mimicry behavior, too. Through many and varied maternal representations, little girls begin to cobble together a framework for the meaning of mothering and motherhood, building a fully formed structure their minds for the performance of the role, so that when it's their turn, they are prepared for the role. This process of amalgamating experiences, cultural images, social policies and theories into a cohesive body of knowledge is called *social construction* and is how each of us come to understand mothering in our own way (Walters, 1992). Like bricklayers from infancy, daughters keep chunks of experiences and shape them into a treasure trove of knowledge about mothering; a cache of information resides in our minds which we can access whenever there's a need.

The link between mothers and daughters may best be summarized as "velvet chains—of security, love, and devotion" (Miller-Day, 2004, p. 4) connecting them across the lifespan. Scholars have noted that the relationship between a daughter and her mother is unique and unlike relationships with fathers, spouses, siblings, parents, or friends (Hampton, 1997; Nelson, 2006). To be clear, it does not follow that because the mother-daughter linkage is unique that it is also positive. You have only to look at bestselling novels or ask a counseling professional to know that this relationship is also fraught with many challenges. Poet Maya Angelou (1969) once wrote, "To describe my mother would be to write about a hurricane in its perfect power. Or the climbing, falling colors of a rainbow" (p. 58). We will come back to the link between mothers and adult daughters in the latter portion of this chapter, but we will begin with a general discussion of the nature of mothering and motherhood.

Rather than glorifying or vilifying mothers, the goal of this chapter is to explore the ways we create meaning about motherhood and mothering. At its heart, this perspective foregrounds agency. Agency refers to the ability to act. As humans we actively participate in cultivating social meanings, such as what motherhood means in contemporary culture. The construction of motherhood takes shape not only in introspective personal ideas and beliefs, but within social interactions, identities, and social institutions (Glenn, 1994, p. 4). The essential goal of this book is to allow you, reader, to consider how these perceptions are formed, molded, and changed over a lifespan. For a detailed history of mother-daughter scholarship from the 1950's forward, see Miller-Day (2004). In the following sections, we begin to explore the current cultural beliefs about motherhood and unpack the terminology. To begin, let's take a look at current scholarship on motherhood and mothering.

DESCRIPTIONS OF MOTHERHOOD AND MOTHERING

Motherhood and mothering continue to be vastly contested terms and ideologi-cally-laden experiences (Hequembourg, 2007). There is a plurality of mothering experiences in the USA with varied motherhood practices, yet understanding cur-rent descriptions are necessary to provide a foundation for our discussion.

Motherhood

Motherhood is the state of being a mother ("Motherhood," n.d., para. 2). The *state* of something is the particular condition at that time ("State," n.d., para. 2). This *condition* is the appearance, quality, or working order of something ("Condition," n.d., para. 2). In essence, *motherhood is the appearance, quality, or working order of someone who is performing the social role of mother.* A social role is a set of connected behaviors, rights, obligations, beliefs, and norms as conceptualized by people in a society (Bandura, 1978). When you talk about mothers, read an article about motherhood, or see a mother on screen, a host of other ideas are attached to the image of a mother you picture. Even now that I am describing the basic defini-tions, you may be picturing a generalized mother figure in your head. That person is enacting a social role and is in a state of being called motherhood.

Fass (2004) describes three types of motherhood: birth motherhood, social motherhood, and caregiving motherhood. The *birth mother* is the person who physically gives birth to the child. Since the development of new reproductive technologies, the concept of birth mother has become more complicated, for the child in the womb may not be the biological offspring of the birth mother. A *social mother* is the person recognized by the social community as a child's mother, even though she might not be the birth mother. This person may have assumed the role of mother in childbirth or through other legal or social means. The caregiver mother engages in child-rearing tasks such as feeding, bathing, dressing, watching over, toilet training, and socializing children—performing the role of *mothering*.

Mothering

In its simplest form, *mothering* is the nurturing of, tending to and caring for another (Worell & Goodheart, 2006). In a broader sense, "Definitions of mothering share a theme: the social practices of nurturing and caring for dependent children. Mothering, thus, involves dynamic activity and always-evolving relationships" (Arendell, 2000, p. 1192). Sociologist Evelyn Nakano Glenn describes mothering as "a historically and culturally variable relationship in which one individual nurtures and cares for another" (1994, p. 3). This last description clarifies that there are variations to motherhood and mothering due to cultural differences or because of the point in time in which mothering was conducted. In addition to context, mothering may vary due to its purpose.

Philosopher Sara Ruddick described the act of mothering as a practice—a socially organized activity based on constitutive aims—resultant from the demand for protection by vulnerable children (O'Reilly & Ruddick, 2009; Ruddick, 1983). This description alerts us to the idea that mothering is based on the goal of protecting children. It's easy to picture a mother making a sack lunch for her child or putting her hand up to a hot forehead. These acts, according to Ruddick (1983) are motivated by the need to protect and preserve offspring. These acts of mothering—this practice—is what she describes as "mothering." The act of mothering is made up of many micro-behaviors, which often occur day after day. While each small act may not seem to protective, the sum of the small things is a big picture of mothering. The practice of mothering can be viewed from *structuralist, interactionist, and resource perspectives.*

Structuralist Perspective

A structuralist view of mothering suggests that role responsibilities of a mother are preexisting in any society (Turner, 2001). To illustrate, let me offer an analogy. Imagine an organization with many members who are working in a big, tall building. The organizational members of Mothers of Mention (M.O.M) are on the 22nd floor and they are advertising for a M.O.M. to manage some junior employees. A woman applies, takes the job, and is now a M.O.M. manager with all associated job responsibilities that entails. She has no say in the scope of her job because it was already decided (probably by men!) before she applied. This structuralist view of a mother's role suggests that any work performed by a mother is considered part of the scope of her work (i.e., mothering). Because she has taken on the title and position, her behaviors in her official capacity are all labeled as a product of that role. From this perspective, a role title leads us to classify her behaviors as mothering. In the simplest form, a structuralist view of mothering would suggest that whatever a mother does is mothering.

Interactionist Perspective

The interactionist view of the mothering argues that mothering emerges from observing interactions with role models (e.g., other mothers) both past and present who orient a woman to what it means to be a mother and how to perform the role, while simultaneously having an influence on those role models (Galvin, Braithwaite, & Bylund, 2004). Let's imagine a woman who decides to join Moms of the Moment (M.O.M), a social group she's heard a lot about from others. Upon joining, she asks what membership entails; the other members tell her a few general tidbits and say that the longer she's a M.O.M, the more she'll figure it out. So, she watches those around her, takes some advice from her new peers, and recalls things she's heard about the group prior to joining. (Now that she's thinking about it, she remembers that her own mother once became a M.O.M). As a result of her membership, the group shifts and changes; her presence in the group alters membership behavior. The role of a mother, from this interactionist perspective, changes based on the ways people act and react within the social group.

An interactionist view of the mother role acknowledges that a person can act differently in a variety of roles and situations, and two very different people may act the same in similar social situations (Turner, 2001). Mothering is a fluid and changing pursuit, understood by each woman independently based upon her past, her present friends and environment, and with a consideration of future goals. Put simply; behaviors are considered "mothering" if the member believes it is so and it is adopted by the social group at large, resulting in an ever-changing list of membership responsibilities.

Resource Perspective. Lastly, we'll consider a resource perspective on mothering. In this line of thought, the social role of mother is considered a tool that can be used for a specific purpose. From this perspective, roles can be thought of as cultural objects, which are nestled within a social system, but also have symbolic meaning (Callero, 1994). Mothers are then seen as acting within a social system, but not wholly governed by that system. Thinking of the role of mother as a "cultural object suggests that roles are much more than a bundle of expectations. Roles are as complex or as simple as the cultural meaning of the object" (Callero, 1994, p. 232).

Let's imagine that the social group above creates a Great Organizational Ornament Decal (G.O.O.D) award for a member who has displayed exceptional social aptitude within the M.O.M organization. This G.O.O.D.-M.O.M can use this award to smooth her way throughout the organization or gain social capital. It is up to her. From the resource perspective, she is individually agentic within her role as a M.O.M and can wield her prize as needed to navigate through the organization as she deems it necessary.

A resource view of the mother role allows us to consider both the system within which mothers operate, but also their agentic "freedom and creative independence" to carve an individual path (Callero, 1994, p. 228). Thinking of the mother role from a resource perspective allows us to consider how a community might shape expectations for mothers, while also valuing a woman's individual performance of the mother role.

It is important to note that systems may also oppress individuals in social roles. Many feminist scholars over the past decades have illuminated the influence of patriarchal ideals on motherhood, noting that when the business of motherhood is male-defined and controlled, it becomes deeply oppressive to women (Rich, 1976). Only through this lens are women made to question themselves and their ability to mother according to social norms (Rich, 1976). "Am I doing what is right? Am I doing enough? Am I doing too much? All mothers' guilt for failing their children is internalized by the institution of motherhood" (Rich, 1976, p. 223). However, when we become aware of the ways we constitute motherhood in a social society, we are afforded the opportunity to reconceive these notions and "recognize that motherhood is not naturally, necessarily, or inevitably oppressive" (O'Reilly, 2016, introduction). Neither should motherhood be considered a universal experience of beauty and bliss. Instead, we define motherhood by the act of mothering. And mothering may be communicatively enacted in a variety of ways.

MOTHERING IDENTITY CONSTRUCTED VIA COMMUNICATION

A new mother begins to think about "who she is" as her identity changes and shifts. Identities are "self-views that emerge from the reflexive activity of self-categorization or identification in terms of membership in particular groups or roles" (Stets & Burke, 2000, p. 226). Essentially, you evaluate yourself—in a social system, in a role, in a setting—and determine who you are and how you fit in, creating various identities. You can be someone who identifies as "a good listener" and "a comedian," for example. You incorporate these identities into your social roles such a "student" or "mother." These can be thought of as preexisting social spaces in a structured system. You can take on new identities or roles as you learn more about yourself as you get older and move through the world. Though identities are something you wear on your shirtsleeve, the way you communicate with others around you reveals your multiple and overlapping identities.

Communication is more than just a method of transmitting ideas; it is fundamental to the creation and construction of our social realities (Leeds-Hurwitz, 2006). The foundational theorists, Berger and Luckmann, wrote about this process in their 1966 book *The Social Construction of Reality*. In it, they described how realities and common-sense thoughts are occurring simultaneously and co-exist as fact, overlapping the experience of the other. Since we cannot know for certain the realities or thought processes of the others with whom we interact, we make educated guesses and create shortcuts in our mind linking a particular behavior to a related guess about its meaning. For instance, when a person smiles, we assess the smile and link it to a meaning in our minds such as kind, sympathetic, or passive-aggressive. According to Berger and Luckmann (1966), the sum total of our social life is made up of millions of these tiny shortcuts where we see an action and relate it to an idea. Over time, we not only react to behaviors, but use them to predict future actions and interactions. When interacting with our role complements, like with her adult daughter, a mother relies on her knowledge of observable patterns to determine her own actions, thus shaping her role as a mother through interactions (Turner, 2001). They create their own roles by "taking the role of the other" and imagining what their role partner may be portraying, which is a cooperative endeavor (Turner, 2001). These role-making moves are not only reliant on her role partner's behaviors, but are also informed by sources inside and outside the family.

Braithwaite, Foster, and Bergen (2017) noted three features of the *social constructionist* perspective that align with the goals of family communication scholars:

- Constructionists value every interaction as essential to human existence
- There is a reflexive relationship between micro (individual-level) and macro (societal-level) discourses, so that social realities become reflected in and supported by larger institutions
- By recognizing the constructed nature of social realities, we are better prepared to identify the impact of hegemonic and taken-for-granted assumptions that are embedded in our everyday communication. (p. 269)

As family members, mothers maintain identities related to womanhood, motherhood, and many other aspects of themselves; they communicate these within family interactions, shaping their role and their social world. Leeds-Hurwitz (2006) described the family itself as a social construct created by those making an effort to construct meaning together. Families are constitutive; that is, constructed through interaction and meaning-making (Galvin, 2006). Mothers co-construct their mothering identities with contributions from others in their lives, describing and explaining what it means to be a mother (Gergen, 1985). Talk among family members and outsiders is what we use to conceive of who we are as a family (Galvin, 2006); we create and define ourselves, our family life, and our position in the world.

What this means is that identities are not preformed and placed inside our heads. Instead, it is through discourse that an idea blooms, we consider it and talk about it with more people, and then believe or reject it. Our beliefs then become the benchmark for how we ought to behave. Rittenour and Colaner (2012) studied mothers in transition. The authors said this link between how a woman defines her identity regarding her role behaviors as a mother is related to how she feels about herself and her life.

MOTHERING AS WORK

As we expand our exploration of what it means to be a mother, let's think about the effort that it takes to mother. Have you ever been to a wedding? They sure can be a lot of fun, but when they're done right, it's also clear that many people put in a lot of work behind the scenes to make it happen. And while work may be fulfilling and purposeful, it is still, well, work! In Chapter 2 (this volume), I presented the idea of daughtering as work, and characterized the various aspects of labor enacted by daughters toward their mothers (Alford, 2016). Forms of labor include kin work (Di Leonardo, 1987), emotion work and emotional labor (Hochschild, 1979), care labor and love labor (Lynch, 2007), and social reproductive labor (Coltrane, 2000).

In addition to these forms of labor that may be enacted by any role performer, Ruddick (1983) coined the term *maternal thinking* to describe the cognitive process essential to mothers caring for someone, stating, "A mother engages in a discipline. That is, she asks certain questions rather than others; she establishes criteria for the truth, adequacy, and relevance of proposed answers; and she cares about the findings she makes and can act on" (Ruddick, 1983, p. 214). This quote points us to the intentionality of mothering; it arises from a need, requires effort, and must be considered within the context where it arose. *Mental work*, for mothers, can be described in the following way:

> I have written and spoken extensively on how mothers, even with involved partners, are the ones who do the maternal thinking: the remembering, worrying, planning, anticipating, orchestrating, arranging and coordinating of and for the household. It is mothers who remember to buy the milk, plan the birthday party, and worry that the daughter's recent loss of appetite may be indicative of anorexia. And while the father may sign the field trip permission form, or buy the diapers, it is the mother, in most households, who reminds him to do so. And delegation does not equality make. (O'Reilly & Ruddick, 2009, p. 27)

Calling mothering work does not reject the notion that it can also be both enjoyable and rewarding. Like many types of work that women may attempt, it's possible for mothering to conjure up many feelings all at the same time. One of the challenges scholars encounter when attempting to reveal the vicissitudes of maternal life is the lack of language to discuss it. About this, Ruddick said, "Overwhelmed with greeting card sentiment, we have no realistic language in which to capture the ordinary and extraordinary pleasures and pains of maternal work" (1983). As we elaborate on mothering and motherhood in this chapter, and as you read the scholars in this book, consider the ways that you might change your own vocabulary to be quite specific when discussing or describing mothers. The value in specificity is clarity for the role performance. The following section discusses some mothering styles and their labels.

MOTHERING STYLES

Like all jobs, there are many ways to tackle mothering. Discussions of mothering styles and strategies have been a hot topic of conversation for the past hundred years and, in the past two decades, have seemingly become ubiquitous with the internet affording 24/7 access to critical opinion. Let's take a brief look at some of the hot-button mothering styles that have garnered recent attention and discussion.

Tiger Mother

Self-proclaimed Tiger Mother Amy Chua (2011b) wrote the bestselling book, *Battle Hymn of the Tiger Mother*, describing the desirability of tough Chinese parenting. In the book she described rejecting her daughters' Mother's Day cards, putting her 3-year-old outside in the cold for disobedience, and so many violin and piano lessons that her daughter began leaving teeth marks on the piano out of rebellion.

> I'm not holding myself out as a model, but I do believe that we in America can ask more of children than we typically do, and they will not only respond to the challenge, but thrive. I think we should assume strength in our children, not weakness. (Chua, 2011a, para. 5)

The essence of the *Tiger Mother* parenting style, according to Chua, is *achievement*. Scholars may disagree with Chua's exact methods and overly-simplistic definition of a Tiger Mother, but agree that it is important to consider the intersectionality of parenting and cultural practices. Juang, Qin, and Park (2013), in a special journal issue dedicated to this topic, said their goal was "to unpack the complexity of Asian-heritage parenting through examining the rationale, practices, and influences of culturally-specific aspects of parenting on child development and well-being" (p. 1).

While Chua may be trying to avoid raising a "praise junkie" she may instead fall into the trap of conditional parenting (Suissa, 2013). Both praise and blame set conditions for children, which can be considered moral directions in a social world (Suissa, 2013). To think about "successful" parenting means considering the moral implications for how we are conditioning our children. Suissa (2013) argues:

> This goes beyond merely modelling forms of polite or socially acceptable behaviour, and involves a process of introducing the child to a world in which the way we talk to each other is expressive of and reflective of the background of moral meaning against which we make sense of the world: what matters and what matters less; what is worthwhile and what is less worthwhile; what is morally significant and what is not. (p. 11)

The answers to these questions—and the ways that we put these responses into practice—informs the social climate and expectations for mothering.

Helicopter Mom

Some moms are claiming the title of Helicopter Parent or *Helicopter Mom* with pride. Green (2012) describes a helicopter mom as one who "hovers" over her children and watches their every move. Personally, Green (2012) says that seeing unsupervised children makes her "break out in a cold sweat" (para. 3). But above all, she argues that being a helicopter mom is about protection for children and believes that "kids are our most precious commodity" (para. 5) Green fears many parents are missing the point about being a helicopter mom and not finding the right balance between freedom and safety when allowing their children to foster their own independence.

In a study of parents and their adult children, the children who received intensive, frequent support reported greater psychological benefits from this type of parenting than those who did not receive "helicopter" parenting (Fingerman et al., 2012). However, in this same report, the mid-to-late life parents who provided the intensive parenting (such as financial, advice, or emotional support) because they saw their adult children as needy, reported lower life satisfaction (Fingerman et al., 2012). A study like this demonstrates that children and adults may have a differing appreciation for various parenting styles, and this may change over time due to cultural norms for how one "ought" to parent.

Free-Range Kids

Quite the opposite from helicopter moms are those who believe that giving children freedom from oversight is key to raising self-sufficient children. Lenore Skenazy (2009), a proponent of *Free-Range parenting* (FRP) says, "Children, like chickens, deserve a life outside the cage" ("About," para. 18). When you hover over a child too closely, "All they are left with is a selection of supervised, sanitized, often pricey activities that allow zero room for creativity. And at the end—I know because I've been there—they get a trophy" (Skenazy, 2008, "Fear Not," para. 5). Dubbed "World's Worst Mom" by national news outlets, Skenazy knows that a lot of people disagree with her strategy, but she happily embraced the term and wrote a best-selling book of the same name.

Instances of FRP have created great discussion among the legal community, where a "neglected" child, found out and about without adult supervision, must be reported to Child Protective Services (CPS) and his parents reported to the state legal system (Vota, 2017). More than any other parenting style, FRP raises questions about potential dangers for children who are unsupervised but should also cause us to question the goals of parenting children and the meaning of freedom in parenting granted by the Fourteenth Amendment of the U.S. Constitution (Vota, 2017). Philosophical discussions of parenting facilitate our understanding of how social systems determine appropriate behaviors, but also give us pause to reflect on how laws, fear, and worry shape our ideas of parenting.

Bad Moms

Some women label themselves as *"bad moms"* in a rejection of an idealized view of motherhood. In her "Bad Mother Manifesto," blogger Catherine Connors extolled her many "bad" choices:

> I am a bad mother according to many of the measurements established by the popular Western understanding of what constitutes a good mother. I use disposable diapers. I let my children watch more television than I'd ever publicly admitted. I let them have cookies for breakfast. (Connors, 2009, para. 2)

Furthermore, she describes the chimera of the "good" mother:

> The Good Mother is everywhere, all at once, and she looks like everything and nothing. She stays at home; she goes to work. She attachment-parents; she's Babywise. She home-schools; she Montessoris. She vaccinates; she doesn't vaccinate. She follows a schedule; she lets her kids run free-range. She co-sleeps; she wouldn't dare co-sleep. She would never spank; she's a strict disciplinarian. She's an Alpha Mom; she's a Slacker Mom; she's a Hipster Mom; she's a Christian Mom; she's a Hipster-Christian-Alpha Mom who slacks off in the summers. She's Everymom; She's NoMom. She brooks no disagreement: if you argue with her, you start a Mommy War. (Connors, 2009, para. 12)

Her description of several mothering dichotomies is a tongue-in-cheek rejection of a possible ideal parenting style, thereby embracing the agency in mothering. When defined as an intentional undertaking, mothering takes on a new meaning of "work" valued for its inherent effort. According to Rutherford (2011), despite claims of differences in strategies for parenting, modern parents agree that children's self-esteem is a measure of good parenting. I have urged you, reader, to think more deeply about what it means to *be* a mother and not just to *do* mothering, so I would add that moms should add measurements of their own self-esteem to considerations of good parenting. Moms, do you feel emotionally competent and self-confident with your parenting? Whatever that looks like for each mom may be a sufficient marker of good parenting.

Mothering Enough

What we can gather from the various mothering styles described above is that moms are trying, putting effort into producing quality results, though these may be disparate. And while many moms are attempting to be the best possible parent, it's also true that there are some moms who don't seem to be doing enough. To be clear, there's a big difference between moms who may give less attention to mothering than others and those who are pathological in their parenting; that is, they are neglectful or have an illness or disease. When mothers do not or cannot provide adequate mothering, their children are impacted. We know from theories in psychology how important it is for a child to be securely attached to a caregiver. Describing Bowlby's (1969) theory of infant attachment to a caregiver, Lyons-Ruth and Jacobvitz (2008) said:

> According to attachment theory, as patterns of interaction are repeated in close relationships over time, children build expectations about future interactions with parents and others that guide their interpretations and behaviors in new situations. As these largely unconscious expectations become elaborated and organized, they are termed internal working models. (p. 667)

Children whose caregivers are present and available develop a secure base and are able to explore their world without worrying if they will have someone to come back to. When a primary caregiver is not available, such as in the case of a mother who is mentally ill or has an addiction, children may develop an insecure attachment. Sroufe (2005) found a strong connection between infant attachment styles and social competency in relationships throughout adulthood.

Though some mothers are unable to properly care for their children, most mothers are doing just fine, even if it seems to the casual observer that they aren't doing enough. Like most forms of labor, there is a minimum input of effort into mothering needed to produce a result, while a maximum effort may be indefinable. You may be wondering what amount of mothering is good enough to produce quality results?

In the 1950's, parenting was a hot topic, with emergent ideas and theories that have guided science and research ever since. Dr. Spock (1946) was telling mothers to show a lot of affection for their children and John Bowlby (1952) discovered that infants attach to their mothers, creating a secure bond that promotes healthy child development.

A mother simply has to be "good enough" to get the job done. Winnicott (1953) describe the good enough mother as starting off with an infant and giving her total attention which lessens over time as a child can handle less-than-perfect parenting. The point is that children do not require around-the-clock care. They adapt over time to frustrations, errors, or lapses on the part of the mother. Winnicott offers this as a reassurance to mothers—babies aren't going to break because moms are imperfectly human. Over the past 65 years since he gave this advice, women have reshaped the ideas of mothering and motherhood, but can always appreciate a bit of reassurance that the kids will be alright!

MOTHERING HER DAUGHTER INTO ADULTHOOD

In their earliest years, children require intense care from mothers. But as they age, the care needs change and the relationship between mothers and children surely follows. Though changes occur, mothers are committed to caring for their children over a lifespan. Mothering needs may change as children enter their mid-life, but women in elderhood still mother their adult children (Mansvelt, Breheny, & Stephens, 2017). While she may no longer cook their meals or enforce curfews, a mother retains her identity even as her children age.

And while mothers may care for and love all of their children, research has shown that mothers' bonds with daughters are uniquely different (Miller-Day, 2004). Among all family relationships, the bond between mother and daughter is most likely to remain significant, even when major life changes occur (Bojczyk, Lehan, McWey, Melson, & Kaufman, 2011).

> The relationship between a mother and daughter may be viewed as having a "life cycle" which is marked by several periods of transition, including the daughter's adolescent years, the daughter's transitions to marriage and motherhood, and the mother's old age and infirmity. (Fischer, 1981, p. 613)

With daughters specifically, mothers tend to hold tight to the mother-daughter bond as this connection is renegotiated over the lifespan. Though her daughter becomes an adult, mothers maintain a mothering identity and offer valuable resources to adult children. One study found that parents view the ties between themselves and their children more positively than do the adult children, which may be because they feel an "intergenerational stake" in their offspring (Fingerman, Sechrist, & Birditt, 2013). And while social expectations may be changing for fathers, it remains that mothers give more support to their grown children and feel more bonded to them (Fingerman et al., 2012; Fingerman et al., 2013).

Put another way; the wise Goldie Hawn said of her daughter, Kate Hudson, "A mother-daughter bond is very different ... As we grow older together, I can't express the amount of love, joy, laughter, sadness we share. She understands me, I understand her. We're girls. We share everything. She's, like, the greatest" (Cagle & Russian, 2017, para. 4). The scholars in this textbook do a wonderful job enumerating the varied experiences of mothering daughters across the lifespan.

WHAT DOES ALL THIS MEAN?

Messages about motherhood are powerful, inescapable, and potentially consequential. In this chapter, I discussed mothering and motherhood messages, revealing the ways messages about the nature of mothering coincide with mothers' communication within and about their families, as well as mothers' feelings about themselves. Mothers behave in a multitude of interesting ways, with the purpose of providing care. What is common for mothers now may not be so in the future, which is the essential nature of social construction.

The key take aways from this chapter reflect on how we society views mothers and how mothers contribute to the social construction of this role. Mothering and motherhood can be thought of as socially derived concepts whose meanings shift over time and place. Our ideas on mothering and motherhood continue to evolve based on the behaviors and attitudes present in a social system. Mothering is a dynamic undertaking enacted differently by every person. Mothers form an identity based on interpreting the expectations of a social system that embraces motherhood to different degrees. The concept of mothering has been highly critiqued and can benefit from the revision of some of these historical thought processes.

Close your eyes and picture a mother. Maybe you see your mother in your mind's eye. Is this person a female? Biologically related? Heterosexual and married to her partner? Is she of sound mind and body? If that's the woman you pictured, I want you to take a moment to reconsider these ideas. Ask yourself, "Is mothering is only for women?" Scholars like Sara Ruddick have been writing about this narrow perspective for decades, saying, "Anyone who commits her or himself to responding to children's demands and makes the work of response a considerable part of her or his life, is a mother" (Ruddick, 1989, xii).

Elaborating on this, Ruddick later said that men "can and often do engage in mothering work" (2009, p. xiii) and that differences between men and women, though not to be ignored, were no different than those between mothers of various races, ethnicities, classes, and cultures; mothering requires no particular sexual commitment and "mothers lead a variety of heterosexual, gay, lesbian, and celibate lives" (2009, p. xii). Many others dispute that the term "mother" could describe anyone other than a woman, arguing that de-gendering the work of a mother devalues it (hooks, 1984). Overall, the word mothering is "semantically overburdened" (Walters, 1992, p. 10), bearing the weight of too many people who would enact it and too many activities to be contained by it.

Beyond gender considerations, I argue that we must investigate mothering outside of the discourse of essential motherhood (Suter, Seurer, Webb, Grewe & Koenig Kellas, 2015) restricted to biological ties among White heterosexual parents (Ruddick, 2009). What about families with multiple mothers—polymaternalism (Park, 2013)—or non-biological links? Consider the narrow view we have when we define motherhood through the act of giving birth or raising living children. Under these conditions, we exclude an entire group of mothers whose pregnancies did not result in a live birth of a child. When we conceive of motherhood solely through biological determination, we overlook loving roles of adoptive mothers, step-mothers, mothers-in-law, lesbian co-mothers, gender non-conforming parenting, and more. Many children thrive when raised by extended family members, legal guardians, or siblings. Some mothers lose their children to illness or death. Other mothers are still children themselves. These contexts provide a rich lens for the exploring the beautiful experience of mothering.

Opening up to novel social spaces without restriction or judgment may help us learn more about differing approaches to mothering and motherhood. I hope this helps you reflect on the ways you discuss mothering and the ways that you listen to those sharing their experiences with the same. As scholars, we must seek out current knowledge, listening to what is said and contemplating what is unsaid or even hidden. Therefore, it is of great importance that we continue to evaluate our conceptions of valuable family roles. I expect that you will critically read this chapter and the rest of this book, asking yourself, "What else do I want to know?" and considering "Do I agree?" I encourage you to continue to ask these questions.

Lastly, I encourage you to think about the ways mothers are in relationship with their children. Particularly with their adult daughters, mothers are agentically cultivating lifelong relationships for the benefit of the entire family system. This takes quite a bit of work on the part of mothers, and although this work looks quite different from baby bottles and soccer games, it is no less valuable or effortful. Mothers of adult daughters continue laboring to make their relationships strong. Through agency, effort, and mindful attention, mothers are actively safeguarding the ones they love throughout their lifetime and creating sustained connections for mutual satisfaction.

WHAT DO WE STILL NEED TO KNOW?

- Healthy debates over the meaning of motherhood serve to keep the work of mothering valued and celebrated. While we see the place of mothers in the care and keeping of future generations as influential and lasting, it is essential to consider new ways to conceive and reconceive the role—both to unburden mothers and give credit where it's due. To do this, we must investigate the roles that are complementary to mothers, but enact care behaviors differently, such as daughters, fathers, and aunts. See my chapter on daughtering (this volume), Floyd and Morman's (2005) discussion of the changing culture of fatherhood, and Sotirin and Ellingson's (2007) elaboration of aunting. We don't have to stop there. Explore sons, grandmothers, and neighbors, too, so we can learn more about the ways communities communicate care aside from mothering. Defining and reconstructing characteristics of "mother" and "not-mother" will allow us to clearly assess their needs and develop appropriate support systems.
- It is important to explore motherhood through varied voices to expand our definitions and reconstruct the standards of mothering. See Dhamoon (2011) for five recommended ways to explore intersectionality. Although intersectionality is a common component of feminist critique, it is a lens that can used to explore any social world. "It is crucial," Dhamoon (2011)

says, "to foreground it as a form of political critique that examines why the social world is configured the way it is and that confronts the work of power" (p. 240).

- As our population continues to live longer, whether healthy or ill, we need to know more about mothering in the "third age." In this "third age," the Baby Boomer mothers of today are post-employment, and—more than any prior generation—healthy, educated, and interested in creating great relationships with their adult children. "The features that characterize the third age are being shaped by the activities of this generation and will continue to evolve with future generations" (Radtke & van Mens-Verhuslt, 2016, p. 47). As life's third-act gains greater attention from scholars, we will come to understand better how we construct the meaning of motherhood across the entire lifespan.

HOW DOES THIS WORK IN REAL LIFE?

- Most mothers care for their children from birth and over a lifetime. Mothers learn how to do mothering through a social system, such as watching her mother as a child, noticing her friends' mothering styles, and gathering subtle messages about mothering through media like books and magazines. Because a mother's role is socially constructed, our idea of mothers continues to flex and change as society does. Can you picture mothers from two hundred years ago managing limits on kids' screen time? Did mothers from even one hundred years ago worry that electing to use an epidural during birth might make them appear to be a weak mother? And fifty years ago, were mothers of college-aged daughters waiting for a daily text message or restricted to writing handwritten letters and weekly phone calls? While we cannot foresee how our society will change (wish we could!), it is certain that the role of mothers will shift right along with it.
- When enacting the role of a mother and performing mothering, a woman is managing her intersecting identities, which impacts the way she mothers. Not only is it impossible to measure all mothers with the same yardstick, it's undesirable! The beauty of mothering and motherhood is the million ways that moms do it differently.
- Recognize that mothers, at any age, are doing the best they can to be good enough for the needs of their children. In some cases that may even mean staying away. When mothers are mentally ill, addicted, or in some other way unable to provide nurturing care, it is reasonable to expect that children will create healthy boundaries with them.

CLASSROOM ACTIVITIES

- Early in the chapter there was a quote suggesting that mothering is a vehicle. Stop to consider this for a minute: What is the nature of a vehicle? How is mothering like a vehicle?
- Find a photo of your mother as a young girl, or the earliest photo available (Bonus: you can keep it and look at it again later, remembering your mom's way of talking, her eyes, her hands). If possible, ask your mother the following questions: Did she want to be a mother from a young age? When she became a mother, what was her biggest surprise? Did she read any parenting books? Who was her support system? What, if anything, does she wish she had done differently as a new mom?
- Do you recall ever saying to yourself, "When I'm a mom, I won't_____." As an exercise, write down all of the things you want to avoid or those behaviors you want to make sure you do when you're a mom. If you've never thought about it, take some time to reflect on your thoughts about yourself as a future mother (or non-mother) and write those down.

REFERENCES

Alford, A. M. (2016) *Daughtering and daughterhood: An exploratory study of the role of adult daughters in relation to mothers* (Doctoral dissertation). The University of Texas, Texas ScholarWorks, Austin. Retrieved from https://doi.org/10.15781/t2bg2hc0w

Angelou, M. (1969). *I know why the caged bird sings*. New York, NY: Random House.

Arendell, T. (2000). Conceiving and investigating motherhood: The decade's scholarship, *Journal of Marriage and Family, 62*(4), 1192–1207. https://doi.org/10.1111/j.1741-3737.2000.01192.x

Bandura, A. (1978). Social learning theory of aggression. *Journal of Communication, 28*(3), 12–29. https://doi.org/10.1111/j.1460-2466.1978.tb01621.x

Berger, P., & Luckmann, T. (1966). *The social construction of reality: A treatise on the sociology of knowledge*. New York, NY: Anchor Books.

Bojczyk, K. E., Lehan, T. J., McWey, L. M., Melson, G. F., & Kaufman, D. R. (2011). Mothers' and their adult daughters' perceptions of their relationship. *Journal of Family Issues, 32*(4), 452–481. https://doi.org/10.1177/0192513X10384073

Bowlby, J. (1952). *Maternal care and mental health: A report prepared on behalf of the World Health Organization as a contribution to the United Nations programme for the welfare of homeless children*. [2nd ed.]. Geneva, Switzerland: World Health Organization. http://www.who.int/iris/handle/10665/40724

Braithwaite, D. O., Foster, E., & Bergen, K. M. (2017). Social construction theory. In D. O. Braithwaite & L. A. Baxter (Eds.), *Engaging theories in family communication: Multiple perspectives* (pp. 267–278). Thousand Oaks, CA: Sage.

Bowlby, J. (1969). *Attachment and loss, Vol. I: Attachment*. New York, NY: Basic Books.

Cagle, J., & Russian, A. (2017, May 12). *Goldie Hawn on her amazing bond with daughter Kate Hudson: "We're girls, We share everything."* Retrieved from https://people.com/movies/goldie-hawn-talks-bond-with-daughter-kate-hudson/

Callero, P. L. (1994). From role-playing to role-using: Understanding role as resource. *Social Psychology Quarterly, 57*(3), 228–243. https://doi.org/10.2307/2786878

Chua, A. (2011a, January 1). *From author Amy Chua.* Retrieved from http://battlehymnofthetigermother.com/

Chua, A. (2011b). *Battle hymn of the Tiger mother.* New York, NY: Penguin Press.

Coltrane, S. (2000). Research on household labor: Modeling and measuring the social embeddedness of routine family work. *Journal of Marriage and Family, 62*(4), 1208–1233. https://doi.org/10.1111/j.1741-3737.2000.01208.x

Connors, C. (2009, June 8). *The bad mother manifesto.* Retrieved from http://herbadmother.com/2009/06/bad-mother-manifesto/

Dhamoon, R. K. (2011). Considerations on mainstreaming intersectionality. *Political Research Quarterly, 64*(1), 230–243. https://doi.org/10.1177/1065912910379227

Di Leonardo, M. (1987). The female world of cards and holidays: Women, families, and the work of kinship. *Signs, 12*(3), 440–453. https://doi.org/10.1086/494338

Fass, P. S. (2004). Mothering and motherhood. In P. S. Fass (Ed.), *Encyclopedia of children and childhood in history and society: A–E.* New York, NY: Macmillan Reference USA.

Fingerman, K. L., Cheng, Y-P., Wesselmann, E. D., Zarit, S., Furstenberg, F., & Birditt, K. S. (2012). Helicopter parents and landing pad kids: Intense parental support of grown children. *Journal of Marriage and Family, 74*(4), 880–896. https://doi.org/10.1111/j.1741-3737.2012.00987.x

Fingerman, K. L., Sechrist, J., & Birditt, K. S. (2013). Changing views on intergenerational ties. *Gerontology, 59,* 64–70. https://doi.org/10.1159/000342211

Fischer, L. R. (1981). Transitions in the mother-daughter relationship. *Journal of Marriage and Family, 43*(3), 613–622. https://doi.org/10.2307/351762

Floyd, K., & Morman, M. T. (2005). Fathers' and sons' reports of fathers' affectionate communication: Implications of a naïve theory of affection. *Journal of Social and Personal Relationships, 22*(1), 99–109. https://doi.org/10.1177/0265407505049323

Galvin, K. M. (2006). Diversity's impact on defining the family: Discourse-dependence and identity. In L. H. Turner & R. West (Eds.), *The family communication sourcebook* (pp. 3–19). Thousand Oaks, CA: Sage.

Galvin, K. M., Braithwaite, D. O., & Bylund, C. L. (2004). Communication and family roles and types. In K. M. Galvin, C. L. Bylund, & B. J. Brommel (Eds.), *Family communication: Cohesion and change* (pp. 168–196). New York, NY: Pearson.

Gergen, K. J. (1985). The social constructionist movement in modern psychology. *American Psychologist, 40*(3), 266–275. http://doi.org/10.1037/0003-066X.40.3.266

Glenn, E. N. (1994). Social constructions of mothering: A thematic overview. In E. N. Glenn, G. Chang, & L. R. Forcey (Eds.), *Mothering: Ideology, experience, and agency* (pp. 1–32). New York, NY: Routledge.

Green, J. (2012, September 11). I'm a helicopter mom, and proud of it. *The Huffington Post.* Retrieved from http://www.huffingtonpost.ca/yummy-mummy-club/helicopter-mom_b_1874556.html

Hampton, M. R. (1997). Adopted women give birth: Connection between women and matrilineal continuity. *Feminism & Psychology, 7*(1), 83–106. https://doi.org/10.1177/0959353597071011

Hequembourg, A. (2007). *Lesbian motherhood: Stories of becoming.* Binghamton, NY: Harrington Park.

Hochschild, A. R. (1979). Emotion work, feeling rules, and social structure. *American Journal of Sociology, 85*(3), 551–557. Retrieved from http://www.jstor.org/stable/2778583

hooks, b. (1984). *Feminist theory: From margin to center.* Boston, MA: South End Press.

Juang, L. P., Qin, D. B., & Park, I. J. (2013). Deconstructing the myth of the "tiger mother": An introduction to the special issue on tiger parenting, Asian-heritage families, and child/adolescent well-being. *Asian American Journal of Psychology, 4*(1), 1–6. http://doi.org/10.1037/a0032136

Leeds-Hurwitz, W. (2006). Social theories: Social constructionism and symbolic interactionism. In D. O. Braithwaite & L. A. Baxter (Eds.), *Engaging theories in family communication: Multiple perspectives* (pp. 229–242). Thousand Oaks, CA: Sage.

Lynch, K. (2007). Love labour as a distinct and non-commodifiable form of care labour. *The Sociological Review, 55*(3), 550–570. https://doi.org/10.1111/j.1467-954X.2007.00714.x

Lyons-Ruth, K., & Jacobvitz, D. (2008). Attachment disorganization: Genetic factors, parenting contexts, and developmental transformation from infancy to adulthood. In J. Cassidy & P. R. Shaver (Eds.), *Handbook of attachment: Theory, research, and clinical applications* (pp. 666–697). New York, NY: Guilford Press.

Mansvelt, J., Breheny, M., & Stephens, C. (2017). Still being "Mother"? Consumption and identity practices for women in later life. *Journal of Consumer Culture, 17*(2), 340–358. https://doi.org/10.1177/1469540515602299

Miller-Day, M. (2004). *Communication among grandmothers, mothers, and adult daughters: A qualitative study of maternal relationships.* Mahwah, NJ: Erlbaum.

Nelson, M. K. (2006). Single mothers "do" family. *Journal of Marriage and Family, 68*(4), 781–795. https://doi.org/10.1111/j.1741-3737.2006.00292.x

O'Reilly, A., & Ruddick, S. (2009). A conversation about maternal thinking. In A. O'Reilly & S. Ruddick (Eds.), *Maternal thinking: Philosophy, politics, practice* (pp. 14–38). Bradford, Ontario, Canada: Demeter Press.

O'Reilly, A. (2016). *Matricentric feminism: Theory, activism, and practice.* Ontario, Canada: Demeter Press.

Park, S. M. (2013). *Mothering queerly, queering motherhood: Resisting monomaternalism in adoptive, lesbian, blended, and polygamous families.* Albany, NY: SUNY Press.

Rich, A. (1976). *Of woman born: Motherhood as experience and institution.* New York, NY: W. W. Norton.

Rittenour, C. E., & Colaner, C. W. (2012). Finding female fulfillment: Intersecting role-based and morality-based identities of motherhood, feminism, and generativity as predictors of women's self satisfaction and life satisfaction. *Sex Roles, 67*(5–6), 351–362.

Ruddick, S. (1983). Maternal thinking. In J. Trebilcot (Ed.), *Mothering: Essays in feminist theory* (pp. 213–230). Totowa, NJ: Rowman & Littlefield.

Ruddick, S. (1989). *Maternal thinking: Towards a politics of peace.* Boston, MA: Beacon Press.

Ruddick, S. (2009). On "maternal thinking." *Women's Studies Quarterly, 37*(3/4), 305–308.

Rutherford, M. B. (2011). The social value of self-esteem. *Social Science and Public Policy, 48*, 407–412. https://doi.org/10.1007/s12115-011-9460-5

Skenazy, L. (2008, June 12). Fear Not! (Or at least—fear less!). *Free Range Kids.* Retrieved from http://www.freerangekids.com/fear-not-or-at-least-fear-less/

Skenazy, L. (2009, January 1). Why Free Range? *Free-Range Kids.* Retrieved from http://www.freerangekids.com/about/

Sotirin, P., & Ellingson, L. L. (2007). Rearticulating the aunt: Feminist alternatives of family, care, and kinship in popular performances of aunting. *Cultural Studies ↔ Critical Methodologies, 7*(4), 442–459. https://doi.org/10.1177/1532708607304538

Spock, B. (1946). *The common sense book of baby and child care.* New York, NY: Duell, Sloan, and Pearce.

Sroufe, L. A. (2005). Attachment and development: A prospective, longitudinal study from birth to adulthood. *Attachment & Human Development, 7*(4), 349–367. https://doi.org/10.1080/14616730500365928

Stets, J. E., & Burke, P. J. (2000). Identity theory and social identity theory. *Social Psychology Quarterly, 63*(3), 224–237. https://doi.org/10.2307/2695870

Stryker, S., & Burke, P. J. (2000). The past, present, and future of an identity theory. *Social Psychology Quarterly, 63*(4), 284–297. https://doi.org/10.2307/2695840

Suissa, J. (2013). Tiger mothers and praise junkies: Children, praise, and the reactive attitudes. *Journal of Philosophy of Education, 47*(1), 1–19. https://doi.org/10.1111/1467-9752.12016

Suter, E. A., Seurer, L. M., Webb, S., Grewe Jr, B., & Koenig Kellas, J. (2015). Motherhood as contested ideological terrain: Essentialist and queer discourses of motherhood at play in female-female co-mothers' talk. *Communication Monographs, 82*(4), 458–483. https://doi.org/10.1080/03637751.2015.1024702

Turner, R. H. (2001). Role theory. In J. H. Turner (Eds.), *Handbook of sociological theory* (pp. 233–254). New York, NY: Springer.

Radtke, H. L., Young, J., & van Mens-Verhulst, J. (2016). Aging, identity, and women: Constructing the third age. *Women & Therapy, 39*(1), 86–105. https://doi.org/10.1080/02703149.2016.1116321

Vota, N. (2017). Keeping the Free-Range parent immune from child neglect: You cannot tell me how to raise my children. *Family and Court Review, 55*(1), 152–167. https://doi.org/10.1111/fcre.12269

Walters, S. D. (1992). *Lives together, worlds apart: Mothers and daughters in popular culture.* Berkeley, CA: University of California Press.

Winnicott, D. W. (1953). Transitional objects and transitional phenomena: A study of the first not-me possession. *International Journal of Psychoanalysis, 34*, 89–97. https://doi.org/10.1093/med:psych/9780190271367.003.0034

Worell, J., & Goodheart, C. D. (2006). *Handbook of girls' and women's psychological health.* New York, NY: Oxford University Press.

CHAPTER FOUR

Reel Mothers AND Daughters

MICHELLE MILLER-DAY,* RIVA TUKACHINSKY,† AND SYDNEY JACOBS‡

The story of motherhood in popular film and television has a history of guiding popular ideals of femininity (Walters, 1992). Images of motherhood both reflect and construct our understandings of womanhood, femininity, and the mother-daughter relationship. From Donna Reed to Kris Jenner mothers depicted in the media, real or fictional, reveal societal beliefs about motherhood. This chapter will review and then examine some representations of the mother-daughter relationship in popular entertainment media such as U.S. television and film, arguing that the mother-daughter relationship is socially constructed through these media portrayals fraught with double-binds and wrapped up in ribbons of sacrifice and friendship.

THE SOCIAL CONSTRUCTION OF THE MOTHER-DAUGHTER RELATIONSHIP

Motherhood, daughterhood, mothering, daughtering and their meanings are not fixed and inevitable. They are the products of history and social ideals, ideas

* Michelle Miller-Day, professor, Chapman University, millerda@chapman.edu.
† Riva Tukachinsky, assistant professor, Chapman University, tukachin@chapman.edu.
‡ Sydney Jacobs, alumna, Chapman University.

embedded within society. As society changes, so too do these ideals. As we grow up in our own social spheres we are not told how to mother or daughter in full detail or how to play the part, but are given a "few cues, hints, and stage directions" (Goffman, 1959, p. 72) by the world around us. Media such as film and television both create and reflect the social constructs of motherhood and daughterhood. *Social constructs* are social categories developed by society and social practice (e.g., what is a "good mother"?) and the study of how humans jointly construct social understandings of these categories is referred to as *social constructionism* (Berger & Luckmann, 1991). Social constructions provide us with the social cues, hints and stage directions for how to enact the roles of mother and daughter.

Motherhood has become one of the biggest media obsessions (Steinberg, 2007) with depictions of motherhood and daughterhood having the power to affects one's perceptions of how mothers and daughters should perform their roles. Mothers and daughters come to understand their relationship "not only through the exigencies of daily life [...] but through the systems of representation and cultural production that help give shape and meaning to that relationship" (Walters, 1992, p. 4). Of interest in this chapter are the depictions of the mother-daughter relationship in film and television over time and how they both reflect the social beliefs of the time and help to change or construct new ideals of motherhood and daughterhood. According to Inglehart and Norris (2003), during the latter half of the 20th century there was a rising tide of change in the U.S., transforming cultural attitudes towards gender and gender roles. Therefore, focusing on select popular film and television from 1950 to 2000 we build on the work of Walters (1992) to explore how ideals for the mother-daughter relationship are, in part, formed by the cultural images in film and television. When we watch a television show or film we are presented with vivid and often contradictory images that provide us with messages about what it means to be a mother or a daughter.

FILM AND TELEVISION REPRESENTATIONS OF MOTHERS AND DAUGHTERS FROM 1950–2017

During World War II, women were heavily relied on to take on jobs previously held by men who were deployed (Goldin, 2006). With this, brought feminist icon Rosie the Riveter proudly claiming, "We can do it!" suggesting women can successfully keep the U.S. running while the men were off to war (Honey, 1985). Yet, once the war ended, men returned to their jobs and women were expected to return to their homes and resume their "primary" roles as wives and mothers (Honey, 1985). During this period, there was an influx of economic growth, the Baby Boom, migration to the suburbs, with the cultural ideal reflecting women as the embodiment of domesticity (Inglehart & Norris, 2003; Sweeney, 2002). During the 1950 media advertisements depicted women with arms full of groceries or cleaning the house looking happy and content, as if there was nothing else they'd rather do (Sweeney, 2002). These depictions conveyed the message that a woman's only goal in life was to please her husband and care for her children and anything otherwise was considered selfish.

The film *Imitation of Life* (Hunter & Sirk, 1959) follows the lives of Lora, a single White mother and aspiring actress and Annie, a single Black mother and housekeeper/nanny over a period of years after World War II. In this film there are two parallel stories that unify around the issue of mothering. Lana Turner plays Lora Meredith, impoverished and trying to break into the theatre while raising her young daughter, Susie. Lora is joined early in the film by Annie and her daughter Sara Jane who are also impoverished but come to live with "Miss Lora" to care for her home and family in exchange for room and board. Annie and Sarah Jane stay on with Lora and Susie over the course of many years witnessing Lora's professional success. In addition to myriad issues pertaining to race and racial equality, throughout the film there is a double-bind message that runs throughout. A *double-bind* is a message promoting two mutually exclusive self-presentations (Johnston & Swanson, 2003). As the country was pushing women out of the workforce and back into the home, social messages conveyed the sense that being a "good mother" was not possible if a woman had a career. During this period, pursuing a career (not just having a job outside the home) and functioning as a good mother were often depicted as mutually exclusive, with the term "career woman" equaling maternal deprivation (Walters, 1992). Therefore, Lora's single-mindedness in pursuing a career is portrayed as narcissistic and neglectful. Lora's daughter, Susie, laments to her mother, "You've given me everything but you" (Hunter & Sirk, 1959). Lora's desire to have a career was not only considered selfish, it was portrayed as aberrant. The message was clear. To become a "good mother" she must sacrifice her career. This narrative is contrasted with the story of Annie and Sarah Jane and sets up good mother-bad mother and good daughter-bad daughter tensions. Annie is portrayed as virtuous, motherly, nurturing, and attentive with Susie turning to her instead of her own mother for solace. But, Sarah Jane who desires to "pass as White" and scorns her Black mother is cast as the bad daughter who rejects her mother and her race only to realize at the end how important her mother was to her. Maternal sacrifice for your children was a popular theme for films of this period, embedded within the social discourses of race and class.

In the 1950s and 1960s the baby boom occurred across the United States. Families grew larger during the baby boom and suburban life became the ideal, while at the same time the percentage of homes with televisions rose exponentially with 83.2% of homes having televisions by 1959 (Baughman, 2006). During this period, Friedan (1963) wrote in her bestselling volume *The Feminine Mystique* which critiqued images of women arguing that women were situated culturally in a mindless void of domesticity:

> In the fifteen years after World War II, this mystique of feminine fulfillment became the cherished and self-perpetuating core of contemporary American culture. Millions of women lived their lives in the image of those pretty pictures of the American suburban housewife, kissing their husbands goodbye in front of the picture window, depositing their station wagons full of children at school, and smiling as they ran the new electric waxer over the spotless kitchen floor ... They were taught to pity the neurotic, unfeminine, unhappy women who wanted to be poets or physicists or presidents. They learned that truly feminine women do not want careers, higher education, political rights. (p. 58, 61)

During the 1960s shows like *Leave It to Beaver* (1957–1963) (Connelly, Mosher, & Conway, 1957) and *The Donna Reed Show* (1958–1966) (Owen, 1958) were some of the more popular domestic situation comedies (sitcoms) of the time, with *the Donna Reed Show* being the first to feature a mother as the protagonist. Over the decades other television shows such as *Cheers* (Burrows, Charles, & Charles, 1982) and *Gilmore Girls* (Sherman-Palladino, 2000) referred to Donna Reed at the epitome of the perfect "good mother" of the '50s and '60s, yet during the series Donna Reed is consistently depicted as trying to break out of the mold of the typical 1950's housewife (Morreale, 2012). In the episode *Male Ego* (Rodolph & Monaster, 1958), Donna's daughter, Mary, gives a moving speech about her mother's values and hard work as a mother and as a valued member of her community. Throughout the episode, the children rely on their mother for virtually all things and she makes significant contributions to her community as well; thus, making the father, Alex, feel unimportant and unnecessary. This exemplifies the "super-mom" ideal of mothers in the '60s—the one who does it all. As life began to revolve around domesticity, mothers were viewed as the source of stability and role models, relying little on their husbands for anything but breadwinning. Moreover, mothers and daughters in sitcoms during this period were depicted as existing in "carefree harmony, disrupted only occasionally by the angst of adolescence" (Walters, 1992, p. 81). By 1965, the feminist movement was increasingly being reflected in television and Donna Reed's domestic bliss no longer captured the public pulse and ratings began to fall (Morreale, 2012). In the mid-1960s new domestic sitcoms emerged, providing satirical depictions of the traditional housewives. For example, Morticia in *The Addams Family* (1964–1966) and Samantha in *Bewitched* (1964–1972) who relied on magic to complete her domestic tasks (O'Reilly, 2010). In addition, through the late 1960s and early 1970s in the United States, family structures became more diverse because of high divorce rates, increasing single parent headed households and blended families, positioning more women as heads of the household than ever before (O'Reilly, 2010).

Due to the shifting view of women and motherhood in the 1970s, sitcoms such as *Maude* (1972–1978) (Parker, 1972) were created, depicting an adult divorced daughter and mother living together (the mother, Maude, being on her fourth husband). The '70s marked the beginning of media's change from focusing on the nuclear family and domestic bliss to an increasingly diverse view of family life in terms of class, race, and family structure. Unlike the '50s, being a working mother with a career in the 1970s tended not to be depicted as selfish, but rather, encouraged as admirable. Moreover, representations of women as sexual beings with healthy (non-deviant) sex lives were rarely seen before the 1970s. Before this, TV shows and movies often depicted husband and wife sleeping in separate beds. For example, in the 1960s, even when real-life husband and wife, Lucille Ball and Desi Arnez, played husband and wife on *The Lucy Show* (1962–1968) (Thompson, 1962) and the show tracked Lucile Ball's real-life pregnancy on the show, the show depicted the couple sleeping in their separate twin beds throughout the entire run of the series. In the 1970s, mothers began to be shown as sexual beings for the first time. *Maude* depicted a mother who is no longer only just caring for her husband and her family, but also for herself. The audience saw Maude as a woman outside of her role as mother. This series created a good amount of social unrest during the run of the series, with some individuals believing that the series encouraged women to leave their husbands and be more independent (Dow, 1996). Not only were women represented as women outside their role as mother, but women were increasingly being depicted as sexual beings. In the episode *Like Mother/ Like Daughter* (Hobin, Lear, & Harris, 1972) Maude was depicted as a sexual rival to her daughter. This episode demonstrated competition between mother and daughter over a man both had dated. The two women were on the same "playing field" with Maude's sexuality and independence as potent as her daughter's. By the '70s media depictions of mothers and daughters reflected a more complex and realistic view of women as sexual beings, working women, and single moms.

In the 1980s we continue to see images of the sacrificial mother, but also an increase in media messages replete with mother blaming. *Mother blaming* refers to casting blame on mothers for her children's behavior and all their problems (Sommerfeld, 1989). Mothers are either idealized or blamed for everything that goes wrong, represented as selfless angels or self-centered witches. During this period, mothers were cherished and praised for everything that went right with their daughters, they were also shamed and blamed for everything that went wrong, often depicting a symbiotic relationship and creating a double-bind. To be a good mother, one had to be friends with daughters, but also be responsible for their successes and failures.

The film *Terms of Endearment* (1983) exemplified both messages of sacrifice and mother-blaming. Throughout the movie, Aurora Greenway and her daughter Emma have a relatively enmeshed relationship. In an enmeshed relationship there is an extreme amount of emotional closeness, and loyalty is demanded. Individuals are very dependent on each other and reactive to one another. There is a lack of personal separateness and little private space is permitted. The energy of the individuals is mainly focused inside the family and there are few outside individual friends or interests (Olson, 2000). Like the symbiotic relationship depicted in a popular book at the time, *My Mother, Myself: The Daughter's Search for Identity* (Friday, 1977), both Aurora and Emma see themselves in each other, depend heavily on each other, but Emma wants to resist the cosmic pull of her mother at every turn. They update each other on their lives daily and always keep in touch, even when Emma moves away. At the same time, they fight constantly, and Emma tries to extricate herself from her mother's need at multiple points during the film. Both Emma and Aurora are depicted as "sacrificial" mothers throughout the film. Emma sacrificed being a career woman to prioritize being a wife and mother to her three children. When Emma visits New York toward the end of the film and meets other women, the divide between housewife and career woman is highlighted. The friends begin to ask Emma if she's planning on going back to work once her toddler is older, in which Emma responds that she's never really worked. The other women are shocked and start to judge Emma for not having a career outside the home. The juxtaposition of the two different types of women in society at the time emphasizes the image of sacrificial mother in the case of Emma. For the widowed Aurora, she was depicted as a woman who prioritized being Emma's mother over pursuing any romantic relationships, despite her dedicated admirers. When Emma becomes an adult and moves away, Aurora finally starts to pursue a relationship and reclaim her womanhood, focusing on herself as a woman instead of solely as a mother.

The tensions between selfish and selfless mothering are also depicted in this film with Aurora refusing to attend Emma's wedding, reacting poorly to the news that she was to be a grandmother, and many instances of not supporting her daughter or her daughter's choices. Emma blamed Aurora for not being a good mother and refusing to show up to her wedding, for not being happy for her and for many of the disappointments in her married life. Yet, she could not extricate herself from her mother's gravitational force.

By the turn of the century, in the early 2000s, mothers in the media often resisted becoming like their mothers and sought to be their daughters' best friends. The era of mom and daughter as best friends emerged evoking the nickname, the "Gilmore years." As the nickname states, the television series the *Gilmore Girls* (2000–2007) (Sherman-Palladino, 2000) provided a clear demonstration of mother as best friend. Lorelai is Rory's mother and Lorelai "made it her purpose to prevent her daughter from making the same mistakes [she] did and therefore give [Rory] all the opportunities she missed out on in her own youth," (Hiddlestone, 2007, p.33). Mother-blaming was still evident in *Gilmore Girls*, with Lorelai blaming her own mother for many of the mistakes she made early in life, but Lorelai and was trying to make up for these mistakes by becoming her daughter's friend. Lorelai's attitude towards parenting was being the "cool" mom and the best friend. This type of relationship defied the typical distance between parent and child standards, being, as close to equality as a parent-child relationship can get (Hiddlestone, 2007). Even though the dynamic is much different than those seen in years before, Lorelai doesn't sacrifice her need to "mother" Rory when also functioning as Rory's best friend.

During the 2000s, with increased programming on television cable and video streaming, there have been increased depictions of mothers behaving badly. Walters and Harrison (2014) argue that as we moved into the 21st century a new type of mother emerged—particularly in non-network cable TV—that presented a radical departure from previous depictions. From the suburban mom/drug dealer of Showtime's *Weeds* (Kohan, 2005) to the wives of *Mad Men* (Hornbacher, 2007) and films such as *Bad Moms* (Block, Lucas, & Moore, 2016) there were depictions of increasingly aberrant mothers. But "unlike aberrant mothers of earlier eras, these mothers are by and large heroines, unapologetically non-normative in their maternal functioning. Their parenting is cursory at best and often downright neglectful, behavior that has typically resulted in sure death for Hollywood mothers of earlier eras" (Walters & Harrison, 2014, p. 38). These mothers are no longer sacrificial, are unapologetically sexual, and oftentimes neglectful of their daughters. Walters and Harrison (2014) note that shows like Desperate Housewives, which feature women very concerned with being great mothers to their children, are also depicted as, "uncontrolled and uncontrollable, full of urges, desires and identities that are antithetical to what we imagine of a good mother." Likewise, with reality TV show moms, mom bloggers, "cool" moms and more, "motherhood in the new millennium is marked by an excess of meaning," (Walters & Harrison, 2014). This "bad mom" depiction is not intended to put women down for ignoring their duties as a mother, but rather, aimed to display their identity as a woman and human being in addition to being a mother—a depiction that has taken decades to be deemed appropriate enough for mass media. Even though they may be "bad," their maternal commitments were rarely doubted and there was a "significant amount of actual labor" occurring …"and the bad mother as anti-hero might be just what we need" (Walters & Harrison, 2014, p. 51). It is unclear what future cultural representations of the mother-daughter relationship will bring, but these are bound to provide messages hinting at what it is to be a "good" or "bad" mother or daughter.

THE STUDY

Examining messages about mothers and daughters in television and film is fun, but it is also important. If we are to understand how popular media has shaped social expectations for mothers and daughters over the years, a critical examination of popular media over time is necessary. To complement the existing feminist and critical cultural evaluations of media we conducted a quantitative content analysis study of network television between 1990 and 2017 to examine how the mother-daughter relationship is depicted over time.

What Were We Interested in Learning?

Guided by important themes identified in previous mother-daughter research we investigated various representations of the mother-daughter relationship in network television asking, *what are the differences in how the mother–daughter relationship is depicted in television between 1990–2017?*

How Did We Go About Learning This Information?

Sample

Fifty-two television episodes that aired on network television between 1990 and 2017 were sampled. To be included in the sample, the show had to meet the following criteria: (a) a scripted live action fiction program (i.e., not reality TV, documentary or animated series); (b) aired for at least two seasons; and (c) prominently featured at least one relationship between an adult/teen daughter and her mother. To meet the third inclusion criterion, either the mother or the daughter had to be part of the main cast on the show and the other character had to be part of the reoccurring cast. If a randomly sampled episode from a television series did not depict both the mother and the daughter, another episode from the show was re-sampled. If more than one mother-daughter dyad was depicted in a given episode, the one most prominently featured relationship was coded. Step mothers were not included in the sample.

Coding

Coding was completed by a trained coder. Eleven (21%) of the episodes were coded both by the coder and one of the authors, to ensure intercoder reliability. Krippendorff's α has been computed to assess reliability for each variable. All disagreements have been resolved by reaching a consensus through discussion.

Variables

Episode-level Variables

The *genre* of each program was coded as either comedy (intended to be humorous and amusing, $n = 16$, 31%, e.g., *The Goldbergs*), drama (realistic characters dealing with emotional themes, $n = 20$, 39%, e.g., *The OC*), or situation comedy (sitcom: comic show with a laughing track, $n = 15$, 29%, e.g., *Step by Step*).

For subsequent analyses, the genres were combined into two main categories—comedy (including both comedy and sitcom) and drama. The *network* on which the episode was originally broadcasted ($\alpha = 1.0$). The *year* when the episode was originally aired ($\alpha = 1.0$). For subsequent analyses, this variable was recoded into decades: 1990–1999 ($n = 20$), 2000–2009 ($n = 15$), and 2010–2017 ($n = 17$). The *total number of dyads* eligible for coding in a given episode was identified. These include all the mother-daughter dyads of recurring/main characters with daughters ages 12 and above. The most prominently depicted dyad was then coded for subsequent characteristics ($\alpha = .95$). Of these dyads, only one dyad per episode was chosen for character-level and relationship-level analysis. There was a 100% agreement between coders as to which dyad should be selected for the character-level analyses. The *prominence* or the extent to which the mother-daughter relationship is central to the narrative of the episode was coded as a major storyline, minor storyline, or a brief reference ($\alpha = .80$). In most of the coded programs (62%) the mother-daughter relationship constituted a main story line, and the rest were deemed minor story lines.

Character-level Variables

The mother and the daughter characters in each episode were coded for demographic and personal characteristics. *Race/ethnicity* for each character (mother and daughter) was coded as White, Black, Latina, Asian, Native American, or Mixed (defined as a combination of at least two non-White ethnicities) ($\alpha = 1.0$ for both the mother and the daughter characters). For *age*, an estimate age-group of the characters has been made. Age categories included: *adolescent* (12–17 years old), *late adolescent* (18–21 years old), *young adult* (22–30 years old), *adult* (31–49 years old), *middle aged* (50–65 years old), or *elderly* (66 years old and above). Given that only relationships with teen or adult daughters were coded, naturally there were no adolescent and late adolescent mothers coded. The reliability for the daughters' age was considerably more reliable ($\alpha = .99$) than the reliability for mothers ($\alpha = .66$). This can be explained by the fact that the daughters' age was more often referenced in the dialogue, or it could be deduced from the life-stage of the daughter (e.g., middle school, freshman in college). *Socio-economic status* was coded as low (i.e., live in poverty or a student), middle (i.e., moderate standard of living with some struggles), high (i.e., financially secure, but does not have to be rich), or unknown (i.e., no information has been provided). Mother: $\alpha = .56$, daughter: $\alpha = .75$.

Mother and Daughter Variables

Several variables emerged from mother-daughter research as well as from media studies that focused our inquiry into media depictions of mothers, daughters, and the mother-daughter relationship. From this literature we selected the following variables to code individually: Sacrificial mother, sexual objectification, and filial comprehending.

Sacrificial Mother. This is the extent to which the mother gives up something of importance so that her daughter can gain something from the mother's sacrifice (Rubenstein, 1998; Walters, 1992; Williams, 1984) was coded on a three-point scale from "1" *not at all* to "3" *very much.* The sacrifice had to be explicit in the narrative ($\alpha = .56$).

Sexual Objectification. The extent to which the character is sexualized/objec-tified was measured on a three-point scale from "1" *not at all* to "3" *very much.* Objectification could occur through provocative clothing, nonverbal behaviors, dialogue (what she says and what others say about her) or being explicitly depicted as an object of sexual desire by other characters (Walters, 1992). Mother: $\alpha = .89$, daughter: $\alpha = .75$.

Filial Comprehending. Filial comprehending occurs when a daughter begins to view her mother as an individual rather than just as a mother (Fisher & Miller-Day, 2006; Miller-Day, 2004). This variable encompasses the daughter's acknowledge-ment that mother is a person, a woman, a professional or assumes another role outside of her role as "mother." Only an explicit message that the daughter sees her mother differently—not as mother but as something else—were coded as achieved filial comprehension, and all other cases were coded as not depicting filial compre-hension ($\alpha = .42$).

Mother-Daughter Relationship-level Variables

The nature of the relationship overall between the mother and the daughter char-acters were coded for a variety of relational dialectics. According to the dialectical perspective, all relationships are constantly changing and fraught with contradic-tions. These contradictions are relational phenomena termed *relational dialectics* (Miller-Day, 2004). Relational dialectics assert that persons in relationships man-age opposing interdependent forces that stand in dialectical association with each other (Montgomery & Baxter, 1998).

Stability/Change. The orientation to change in the mother-daughter relationship in an episode was coded as a function of the extent to which the characters resist or accept change in their relationship ($\alpha = .89$). Categories included (1) recep-tive to change through the episode, (2) neutral/mixed throughout the episode, (3) resistant to change throughout the episode, (4) transition from resistance to acceptance, or (5) transitioning from acceptance to resistance.

Powerful/Powerless. The orientation to power in the mother-daughter relationship in the episode was coded based on the emotional, financial, and other resources that the characters possess relative to each other (α = .76). Categories included (1) daughter more powerful through the episode, (2) neutral/mixed throughout the episode, (3) mother more powerful throughout the episode, (4) transition from mother to daughter, or (5) transitioning from daughter to mother.

Openness/Closedness. The relationship was coded for the extent to which the characters share feelings, ideas, and information, versus keeping information restricted, private, and concealed from the other character (α = .73). Disclosure was coded as (1) closed through the episode, (2) neutral/mixed throughout the episode, (3) open throughout the episode, (4) transition from closed towards more open, or (5) transitioning from open to more closed.

Family Role/Friend. The mother-daughter relationship is rated according to the characters' orientations to each other as either based on sociological roles as rigid mother/daughter roles, or more like peers and friends. The relationship was coded based on explicit depictions of rigid sociological role interactions (clear boundaries, obeying behaviors) or friend-like behaviors (e.g., daughter privy to mother's relationships, engaging in activities like consuming recreational drugs together, etc.) (α = .65). Categories included: (1) mother-daughter roles, (2) mixed mother-daughter but also some friends roles throughout the episode, (3) friends throughout the episode, (4) transition from rigid roles towards friends-like, or (5) transitioning from friendship to more rigid roles.

Competition/No Competition. The mother-daughter relationship is rated as (1) competitive, (2) neutral or mixed—competitive in some cases but not others, (3) non-competitive, (4) moving from competitive to non-competitive, or (5) moving from non-competitive to competitive. To be coded as competitive to any extent, the narrative explicitly depicted a competition for some resource such as attention or a reward (α = .49).

Comforting/Hurtful. The characters' caring orientation towards each other was coded for explicitly hurtful or comforting behaviors: (1) hurtful, (2) neutral or mixed, (3) comforting, (4) moving from hurtful to comforting, or (5) moving from comforting to hurtful (α = .74).

Mother-Centered/Daughter-Centered. The storyline was coded for the focal character of the story whose perspective is most represented: (1) daughter-centered, (2) equally balanced, (3) mother-centered (α = .73).

What Did We Learn?

Characteristics of Mothers and Daughters in the Shows

On average, each show depicted two mother-daughter dyads (M = 2.02, SD = 1.08, range 1–6). The coded programs featured almost exclusively White upper-class families. The only ethnic minority depicted was Black, constituting only 10% of the mothers and the daughters coded. Only 10% of daughters and 8% of mothers were low/middle SES. Most (66%) of the daughters in the sample were teenagers ages 12–17 with mothers typically (75%) in their 30s and 40s.

The narrative was often (52%) told from the point of view of the daughter whereas only 29% of the shows represented the mother's perspective alone. Most (64%) of the daughters did not reach filial comprehension. Filial comprehension was particularly present in older daughters (63–71% in daughters ages 22–49), while none of the daughters ages 18–21 and only 27% of daughters ages 12–17 achieved it ($\chi^2(3)$ = 9.21 p < .05, η = .42).

Sacrificial mothers were uncommon. Overall, 78% of the mothers were *not at all* sacrificial and a mere 6% of the mothers were highly sacrificial.

There were no differences between levels of sexual objectification of mothers and daughters. For the most part, both mothers (67%) and daughters (58%) were not objectified sexually with only 10% of mothers and 8% of daughters highly objectified sexually.

Dialectical Nature of the Shows' Mother-Daughter Relationships

Overall, mother-daughter relationships on television during this period evolved throughout any given episode, typically characterized as moving from resistance to change at the beginning of the episode to acceptance of change at the end of the episode (50%), and from being closed to more open (39%). Ultimately, considering the note on which the episodes ended, 73% of the relationships were receptive of change and 58% of them were open. Relationships were also mostly positive, typically ending on a comforting and non-competitive note. Many of the relationships were comforting throughout the episode (39%) and others transitioned from being hurtful to comforting (23%) over the course of the episode. Most (58%) of the relationships also become less competitive. Nonetheless, the relationships were usually rigid (69%) with characters assuming clear sociological roles of a mother and daughter. Accordingly, in 43% of the relationships, mothers had more power than did their daughters, and in another 17% the power in the relationship gravitated towards the mother over the course of the episode. Notably, this was more characteristic of dramatic shows than comic programs. Almost all (90%) of the families in dramas were set in rigid roles, compared to only 58% of families in comedies and sitcoms ($\chi^2(2)$ = 6.38, p < .05, η = .35). Similarly, compared to dramas, comic shows featured more mixed power (25% vs. 10%).

Changes Across Time

There were no significant differences in the pattern of portrayals of mother-daughter relationships over the course of the three decades under consideration. The only exceptions were stability and filial comprehension. It appears that there is a tendency for more resistance to change over time. In the 1990s 80% of the dyads were receptive to change compared to 73% in the 2000s, and just 65% in the 2010s. Instead, the 2010s shows depict more mixed reactions to change ($\chi^2(4)$ = 9.46, p = .05, η =.07). Likewise, there is a significantly higher level of filial comprehension in the more recent seasons, growing from merely 20–25% in the 1990s–2000s to 65% in the 2010s ($\chi^2(2)$ = 8.75, p < .05, η = .41).

WHAT DOES ALL THIS MEAN?

In this chapter we discussed how representations of the mother-daughter relationship in popular U.S. television and film help construct ideals of what it is to be a (good) mother and daughter and provide us with social cues and hints for how to enact these roles. Yet, these media portrayals are fraught with double-binds and images of maternal sacrifice as well as mother-daughter friendship.

Although representations of mother-daughter relationships may have changed significantly in cable television (Walters & Harrison, 2014), our study suggests that on network television there has not been much change over time in depictions of mothers and daughter, except for filial comprehension depictions. Over time, network television included significantly more depictions of daughters acknowledging their mother as a person with her own goals and desires and not just as her mother. Seeing a woman outside her role of mother is an important stepping stone in making progress for women who may embrace several identities in their lifetime. The study also reveals that network television over the past thirty years represented mother-daughter relationships privileging open communication, embracing change, revealing secrets, and moving toward increased connection. Interestingly, it is the comedies that tend to portray mothers as less powerful and less authoritative (more friend-like) and viewers are invited to laugh at this model and reject it. This may suggest a changing social dynamic; yet more research is needed to investigate this. Of note is the lack of sacrifice observed in the television episodes coded in the study. This is in contradiction to previous media and feminist studies reporting that the sacrificial mother has been ever present in media representations from the early 1900's to the turn of the 21st century (Rubenstein, 1998; Walters, 1992).

The study presented in this chapter has its limitations. Overall, the dataset depicts a very narrow set of families with mothers and daughters. There are very few non-White and low/middle class families and adult daughters with elderly mothers almost non-existent. This is consistent with other content analysis work on television programming—underrepresentation of ethnic minorities and older adults (e.g., Robinson & Skill, 1995; Tukachinsky, Mastro, & Yarchi, 2015).

WHAT DO WE STILL NEED TO KNOW?

- Is media moving away from the image of mother-daughter best friend toward a different cultural model?
- What social, political, economic, and organizational factors play a role in determining how mother-daughter relationships are depicted in the media?
- What other forms of media might shape our cultural ideas of what it is to be a (good) mother or daughter?
- Are there differences between television and other entertainment media portrayals and if so, what causes these differences?
- What are representations in entertainment media of mother-son, father-son, and father-daughter relationships?
- The current study only looked at a snapshot of each mother-daughter relationship within a single episode. Would the findings be different if study examined relationships as they evolve over the course of a full season? How/why?
- Social constructionism suggests that exposure to messages about mothering and daughtering in television and film would shape women's attitudes about how to mother and daughter, but data from viewers is needed to assess the actual media effects.

HOW DOES THIS WORK IN REAL LIFE?

- Why might it be important to show more television representations of daughters viewing their mothers as women with individual needs and goals, instead of just as mothers?
- Would it be useful to do similar investigations of mother-son, father-son, and father-daughter representations? What do you think we might find?
- Compare the results of this study to the content analysis of a representation of fathers from 1950s to 1990 (Scharrer, 2001). Would it be valuable to replicate that study in the context of mothers rather than fathers? Based on the findings of the current study, how do you expect the results to be similar or different to those in Scharrer's study?
- How does diversity behind the camera (e.g., assuming roles of directors, script writers, and producers) have implications for representations of mothers and daughters?

- If you were able to influence the media industry, would you encourage script writers and directors to make any changes in their current representations of mother-daughter relationships? What would you suggest and why?
- How do you think these television representations influence the viewers? Can you think of short term and long-term effects? Consider the potential effects on different groups of viewers (young or prospective mothers, teenage daughters, fathers, members of different racial groups, etc.)
- How do you viewers respond to the different types of relationship in the media? Do they relate to different characteristics? What characters do they identify with the most? Again, consider the reactions of viewers from different social groups.
- Do you think that media reflect existing social and cultural norms or do media contribute to shaping social and cultural norms? How could we empirically distinguish between these "chicken and the egg" processes?
- What did you expect the researchers to find? Were you surprised by the results? In your opinion, are the results of this study are "good" or "bad"? In what ways?

CLASSROOM ACTIVITIES

- Select two of the following films to watch and then compare and contrast how the mother-daughter relationship is represented during the different time periods. How might the cultural and economic contexts of that decade have shaped the messages in the films?
  - *Imitation of Life* (Hunter & Sirk, 1959)
  - *Carrie* (Monash & De Palma, 1976)
  - *Terms of Endearment* (Brooks, 1983)
  - *The Joy Luck Club* (Bass & Wang, 1993)
  - *Thirteen* (London & Hardwicke, 2003)
- View the "Tush Push and Some Radishes" episode (Season 4, Episode 18) of the television series *Mom*. Identify and discuss the dominant relational dialectics in a mother-daughter relationship?
- Prior to the class, students can be assigned to invent a new television sitcom or drama and write a one-page synopsis of a pilot episode for this show. Students should describe the main characters and the events taking place during the episode. In class, students can break down into groups and analyze each other's synopses asking the following questions: (1) Does the show have a mother/daughter dyad? (2) If so, what are the theoretically

meaningful characteristics of mothers and daughters? (3) To what extent these mothers/daughters are consistent or inconsistent with what we see on the screen today? Discuss how students came up with these characteristics and how these student-based ideas are similar to or different from current media representations and why.

REFERENCES

Ackerman, H. (Executive Producer). (1964). *Bewitched* [Television series]. Hollywood, CA: Warner Brothers.

Bass, R. (Producer), & Wang, W. (Director). (1993). *The joy luck club* [Motion picture]. Hollywood, CA: Hollywood Pictures.

Baughman, J. L. (2006). *The republic of mass culture: Journalism, filmmaking, and broadcasting in America since 1941*. Baltimore, MD: JHU Press.

Berger, P., & Luckmann, T. (1991). *The social construction of reality: A treatise in the sociology of knowledge*. London, UK: Penguin Books.

Block, B. (Producer), Lucas, J., & Moore, S. (Directors). (2016). *Bad moms* [Motion picture]. Hollywood, CA: Billblock media.

Brooks, J. L. (Producer/Director). (1983). *Terms of endearment* [Motion picture]. Los Angeles, CA: Paramount Studios.

Burrows, J., Charles, G., & Charles, L. (Executive producers). (1982). *Cheers* [Television series]. Los Angeles, CA: Paramount Studios.

Connelly, J., Mosher, B., & Conway, D. (Creators). (1957). *Leave it to Beaver* [Television series]. Studio City, CA: CBS Studio City.

Dow, B. J. (1996). *Prime-time feminism: Television, media culture, and the women's movement since 1970.* Philadelphia: University of Pennsylvania Press.

Fisher, C., & Miller-Day, M. (2006). Communication over the life span: The mother-adult daughter relationships. In K. Floyd & M. Morman (Eds.), *Widening the family circle: New research on family communication* (pp. 3–16). Newbury Park, CA: Sage.

Friday, N. (1997). *My mother/myself: The daughter's search for identity*. New York, NY: Delta.

Friedan, B. (1963). *The feminine mystique*. New York, NY: W. W. Norton.

Goffman, E. (1959). *The presentation of self in everyday life*. New York, NY: Doubleday.

Goldin, C. (2006). The quiet revolution that transformed women's employment, education, and family. *American Economic Review, 96*(2), 1–21.

Hiddlestone, J. (2007). Mothers, daughters and Gilmore girls. In J. Crusie & L. Wilson (Eds.), *Coffee at Luke's: An unauthorized Gilmore girls gabfest* (pp. 31–42). Dallas, TX: Benbella Books.

Hobin, B. (Director), Lear, N., & Harris, S. (Writers). (1972, October 3). Like mother, like daughter [Television series episode, season 1, episode 4]. In R. Parker (Executive producer). *Maude* [Television series]. Hollywood, CA: Tandem Productions.

Honey, M. (1985). *Creating Rosie the riveter: Class, gender, and propaganda during World War II*. Amherst, MA: University of Massachusetts Press.

Hornbacher, S. (Executive producer). (2007). *Mad men* [Television series]. Los Angeles, CA: Lionsgate.

Hunter, R. (Producer), & Sirk, D. (Director). (1959). *Imitation of life* [Motion picture]. Hollywood, CA: Universal Pictures.

Inglehart, R., & Norris, P. (2003). *Rising tide: Gender equality and cultural change around the world.* Cambridge, UK: Cambridge University Press.

Johnston, D. D., & Swanson, D. H. (2003). Undermining mothers: A content analysis of the representation of mothers in magazines. *Mass Communication and Society, 6*(3), 243–265. https://doi.org/10.1207/S15327825MCS0603_2

Kohan, J. (Executive producer). (2005). *Weeds* [Television series]. Los Angeles, CA: Lionsgate.

London, M., (Producer), & Hardwicke, C. (Director). (2003). *Thirteen* [Motion picture]. Los Angeles, CA: Twentieth Century Fox.

Lorre, C. (Writer), & Widdoes, J. (Director). (April 6, 2017). Tush Push and Some Radishes. [Television series episode]. In N. Backay (Producer), *Mom.* Burbank, CA: USA.

Miller-Day, M. (2004). *Communication among grandmothers, mothers, and adult daughters: A qualitative study of maternal relationships.* Mahwah, NJ: Lawrence Erlbaum.

Monash, P. (Producer), & De Palma, B. (Director). (1976). *Carrie* [Motion picture]. Red Bank, NJ: Red Bank Films.

Montgomery, B. M., & Baxter, L. A. (1998). *Dialectical approaches to studying personal relationships.* Mahwah, NJ: Lawrence Erlbaum.

Morreale, J. (2012). *The Donna Reed show.* Detroit, MI: Wayne State University Press.

Olson, D. H. (2000). Circumplex model of marital and family systems. *Journal of Family Therapy, 22*(2), 144–167.

O'Reilly, A. (2010). Mothers in media. *Encyclopedia of Motherhood, 1,* 748–749.

Owen, T. (Producer). (1958). *The Donna Reed show* [Television series]. Burbank, CA: ABC.

Parker, R. (Executive producer). (1972). *Maude* [Television series]. Hollywood, CA: Tandem Productions.

Perrin, N. (Producer). (1964). *The Adams family* [Television series]. Hollywood, CA: General Service Studios.

Robinson, J. D., & Skill, T. (1995). The invisible generation: Portrayals of the elderly on prime-time television. *Communication Reports, 8*(2), 111–119. https://doi.org/10.1080/08934219509367617

Rodolph, O. (Director), & Monaster, N. (Writer). (1958, October 15). Male ego [Television series episode, season 1, episode 4]. In W. Roberts (Creator), *The Donna Reed show.* New York, NY: ABC Studios

Rubenstein, C. (1998). *The sacrificial mother: Escaping the trap of self-denial.* New York, NY: Hyperion Books.

Scharrer, E. (2001). From wise to foolish: The portrayal of the sitcom father, 1950s–1990s. *Journal of Broadcasting & Electronic Media, 45*(1), 23–40. https://doi.org/10.1207/s15506878jobem4501_3

Sherman-Palladino, A. (Producer). (2000). *Gilmore girls* [Television series]. Burbank, CA: Warner Brothers.

Sommerfeld, D. P. (1989). The origins of mother blaming: Historical perspectives on childhood and motherhood. *Infant Mental Health Journal, 10*(1), 14–24.

Steinberg, E. (2007). *Finding your inner mama: Women reflect on the challenges and rewards of motherhood.* Boston, MA: Trumpeter.

Sweeney, M. M. (2002). Two decades of family change: The shifting economic foundations of marriage. *American Sociological Review, 67,* 132–147.

Thompson, T. (Producer). (1962). *The Lucy show* [Television series]. Culver City, CA: Desilu Studios.

Tukachinsky, R., Mastro, D., & Yarchi, M. (2015). Documenting portrayals of race/ethnicity on primetime television over a 20-year span and their association with national-level racial/ethnic attitudes. *Journal of Social Issues, 71*(1), 17–38. https://doi.org/10.1111/josi.12094

Walters, S. D. (1992). *Lives together/worlds apart*. Berkeley, CA: University of California Press.

Walters, S. D., & Harrison, L. (2014). Not ready to make nice: Aberrant mothers in contemporary culture. *Feminist Media Studies, 14*(1), 38–55. https://doi.org/10.1080/14680777.2012.742919

Williams, L. (1984). Something else besides a mother: Stella Dallas and the maternal melodrama. *Cinema Journal, 24*(1), 2–27. https://doi.org/10.2307/1225306

CHAPTER FIVE

Memorable Moments

Turning Points in the Mother-Daughter Relationship from Childhood to Mid-Life

MICHELLE MILLER-DAY*

Thinking back through my lifetime and the memories I have of my relationship with my mother, I can point to a handful of memorable moments that either increased or decreased my experience of intimacy in the relationship. One of my earliest memories of a memorable moment in our relationship is the time when I was five-years-old and I burned my hand on our stove. My mother was angry with me. I had expected her to care for me, comfort me, and sympathize with my pain. Instead, exhausted from spending the past week sitting by my brother's bed in the hospital, her temper was short, and the last thing she wanted was to deal with another sick or injured child. She yelled at me, bandaged my hand, and made me go to bed. I recall lying awake and crying. Crying in pain, but also self-pity. How could she spend so much time with my brother and then when I get hurt, I get into trouble? Of course, at the age of five I did not understand that my mother was exhausted and feeling stressed about my brother's illness. In my world, I felt neglected and betrayed. For me, this was memorable, and it decreased my feelings of closeness to my mother.

Memorable moments that occur in our relationships that serve to increase or decrease intimacy are called *relational turning points*. Turning points are "events or relational incidents that are associated with change or transformation in a relationship" (Baxter & Wolf, 2009, p. 1652). Miller-Day (2004) indicates that turning points result in the recalibration of the mother-daughter relationship. Once these

---

* Michelle Miller-Day, professor, Chapman University, millerda@chapman.edu.

turning points occur, we consider the mother-daughter relationship and adjust our perceptions and expectations of the relationship. I experienced several turning points in my relationship with my mother in my lifetime, with her death last year providing our final significant relational turning point. Some turning points resulted in me pulling away from my mother (such as the example above), and some brought me closer to her (e.g., attending my first Broadway show with her). Thankfully, I had many more upward turning points bringing me closer to my mother, than downward turning points pulling me away from her. This chapter will explore some of the most common relational turning points in the mother-daughter relationship, with a specific focus on social support—one of the most commonly reported types of turning points in the mother-daughter relationship.

MOTHER-DAUGHTER TURNING POINTS: *"I REMEMBER WHEN ..."*

Using retrospective interviews and asking individuals to graph their relational turning points across time, several scholars have examined turning points in mother-child relationships from childhood to mid-life. These studies are designed to identify moments that serve to constitute, reinforce, or redefine family bonds and relational intimacy (Miller-Day, Fisher, & Stube, 2013). This type of research typically asks adult individuals to think back and remember the turning points in their mother-child relationship, noting details of what occurred and how they experienced this relational transition (see for example, Fisher & Miller-Day, 2006; Golish, 2000; Miller-Day, 2004; Miller-Day et al., 2013).

Findings of this research reveal that turning points in mother-daughter relationships can include both grand, life-altering moments—such as a daughter's pregnancy and childbirth—or more intimate relational events, such as a shared activity like attending a Broadway musical together. The following discussion identifies the primary types of turning points reported by both mothers and daughters in previous research.

Types of Mother-Daughter Turning Points

Social Support

Interactions involving the provision or receipt of social support are categorized as one of the most common types of relational turning points. Mattson and Hall (2011) define *social support* as a "transactional communicative process, including verbal and/or nonverbal communication, which aims to improve an individual's feelings of coping, competence, belonging, and/or esteem" (p. 184). Social support is one of the most important and fundamental forms of family communication, and it has been argued that one of the primary functions of the family is to provide social support to its members (Segrin & Flora, 2005). For most children, the family is the primary source of social support and affection (Furman & Buhrmester, 1985; Levitt, Guacci-Franco, & Levitt, 1993). There are several different types of support, but research on turning points finds that receiving and providing social support from mothers and daughters is consequential to the mother-daughter connection. Receiving or providing social support was the most frequently listed turning point for both daughters and sons in Miller-Day et al.'s (2013) study of mother-daughter and mother-son relationships. For example, participants recalled the importance of receiving support ("On the night of graduation, my mom cried and said she was so proud of me and all my accomplishments") or providing support ("I just listen to her and help her with her problems") to the health of the relationship (Miller-Day et al., 2013, p. 10). Support can include assisting with tasks, providing financial assistance, expressing love, providing encouragement, empathizing, and offering and accepting advice. Harrigan and Miller-Ott (2013) found that supportive communication between mothers and daughters has been shown to ease the interaction between stress, life events, and depression. Previous research on mother-adult daughter relationships reveals that daughters report a greater desire to obtain support from mothers than sons (Trees, 2000) and come to expect emotional and instrumental support in their mother-daughter relationships (Fisher & Miller-Day, 2006). The expectations we hold about what is supportive in different contexts may lead to disappointment when our mother negatively violates that expectation or leads to surprise when she performs an unexpected act of support.

Shared Activities

Both mothers and daughters indicate that shared activities can be a type of turning point that can impact the mother-daughter relationship (Fisher & Miller-Day, 2006; Miller-Day et al., 2013). Activities can be isolated memorable events such as special vacations or attending a specific performance, or they can be more common rituals or traditions shared between the women, such as getting their hair or nails done together annually on each other's birthday. Having uninterrupted "mother-daughter time" can serve to reconnect mothers and daughters, strengthening their bond (Miller-Day, 2004).

Conflict

Conflict is an "expressed struggle between at least two interdependent parties who perceive incompatible goals, scarce resources, and interference from the other party in achieving their goals" (Beebe, Beebe, & Redmond, 2016, p. 210) and it can be constructive or destructive to a relationship. An argument can be a sincere effort to work out differences or an opportunity to release hostility and assign blame. Blame suggests "it is not my fault, it is hers" and mother-blaming can last a lifetime, causing irreparable damage to the mother-daughter relationship (Caplan, 2002). For many women, the height of mother-daughter conflict occurs in adolescence (Golish, 2000), with both mothers and daughters reporting versions of "We yelled a lot about everything," "We fought about priorities," and "We argued about boys" in adolescence. Human development literature indicates that the developmental tasks of middle-aged mothers and adolescent daughters are interrelated (Bassoff, 1988) with both midlife mothers and adolescent daughters experiencing the stress of separation and self-definition. Adolescent daughters struggle developmentally to separate from mothers while attaining a unique identity, while mothers struggle with a sense of loss and rejection as the daughter pulls away from her. Moreover, mothers of adolescent daughters tend to also struggle for a new identity "between an outgrown past and uncertain future" (Rubin, 1979, p. 124) creating a fertile ground for conflict. For some women, conflict and blame is a feature of the mother-daughter relationship across the lifespan (Caplan, 2002; Secunda, 1991; Tannen, 2006). Conflict is most often reported as a downward turning point by mothers and daughters, but the successful management of conflict can also powerfully connect women (Tannen, 2006). For example, a daughter in Miller-Day (2004) shared that her mother "did not agree with my decision [to go to a college in another state], but she said that she could understand why I made the decision and told me that she would support this decision and pay for my tuition. I see this as a time when our relationship got better." Laughing, she added, "She did add the condition that I had to call her every Sunday ... but that's fair."

Emotional Distance

Miller-Day et al. (2013) reported maternal emotional distance as another type of significant turning point for both sons and daughters, with significantly more daughters indicating that emotional distance served as a downward turning point in their relationship with their mothers. Emotional distance refers to the extent that an individual has removed themselves from others emotionally and relationally. Examples of emotional distance as turning points might be "She just pulled into herself and wouldn't let me in no matter how much I reached out to her" or "She was cold and distant, more interested in scrolling through posts on her phone than in talking with me." This kind of downward turning point can be especially damaging to a mother-daughter relationship (Miller-Day, 2004). As indicated in chapter two, daughters, as well as mothers, have an equal responsibility to maintain and be emotionally present in the relationship.

Criticism

Criticism is the expression of disapproval of someone or something or negative feedback based on perceived faults or mistakes (Baron, 1990). Criticism is a particularly potent type of turning point because women are particularly sensitive to criticism (Tannen, 2006) with daughters reporting maternal criticism as a turning point in the mother-child relationship significantly more than sons (Miller-Day et al., 2013). Examples of memorable criticism that serve as turning points include, "My mom said she wanted a different daughter," "she didn't like my performance [on a test, in a sport, or performing art] and is disappointed in me," "she wouldn't let up on me about my weight," and "she told me that I was a bad mom" (Miller-Day et al., 2013). Criticism from mothers and daughters can cause a downward spiral in mother-daughter closeness, and chronic critical communication can contribute to destructive interaction patterns with negative consequences for both mothers' and daughters' mental health (Caplan, 2002; Miller-Day, 2004; Miller-Day, 2017).

Crisis

Mothers and daughters often experience major disruptions in the relationship due to a particular crisis event that causes a significant decrease in closeness (Golish, 2000). These crises are myriad but can include events such as parental divorce, family illness/death, or a teen pregnancy (Golish, 2000; Miller-Day, 2004). Many crises can decrease closeness between a mother and daughter, but some can bring them together; such as the death of a mother's mother. The passing of the maternal grandmother often brings women together over shared grief, sympathy, and sometimes relief (Miller-Day, 2004).

Daughter's Transition into Adulthood

A type of turning point that often causes a strain in the mother-daughter relationship is when daughters push mothers away in their search for their own autonomy and identity as an adult. Golish (2000) describes rebellion as a stage when teenagers and young adults need autonomy and independence from their parents and they may reject or challenge parents' values. Daughters' transition to adulthood may be threatening to some mothers, especially those who live their lives vicariously through their daughters, resulting in mothers feeling personally rejected (Miller-Day, 2004). The transition into adulthood is most often reported as an upward turning point for daughters, as they move into adulthood many young women experience increased open communication and feel more equal to mothers (Lefkowitz, 2005). As daughters transition into adulthood, they will often balance the inevitable exclusion of mother from everyday activities with a conscious attempt to increase personal disclosures and openness (Miller-Day, 2013). Moving away to college is a highly memorable turning point for most mothers and daughters, along with other life events such as engagement, wedding planning, and marriage (Fisher & Miller-Day, 2006).

Physical Distance

The transition to adulthood, for many daughters, includes moving out and living independently for the first time—living on their own or cohabiting, in college, or joining the military. Some research indicates that physical proximity to parents during emerging adulthood can have a negative impact on parent-child relationships (Arnett, 2000). Living with or near mothers during this developmental period can create conflict because mothers may believe they must still monitor their daughter and the daughter may not be able to pursue new experiences (Arnett, 2000). One woman in Miller-Day (2004) stated:

> When I got away from home. That's when I really could see myself and myself in relation to her differently. My mother always treated me as sickly and I didn't know I was not sick until I … got away from home. She had designated me the sickly one, and all I had was like my tonsils out and a broken arm, and maybe some headaches. The headaches were probably from being nervous and I just think that had to be her influence on me because when I left town I was not sickly. I was quite healthy and I'm fine. So, I had to get away from her to see the influence, the bad influence, she had on me. (pp. 84–85)

When daughters live with their mothers, they may have difficulty differentiating from mother and becoming an autonomous person, but this does not mean disconnecting from mother emotionally. A daughter's healthy development often requires staying emotionally connected to her mother while she develops her own unique personal identity (Caplan, 2002; Miller-Day, 2004). While living in close proximity, this connection tends to be maintained through interacting with one another; however, when daughters transition into adulthood and out of the home, strategies for maintaining mother-daughter connection shift (Harrigan & Miller-Ott, 2013). When there is more physical distance between a mother and daughter, research suggests that mothers provide more emotional support than if they lived at home (Harrigan & Miller-Ott, 2013). When living apart, maternal warmth and support can ease daughters' stress and depression, daughters are often better adjusted than those who stay at home and relationships with mothers can improve (Harrigan & Miller-Ott, 2013; Lefkowitz, 2005). If a mother is highly enmeshed in her daughter's life, however, increased distance may not provide an upward turning point, and the distance may be threatening. In an *enmeshed* adult mother-daughter relationship, there may be extreme emotional closeness with a lack of personal boundaries (Miller-Day, 2004). This is reflected in the following quote from a daughter in Miller-Day (2004):

> After I got divorced and returned to live back home with my mother temporarily, my mom said, "When you got married, in my heart I felt that I had lost you. Now I feel like I have you back." That comment really shocked me. I don't think she ever lost me. My God, I just lived a little bit away. What happened was that someone else had my full attention, and she

didn't want to share me. She never lost me, we just had to figure out a way that she could share me. (p. 85)

Daughter's Pregnancy/Childbirth

Daughters' pregnancy and childbirth are highly salient in the relational lives of mothers and daughters (Fischer, 1987) and are a frequently reported type of turning point. As a daughter transitions into becoming a mother herself, she often turns to her mother for support and mothers begin to see daughters as adults, necessitating a redefinition of the mother-daughter relationship. A daughter's pregnancy can be perceived as an upward turning point, ushering the daughter into motherhood (Fischer, 1981). Yet, under certain conditions, it may be experienced as a downward turning point if the pregnancy was unintended or if the daughter is a teen and/or unmarried. Miller (1995) reported the experience of a pregnant teen daughter in the early 1970s who was sent to live in a residence for unwed mothers. When returning home for a weekend with her siblings and parents, her mother required her to hide on the floor of the car with a coat thrown over her to avoid being seen by neighbors. Both mother and daughter perceived the other as actively trying to humiliate her. One need only watch an episode of the television show "Teen Moms" to understand how a daughter's pregnancy can serve to unify or divide mothers and pregnant daughters.

Filial Comprehending

The birth of her own child often allows a daughter to see her mother in a new way, reinforcing or challenging the bond between the two women. New mothers often begin to see their mothers not just in her social role as "mother," but as a person with her own goals, needs, fears, values, and desires. This change has been called seeing the woman behind the role (Miller-Day, 2004) and filial comprehending (Nydegger, 1991). This is not restricted to a daughter who gets pregnant. This type of turning point occurs when a daughter begins to view her mother as an individual, and not just as her mother. Adolescents often do not think of their mothers as individual people with lives apart from mothering, but this point of change occurs for many women in young adulthood and certainly by mid-life. A daughter in Miller-Day et al. (2013) shared, "We got to know each other as adults because we were only talking once or twice a week. Our relationship changed a lot once I moved to college, and I feel like an adult rather than just her kid." When filial comprehending happens, a reframing occurs, seeing mothers in "a different light," including seeing them as sexual beings (Miller-Day, 2004). One woman in the Miller-Day (2004) study reported finding a sex toy in her mother's drawer and this forced her to think of her mother in a new way. Another discussed how her mother's musical talent ushered in filial comprehending:

[My mom has] a lot of musical talent. She would practice and perform, you know, like at church, and all the weddings and the funerals. So, I just always looked up to her and saw her for who she was. How other people see her. I think this is where we really started moving into being friends. (Miller-Day, 2004, p. 94)

Research provides evidence that daughters who experience this turning point and achieve "filial maturity" may experience fewer tensions in the mother-daughter relationship (Fingerman, 2001; Nydegger, 1991).

Caregiving

Another type of turning point is caregiving. When a mother provides care for daughter during a pregnancy, illness, or injury ("she took care of me when I had my wisdom teeth out" or "when I broke my leg") or when the daughter assumes caregiving responsibilities for her mother, these can serve to alter closeness in the mother-daughter relationship. As indicated throughout this chapter, women come to expect care and support from their mothers and daughters. In later life, daughters caring for mothers is one of the most commonly represented caregiving relationships in Western culture (Cicirelli, 1993). As the daughter shifts into the caregiver role for frail mothers, this relationship is often referred to as a "role-reversal"; however, mothers will always remain the parent and the daughter the child. A loss of the quality of the previous relationship exists but does not mean it is a "reversal." It merely requires a renegotiation of the relational framework (Fisher, 2014).

These types of turning points represent findings from several studies examining mother-daughter turning points and paint a picture of the complexity of the relationship across the lifespan. *Social support* is one of the most common types of turning points reported by both daughters and sons when describing turning points in the mother-child relationship (Miller-Day et al., 2013). But, what do those turning points look like? To examine these questions more closely, the remainder of the chapter will define and discuss social support in more detail, unpacking the concept, and then examine the different types of social support eliciting relational turning points.

Social Support Unpacked

I indicated earlier in the chapter that Mattson and Hall (2011) defined social support as a "transactional communicative process, including verbal and/or nonverbal communication, which aims to improve an individual's feelings of coping, competence, belonging, and/or esteem" (p. 184). Essentially, social support is communication conveying the message that the person is cared for, has assistance available, and that he or she is part of a supportive social network. Feeling supported leads to positive physical and mental health outcomes (Sarason, Sarason, & Pierce, 1990).

Not only does a person receiving social support receive these health benefits, but the person providing social support can derive an increased sense of worth and personal strength. The health benefits of social support are both mental and physical (Sarason et al., 1990) and can include psychological adjustment, improved efficiency, better coping with upsetting events, resistance to disease, recovery from disease, and reduced mortality (Burleson, 1990). The *stress-buffering hypothesis* explains that social support can shield the adverse effects of stress, with high stressed individuals experiencing less overall physical and psychological symptoms if they also have social support (Burleson, 1990). The stress-buffering effect is particularly salient with family support.

Family Support

Family support is one of the most essential and fundamental forms of family communication, and it has been argued that one of the primary functions of the family is to provide social support to its members (Segrin & Flora, 2005). Franco and Levitt (1998) found that children reported more support from their close family members than from any other sources. Support from family members has been found to result in many positive outcomes for adolescents including better mental and physical health and the ability to better adapt to stress (Burke & Weir, 1978; Franco & Levitt, 1998).

A lack of support from family has been associated with hopelessness, depression, suicidality, and substance abuse (Andrews, Martin, & Hasking, 2012), especially for multiethnic sexual minority youth (Newcomb, Heinz, & Mustanski, 2012). Garnefski and Diekstra (1996) discovered that students without supportive families were four times more likely to have behavioral problems or emotional problems and eight times more likely to have both behavioral and emotional problems than those with supportive families. The importance of family support in children's well-being increases the need for us to have a more thorough understanding of the different types of social support and the role family support plays in mother-daughter turning points.

Types of Social Support

The first type of social support, and probably the most common, is *emotional support*, which is "communication that meets individual's emotional or affective needs" (Mattson & Hall, 2011, p. 185). Emotional support increases empathy, connection, and enhances mood and decreases stress, but it doesn't try to fix a person's problems (Sarason et al., 1990).

Esteem support is "communication that bolsters an individual's self-esteem or beliefs in their ability to handle a problem or perform a needed task" (Mattson & Hall, 2011, p. 186). Esteem support refers to expressions of confidence, respect, and validation that serve to bolster one's self-concept (Xu & Burleson, 2001). This type of support has a lot to do with encouraging another person and letting them know they can overcome a challenge. You give the support verbally like emotional support, but in a way that inspires a person to face a problem.

Network support is communication that reminds people that they are not alone in whatever situation they are facing because there is a network of people available to give the needed support. It entails generating feelings of social connection and creating a sense of belonging (Xu & Burleson, 2001).

Informational support has also been defined as the availability of advice, guidance, and information about community resources (Wills, Blechman, & McNamara, 1996). The fact that informational support provides advice or a new perspective on the problem, rather than merely providing information, is what distinguishes this form of support from the process of information provision (Goldsmith, 2004). Burke and Weir (1978) found that informational support was positively related to adolescents' well-being.

Tangible or Instrumental support refers to concrete types of assistance. This includes things that others physically do or provide to assist, such as when parents give children money so that they can pay rent for the month, giving assistance with important instrumental tasks including paying bills, providing transporta-tion, decision-making, and completing daily activities (Wills et al., 1996).

Understanding the various types of social support led me to wonder if specific types of support were prompting reports of transitions and turning points in the mother-daughter relationship for daughters. I wondered, *what types of social support do daughters perceive most salient to the mother-daughter relationship?* Therefore, I conducted a turning point study with daughters. The remainder of this chapter describes this study and what I learned.

THE STUDY

What Was I Interested in Learning?

The research question guiding the current study was, *what are the types of social support young adult daughters perceive as creating turning points in the mother-daughter relationship?*

How Did I Go about Learning This Information?

Sample

To answer our question, we recruited 172 daughters to participate in the study at a university on the west coast of the United States. Participants received 2% extra course credit for their participation. To examine developmental periods prior to adulthood, a college-aged population was deemed appropriate to provide retrospective reports. The ages reflected the composition of the general education course population including two age groupings 18–20 (N = 129) and 21–25 (N = 43). Participants answered the study questions about biological mothers (N = 171) and adoptive mothers (N = 1).

Data Collection

After providing consent, participants were directed to a web page asking them to "list two to seven memorable moments in your lifetime that have either increased or decreased your feelings of emotional closeness with your mother. These will be referred to as 'turning points' in your relationship." Then, for each of the turning point (TP) listed, participants were asked to enter a description of that experience. All reports are anonymous.

Data Analysis

For the purposes of this chapter, my analysis focused only on TPs coded as social support. The primary task in the study was to categorize the types of social support participants perceived as contributing to mother-daughter relational turning points. To do this, qualitative content coding was completed with the open-ended data. The coding system began with a list of a-priori codes including: providing or receiving emotional, esteem, network, informational, or tangible support. Analytic induction was employed to compare and contrast each social support TP to determine its type of support or identify novel types. No novel types of support were identified and a co-analyst coded a random selection of 10% of the social support TPs to assess coding agreement. Intercoder agreement was calculated and deemed acceptable using Krippendorf's Alpha coefficient (.88).

What Did I Learn?

Daughters identified a total of 256 TPs and of those, 116 related to social support (45.3%). Table 5.1 illustrates the definitions employed to determine types of turning points, examples from the data, and the total number of TPs provided by daughters in that category.

I discovered that emotional and tangible support were most frequently associated with transformation in the mother-daughter relationship. The *emotional support* that participants mentioned tended to focus on disclosure, listening, and assisting each other through difficult times, such as periods of stress or the death of a loved one. Disclosure and non-disclosure of private information consistently represented upward turning points for daughters. Disclosure of mother's private information and supportive comments during times of daughter's stress were most salient, for example:

> A few weeks after I told my mom that I was gay she approached me and said that she had spoken with one of her close friends to try and figure things out. It was probably the first breakthrough in solid communication, where she started to feel a little more comfortable with the idea that I'm gay. In the months after that communication had returned to normal. I felt supported, like she was on my side. Several years after the event, communication with my mom is stronger than it has ever been.

In a similar situation, another daughter who had shared her sexual identity as a lesbian with her mother commented that "she kept secret my disclosure about being gay," consequently "I can tell her anything; she is my advocate."

"Being there for me" and "listening" were powerful, memorable forms of support for daughters. "She was there for me when …" and "she listened to me while I [yelled, broke down, cried] …" Many of the examples were nonverbal, including "she held me on her lap while I cried," "she hugged me," and "she cried for my loss." Finally, many turning points indicated how profound it was to help a mother through her time of need, especially during times of loss, such as the death of a parent or sibling, "helping her write his eulogy" and "just being there to hug her while she cried." Descriptions of these TPs typically extolled the benefits of providing as well as receiving support. Of the 50 turning points in this category, only five represented a downward TP, resulting in a decrease in closeness. These downward TPs were similar but in opposition—describing *a lack of* listening, supportive statements, or nonverbal cues of support during a time of stress.

Tangible Support

Tangible support was the second most frequently reported type of support linked to turning points. Tangible support incidents referenced provision of materials things ("she bought me a car," "she bought me a special necklace," "buying me ice cream and renting movies for me while I moped around after breakup"), the provision of favors when someone was experiencing a time of stress or illness ("I helped her with basic things like showering or running errands for her after her surgery"), or providing simple assistance with tasks ("she helped me with college applications," "she taught me to drive"). There were also many examples of mothers "selflessly" volunteering their time to coach a sport, provide transportation, or provide resources to support daughters' interests.

Mothers provided *esteem support* to boost their daughter's self-esteem, make them feel better, and to give their daughter's the confidence to overcome challenges. Esteem support was provided in times of relationship breakups, fights with friends, and disappointments surrounding failed auditions, classes, and disappointing performance in sports. Esteem support was often described in tandem with

Table 5.1. Daughters' Perceptions of Types of Turning Points in the Mother-Daughter Relationship.

Type of Social Support	Definition of Social Support	Example from Data	Total Number of Turning Points
Emotional	Communication that meets an individual's emotional or affective needs. Emotional support is there to make someone feel better or enhance their mood, but it doesn't try to actually fix a person's problems.	"As soon as I walked in I just fell to the couch where my mom was, and after I told her what happened, she held me in her lap and let me cry. She didn't make me feel bad or worse about it she just let me cry and told me it was going to be okay."	50 (43%)
Tangible	Any kind of instrumental assistance given. Things they do for the other to provide assistance.	"My mom basically helped me through a very difficult time, taking me to my multiple doctor's appointments and staying by my side when she knew I was in pain."	32 (28%)
Esteem	Communication that bolsters an individual's self-esteem or beliefs in their ability to handle a problem or perform a needed task.	"This turning point was all about building my self-concept up. I was feeling very depressed and down on myself, and I felt that I had let everyone down. I feel that this turning point was important because she didn't give me the generic speech of 'it's just a sport, blah, blah, blah.' She told me the truth. She told me it sucked and it's probably going to suck for a while, but that I should never hang my head. The real accomplishment was making it to that point, not the outcome."	19 (16%)

(Continued)

Table 5.1. (*Continued*)

Information	Communication that provides valuable or necessary information. When a person needs someone else to help weigh the options and provide adequate information to come to a conclusion.	"I was thinking about changing my college major and she talked with me throughout the whole debate and made arguments."	14 (12%)
Network	Communication that provides affirmation of an individuals' belonging to a network rather than focusing on self-esteem or emotions. Network support is communication that reminds people that they are not alone in whatever situation they are facing.	"My whole family and I all visited my mom in the hospital and let her know she wasn't alone, that we would all help with her recovery."	1 (<.01%)

Source: Author.

other forms of support. For example, the following turning point included esteem support (she made me feel better about myself), emotional support (talking with me and hanging out with me) and tangible support (baking):

> When I was cut from my school volleyball team, I was extremely upset for a week. Every day that week my mom made sure to make me feel better by talking to me, baking for me, hanging out with me, etc. Even when I didn't feel like talking, she always knew exactly what to say. If it weren't for her, I would have been upset throughout the whole season rather than just one week. She knew exactly what was right for me even though I didn't. She made me feel better about myself by convincing me that I am so much better than I think I am and she listed every possible nice thing she could and it made me feel great.

Informational support was one of the least common types of support linked to relational turning points. These referred to general maternal advice and direction, but also about specific information such as substance use prevention and sexual health. Finally, there was only one example of *network support*, perhaps because our research question asked about turning points in the dyad and not the family system.

WHAT DOES ALL THIS MEAN?

Across our lives, we will experience many changes in our mother-daughter relationships. We will inevitably move toward and away from each other across our lifetime, with velvet ties of emotional connection binding us over the years. Memorable incidents that create changes in our relational intimacy are called turning points and these turning points require us to recalibrate the mother-daughter relationship. Scholarship has identified several salient turning points in the mother-daughter relationship including social support, shared activities, conflict, crisis, daughter's transition to adulthood, proximity, daughter's pregnancy/childbirth, filial comprehending, and caregiving.

Social support is commonly listed as a category or type of mother-daughter turning point; therefore, I conducted a new study to further examine socially supportive mother-daughter relational turning points. Findings from this study indicate that mothers' emotional and tangible support are perceived by daughters as the most consequential in mother-daughter relationships. Daughters feel closer to their mothers when mothers talk with them, listen to them, and are present for them during hardship. Equally, daughters feel closer to mothers when they can reciprocate and provide emotional and tangible support to their mothers.

Thinking back through my lifetime and the memories I possess of my mother, I appreciate both the upward and downward turning points in my relationship with her and am heartened that at the end of her life I could provide her with emotional support. She may not have always been a perfect mother, but she was the only mother I had. I find perfection in the memory of knowing her.

WHAT DO WE STILL NEED TO KNOW?

- Are there differences in turning points for ethnically diverse mothers and daughters? Much of the mother-daughter research has been conducted with primarily White samples.
- Are turning points similar for stepmother-stepdaughter relationships or mother-daughter relationships in alternative family forms?
- What are mothers' expectations surrounding social support from their daughter? What are the implications of these expectations for relational intimacy?
- More information is needed on those turning points specific to mothers and daughters such as the unique impact of maternal criticism and emotional distance on the mother-daughter relationship.

HOW DOES THIS WORK IN REAL LIFE?

- Think about your daughtering (or son-ing) and consider how you might best provide social support to your mother. What kinds of support does she provide you? Where are improvements needed? How do you want things to change?
- Think about your daughtering (or son-ing) and consider how you have contributed to relational turning points with your mother. In what ways has your behavior over the years served to increase or decrease intimacy with her?
- When you consider the support you receive from your mother, how would you like her to better support you? How might you approach your mother to ask her to better support you?

CLASSROOM ACTIVITIES

- *Identify your turning points.* Think back across your mother-daughter/son relationship and identify at least two relational turning points. For each turning point, note if it increased or decreased intimacy with your mother.
  - Take each TP and develop a story surrounding it, elaborating on how the TP affected your relationship. Provide as much description and detail as possible.
  - Are your TPs the same as one of the types of TPs discussed in this chapter? If so, which ones? If not, what is the new type of TP?
- *Scenario:* Your mother was widowed two years ago. She has just started dating again and is currently going out with a guy who seems nice. Well, last night she told you that this guy shoved her and she fell and broke her ankle. She is very upset and doesn't want to burden you, but she needs your help getting some basics done around the house. Not to mention, she is worried about medical expenses because she is no longer on your dad's medical insurance. As her son or daughter, come up with examples of how you could enact each type of social support for your mother:
  - Emotional
  - Esteem
  - Network
  - Information
  - Tangible

REFERENCES

Andrews, T., Martin, G., & Hasking, P. (2012). Differential and common correlates of non-suicidal self-injury and alcohol use among community-based adolescents. *Advances in Mental Health, 11*(1), 55–66. https://doi.org/10.5172/jamh.2012.11.1.55

Arnett, J. J. (2000). Emerging adulthood: A theory of development from the late teens through the twenties. *American Psychologist, 55*(5), 469–480. https://doi.org/10.1037/0003-066X.55.5.469

Baron, R. (1990). Countering the effects of destructive criticism: The relative efficacy of four interventions. *Journal of Applied Psychology, 75*(3), 235–245. https://doi.org/10.1037/0021-9010.75.3.235

Bassoff, E. (1988). *Mothers and daughters: Loving and letting go.* New York, NY: New American Library.

Baxter, L. A., & Wolf, B. (2009). Turning points in relationships. In H. T. Reis & S. Sprecher (Eds.), *Encyclopedia of human relationships* (pp. 1652–1653). Thousand Oaks, CA: Sage.

Beebe, S. A., Beebe, S. J., & Redmond, M. V. (2016). *Interpersonal communication: Relating to others* (8th Edition). Scarborough, ON: Prentice-Hall Canada.

Burke, R. J., & Weir, T. (1978). Benefits to adolescents of informal helping relationship with their parents and peers. *Psychological Reports, 42*(3), 1175–1184. https://doi.org/10.2466/pr0.1978.42.3c.1175

Burleson, B. R. (1990). Comforting as everyday social support: Relational consequences of supportive behaviors. In S. Duck (Ed.), *Personal relationships and social support* (pp. 66–82). London, UK: Sage.

Caplan, P. (2002). *The new don't blame mother: Mending the mother-daughter relationship.* New York, NY: Routledge.

Cicirelli, V. G. (1993). Attachment and obligation as daughters' motives for caregiving behavior and subsequent effect on subjective burden. *Psychology and Aging, 8*(2), 144–155. https://doi.org/10.1037/0882-7974.8.2.144

Cohen, S., & Wills, T. A. (1985). Stress, social support, and the buffering hypothesis. *Psychological Bulletin, 98*(2), 310–357. https://doi.org/10.1037/0033-2909.98.2.310

Fingerman, K. L. (Ed.). (2001). *Aging mothers and their adult daughters: A study in mixed emotions.* New York, NY: Springer.

Fischer, L. R. (1981). Transitions in the mother-daughter relationship. *Journal of Marriage and the Family, 43*(3), 613–622. https://doi.org/10.2307/351762

Fischer, L. R. (1987). *Linked lives: Adult daughters and their mothers.* New York, NY: Harper & Row.

Fisher, C. L. (2014). *Coping together, side by side: Enriching mother-daughter communication across the breast cancer journey.* New York, NY: Hampton Press.

Fisher, C., & Miller-Day, M. (2006). Communication in mother-adult daughter relationships. In K. Floyd & M. Morman (Eds.), *Widening the family circle: New research on family communication* (pp. 3–16). Newbury Park, CA: Sage.

Franco, N., & Levitt, M. J. (1998). The social ecology of middle childhood: Family support, friendship quality, and self-esteem. *Family Relations, 47*(4), 315–321. https://doi.org/10.2307/585262

Furman, W., & Buhrmester, D. (1985). Children's perception of the personal relationships in their social networks. *Developmental Psychology, 21*(6), 1016–1024. https://doi.org/10.1037/0012-1649.21.6.1016

Garnefski, N., & Diekstra, R. F. W. (1996). Perceived social support from family, friends, school, and peers: Relationship with emotional and behavioral problems among adolescents.

Journal of American Academy of Child and Adolescent Psychiatry, 35(12), 1657–1664. https://doi. org/10.1097/00004583-199612000-00018

Goldsmith, D. J. (2004). *Communicating social support.* Cambridge, UK: Cambridge University Press.

Golish, T. D. (2000). Changes in closeness between adult children and their parents: A turning point analysis. *Communication Reports, 13*(2), 79–97. https://doi.org/10.1080/08934210009367727

Harrigan, M. M., & Miller-Ott, A. E. (2013). The multivocality of meaning making: An exploration of the discourses college-aged daughters voice in talk about their mothers. *Journal of Family Communication, 13*(2), 114–131. https://doi.org/10.1080/15267431.2013.768249

Lefkowitz, E. S. (2005). "Things have gotten better": Developmental changes among emerging adults after the transition to university. *Journal of Adolescent Research, 20*(1), 40–63. https://doi. org/10.1177/0743558404271236

Levitt, M. J., Guacci-Franco, N., & Levitt, J. L. (1993). Convoys of social support in childhood and early adolescence: Structure and function. *Developmental Psychology, 29*(5), 811–818. https://doi. org/10.1037/0012-1649.29.5.811

Mattson, M., & Hall, J. G. (2011). Linking health communication with social support. In *Health as communication nexus: A service learning approach* (pp. 181–219). Dubuque, IA: Kendall Hunt.

Miller, M. (1995). An intergenerational case study of suicidal tradition and mother-daughter communication. *The Journal of Applied Communication Research, 23*(4), 247–270.

Miller-Day, M. (2004). *Communication among grandmothers, mothers, and adult daughters: A qualitative study of maternal relationships.* Mahwah, NJ: Lawrence Erlbaum.

Miller-Day, M. (2013). Two of me: Mothers and daughters in connection. In A. Deakins, R. Lockridge, & H. Sterk (Eds.), *Mothers and daughters: Complicated connections across cultures* (pp. 89–104). Lanham, MD: Rowman & Littlefield.

Miller-Day, M. (2017). Necessary convergence communication theory: Submission and power in family communication. In. D. O. Braithwaite, E. A. Suter, & K. Floyd (Eds.), *Engaging theories in family communication: Multiple perspectives* (2nd ed., pp. 221–232). New York, NY: Routledge.

Miller-Day, M., Fisher, C. L., & Stube, J. (2013). Looking back and moving forward: Toward an understanding of mother-daughter and mother-son relationships. In K. Floyd & M. Morman (Eds.), *Widening the family circle II: New research on family communication* (pp. 1–17). Newbury Park, CA: Sage.

Newcomb, M. E., Heinz, A. J., & Mustanski, B. (2012). Examining risk and protective factors for alcohol use in lesbian, gay, bisexual, and transgender youth: A longitudinal multilevel analysis. *Journal of Studies on Alcohol and Drugs, 73*(5), 783–793. https://doi.org/10.15288/jsad.2012.73.783

Nydegger, C. N. (1991). The development of paternal and filial maturity. In K. Pillemer & K. McCartney (Eds.), *Parent-child relations throughout life* (pp. 93–112). Hillsdale, NJ: Lawrence Erlbaum.

Rubin, L. (1979). *Women of a certain age: Individual search for self.* New York, NY: Harper.

Sarason, B. R., Sarason, I. G., & Pierce, G. R. (1990). *Social support: An interactional view.* New York, NY: Wiley.

Secunda, V. (1991). *When you and your mother can't be friends: Resolving the most complicated relationship of your life.* New York, NY: Delta.

Segrin, C., & Flora, J. (2005). *Family communication.* Mahwah, NJ: Lawrence Erlbaum.

Tannen, D. (2006). *You're wearing that? Understanding mothers and daughters in conversation.* New York, NY: Ballantine Books.

Trees, A. R. (2000). Nonverbal communication and the support process: Interactional sensitivity in interactions between mothers and young adult children. *Communication Monographs, 67*(3), 239–262. https://doi.org/10.1080/03637750009376509

Wills, T. A., Blechman, E. A., & McNamara, G. (1996). Family support, coping, and competence. In E. M. Hetherington & E. A. Blechman (Eds.), *Stress, coping, and resiliency in children and families* (pp. 107–133). Mahwah, NJ: Lawrence Erlbaum.

Xu, Y., & Burleson, B. R. (2001). Effects of sex, culture, and support type of perceptions of spousal social support: An assessment of the "support gap" hypothesis in early marriage. *Human Communication Research, 27*(4), 535–566. https://doi.org/10.1111/j.1468-2958.2001.tb00792.x

PART TWO

Enacting THE Mother-Daughter Relationship Across THE Lifespan

... Of the many family roles women may assume during the course of their lives—sister, girlfriend, aunt, niece, mother or even grandmother—only one is universal among women: The role of daughter. (Miller-Day, 2013)

REFERENCE

Miller-Day, M. (2013). Two of me: Mothers and daughters in connection. In A. Deakins, R. Lockridge, & H. Sterk (Eds.), *Mothers and daughters: Complicated connections across cultures* (pp. 89–104). Lanham, MD: Rowman & Littlefield.

CHAPTER SIX

Pregnancy AND Disability

DENISE LAWLER*

Becoming a mother is a life transition accompanied by myriad emotions and challenges; it is surely an experience that impacts a woman psychologically, cognitively, socially, and emotionally. Picture one of those whirly-swirly rides at the amusement park. You get a strange feeling after riding it, but you still look the same to any casual observer. Likewise, the sense of life-changing transition and overwhelming responsibility that attend pregnancy and motherhood can send anyone reeling. Add in a context of stigmatization and exclusion—significant concerns for women with disabilities—and things become quite hairy. It's like riding the whirly-swirly ride alone with a broken seatbelt.

Put yourself in the place of pregnant woman with a disability and imagine telling a physician that you are pregnant. Instead of being congratulated and offered practical medical and health care, you are questioned, judged, or perhaps even reprimanded. This is a common reality for mothers with a disability who have their mothering choices and abilities immediately evaluated in light of their physical or sensory attributes. Reactions like these can make a big dent in a woman's self-confidence (Lawler, 2013). Let me pause here and ask you, have you ever thought about this?

If this phenomenon is new to you, then you won't be surprised to learn that the experience of becoming and being a mother with a disability in contemporary society are relatively undocumented (Lawler, 2013). Mothers with a disability and

* Denise Lawler, assistant professor, Trinity College Dublin, Lawlorde@tcd.ie.

their families are somewhat invisible to policymakers and health service providers because—while many resources and services exist for new mothers—most policies and services do not recognize that women with a disability can be capable parents (Lawler, 2013). It is safe to say that systems, resources, health, and social services for women mothering with a disability range from limited to non-existent. The resultant lack of awareness effectively excludes new mothers with disabilities from integrating into communities, leaving them unable to access appropriate resources, including parenting classes (specifically for parents with a disability) or consultations with disability agencies where assistance can be sourced to aid with the physical and sensory elements of parenting.

In this chapter, I discuss the progression of becoming a mother for those with disabilities and describe the impact on the construction of the self and one's identity. I also show how women's relationships with others, especially their own mothers, are important to the construction of their identity and sense of self. Sourcing a precise definition for self and identity can be difficult. Some suggest that self and identity are "large, amorphous, and changing phenomena that defy hard and fast definitions" (Ashmore & Jussim, 1997, p. 5), while others suggest both are related and interconnected and how at both have a number of associated concepts including, self-awareness and reflexivity (Kralik & Telford, 2010).

For the purpose of this chapter self and identity are considered to be related, interconnected and interchangeable. In the chapter I describe how a woman's identity is shaped through relationships and interactions with others, especially healthcare providers encountered when accessing healthcare services during pregnancy and early motherhood. The chapter begins by defining what is meant by the self and the different representations of the self. Following that I explain how the language used to define "disability" can influence how women with a disability are perceived and treated by others in contemporary society. Lastly, the chapter ends with a discussion of the impact of new motherhood on women with a disability.

DEFINING THE SELF AND REPRESENTATIONS OF THE SELF

Describing what is meant by the term "the self" is complex because it is difficult to convey what the self is and how it may function (Onorato & Turner, 2001). Some authors define the self as an organized set of essential possesses that confers an ability to consider, observe and evaluate, to take account, to plan and to construct itself, an object that can be modified in different situations (Burke & Stets, 2009; Smith, Coats, & Murphy, 2001). In essence, *the self* is an entity comprised of a mind and body, character and personality, which is informed and can adjust to the setting and environment it is located in. Furthermore, the self has an innate ability to determine the aspects to present to others and the elements to disguise. It is the self, introduced to others, that informs and influences how other people perceive it. These perceptions, created by others, are then internalized by the self to form a sense and an understanding of the self and one's identity (Kralik & Telford, 2010).

The self can be considered in three representations: the "individual self," the "relational self" and the "collective self" (Sedikides & Brewer, 2001, p. 1). All three representations are social in origin, coexisting in each person and are conceptualized as "an integrated system in which interplay, integration, and interdependence are the modus operandi" (Deaux & Perkins, 2001, p. 300; Sedikides & Brewer, 2001).

For the purpose of this chapter, our focus is on the relational self. The relational self comes into existence as part of a unit, defined by the relationships we, as persons, engage in, created through our interactions with and the appraisals of others, especially significant others (Sedikides & Brewer, 2001). So, in a sense, it is the relationships with others—as we assimilate and integrate the perspectives, resources, and identities of those others, especially significant others—that extend and expand the self (Aron & McLaughlin-Volpe, 2001).

As many authors in this text have similarly described, from early childhood, girls with a disability construct the self through symbolic relationships and interactions with others, especially significant others, located in their social world. Construction of the self also occurs through the role models girls choose to emulate, life experiences, and interpretation of those lived experiences (Blumer, 1998; Cooley, 1964; Mead, 1934). It is during this construction of the self that girls and young women with a disability decide whether to incorporate their disability into the self they have constructed or to leave it out. In many ways, it is like building a house and deciding which design elements to incorporate; does that house have two floors with both an elevator and stairs?

The construction process, hammering and nailing her personal design details into place, results in a construction of an identity that is (i) positive, (ii) neutral or (iii) negative relative to her disability. A positive evaluation means that a woman considers identity as a part of the self, and a "disability identity" is adopted—she chose to add the elevator to the house. A neutral evaluation of her disability during construction means she is non-committal, assuming neither a positive nor a negative position about her disability when constructing the self—she chose both an elevator and stairs. Lastly, a negative self construction means that a woman perceives her disability to be a negative characteristic and she rejects an identity that incorporates disability—she chose to build stairs in her house, which can make it difficult to get upstairs.

A Mother's Influence on Sense of Self

Relationships women form with others are influential to creating assumptions about and an understanding of self, providing meaning and a sense of purpose.

Assumptions about one's self guide our self-evaluations and tell us how to feel about any given aspect of our bodies or our lives. Such assumptions reside at the core of a woman's being, providing her with the necessary information to autonomously negotiate life, serving as a guide and filter for her life experiences and instilling a sense of meaning and self-worth (Janoff-Bulman, 1992). The mother-daughter relationship is especially meaningful in the creation of such assumptions and understanding of the self for women with disability.

As a girl with a disability grows up, her experience of being mothered (i) instills a desire to become a mother (Lawler, 2013), (ii) generates an expectation that this desire will be realised, and (iii) creates an assumption that she can be a good, competent, responsible mother when the time comes (Lawler, Begley, & Lalor, 2015). Mothers of daughters with disabilities are especially instrumental in creating a sense of sameness and inclusiveness for their daughters. When mothers of daughters with a disability treat them the same as other siblings who do not have a disability, making no allowances for physical or sensory differences, a sense of belonging, sameness, and inclusiveness swells within the daughters. When mothered this way, daughters assume that their disabilities are not an impediment, but simply another aspect of herself (which they may evaluate as a positive, neutral, or negative characteristic).

Women with a disability welcome the sense of sameness, inclusiveness, and equality promoted and evoked by their mothers and others (Lawler et al., 2015). The unrelenting sense of confidence in their daughters' abilities builds a sense of self-sufficiency in the daughter who has a disability.

As you might expect, there are some mothers who approach their daughters' disabilities differently. When mothers and others have difficulty accepting their daughter's disability, the result is a feeling of vulnerability. This sense of vulnerability does dissipate over time, as women age, becoming more resilient and confident, but can re-emerge again when encountering obstacles. Patriarchal, negative attitudes and behaviors create barrier for women with disabilities to interact with others. Vulnerability may also emerge when encountering infrastructural challenges in a new mother's physical environment. Without a doubt, relationships with others are instrumental in the construction of the self and one's identity but so too is the construction and consideration of disability in contemporary society (Shakespeare, 2006; Watson, 2002).

Constructions of Disability in Contemporary Society

Perceptions of women with a disability, including the ways in which they are accepted and treated in contemporary society, stem from each person's understanding of the term "disability" and personal evaluations of what living with a disability is like (Raman & Levi, 2002). From these perspectives, each of us frames disability in a certain light, like wearing glasses of different colors that cause us to see something one way or another, and leading us to snap evaluations of those who are living with disabilities. These are mental shortcuts we all make, though we are often unaware that we created these mental connections in the first place.

There are three distinctive ways to think about the lived experience of disability. The first is the functionalist, biomedical construction, focusing primarily on how a person's impairment results in the person being perceived as inadequate and different. The second is a biopsychosocial construction which asserts that is not the person's impairment that renders them disabled, but the social and physical challenges encountered in society that inhibit a full and independent participation in one's community. These are the dominant models that most use to think about disability (Patston, 2007; Swain & French, 2000; Tate & Pledger, 2003).

However, a new model developed by people with disabilities who are seeking full participation and equal rights, emerged at the turn of the century (Swain & French, 2000): the affirmation construction of disability. The affirmation model rejects the tragic notion of disability and impairment espoused by the functionalist, biomedical construction. The affirmation construction of disability recognizes and acknowledges that people with a disability are capable of establishing their own sense of self and determining their identity (Swain & French, 2000). The affirmation construction challenges the notion that people with a disability are to be pitied and questions how a person's identity and self are defined by the presumptions of others, most significantly, people with no disability.

As you read this, if you are a non-disabled person, take a moment to reflect on how you have perceived people with a disability whom you have encountered. Is their disability the first thing you think about to describe this person? Would you say that "non-disabled" is the first thing that others think of when they encounter you? The affirmation construction of disability creates a path for us to consider people with a disability in many lights, not only through the identity lens of disability. Additionally, an affirmation construction rejects the presumption that people with a disability are dependent and anomalous. This construction promotes acceptance and appreciation of the value and validity of the life of a person with a disability in its many and varied aspects. This construction dispels the dominant perception of normality. Instead, it allows for the recognition, acknowledgment, and celebration of diversity—irrespective of ability or disability.

Now that you have a better understanding of how disability is constructed, let's turn to the intersection of pregnancy and disability. As I noted earlier, it is not uncommon for women with a disability to encounter prejudice concerning their right and/or ability to mother. Indeed, some sectors of society believe that women with a disability should not be mothers (Prilleltensky, 2003).

The fact remains uncontested that women with a disability are more likely to encounter a myriad of challenges when accessing healthcare during pregnancy and early motherhood; these challenges are physical, attitudinal, and communicational in nature. Take a moment to think of a healthcare setting. In this environment, the prime modes of communication are oral communication and nonverbal gestures and facial reactions. For those with physical or sensory disability, these settings can prove challenging, and that starts by just getting in the door and letting the receptionist know you've arrived for your appointment. Because of their disability alone, women are rarely considered by healthcare providers to be independent agents. This includes providers such as nurses, physicians, or pharmacists. Instead, they are perceived as dependent on others, different, needing caretaking, requiring sympathy, and someone to be pitied. This is communicated to them with language and behaviours that are stigmatising, insulting, derogatory, and offensive (Barnes & Mercer, 2003; Begley et al., 2010; Lawler et al., 2015)—and that starts by just getting in the door.

Such behaviors manifest when healthcare providers, for no other reason other than her disability, refer the woman to social services or call child-protective services, citing her in/ability to mother as an issue of concern. Imagine if someone called protective services based solely on the race of the mother, or because of her sexual orientation. If this occurred, there would be absolute outrage, but when it happens to women with a disability, it's perceived as an act of benevolence.

Shockingly, Lawler (2013) and Lawler, Begley, and Lalor (2015) reported situations where healthcare providers called meetings with family members—without the pregnant woman's consent or involvement—where they discuss concerns about her physical or sensory inability. These discussions often cast the mother's disability as an impediment, hindering her ability to mother her own baby, and interventions are recommended (Lawler, 2013, 2015). Instances like these have a profound impact on a new mother's identity, self-confidence, self-esteem, and self-worth (McKay-Mofatt & Rotheram, 2007; Smeltzer, 2007; Thomas & Curtis, 1997). On the other hand, affirming and empowering messages about the sexuality of women with a disability, especially from a loved one, instill a sense of normality and nullify the asexual myth that surrounds these women. As a result, women with a disability plan and expect that someday, they will become mothers as part of their normal life trajectory.

Mothering with a Disability

The process of becoming a birth and/or social mother encompasses physical and psychological changes that result in women adapting and re-orientating the self to embrace motherhood as a fundamental part of their lives (Lawler et al., 2015; Redwood, 2007). Over the years numerous theories regarding the transition to motherhood have evolved, but these are primarily from the perspective and experiences of women with no disability, while very few studies have included women with a disability. Studies that include women with a disability tend to focus on the issue of accessibility, profiling the challenges that women with a disability encounter while accessing healthcare services and care during pregnancy and early motherhood few have investigated the women's transition to motherhood (Prilleltensky, 2003; Smeltzer, Sharts-Hopko, Ott, Zimmerman, & Duffin, 2007). During the transition and act of becoming a mother, women with a disability undergo a reorganization of the self, at a conscious and subconscious level, resulting in the development of an identity that includes motherhood, one where their disability does not take precedence (Oakley, 1980).

Beginning with the decision to become a mother, a mother with a disability is often met with skepticism from persons without a disability (Begley et al., 2010; Lawler et al., 2015) and when women with a disability become mothers their capacity and ability to be good, competent and responsible mothers are questioned (Kallianes & Rubenfeld, 1997; McKeever, Angus, Lee-Miller, & Reid, 2003). These women go to great lengths to present themselves as capable, competent, confident and responsible mothers while simultaneously fearing that if they do not meet society's expectations of what it is to mother, they are at a real risk of losing custody of their child(ren) (Lawler, 2013).

When mothers with a disability sense they must prove their abilities, they begin to question a fundamental assumption of the self: that they can be good, competent, responsible mothers who also happen to have a disability (Janoff-Bulman, 1992; Lawler et al., 2015). This need to prove mothering ability leads many women to reconstruct their expectations of the self and, if negative enough, may induce a psychological and emotional crisis of varying intensity (Stroebe & Schut, 2010). Through the renogiation of her identity, she emerges with a new self that embraces motherhood, discussed further in the next section.

Managing Mothering with a Disability

For those with a disability, managing mothering might include the sourcing of extra support to accomplish tasks or provide emotional reassurance (Prilleltensky, 2003; Sheerin, Keenan, & Lawler, 2014) For instance, a new mother might employ a nanny or assistant. She may use devices that help her mother, such as a mattress that sets off an alarm if her child leaves his bed. Though the use of devices may be seen as "helpers" for mothering, healthcare providers often miss the key point that a mother's disability can enhance her mothering abilities and practices (Malacrida, 2009). Through hyper-vigilance and technological gadgets, mothering with a disability can result in a child that is better minded. Using every resource is second nature to a mother with a disability, while those new mothers without disability may not realize how to seamlessly incorporate these mothering aids into their lifestyle. A mother with a disability draws from her past experiences of experience adapting to new situations and finding a way, then applies this to the context of parenting.

There are, however, some women with a disability who flounder during the transition to parenthood. Based on a feeling of helplessness and inability from her foundational self, this type of new mother can be battered by the onslaught of negative assumptions and attitudes around her (Peterson, Maier, & Seligman, 1995). Though it may appear paradoxical, passivity may be a strategy that a new mother with a disability uses to take back control over her interactions and a strategy to avoid conflict. Passivity may help manage non-affirming interactions, and a new mother with a disability may consciously disconnect and disengage from any meaningful interaction without question rather than seek and probe for alternative ways of doing things. As a result, the provider sees a woman who will do as instructed, leading to an assumption that she *needs* to be told what to do. Whether through enterprise or indifference, the point is that women with disabilities find a way to mother; every way a woman mothers ought to be valued.

Impact of Motherhood on Women with a Disability

Motherhood represents a sense of achievement for women with a disability, enhancing their self-esteem and engendering a positive contribution to their identity. Motherhood reveals a sense of purpose and sameness. Essentially, motherhood provides women with disabilities with a focus, affirming their sense of femininity, as it does for new mothers of any ability. What emerges are new assumptions and understandings of the self as a mother (Lawler, 2013).

One act that is critical to the establishment of a new understanding of the self and identity as a mother is the act of letting go. Letting go is where the mother consciously relinquishes aspects of the pre-motherhood self that is considered incompatible with their new mothering identity. This internal feeling is manifested in behavior and actions, whereby there is a modification of social behavior, alteration of physical appearance, a reprioritizing of life and personal goals, and a reconfiguration of interpersonal relationships (Lawler et al., 2015). This is where many women transform through the birth of their child into someone wholly new and different from the inside out. It is through this act of letting go and by engaging with motherhood, finding confidence in activities others thought them incapable of, that their self-confidence increases and they newly see a greater awareness of what is truly worthwhile in life. The act of letting go causes the sense of vulnerability to turn steely. Life takes on new meaning as the old self is bolstered and the new mothering self emerges as a strong fortress ready to face any storms that may come her way.

Thus, *being a mother*, not physical or sensory disability, becomes a woman's defining attribute. Motherhood engenders a sense of pride, purpose, self-worth, and value; it re-establishes the sense of belonging and place imbued by significant others during childhood. With motherhood, women engage in the process of affirming the attributes of the self that they value while recognizing other elements that need changing or modifying. They identify their strengths and limitations, establish more supportive and fulfilling relationships, rethink and reprioritize their life goals and plans, and willingly relinquish entities of the self that are considered incompatible with the self as a mother. Their child(ren) and their role as a mother take precedence over less-essential aspects of the women's life. Planning for the future becomes a priority as feelings of hope and potential replace doubt and indecision.

In contrast, a small body of literature has examined a sense-of-loss experienced by women with no disability during the transition to motherhood (Barclay, Everitt, Rogan, Schmied, & Wyllie, 1997; Oakley, 1979). Rather, a feeling of loss does not resonate with the experiences of women with a disability, where they instead find a rebirth (pun intended). Motherhood is, for women with a disability, a life-changing psychosocial event representing a meaningful *gain* that has a significant impact on all aspects of the women's life. New information that evolves from becoming a mother, being a mother, and doing mothering provides a sense of what is worthwhile in life. Motherhood is a new chapter in a woman's life story, one that incorporates new assumptions and understanding of the self, one with new direction and purpose (Lawler et al., 2015).

WHAT DOES ALL THIS MEAN?

For women with a disability, significant others, such as her mother, are instrumental in the establishment of their identity and assumptions of self in early childhood and across the lifespan. These interactions provide a foundation from which a sense of self-worth evolves. All women develop assumptions about who they are from an early age, and these assumptions are adjusted as they mature. For those with disabilities, identity development in childhood must also incorporate a prevailing perspective of disability's impact on their life.

Early childhood interactions can either imbue them with the belief that they are invulnerable or undermine it, later becoming women who view their disability with optimism or pessimism. These assumptions and understandings of the self reside at the core of the women's psyche, informing the self and serve as both guide and filter for life experiences, especially as they approach the transition to motherhood. Support and affirming actions of others motivate the women to pursue their life goals, including that of becoming a mother. Becoming a mother, being a mother, and doing mothering are—for women with a disability—redefining events that are a catalyst for recognizing their abilities over their inabilities.

Being a mother bestows a status and a sense of value and purpose that may be non-existent during pre-motherhood life. Motherhood provides women with a disability with a sense of purpose and being, affords her a sense of normality and sameness where her ability to mother (not her disability) becomes her defining attribute. Being a mother engenders a sense of pride, purpose, self-worth, and value, and reinstates the sense of belonging begun in childhood.

Healthcare providers have a responsibility to care for all aspects of a woman's health, including both emotional and physical needs. During pregnancy and motherhood, healthcare providers must provide quality of care to all women including women with a disability. This care must not assume a danger to her child at its base, but instead recognize the adaptability of mothers with disabilities who will always find a way. For these changes to occur, I propose the following service initiatives (Lawler, 2013):

> Health services providers are to be provided with disability and diversity training and awareness; All women's needs are assessed at the first point of contact with the healthcare services, and an individualized plan of care be devised, implemented and evaluated in partnership with each woman; Equality, diversity, and disability training be included in all education programmes for healthcare providers; Specialist posts should be implemented in each healthcare unit to support women with a disability during the continuum of pregnancy, childbirth, and early motherhood; Healthcare providers collaborate with and develop a mechanism of referral to appropriate voluntary and non-voluntary disability agencies to identify, source and enhance support and resources for parents with a disability.

Implementation of these suggestions will move the healthcare industry one step closer to recognizing women with disabilities with a lens of equality and create an environment of truly holistic care for these women and their families.

WHAT DO WE STILL NEED TO KNOW?

- Researchers must explore how mothers with disabilities reconstruct their mother identity as the child(ren) develop. Most research is focused on the transition to motherhood, but studying motherhood and identity during the experience of childbirth and the first 6 weeks post birth will reveal a rich area for growing our knowledge of this population.
- More information is needed on fathers with a disability. Researchers should similarly explore the experiences of fathers with a disability and their experiences.

HOW DOES THIS WORK IN REAL LIFE?

- Society recognizes and acknowledges that all persons, regardless of ability, have a right to be treated with respect and dignity. This could be achieved through the meaningful enenagement, consultation, recognition and involvement of all citizens in the shaping of society.

- Human rights of all people are protected and promoted in society realised in instruments such as legislation, policies, procedures and guidelines that shape and inform how people are recognized and treated in society.
- Parents, especially mothers, continue to develop positive, affirming relationships with their children regardless of their ability and disability. Support and education may be needed to help parents do this. There should be a government committee established to provide such support and education.
- Healthcare providers recognize and acknowledge the capacity and abilities of women with a disability. Disability agencies such as Through the Looking Glass (TLG) and research agencies such as the National Institute on Disability and Rehabilitation Research (NIDRR) continue to lobby for the rights of parents with disability and provide evidence on the optimal care that when implemented would assist in meeting the needs of pregnant women and parents with a disability.

CLASSROOM ACTIVITIES

- As a point of discussion for a classroom activity, consider what is needed in society to (i) recognize, acknowledge and treat people with disability with respect and dignity, and (ii) promote and protect their fundamental human rights.
- Spend one day with a person with a disability and experience first-hand their experiences of living with a disability in contemporary society. Write a one-page reflection on this experience.
- Reflect and consider the impact women and other immediate family members may have on the construction of your sense and understanding of self. Are there any aspects of you or your body that a significant person spoke of in a negative way? How does that make you feel? Do you agree or have you changed your conception of this personal aspect?
- Find a video online of someone with a disability doing something in a new way. Would you consider doing this activity the same way? Discuss as a class why or why not.
- Discuss as a class the notion of "pity." When do we feel this emotion? How do we express it? What is gained by the expression of pity? What is lost?
- Complete a case study on the experiences of a pregnant woman with a disability, document her experiences accessing healthcare and engaging with healthcare providers through the continuum of pregnancy, birth and early motherhood (first 6 weeks post-birth of the baby).

REFERENCES

Aron, A., & McLaughlin-Volpe, T. (2001). Including others in the self: Extensions to own and partner's group membership. In C. Sedikides & M. B. Brewer (Eds.), *Individual self, relational self, collective self* (pp. 89–108). Philadephia, PA: Psychology Press.

Ashmore, R. D., & Jussim, L. (1997). *Self and Identity: Fundamental Issues*. Oxford, UK: Oxford University Press.

Barclay, L., Everitt, L., Rogan, F., Schmied, V., & Wyllie, A. (1997). "Becoming a mother": An analysis of women's experience of early motherhood. *Journal of Advanced Nursing, 25*, 719–728.

Barnes, C., & Mercer, G. (2003). *Disability*. Cambridge, UK: Polity Press.

Begley, C., Higgins, A., Lalor, J., Sheerin, F., Alexander, J., Nicholl, H. ... Kavanagh, R. (2010). *The strengths and weakness of the publicly-funded Irish health services provided to women with disabilities in relation to pregnancy, childbirth and early motherhood*. Dublin, Ireland: National Disability Authority.

Blumer, H. (1998). *Symbolic interactionism: Perspective and method*. Berkeley, CA: University of California Press.

Burke, J. P., & Stets, J. E. (2009). *Identity theory*. Oxford, UK: Oxford University Press.

Cooley, C. H. (1964). *Human nature and the social order*. New York, NY: Scribner's.

Deaux, K., & Perkins, T. S. (2001). The kaleidoscopic self. In C. Sedikides & M. B. Brewer (Eds.), *Individual self, relational self, collective self* (pp. 299–313). Philadelphia, PA: Psychology Press.

Janoff-Bulman, R. (1992). *Shattered assumptions:Towards a new psychology of trauma*. New York, NY: Free Press.

Kallianes, V., & Rubenfeld, P. (1997). Disabled women and reproductive rights. *Disability and Society, 12*(2), 203–222.

Kralik, D., & Telford, K. (2010). *Shifts in self and identity*. Wayville: University of South Australia.

Lawler, D. (2013). *Reconstructing myself: The transition to motherhood for women with a disability* (Doctoral dissertation). Trinity College Dublin, Ireland.

Lawler, D., Begley, C., & Lalor, J. (2015). (Re)constructing myself: The process of transition to motherhood for women with a disability. *Journal of Advanced Nursing, 71*(7), 1672–1683.

Malacrida, C. (2009). Performing motherhood in a disablist world: Dilemmas of motherhood, feminity and disability. *International Journal of Qualitative Studies in Education, 22*(1), 99–117.

McKay-Mofatt, S., & Rotheram, J. (2007). Maternity services and women experiences. In S. McKay-Moffat (Ed.), *Disability in pregnancy and childbirth* (p. 49–72). Edinburgh, Scotland: Churchill Livingstone.

McKeever, P., Angus, J., Lee-Miller, K., & Reid, D. (2003). It's more of a production: Accomplishing mothering using a mobility device. *Disability and Society, 18*(2), 179–197.

Mead, G. (1934). *Mind, self and society*. Chicago, IL: University of Chicago Press.

Oakley, A. (1979). *From here to maternity: Becoming a mother*. Harmondsworth, UK: Penguin.

Oakley, A. (1980). *Women confined: Towards a sociology of childbirth*. Oxford, UK: Martin Roberston.

Onorato, R. S., & Turner, J. C. (2001). The "I" the "me" and the "us": The psychological group and self concept maintainance and change. In C. Sedikides & M. B. Brewer (Eds.), *Individual self, relational self, collective self* (pp. 147–170). Philadelphia, PA: Psychology Press.

Patston, P. (2007). Constructive functional diversity: A new paradigm beyond disability and impairment. *Disability and Rehabilitation, 29*(20–21), 1625–1633.

Peterson, C., Maier, S. F., & Seligman, M. E. P. (1995). *Learned helplessness: A theory for the age of personal control.* New York, NY: Oxford University Press.

Prilleltensky, O. (2003). A ramp to motherhood: The experience of mothers with physical disabilities. *Sexuality and Disability, 21*(1), 21–47.

Raman, S., & Levi, S. J. (2002). Concepts of disablement in documents guiding physical therapy. *Disability and Rehabilitation, 24*(15), 790–797.

Redwood, T. (2007). *Becoming a mother: A phenomological exploration of transition to motherhood, its impact and implications for the professional lives of nurses, midwives and health visitors* (Doctoral dissertation). University of East Anglia, Norwich.

Sedikides, C., & Brewer, M. B. (2001). Individual self, relational self, and collective self: Partners, opponents or strangers? In C. Sedikides & M. B. Brewer (Eds.), *Individual self, relational self, collective self* (pp. 1–3). Philadelphia, PA: Psychology Press.

Shakespeare, T. (2006). *Disability rights and wrongs.* London, UK: Routledge.

Sheerin, F., Keenan, P., & Lawler, D. (2014). Mothers with intellectual disabilities: Interactions with children and family services in Ireland. *British Journal of Learning Disabilities, 41*, 189–196.

Smeltzer, S. (2007). Pregnancy in women with physical disabilities. *JOGNN: Journal of Obstetric, Gynaecology and Neonatal Nursing, 36*(1), 88–96.

Smeltzer, S., Sharts-Hopko, N. C., Ott, B. B., Zimmerman, V., & Duffin, J. (2007). Perspectives of women with disabilities on reaching those who are hard of hearing. *The Journal of Neuroscience Nursing: The Journal of the American Association of Neuroscience Nurses, 39*(3), 163–171.

Smith, E. R., Coats, S., & Murphy, J. (2001). The self and attachment to relationship partners and groups. In C. Sedikides & M. B. Brewer (Eds.), *Individual self, relational self, collective self* (pp. 109–122). Philadelphia, PA: Psychology Press.

Stroebe, M. S., & Schut, H. (2010). Meaning making in the dual process model of coping with bereavement. In R. A. Neimeyer (Ed.), *Meaning reconstruction and the experience of loss* (4th ed., pp. 55–73). Washington, D.C.: American Psycological Association.

Swain, J., & French, S. (2000). Towards an affirmation model of disability. *Disability and Society, 15*(4), 569–582.

Tate, D. G., & Pledger, C. (2003). An integrative conceptual framework of disability. *American Psychologist, 58*(2), 289–295.

Thomas, C., & Curtis, P. (1997). Having a baby: Some disabled women's reproductive experiences. *Midwifery, 13*(4), 202–209.

Watson, N. (2002). Well, I know this is going to sound very strange to you, but I don't see myself as a disabled person: Identity and disability. *Disability and Society, 17*(5), 509–527.

CHAPTER SEVEN

Sustaining AND Draining?

Adoptive Mothers' Enactment of Rituals in Open Adoption Relationships

COLLEEN WARNER COLANER,* HALEY KRANSTUBER HORSTMAN,† AND MARIA BUTAUSKI‡

Chances are you know someone who has been touched by adoption. Placing a child for adoption not only changes the life of the adoptee; it also affects every member of the adoptive and birth family. This includes people in the current adoptive and birth families, such as siblings, grandparents, aunts/uncles, and cousins. This also includes the adoptee's future family, such as future children and spouse(s). When we think about all this together, tens of millions of people are connected to adoption in some way. Among the three of us writing this chapter are many connections to adoption: Colleen is an adoptive mother, Haley is an adoptee, and Maria plans to adopt children with her wife in the future.

As communication researchers with both personal and professional connections to adoption, we think a lot about how families talk about adoption. After the legal side of adoption is settled, adoptive families need to think about how they talk about adoption and how that talk affects the adoptee. That is why adoption scholars talk about adoption as created through "law and language" (Galvin & Colaner, 2013). The purpose of this chapter is to look more closely at one type of communication common in adoptive families: family rituals. Because mothers tend to be the most involved in creating and sustaining family rituals, we think

* Colleen Warner Colaner, University of Missouri, colanerc@missouri.edu.
† Haley Kranstuber Horstman, University of Missouri, horstmanh@missouri.edu.
‡ Maria Butauski, University of Missouri, mcbvh8@mail.missouri.edu.

about adoptive mothers' ritual use with an eye towards critical feminist theorizing. Applying feminist theory to adoptive mothers' ritual communication helps us understand how important but also effortful family rituals can be.

FAMILY RITUALS, KINKEEPING, AND CRITICAL FEMINIST THEORIZING

Family rituals are very important for many families. One of the biggest things family rituals do is to create, maintain, and celebrate *family identity*, or a sense of what it means to belong to a specific family group (Galvin, 2006). Family rituals create family identity by honoring its past, present, and future. This helps to create a sense of home (Baxter & Braithwaite, 2006) and closeness among family members (Crespo, Kielpikowski, Pryor, & Jose, 2011). Many families have specific rituals surrounding holidays, religious ceremonies, birthdays, reunions, storytelling, vacations, and bereavement/loss of family members (McCoy, 2011). Scholars have organized rituals in three different types: family celebrations, family traditions, and patterned family interactions (Galvin, Braithwaite, & Bylund, 2016). Most people probably first think of rituals in terms of *family celebrations*, such as holidays and special events. These types of rituals are connected to specific days on the calendar such as Christmas or Hanukkah, Halloween, and Thanksgiving as well as individual birthdays. For example, when Haley was young, her mom used to make green shamrock-shaped pancakes on St. Patrick's Day to celebrate their Irish heritage. Maria and her fiancé Abi celebrate the new year with a spread of twelve fruits (one for each month of the year to come), a ritual connected to Abi's Filipino ethnicity.

Rituals also take the place of *family traditions*, involving unique family occasions. Colleen's family, for example, celebrates the Super Bowl every year with a gathering of friends and family to celebrate her husband's family connections to football. Haley and her mom made May baskets each year to celebrate May Day and her mother's love of flowers.

Finally, rituals can involve *patterned family interactions* or everyday routines that are meaningful to members of the family. Bedtime rituals are an important part of Colleen's family, as her young daughters depend on a specific order of stories, songs, and snuggles to fall asleep. Rituals give meaning to the special days and moments that make up family life.

Kinkeeping and Critical Feminist Theorizing

More and more researchers are beginning to think about rituals with an eye to critical feminist theories. Simply put, critical feminist theories "identify, critique, and attempt to change" the ways that women are treated unfairly because of their sex and gender (Wood, 2008, p. 326). Critical feminist theories draw attention to women's experiences, perspectives, and knowledge in everyday life. This perspective is helpful for pointing out aspects of women's experiences that no one really noticed before. For example, thinking about women doing more housework and childcare than men helps us appreciate work that tends to be taken for granted (Wood, 2008).

Applying critical feminist theorizing to family rituals helps us understand that mothers tend to initiate, organize, and sustain family rituals (Rosenthal, 1985). The work required to keep family rituals running and successful is called *invisible emotional labor*, meaning that remembering to do family rituals and making the rituals happen takes a lot of work that is usually not noticed or celebrated. Scholars have named this emotional labor *kinkeeping*, explaining it as "remembering birthdays, sending cards, preparing for holidays, [and] keeping in touch with relatives," (Shaw & Lee, 2012, p. 395). Mothers tend to do most of the work to keep rituals going by planning celebrations, gathering family members together, buying and giving gifts, and planning and preparing food for family celebrations (di Leonardo, 1987). Mothers tend to be responsible for the small details that keep family gatherings running smoothly, such as making sure there are enough plates, napkins, and silverware for everyone coming to the family reunion. Although this level of planning seems relatively unimportant, it is a task that is central to the success of the event and requires mental energy that is often considered a given by other family members. From a critical feminist perspective, mothers' work to make family rituals successful should be examined.

Mothers' kinkeeping tends to be a stressful experience for many women (Rosenthal, 1985). Gerstel and Gallagher (1993) noted that kinkeeping usually involves working with numerous family members, such that women have to juggle many demands and responsibilities which can be stressful. In all, mothers' work to make family rituals happen is important for creating family cohesion yet results in increased stress for women. Thus, rituals are sustaining yet draining from a critical feminist perspective.

Adoptive Mother's Ritual Enactment

Family rituals are very important to adoptive families. Because adoptive families are not genetically related, they violate expectations that society has about what family is supposed to be (Baxter, 2014). Because of this, communication becomes an important way that adoptive families make sense of their relationships, both when talking to other members of the adoptive family as well as talking to outsiders about the family. Rituals are one important way that adoptive families communicate to celebrate the family's unique history and form. For example, Haley's parents celebrated her adoption on the anniversary of the adoption becoming official with a fun family activity and a small gift, such as going out to breakfast or getting a new T-shirt. Colleen does a similar celebration with her daughters on their adoption anniversary, allowing each girl to pick out a fun cake and plan a family outing each year.

Adoption rituals are clearly important for keeping the adoptive family connected. However, adoption rituals are also important for staying in touch with birth family members (Fiese et al., 2002). Open adoptions occur when birth parents are known and included in adoptive family life. The specifics of how much and what type of communication happens with the birth family is different in every family (Colaner & Scharp, 2016). This may be because open adoption agreements are not legally binding but rather "handshake agreements" between adoptive and birth families about the type and amount of contact the families will have in the future (Grotevant, McRoy, Wrobel, & Ayers-Lopez, 2013). Adoptive and birth families make agreements when the child is placed with the adoptive family about expectations about regular contact such as sending monthly photos, attending annual visits, and celebrating certain holidays together (such as the child's birthday or Christmas) (Colaner & Scharp, 2016). At its core, these conversations create expectations about the kinds of rituals that will keep the adoptive and birth families connected through the ritual forms of family celebrations, family traditions, and patterned family interactions. Although rituals seem to play a big role in keeping birth and adoptive families connected, we do not actually know a lot about the specific types of rituals these open adoptive families use. To get more information about these rituals, we were interested in conducting a study to explore the rituals adoptive families use to stay in touch with birth families.

THE STUDY

What Were We Interested in Learning?

In this study we were specifically interested in the mother's perceptions of the rituals adoptive families use to stay in touch with birth families. We were specifically interested in mothers' perceptions for two reasons. First, mothers tend to be the family member who makes rituals happen for the family (Friedman & Weissbrod, 2004). Second, adoptive mothers tend to be the *gatekeepers* in the open adoption relationship (Hays, Horstman, Colaner, & Nelson, 2015), meaning that they serve as the central person communicating with the birth parents on behalf of the family. Adoptive mothers wear many hats in the open adoption relationship, "including their roles as parents, their relationships with the birth parent, and the relationships between the birth parent and the adopted child" (p. 932). Because adoptive parents are the legal parents (Grotevant, 2009), and mothers tend to be the kinkeepers of family relationships (Shaw & Lee, 2012), adoptive mothers tend to be responsible for sustaining the relationship with the birth parents. To learn more about this kinkeeping work, we asked the following research questions:

RQ1: *What kind of rituals do adoptive mothers enact with or surrounding their adopted child's birth families?*
RQ2: *What biological family members are present in these rituals?*

Because rituals are so important for feelings of family closeness and identity (Crespo et al., 2011), it is likely that rituals are related to adoptive mothers' feelings about the relationship with the birth parent. Rituals can also help the adoptee feel closer to the birth mother, especially from the perspective of the adoptive mother who serves as the gatekeeper of the open adoption relationship. Thus, the following hypothesis is posed:

H1: *Adoptive mothers with birth parent rituals will have higher levels of (a) adoptive mother–birth parent relational satisfaction and (b) perceived birth parent–adoptee relational closeness when compared to adoptive mothers without rituals.*

Rituals tend to be specific to individual families, which each family having a different way of doing rituals (Bruess & Pearson, 1997). Because rituals mean different things to different people, the type of ritual that the family uses might not be as important as how the adoptive mother feels about the ritual. Thus, we were interested in the adoptive mothers' satisfaction with the ritual. Thus, we posed the following hypothesis.

H2: *Adoptive mother ritual satisfaction is associated with (a) adoptive mother–birth parent relational satisfaction and (b) adoptive mother perception of birth parent–adoptee relational closeness.*

Not all adoptive families will have rituals with the birth family. We were also interested in how a lack of rituals would relate to the open adoption relationship. On one hand, adoptive mothers may be relieved to not have the additional emotional labor that comes with making rituals happen. On the other hand, adoptive mothers may miss the relationship building that comes with ritual use. To learn more about this, we asked the final research question:

RQ3: *How satisfied are adoptive mothers with not having rituals in their open adoption relationship?*

How Did We Go About Learning This Information?

To answer our questions and hypotheses, we asked a group of adoptive mothers to complete a survey about their rituals and family relationships. We put together an online survey, and we sent the link to several adoption agencies. These agencies sent the link to families who worked with their agency. Participants voluntarily completed the online survey after giving consent to join the research study. Any names in the responses were changed to pseudonyms to protect confidentiality. About 300 adoptive mothers completed the set of questions about adoption rituals. Most of these mothers identified as White. The mothers were between 26–72 years old, with the average age being 39 years.

We asked these mothers to describe the kinds of rituals that they used to stay in touch with their child's birth family. There were text boxes for them to describe up to four different rituals. This gave us details about 274 different family rituals. We put these rituals into categories based on similarity to come up with a list of common rituals.

We also asked the adoptive mothers questions about how they felt about the rituals. For example, they responded to questions such as "These rituals are important to my family" on a scale of (1) *strongly disagree* to (5) *strongly agree*. The mothers who did not have rituals with their birth family were asked, "How satisfied do you feel about NOT having rituals with your child's birth parent?," also on a scale of (1) *strongly disagree* to (5) *strongly agree*. We also asked all the mothers questions to find out how they felt about their relationship with the birth mother and how close they thought their child was to the birth mother, again on a scale of 1 to 5. This data helped us understand adoptive mothers' experiences so that we could answer our hypotheses and research questions.

What Did We Learn?

Ritual Type

Our data helped us understand there are two types of rituals that open adoptive families use: event-based rituals and communication-based rituals. The list in Table 7.1 shows all the rituals and how often adoptive mothers mentioned each one. Below, we describe each ritual and give examples from the adoptive mothers' descriptions.

Table 7.1. Ritual Type and Frequency.

Ritual	Frequency
Event-based rituals	
Child birthday	92 (33.6%)
Christmas	50 (18.2%)
Small holidays	34 (12.4%)
Birth family birthday	26 (9.5%)

Ritual	Frequency
Special occasions	26 (9.5%)
Birth family visits	26 (9.5%)
Mother's Day	14 (5.1%)
Adoption anniversary	6 (2.2%)
Agency events	4 (1.5%)
Father's Day	3 (1.1%)
Communication-based rituals	
Exchanges	78 (28.5%)
Phone calls	16 (5.8%)
Storytelling	7 (2.6%)
Video chats	7 (2.6%)
Praying	4 (1.5%)

Source: Authors.

Event-based Rituals

Most of the rituals are event-based rituals. These events, tied to the U.S. calendar as well as the unique family calendars, provided predictable rhythms of contact between adoptive and birth families.

Child's Birthday. Several rituals surrounded the adopted child's birthday, including meeting with the birth family, sending updates to the birth family, or inviting the birth family to the child's party. For example, one mother mentioned, "We have always visited with his birth mom on his birthday. We bring cupcakes and candles and sing to him, all together." Birthdays created a consistent time for the birth and adoptive families to visit. For birth families who are not able to visit face-to-face, birthdays offered a valuable time to connect, such as this mother explained: "Our Birth Mom calls every year and sings our son [the song] 'happy birthday' on FaceTime and then we open the gift that she sent us while she watches." The child's birthday offered a unique time to connect with the birth family, given their attachment to the child's birth.

Birth Family Birthdays. Adoptive families also celebrated birth family members' birthdays. At times, birth family members were actively involved, such as this mother explained, "We celebrate our son and his bio[logical] brother's birthdays when we travel to visit. We have a family party with both boys and whatever family members are invited by our son's first mom." Other times, however, the ritual is conducted about, but not with, the birth family member: "We celebrate our son's first mom's birthday at [our] house with a cake and we send her a card. For any family member's birthday we put up a happy birthday banner and a string of lights about 2 weeks before and we start talking about that person's birthday and what we will do to celebrate it. Our son's first mom has not wanted face-to-face contact so she is not there but we hope someday she will be." Thus, ritualistic celebrations of family members created connections to individuals who may not be actively connected to the family at the moment.

Adoption Finalization Anniversary. Sometimes referred to as "Gotcha Day," adoption finalizations mark the date in which the child became a legal member of the adoptive family. Rituals surrounding a celebration of the adoption finalization included talking about or celebrating the adoption, sending updates to the birth mom, or meeting with birth family members on this day. Families celebrated with the birth family ("Adoption Day Celebration—call or send photos on the special day") or remembered the birth family in private family celebrations ("We officially took custody on Valentine's Day and brought our child home. So each Valentine's day we also celebrate the great love our birthmother has for our child").

Mother's Day. Adoptive families had rituals surrounding Mother's Day in which they communicated with the birth mother, either directly ("We acknowledge our son's birthmother with a card and a call. This year we timed our visit to coincide with Mother's Day and all went out to a restaurant. We also brought flowers") or indirectly ("I send a card to her, child makes something for her"). Some families created a Birthmother's Day surrounding Mother's Day, as this mother explains ("We take her out to lunch to celebrate Birthmothers Day, traditionally the Saturday before Mother's Day").

Father's Day. Similarly, adoptive mothers mentioned connecting with birth fathers around Father's Day, such as this mother explains, "(the birth family and we) exchange cards on Father's [Day]." Interestingly, one adoptive mother explained celebrating the adoptive and birth father in equivalent ways, stating that they celebrated by, "making Father's Day presents for the dads in our lives."

Christmas. Adoptive mothers described extensive rituals around Christmas, involving cards, gifts, and time spent with the birth family. Christmas tended to mark a special time of connection for these open adoption relationships. One mother explained that she buys matching ornaments for the child and birth mother each year as well as "some other small gifts plus a school picture." The Christmas celebrations also afforded the opportunity to visit with extended birth family members, as this mother explains, "Our son's birth mother's family has a huge Christmas/New Year's get-together every year. The house is packed with tons of relatives. The highlight is the white elephant gift exchange."

Other Holidays. In addition to Christmas, other holidays were celebrated with the birth family each year, such as Easter ("My daughter dyes Easter eggs with her bio grandmother every year"), Halloween ("My daughter's [birth] mother is the one who takes her trick or treating"), Thanksgiving ("Usually a day or two before [Thanksgiving] we will have a FaceTime session with each birth parent"), and summer holidays ("We usually get together during the summer during one of the long weekends for fireworks and dinner").

Special Occasions. In addition to holiday celebrations, special occasions such as baptisms, graduations, and annual family photos were mentioned as routine times to connect with the birth family. Some adoptive mothers described being involved with the birth family's wedding celebrations, stating, "Both my adopted and bio son were in my adopted son's mom's wedding." Routine events such as adoptees' sporting and school events were also mentioned, such as this adoptive mother stated, "She has been invited and has come to see gymnastics, soccer, and a dance recital. This arrangement feels comfortable and non-intrusive. Our daughter enjoys having grandma [Sue] there and sometimes asks about her (will she be there?)"

Agency Events. Adoptive mothers described formal agency meetings for birth and adoptive families. For example, "Our adoption agency hosts a summer picnic each year to reunite families and we invite the birth parents and extended family but they don't always show up." Importantly, birth family members may not attend each year, but adoptive mothers routinely invited them. Thus, the invitation as well as attending the adoption agency event is considered a ritual for the adoptive mothers.

Birth Family Visits. Face-to-face visits were important to adoptive mothers as they maintained a relationship with the birth family. Birth family visits also included sleepovers, babysitting, and casual visits, such as this mother explained, "When we are back in town, we call our birth mother and our son spends time with her. They go out to eat or hang at her house." These visits often have ritual elements in which the same behaviors are conducted each visit, as this mother explains, "We go for ice cream at the same place every time we visit birth mom." Some families also tried to create predictability about the ritual enactment, such as this mother, "We make an effort to have face-to-face visits at least once a month."

Communication-based Rituals

In addition to rituals surrounding family events, adoptive mothers also described communication-based rituals. These rituals also happened along with special events (i.e., holidays, special occasions) as described above, so there is some overlap with the events-based list. Yet, communication-based rituals reference the ways that discourse occurs in families toward the goal of making sense of their family unit.

Storytelling. Adoptive mothers talked about routine communication about birth families in the form of storytelling. Some mentions involved reading books about adoption ("Read a story each night that is specific to adoption ..."), talking specifically about the child's adoption or birth family ("My daughter's mom sent her a recordable storybook that we listen to"), or telling the adoptee's birth story ("We read adoption books to our daughter regularly. We also have a book that we created specifically about our daughter's adoption, including pictures of her birth mother"). Storytelling tended to occur at bedtime as part of a bedtime routine.

Prayer. Prayer rituals were another common component of bedtime routines. Birth family members were specifically mentioned in prayer rituals: "After jammies and book reading, we say prayers. We often say prayers for our son's birth family including his first mom and his 2 siblings she is raising." Prayer rituals differed from storytelling in that they were specifically spiritual or religious in nature.

Exchanges. Coinciding with ritual gatherings, holidays, and celebrations, many adoptive mothers discussed sending, giving, or receiving pictures, gifts, letters, or cards. Exchanges occurred via mail and in person. One adoptive mother explained that giving gifts to the birth mother was itself a ritual, "We gave her a charm bracelet when he was born with a 'forget me knot' charm, to assure her we would not forget her. Now we give her a charm to celebrate different holidays or events, such as her graduation." More commonly, adoptive mothers discussed exchanges as embedded in holiday rituals, such as sending gifts at Christmas, cards on Mother's Day, and pictures on the child's birthday.

Phone Calls. Adoptive mothers described commemorating holidays and birthdays with phone calls. For example, one adoptive mother explained, "we talk on the phone with our son's [birth mom] every time it is our son's birthday." For some, phone calls were a replacement for face-to-face visits due to living in geographically distant areas.

Video Chats. Similarly, video chats (i.e., Skype, FaceTime) with the birth family were used at holidays and special occasions. Presumably, video chatting is used as a replacement for face-to-face visits, as this adoptive mother suggests, "We can't spend holidays together, but we send boxes of goodies and FaceTime on holidays."

Birth Family Member Presence in Rituals

Our second research question helped us pinpoint which birth family members were involved in these adoptive family rituals. Table 7.2 shows how often different family members were included in the rituals. Birth mothers were most commonly referenced, followed by birth family generally, birth father, birth siblings, and birth grandparents. Importantly, in 81 rituals (29.6%) adoptive mothers did not make specific mention of anyone from their child's biological family but rather explained the ritual generally.

Table 7.2. Frequency of Birth Family Member in Ritual.

Birth family member in ritual	Frequency
Birth mother	130 (47.4%)
Birth family	75 (27.4%)
Birth father	37 (13.5%)
Birth siblings	16 (5.8%)
Birth grandparents	14 (5.1%)

Source: Authors.

Ritual Satisfaction and Relational Quality

Our hypotheses compared adoptive mothers who had rituals to mothers who did not have rituals. We found that adoptive mothers with rituals tended to more satisfied with their relationship with the birth family. Those mothers with adoption rituals also felt that their child had a closer relationship with the birth family. We also found that mothers who were satisfied with their adoption rituals also tended to feel satisfied with their relationship with the birth family; they also felt that their child was closer to the birth family when they felt satisfied with the rituals. These findings meant that both of our hypotheses were supported.

Our third research question asked about ritual quality for adoptive mothers who did not use rituals. We found that adoptive mothers without adoption rituals tended to still be pretty satisfied with their relationship with the birth family.

WHAT DOES ALL THIS MEAN?

We have pulled together research, theory, and adoptive mothers' experiences to learn more about the rituals adoptive mothers use to connect with their children's birth families. Bringing all this together helps us understand the importance of rituals for family life, especially for adoptive families who really rely on communication to create a family identity. Thinking about the experiences of the adoptive mothers through the lens of critical feminist theorizing helps us understand a bit more about the invisible work that is required to keep adoption rituals going.

Ritual Usage and Types

We already knew that rituals are an important way adoptive families communicate to create a family identity (Galvin, 2006). We can now also see that rituals play a vital role in connecting adoptive and birth families. This is especially clear when we think about the finding that mothers who use rituals with the birth family feel more satisfied and think that their child has a closer relationship with the birth parent when compared to adoptive mothers who did not have rituals. This makes sense when we think about how important rituals are for feelings of family togetherness (Crespo et al., 2011). The rituals that the adoptive mothers described show how these rituals create a place for the birth family in the adoptive family's life. Having regular, planned contact with the birth family helps to make sure that birth family is a consistent presence in the adoptee's upbringing. These rituals serve as a form of relational maintenance, keeping the families connected and close to one another.

At the same time, we have to be careful about our claims connecting rituals and feelings about the relationship. Because of the way that we studied adoptive mothers' experiences, we cannot say which came first—the ritual or the satisfaction. We suggest above that rituals help the families feel closer, but it is also possible that adoptive mothers use rituals because they feel the relationship is worth celebrating. If a birth mother is close with the adoptive family, it may be more likely that that birth mother is incorporated into the adoptive family's holidays; adoptive mothers who do not have a close, satisfying relationship with the birth family may not have the type of relationship that can support an ongoing ritual. For example, one adoptive mother reported, "My child's [birth] mother is invited to every birthday celebration of our daughter. BUT she has never come." Here we see that the birth mothers' lack of involvement perhaps says something about the relationship in a larger sense, that the relationship is lacking the closeness that is needed to perform a ritual. In this sense, ritual use both affects and reflects the open adoption relationship.

When we think about the types of rituals adoptive mothers described, we see a lot of overlap with rituals reported by traditional families (Fiese et al., 2002). Family gatherings and routines, for example, have been reported as common family rituals for more than 50 years. Adoptive families' rituals in this way demonstrate the way that families function in a more universal way, regardless of biological connectedness. Other rituals were, however, are exclusive to the open adoption relationships, such as adoption finalization anniversaries, agency meetings, and adoption storytelling rituals. Because adoption is a unique relationship, it makes sense that there are unique rituals. Each adoptive mother described a different combination of rituals, and the way that the rituals were carried out were individualized to each family. Thus, ritual use is very personal and specific to each open adoption relationship.

Birth Family Ritual Involvement

We can also learn a lot about adoption rituals by thinking about who from the birth family was involved. Many of the rituals involved several members of the birth family. Biological fathers, grandparents, and siblings had a prominent role in ritual enactment. Adoption researchers typically only think about the birth mother (Galvin & Colaner, 2013), but we can see from the adoptive mothers' experiences that rituals connect the adoptive family to many members of the birth family. Most people do not think about birth fathers, but the adoptive mothers that we talked to mentioned birth fathers in 13.5% of the responses. Also, birth or half-siblings were mentioned in 5.8% of the rituals described, and biological grandparents were mentioned in 5.1% of the responses. Some of the rituals involved specific activities with just grandparents, such as the child who dyes Easter eggs with her biological grandmother every year. This could mean that the grandmother simply desires a relationship with her biological granddaughter, or perhaps the adoptee's birth parents are not interested in maintaining contact, so the grandmother took on the role. We need to keep thinking about how adoptees stay connected to multiple members of their birth families, how those different relationships come about, and how connecting to biological parents, siblings, grandparents and other members of the adoptive family might affect the adoptee in different ways.

Critical Feminist Theorizing and Ritual Use

We have seen how important rituals are for adoptive families. It is also important for us to consider rituals through the lens of critical feminist theorizing to understand how these rituals can potentially be draining for adoptive mothers. For example, adoptive mothers mentioned Christmas a lot when talking about their adoption rituals. Other researchers have written about how mothers tend to feel overwhelmed by Christmas rituals because it takes a lot of emotional energy to make the holiday season meaningful and memorable for the family (Kudak, 2013). Although our participants did not specifically mention other holidays, we can extend this logic to other holidays as well, such as Hanukah and Kwanza. Rituals involving birth members during the holiday season place an extra layer of emotional, mental, and time-consuming work on adoptive mothers at an already demanding time.

Adoptive mothers also mentioned rituals that celebrate Mother's Day and Father's Day. Adoptive mothers tended to perform rituals with birth mothers around Mother's Day, such as getting together for a meal or sending cards, gifts, and flowers. Thus, adoptive mothers gave their energy to celebrate the birth mother at a time reserved for honoring their own contributions to their family. Similarly, adoptive mothers talked about sending the birth father pictures and gifts on Father's Day. This requires adoptive mothers to complete two rounds of Father's Day preparations. Thus, these holiday rituals provided important connections to the birth family, but rituals also created an extra layer of work for adoptive mothers at times that were already demanding (di Leonardo, 1987).

It is important to think about how much of an adoptive mothers' ritual work is invisible. Many of the reported rituals were done with the birth family on behalf of the child. For example, a mother mentioned that her "child makes something for [the birth mother]" on Mother's Day. Thus, the gift comes from the daughter, but the adoptive mother coordinated the creation and sending of the gift. Other mothers mentioned arranging yearly family photo sessions that include the adoptive and birth families. In essence, the rituals aim to create connections between the child and the birth family. Here, the adoptive mothers' effort is behind the scenes to sustain rituals between other members of the open adoption relationship.

Taking all of this together, we now know more about rituals, adoptive mothers, and the invisible emotional labor related to creating and performing rituals. Rituals are some of the most fun things that families do together. When we think back on our favorite moments with our childhood families and our current families, rituals tend to come to mind as the high notes of these relationships. For adoptive families, rituals are important for celebrating what makes the adoptive family unique. Now that we have spent a lot of energy thinking about what rituals do for our family and what it takes to make a ritual successful, we can better appreciate our own family rituals. We can also notice mothers' emotional labor that keeps rituals alive and makes them special. If that work is something that you used to take for granted, you can thank your mother for her work and tell her that you appreciate the rituals that keep the family strong.

WHAT DO WE STILL NEED TO KNOW?

- In open adoption, we see that adoptive mothers enact rituals to create and sustain relationships with the birth family, but we know less about the decision-making processes behind these rituals. What do you think adoptive parents consider and discuss when deciding how to best maintain relationships with birth family members? In what situations do you think adoptive fathers would have a greater role in planning and enacting these rituals?

- What do rituals look like in multicultural families? Families with fewer resources?
- Are more people involved or does the majority of kinkeeping responsibilities still fall into the hands of mothers?
- Do adoptive mothers want more help with the planning and execution of family rituals? Why or why not?
- What do fathers want? As families become more diverse, do fathers desire to become more involved in kinkeeping? Why or why not? Under what circumstances do you think other family members take on the role of kinkeepers?

HOW DOES THIS WORK IN REAL LIFE?

- We know that planning family rituals can be exhausting for mothers, especially around holidays when there is so much to do. Adoptive mothers put in a great amount of work to help make holidays like Christmas and Mother's Day special for their child and the birth family. Think of ways *you* can help make these holidays special for your family. Plan your own gifts and consider creating new rituals. Think about what kind of legwork *you can do* to make these holidays special for them.
- A little bit of gratitude goes a long way. Don't forget to tell your mom how much you appreciate everything she does for you and the family, especially during busy times of the year!
- Think about the people in your life who are touched by adoption. If they are open to talking about the adoption, ask them what kind of rituals they have used to stay connected. Think about some ways that you can celebrate and support their rituals.

CLASSROOM ACTIVITIES

From this chapter, we learned about the importance of family rituals and the central role mothers play in organizing and enacting family rituals. What are your favorite family rituals? What are your not-so-favorite family rituals? Do you remember rituals from when you were younger that your family no longer does?

- List of all your family rituals.
- List rituals you remember from your childhood that your family no longer does.

- With a partner, discuss the role your mother and other maternal figures in your family played to make the family rituals happen? Do you remember them being especially stressed? Why did your family stop doing family rituals you used to have in the past? How can other family members get involved in organizing family rituals? How can you be a part of helping carry out family rituals in the future?
- After discussing with a partner, take 3–5 minutes of reflective writing time. Knowing what you know now about the work mothers put into planning and executing family rituals, reflect on the following questions:
  - How can I help with the planning of family rituals to ease the burden on my mom and other maternal figures in my family?
  - What can I do to ensure that, when I have my own family, we have valuable family rituals? How can I get more family members involved in the planning and execution of family rituals?
  - After reflection time, discuss as a class.

REFERENCES

Baxter, L. A. (2014). Introduction to the volume. In L. A. Baxter (Ed.), *Remaking "family" communicatively* (pp. 3–16). New York, NY: Peter Lang.

Baxter, L. A., & Braithwaite, D. O. (2006). Rituals as communication constituting families. In L. Turner & R. West (Eds.), *Family communication: A reference of theory and research* (pp. 259–280). Thousand Oaks, CA: Sage.

Bruess, C. J., & Pearson, J. C. (1997). Interpersonal rituals in marriage and adult friendship. *Communications Monographs, 64*(1), 25–46. https://doi.org/10.1080/03637759709376403

Colaner, C. W., & Scharp, K. M. (2016). Maintaining open adoption relationships: Practitioner insights on adoptive parents' regulation of adoption kinship networks. *Communication Studies, 67*(3), 359–378. https://doi.org/10.1080/10510974.2016.1164208

Crespo, C., Kielpikowski, M., Pryor, J., & Jose, P. E. (2011). Family rituals in New Zealand families: Links to family cohesion and adolescents' well-being. *Journal of Family Psychology, 25*(2), 184–193. https://doi.org/10.1037/a0023113

di Leonardo, M. (1987). The female world of cards and holidays: Women, families, and the work of kinship. *Signs: Journal of Women in Culture and Society, 12*(3), 440–453. https://www.jstor.org/stable/3174331

Fiese, B. H., Tomcho, T. J., Douglas, M., Josephs, K., Poltrock, S., & Baker, T. (2002). A review of 50 years of research on naturally occurring family routines and rituals: Cause for celebration? *Journal of Family Psychology, 16*(4), 381–390. https://doi.org/10.1037/0893-3200.16.4.381

Friedman, S. R., & Weissbrod, C. S. (2004). Attitudes toward the continuation of family rituals among emerging adults. *Sex roles, 50*(3–4), 277–284. https://doi.org/10.1023/B:SERS.0000015558.21334.6b

Galvin, K. (2006). Diversity's impact on defining the family. In L. H. Turner & R. West (Eds.), *The family communication sourcebook* (pp. 3–19). Thousand Oaks, CA: Sage.

Galvin, K., Braithwaite, D., & Bylund, C. (2016). *Family communication: Cohesion and change* (9th ed.). New York, NY: Routledge.

Galvin, K., & Colaner, C. (2013). Created through law and language: Communicative complexities of adoptive families. In K. Floyd & M. T. Morman (Eds.), *Widening the family circle* (2nd ed., pp. 191–209). Thousand Oaks, CA: Sage.

Gerstel, N., & Gallagher, S. K. (1993). Kinkeeping and distress: Gender, recipients of care, and work-family conflict. *Journal of Marriage and the Family, 55*(3), 598–608. https://doi.org/10.2307/353341

Grotevant, H. D. (2009). Emotional distance regulation over the life course in adoptive kinship networks. In G. M. Wrobel & E. Neil (Eds.), *International advances in adoption research for practice* (pp. 295–316). Hoboken, NJ: Wiley-Blackwell.

Grotevant, H. D., McRoy, R. G., Wrobel, G. M., & Ayers-Lopez, S. (2013). Contact between adoptive and birth families: Perspectives from the Minnesota/Texas adoption research project. *Child Development Perspectives, 7*(3), 193–198. https://doi.org/10.1111/cdep.12039

Hays, A. H., Horstman, H. K., Colaner, C. W., & Nelson, L. R. (2015). "She chose us to be your parents": Exploring the content and process of adoption entrance narratives told in families formed through open adoption. *Journal of Social and Personal Relationships, 33*(7), 917–937. https://doi.org/10.1177/0265407515611494

Kudak, A. (2013, November). *"We rack our brains all year to make it special": The discursive construction of mothers' holiday ritual roles.* Paper presented at the National Communication Association, Washington D. C.

McCoy, R. (2011). African American elders, cultural traditions, and the family reunion. *Generations, 35*(3), 16–21.

Rosenthal, C. J. (1985). Kinkeeping in the familial division of labor. *Journal of Marriage and Family, 47*(4), 965–974. https://doi.org/10.2307/352340

Shaw, S. M., & Lee, J. (2012). *Women's voices, feminist visions: Classic and contemporary readings.* New York, NY: McGraw-Hill.

Wood, J. T. (2008). Critical feminist theories. In L. A. Baxter & D. O. Braithwaite (Eds.), *Engaging theories in interpersonal communication: Multiple perspectives* (pp. 323–334). Thousand Oaks, CA: Sage.

CHAPTER EIGHT

Mother-Daughter Communication About Sex AND Sexuality Across THE Life Course

WENDY K. WATSON* AND SANDRA L. FAULKNER†

> How would I raise my daughter? I'm not going to raise her to have sex real early. I think
> that's a universal … You always tell your daughter not to have sex early … But I'm going to
> tell my daughter you can get pregnant. Everybody probably should tell their daughter that.
> You don't need all the emotional baggage that comes along with it … I was raised as what
> my role would be as a female, not what I think I can [be] in the future as a doctor or lawyer.
> Like, for example, my mom would teach [me] a couple of things on how to cook: *What's
> your husband going to eat? What are your kids going to eat?* Not you're going to starve if you
> don't know how to cook. And I want to raise my daughter [to understand that] sex is not a
> bad thing. Sex is bad when you treat it irresponsibly.
> —QUOTED IN FAULKNER (1999)

The above quote demonstrates the importance of mother-daughter talk about sex and sexuality, especially because this topic is so charged in society, at large, and often within families, in particular. The mother-daughter relationship is complex and valuable as it changes across the life course following the changing needs of both mothers and daughters (Fingerman, 2000; Sheehan & Donorfio, 1999). This relationship has to be continually renegotiated as mothers and daughters grow individually and in relation to one another. Family talk about sex and sexuality is important given that families are children's primary sexuality educator (for review,

* Wendy K. Watson, associate professor, Bowling Green State University, wwatson@bgsu.edu.
† Sandra L. Faulkner, professor, Bowling Green State University, sandraf@bgsu.edu.

see Flores & Barroso, 2017). "Parent-child sex communication is the bidirectional communication between parents (or parent figures) and their children about sex-related issues including sex, sexuality, and sexual health outcomes" (Flores & Barroso, 2017, p. 532). Patterns of discussion often mirror those from our family of origin with mothers handling discussions of sex and sexuality with their daughters as their mothers did with them. For example, Jen (2017) interviewed women ages 57–93 and discovered they believed that daughters ought to be the ones to set boundaries and be in control of their sexual relationships. Although this research did not explore how these women might have replicated these messages with their own daughters, their memories of these messages from their own mothers persisted decades later.

In this chapter, we discuss conversations and silence between mothers and daughters about sex and sexuality across the life course. "Sexual communication skills represent a tool for negotiating sexual experiences, exploring the meaning of sexuality, and acquiring information about sexuality" (Faulkner & Mansfield, 2002, p. 311). As with many topics of conversations between mothers and daughters, mothers may see their role to educate and even protect their daughters, and as such may not often share their own experiences with sex and sexuality. This may be because of feelings of powerlessness, inadequacy, and discomfort often accompany sexual talk. For example, participants in Daniluk's (1998) phenomenological study of women's sexuality believed that structural barriers (e.g., media, religion, sexual violence, and medicine) harmed their sexual health, and their experience of womanhood was intimately connected with feelings of powerlessness. Women need more language to talk about sexual issues, a topic area that is already impoverished. Not knowing how to communicate about sexual issues can create a lack of confidence and comfort, which in turn make barriers to open talk about sex and sexuality between mothers and daughters (Faulkner & Mansfield, 2002). Levels of personal disclosure vary per individual, but sex is seen in our society as private, and discussion of sex and sexuality are influenced by culture, gender, personal expectations, motivations, and attitudes. Thus, we see Communication Privacy Management Theory as a useful framework for studying and understanding communication and sex and sexuality in the mother-daughter relationship (Petronio, 2002).

PRIVACY MANAGEMENT THEORY AND TALK ABOUT SEX AND SEXUALITY

The development and maintenance of our close relationships depends in part on our disclosure decisions; what and how we decide to reveal and conceal has implications for our relational development, trust, and solidarity. *Self-disclosure* is verbal communication that reveals something private about the self; it can deepen our close relationships and be a way to maintain them as well as create chaos, discord, and decline (Petronio, 2002). Talking about sex and sexuality is an example of private information that mothers and daughters may choose to discuss—openly, partially, or not at all. *Communication Privacy Management* (CPM) addresses how we balance the need to make public disclosures with the need for privacy and emphasizes the co-owned nature of information (Petronio, 2002). In our close relationships, we expect others to disclose, and this represents a reciprocal process.

Because disclosure of private information such as sexual behavior and sexual preferences involves risk, we manage the disclosure and receipt of personal information using "metaphoric boundaries" that serve as a form of protection of the self and one's relationships and a way to decrease the possibility of losing face (for a discussion of facework see Goffman). We have multiple goals for revealing and concealing our personal information in addition to our experiences of consequences for these decisions. For instance, in the case of mother-daughter conversations about sex and sexuality, we may be interested in maintaining the relationship and our preferred identities (e.g., moral daughter, good mother), accomplishing parenting goals and keeping one another safe. It is essential to disclose positive and negative information about sex and sexuality to obtain needed support and achieve our relational goals, but if the person we disclose to is judgmental, indiscreet, and/ or reacts poorly, there can be poor consequences for our health and relationships (Kelly & Macready, 2009).

Culture, gender, context, cost-benefit ratios, and motivation are important influences on the disclosure process because they highlight important reasons we disclose or do not disclose private information (Petronio, 2002). For instance, Faulkner's research on Latinas' disclosure of sexual information to family and romantic partners revealed that women were motivated to disclose if they felt comfortable and expected or received a positive response to talk (Faulkner & Mansfield, 2002; Faulkner, 2003). Women in Faulkner's study (1999) wanted to be seen as moral and were motivated to keep relationships positive; they often felt trapped between a dialectic of cultural discourses of romantic relationships as being sexual and cultural expectations for chasteness. Daughters engaged in open conversations with their mothers if there was a reciprocal relationship; women remained quiet about sex because of family ignorance, fear of admitting sexual activity, and precedence of silence (Faulkner & Mansfield, 2002). However, being silent about sexual issues represented the most common experience cited by participants in and out of their homes. According to women, talking about sex was taboo and did not occur much at home or at school. Some women did not even hear a "birds and bees" talk because it was assumed that this information would be provided once they married. Some mothers felt that their daughters were too young to learn about sex, but they remained silent even when the women became older. Flores and Barroso's (2017) meta-analysis of adolescent mother-daughter communication about sex found instances of silence around sexual talk:

> Mothers who are approachable foster trust and are able to assess daughters' readiness to talk. Mothers with the highest responsiveness had significantly increased odds of discussions about abstinence, puberty, and reproduction. Meanwhile, paternal discomfort is interpreted as a lack of caring, or being judgmental of children's thoughts or actions, and keeps daughters away. (p. 540)

Thus, mothers can foster trust with their daughters by demonstrating comfort and efficacy with sexual talk. In the next section, we move on to talk about the content and context of sex and sexuality conversations between adolescent daughters and mothers using CPM as a framework.

ADOLESCENTS AND MOTHER-DAUGHTER TALK ABOUT SEX AND SEXUALITY

In the United States, we often seek to monitor and control women's sexuality (Flores & Barroso, 2017). Cultural messages about sexuality often conflict with what women feel physiologically, emotionally, and spiritually. Many women are not equipped with the skills to negotiate the kind of sex they desire. Other women feel pressure to be sexual in ways that may not feel good to them bodily and emotionally. Women must negotiate sex and sexuality in a patriarchal context, which does not center their experiences and desires. In addition, there are ethnic differences in mother-daughter conversations about sex; one study reported that non-White participants reported less comfort in sexuality conversations (Meneses, Orrell-Valente, Guendelman, Oman, & Irwin, 2006). When women are adolescents, what this may mean is withholding information from girls about sex and providing only abstinence-only education in schools. Young women face challenges to their sexuality because of all of the messages they receive and do not receive about their sexuality. Conceptions of women's sexuality are usually negative and fraught with contradictions. Feelings of shame, neediness, and fear encompass the scope of women's sexual world (Wolf, 1997). Wolf (1997) paints a picture of sexual restriction in her ethnographic study of upper-middle-class white women. Looking back on girlhood, these women in their twenties and thirties describe how they feared being seen as sexually available, and they relayed stories of shame for their naked bodies and their emerging sexuality. Hite (1994) found similar results in her study on sexuality and the family. Eighty-one percent of girls reported that their mothers told them not to be too sexy, or else they may be labeled a "tramp" or "slut," and 63% described such messages emanating from their fathers. Mothers may not talk about sex and sexuality with their daughters because of shame, feelings of inadequacy, and not finding the right time (Coffelt, 2010). That leaves daughters with few examples of open and honest talk about sex and sexuality.

It has long been the fear that if girls were educated about sex, they would engage in sex more, which is seen by most people as an undesirable outcome. The content of many mother-daughter conversations about sex centers on morals, pregnancy, negative consequences of sexual behavior, general information about sexual health, and sexual behavior as a threat to health (McKee & Karasz, 2006; Sneed, Somoza, Jones, & Alfaro, 2013), rather than private topics such as desire, emotional issues, and orgasm (Rosenthal, Senserrick, & Feldman, 2001). Mothers who were educated about the negative consequences of sexual behavior pass on this type of education to their daughters with the goal of protecting their daughters from disease, unplanned pregnancy, and obtaining a negative reputation (Jen, 2017). The type of talk that occurs in these conversations about sex seems to matter. African American girls in Usher-Seriki, Bynum, and Callands' (2008) study were less likely to engage in sexual intercourse when they had a close relationship with their mothers, and when their mothers talked about the moral reasons not to participate in premarital sex and the potential negative consequences. On the other hand, daughters were more likely to engage in sexual activity when their mothers talked about sex often and freely and did not evaluate pre-marital sex negatively. Thus, relational quality and the communication about values influence mother-daughter conversations about sex and sexuality.

As with the negotiation of boundaries, the dialogue between mother and daughter about sex can be initiated or controlled by either mother or daughter. Therefore, a daughter's questions can begin this discussion, or mothers may make the decision that it is time to talk about sex. Adolescents prefer discussing sex with their same-sex parent (Crohn, 2010), so daughters most often seek out their mothers than fathers for discussions of sex (Flores & Barroso, 2017). Other research suggests that older adolescents seek out peers first, then mothers, followed by fathers for sexuality information with mothers being predominantly responsible for sexuality education (Heisler, 2005). College-aged daughters also recalled their mothers talking more about sex, feeling more comfortable talking with mothers compared with fathers and characterized these conversations as more open (Heisler, 2005). Open communication about sexuality with a reciprocal flow is preferred by daughters, but this is often difficult to enact (McKee & Karasz, 2006). When a parent is receptive, informal, and composed, children are less anxious and avoidant of conversations about sex (Afifi, Joseph, & Aldeis, 2008). *How* mothers talk about sex and sexuality may be more important than the *frequency*. Mothers must be seen as approachable to foster open communication, and they are often considered by daughters to be relationship experts so it may be best to view communication about sex between mothers and daughters as a dialectic ranging from challenging to not challenging (Coffelt, 2010). Coffelt (2010) used a qualitative dyadic approach to study mother-daughter communication about sex and discovered that sex was viewed as a natural topic, but that the younger a daughter, the more awkward and uncomfortable it felt to her, and that some topics, such as personal details about sexual activity, were too private to share.

Mothers may seek assistance or guidelines about age-appropriate sex education or may provide information as seems appropriate. For example, many women in Faulkner's (1999) study about sexual talk among Latinas and their parents, partners, and friends described how they were provided with information on sex in the form of books and pamphlets that contained general information about body parts, sexual functioning, and STDs. These women's parents often gave them books because sex was not discussed openly; few women participated in mother-daughter conversations in addition to reading written material, resulting in feelings of being cheated.

Due to experiences such as these, women whose mothers did not talk with them about sex tend to plan for the kinds of things they could say to their own daughters. Women in the Faulkner (1999) study wanted their own daughters to understand that they possess worth beyond their sexuality, that they need not play traditional roles in the family. Accordingly, those interviewed believed that women should be taught about sex and the consequences of sex in a non-judgmental manner. They wanted sex to be viewed as something positive and enjoyable. Most of the women in this study hoped that their daughters would wait until they were responsible and emotionally able to handle sex, but they wanted to them to feel the support they were lacking. And as with other boundary negotiation, this is not a one-time discussion. As children and teenagers grow, learn, and experience, they may have more questions or concerns that they bring to their mothers. For example, Faulkner (2018) used collage about her personal experience talking with her young daughter about sex and sexuality as a feminist mother as an act of resistance against damaging cultural expectations about women's sexuality (Faulkner, 2018). This work questions restrictive cultural expectations about women's sexuality that may conflict with personal desire (Faulkner, 2017a). Faulkner (2018) represented conversations between a mother and a young daughter as dialogue poems to show the context, scene, and feel of mother-daughter conversations about sex and sexuality (Faulkner, 2017b).

@Breakfast

Daughter:	If you are 15 and you have a baby, do you kill your baby?
Mother 1:	[Thinking … infanticide? Take a bite of oatmeal for more time to respond.]
Father:	Someone can adopt the baby.
Mother 2:	[Oh! 15 and *pregnant*]. Are you asking about abortion? You can prevent pregnancy. Abortion is a back-up if contraception fails.

Daughter:	You kill your baby?
Mother 2:	You are not killing babies [blasted baby-killer rhetoric]! It is an embryo. The goal is to not get pregnant in the first place. [An embryo is a sack of cells.]
	Time to go to school. Did you do your homework?
	[Why does she ask these questions when there is something else to do?]
	[Is there ever a good time?]
Daughter:	What's for dinner?
Mother 1:	(looking at the *headlines* about anti-abortion bills and quickly igniting into a ball of middle-aged fire) Calling the Governor.

@Bedtime

Daughter:	[reading from the age-appropriate book about bodies and sexuality]. Does a penis go into a vagina?
Mother:	[Sigh. So tired. Want to read my own book and go to sleep.] Uh-huh.
Daughter:	You told me I could ask you anything.
Mother:	[Mustering the will] I did. And you can. [Puts down book] What else do you want to know? (Faulkner, 2018, p. 38)

What mothers and daughters do not talk about can be equally important in the formation of sexual self-concepts and beliefs. The silence surrounding many issues regarding sexuality communicates powerfully. Hite (1994) documents family silence about sexuality, beginning with the denial of menstruation and continuing with dating. Most women in her study (79%) tell of how their parents pretended that dating and sexual feelings were not occurring. Early on from childhood, girls learn that sexuality is something not to be discussed with family members. Brock and Jennings (1993) interviewed thirty women, average age of 35.5 about what they wish their mothers had told them about sex. Over half of the women said that their mothers did not talk with them about sex. If their mothers had provided sex education, most of the women said that the messages were negative and non-verbal, containing warnings about sex, stressing how much trouble it could cause. The participants wished that their mothers had talked openly with them about birth control and anatomy and had been positive about sex. Dennis and Wood (2012) also discovered that many African American women could not recall sustained conversations about sex with their mothers, and they wished that they had experienced open and honest conversations. Those women who did recall open and honest conversations felt like it made them stronger women and created closeness between themselves and their mothers. Daughters want to talk to their mothers about sex and sexuality, rather than being silent. Given this desire, what do we know about what happens in conversations about sex and sexuality past adolescence?

MOTHER-DAUGHTER TALK ABOUT SEX AND SEXUALITY IN LATER YEARS

What is typically not covered in research literature is the conversation that may go the other direction, in other words, mothers asking advice from daughters about sex, or daughters inquiring into their mother's sexual behaviors. Sex is seen as a private issue and is mostly explored from the perspective of the individual. Not only is sex seen as private and personal, when it is researched as a dyadic topic, but that dyad consists of the woman/mother and her partner, not mother and daughter. When there is research on communication about sex or sexuality in later life, the research explores the communication (or lack thereof) between older women and their physicians (Gott, Hinchliff, & Galena, 2004; Hinchliff & Gott, 2011; Hughes & Lewinson, 2015), within long-term care facilities (Dinapoli, Breland, & Allen, 2013; Reingold & Burros, 2004; Roelofs, Luijkx, & Embregts, 2014), and nego-tiation of condom use as prevention of HIV/STIs (DeLamater & Koepsel, 2015; MacDonald, Lorimer, Knussen, & Flowers, 2016; Spring, 2015).

One reason that literature on women's later life sexuality is scarce is because older women are viewed by society as asexual (Gott & Hinchliff, 2003; Gott et al., 2004; Reingold & Burros, 2004). They are often not seen as sexual beings. This factor is noted in literature that examines sex in long-term care facilities (Breland, 2014; Reingold & Burros, 2004) and the absence of this discussion by physicians who work with older adults (Gott et al., 2004). One of the main reasons that HIV education for older adults is challenging is because older adults are not seen at risk for the disease, largely because they are not seen as sexual beings (Beaulaurier, Fortuna, Lind, & Emlet, 2014). Yet, emerging issues with sexually transmitted diseases and sexual activities in long-term care facilities have shown that not to be true (Beaulaurier et al., 2014).

If older women wish to begin a new, sexual relationship, it can be challeng-ing to obtain information about how their bodies might be different from earlier points in time or how sex might be different at this stage in life. Where does that information come from? Research finds that older women do not talk to physicians or friends about sex (Radosh & Simkin, 2016). Daughters might have gone to their mothers when they needed information, but the reverse is not often the case. When adult daughters and mothers communicate, research demonstrates that it is mostly regarding health of the mother, caregiving, and support—topics where the daughters may act in the role of leader or provider (Donorfio & Sheehan, 2001; Sheehan & Donorfio, 1999; Walker, Shin, & Bird, 1990). This concept is referred to in the literature as role reversal, where the daughter may now feel that she is in the "mother" role, perhaps even in charge of her mother (Sheehan & Donorfio, 1999). This new aspect of the relationship can be challenging for both mother and daughter, although it is important to note that in this research, even when both mothers and daughters are interviewed (together or separately), they are typically interviewed about their individual experiences, not about how they communicate their opinions and feelings to the other person (Lefkowitz & Fingerman, 2003; Sheehan & Donorfio, 1999). Therefore, women in mid and later life who wish to begin a new sexual relationship, are not utilizing the relationships with their adult daughter as they might with other areas of concern in their lives.

One example of this type of research that involves sexuality is in long-term care facilities. The research does not examine communication between mothers and daughters, but it does point out that adult children, often daughters, are called upon to make decisions about sexual behaviors when an older adult, often with cognitive impairment, is in a long-term care facility (Dinapoli et al., 2013; Makimoto, Kang, Yamakawa, & Konno, 2015). The challenge for long-term care facilities is when a person with dementia (PWD) wishes to engage in sexual behaviors or is seen doing so (Dinapoli et al., 2013; see Roelofs et al., 2014 for review). The facility will often turn to the person's guardian for advice or permission or assistance. The adult child can then find him/herself in a position of making decisions about their parent's sexuality.

What research does not investigate much is how communication about sex may change for mothers and daughters as they age. It is possible to sneak around the edges of this topic by examining the research on dating and remarriage in later life. Even though there is not necessarily dyadic research looking at mothers and daughters, there is some literature exploring how mothers navigate the needs or concerns of their adult children as they date or remarry after widowhood or divorce (Carr & Boerner, 2013; van den hoonaard, 2002). But if we take a hard look at the available literature, we see that research on women/mothers in long-term marriages does not delve into how these mothers might communicate about sex with their daughters. The following section will discuss women's sexuality later in the life course.

Sexuality in Later Life

Though there is research investigating women's sexual behaviors and sexuality in later life, it consists mostly of interview or survey data with individuals about their own attitudes and behaviors, and not research with couples (for exception see Lodge & Umberson, 2012; Waite, Iveniuk, Laumann, & McClintock, 2017) or communication between mothers and daughters. In a nationally representative study over more than 3000 participants ages 57–85, Lindau et al. (2007) found that many older adults remain sexually active although behavior does decline with age. Aging and internalizing society's attitudes about older women and sex can also negatively impact women's feelings of being sexual (Jen, 2017) and their feelings about their aging bodies (Thorpe, Fileborn, Hawkes, Pitts, & Minichiello,

2015). Even though declining sexual behavior with age is a consistent finding in the literature (Lindau et al., 2007; Thomas, Hess, & Thurston, 2015), there is also ample research to demonstrate that many women are still interested in sex in later life (Hurd-Clarke, 2006) and see themselves as sexual beings despite being old in a society that does not see them as sexual (Montemurro & Siefken, 2014; Watson, Stelle, & Bell, 2017).

One factor that impedes sexual desire and behavior in later life is the lack of a partner (DeLamater & Sill, 2005; Gott & Hinchliff, 2003; Lindau et al., 2007; Thomas et al., 2015). For heterosexual women, desiring a partner can be problematic given the ratio of men to women in later life. Engaging in sexual behaviors with a male partner may be desired for women for whom there is not an available partner. However, Gott and Hinchliff (2003) found that for some of their participants, not having a partner dampened their interest in sex. Another factor that has been found to inhibit sexual activity in later life is health. People in poor health are less like to be sexually active (Brown & Shinohara, 2013; DeLamater & Koepsel, 2015; Gott & Hinchliff, 2003; Jen, 2017; Lindau et al., 2007; Santos-Iglesias, Byers, & Moglia, 2016).

One population largely ignored when exploring sexuality and aging is lesbians. Jen's (2017) small sample of 13 women included six women who identified as lesbian although all had previously been in relationships with men. In her study exploring topics of sexuality, gender, aging, and living environment, Jen found one distinction between how lesbian and heterosexual women experienced their sexuality in later life was that lesbians found a lack of attraction to men freeing from society's control over their sexuality.

Let's circle back to one area of mother-daughter communication noted above: when older mothers are receiving care in a long-term care facility, daughters may be contacted when the older adult is sexually active. This topic is of particular note when the mother is lesbian or bi-sexual. To date, literature has not explored this topic, but research has demonstrated that older lesbian and bisexual women do express concern about quality of care and potential discrimination when they need to access healthcare, home healthcare, or nursing home care (Grigorovich, 2016; Hillman, 2017; McParland & Camic, 2016; Westwood, 2016).

In another sexually-diverse study, Averett, Yoon, and Jenkins (2012) used an online survey to explore experiences of 456 women (92% self-identified lesbians, 4% bisexual, 2% gay) between the ages of 51 to 86 (M = 63.06). The women felt very positive about being lesbian with the average age of recognizing their attraction to other women around age 18. About half of the women had previously been married to a man. When completing the survey, 60.5% of the women were currently in a romantic (i.e., emotional, physical, or sexual) relationship with a woman with over half of the participants labeling this relationship as a "lifetime partnership." As with research with heterosexual women, this study found a decrease in the belief in the importance of sex with increasing age. When asked how their relationships had changed as they had aged, these women noted more continuity than change, with change focusing on individuals (as opposed to the relationship) being more mature and stable.

WHAT DOES ALL THIS MEAN?

In this chapter, we have discussed how women in the U.S. culture are surrounded by messages about sex and sexuality, but rarely have open, honest conversations about it and what it means in our lives and relationships. Communicating about sex and sexuality are quite important to relationships. Over a lifetime, mothers and daughters continue to renegotiate their relationship as they both age and change. Thus, it is vital to keep communication lines open as we know that talk about sex and sexuality is not a one-shot encounter.

Through the lens of CPM theory, we discovered that mothers and daughters self-disclose on sexual health topics in uniquely personal ways. Mothers often base their discussions (or lack thereof) with their daughters about sex on how *their* mothers handled the topic with them. We can also take that to mean, that the conversations mothers are having with their adolescent and adult daughters today are influencing sexual conversations that these daughters will have later in life with their own children. So, any small changes that you, the reader, make in your relationship to open the lines of communication between you and your mother can positively reverberate across the decades.

We described how open and reciprocal communication about sex and sexuality is ideal, but mothers may not want to discuss sex with their daughters because of a desire to keep their own past or behaviors private. This is part of the culture of silence surrounding sexual communication that creates barriers for women in a patriarchal society. Mothers may also be silent on sexual matters because, although they may want to educate their daughters about sex, they are simultaneously attempting to protect their daughters from labels and shame that society imposes on women about their own bodies and sexuality. Unknowingly, mothers who choose silence instead of open communication on sexual topics with their daughters can contribute to unhealthy societal conceptions of women's sexuality. Silence can continue into older adulthood when older women have questions about sex but do not seek answers or advice from their adult daughters. For many older women, they can talk with their adult daughters about addictions, finances, caregiving, and health, but not about sex or sexuality because society tends to characterize older adults as asexual. The result is that discussions about sex are not broached by healthcare professionals or seen as matters of importance in long-term care facilities. In later life, daughters are asked to make decisions about their mothers' sexual health but have little knowledge of her as a sexual being. It takes open and bidirectional communication about sex for this to change.

We hope the readers of this chapter have learned that sex is important across the life course for women and that the mother-daughter relationship can be a vital source of information for both parties as they age.

WHAT DO WE STILL NEED TO KNOW?

- As we consider the future of research on mother-daughter communication about sex and sexuality, we acknowledge that the focus in the literature will continue to be on adolescents and adult mothers, however, we must ask, how does this communication change as mother and daughter both age? As this relationship often changes from a vertical or hierarchical one to a more horizontal one, with older mothers regularly reporting their adult daughter as a close friend and confidant, does this friendship extend to a bi-directional discussion of sex and sexuality?
- If midlife and older women are re-entering the dating world and/or interested in being sexually active with someone new, with whom do they talk about these desires and experiences? How do they learn about HIV/AIDS and how to protect themselves from disease? If an older woman has been in a long-term marriage and is experiencing biological changes that impact her sexual desire, how does she address those concerns? With whom does she risk vulnerability through self-disclosure?
- Research on older mother-adult daughter communication is primarily focused on issues of mother's health and caregiving and support needs. What about the significant portion of mid and later life when the aging mother is not in need of caregiving support?

We want to see research that explores the mother-daughter relationship, especially concerning conversations about sex and sexuality.

HOW DOES THIS WORK IN REAL LIFE?

Tips for real mother/daughter communication about sex and sexuality:

- Go for open, honest, and quality conversation.
- Think about self-disclosure and talk about sex and sexuality as a form of relationship building.
- Educate yourself on sex and sexuality. Ask questions. Be okay with stumbling.

- Think about the kinds of talk about sex and sexuality you would like to have and rehearse. Write it down if you need to.

CLASSROOM ACTIVITIES

- Write two dialogues about sex between a mother and daughter like the one that Faulkner (2018) presents in this chapter. One dialogue can be based on a recalled conversation from personal experience or a conversation presented in the media. In the second dialogue, imagine an ideal conversation or series of discussions based on openness, comfort, and non-judgment. Vary the ages of participants in the conversations.
- What could you do as a parent to increase the likelihood of your teenagers being a sexually healthy, responsible, and confident person?
- What is the line between responsible parental supervision and overly intrusive or excessive parental interference? How can mother-daughter communication about sex and sexuality be more comfortable, open, and honest?
- On the societal level, what could be done to help families raise sexually healthy, responsible, and confident children?
- Think about how you would handle a conversation with an older adult, perhaps your mother, about sex. How would you be respectful about her questions and convey accurate, appropriate information?

REFERENCES

Afifi, T. D., Joseph, A., & Aldeis, D. (2008). Why can't we just talk about it? An observational study of parents' and adolescents' conversations about sex. *Journal of Adolescent Research, 23*(6), 689–721. https://doi.org/10.1177/0743558408323841

Averett, P., Yoon, I., & Jenkins, C. (2012). Older lesbian sexuality: Identity, sexual behavior, and the impact of aging. *Journal of Sex Research, 49*(5), 495–507. https://doi.org/10.1080/00224499.2011.582543

Beaulaurier, R., Fortuna, K., Lind, D., & Emlet, C. (2014). Attitudes and stereotypes regarding older women and HIV risk. *Journal of Women & Aging, 26*(4), 351–368. https://doi.org/10.1080/08952841.2014.933648

Breland, L. (2014). Lost libido, or just forgotten? The legal and social influences on sexual activity in long-term care. *Law & Psychology, 38*, 177–192.

Brock, L., & Jennings, G. (1993). Sexuality Education: What daughters in their 30s wish their mothers had told them. *Family Relations, 42*(1), 61–65. https://doi.org/10.2307/584923

Brown, S., & Shinohara, S. (2013). Dating relationships in older adulthood: A national portrait. *Journal of Marriage and Family, 75*(5), 1194–1202. https://doi.org/10.1111/jomf.12065

Carr, D., & Boerner, K. (2013). Dating after late-life spousal loss: Does it compromise relationships with adult children? *Journal of Aging Studies, 27*(4), 487–498. http://doi.org/10.1016/j.jaging.2012.12.009

Coffelt, T. (2010). Is sexual communication challenging between mothers and daughters? *Journal of Family Communication, 10*(2), 116–139. https://doi.org/10.1080/15267431003595496

Crohn, H. (2010). Communication about sexuality with mothers and stepmothers from the perspective of young adult daughters. *Journal of Divorce & Remarriage, 51*(6), 348–365. https://doi.org/10.1080/10502551003652108

Daniluk, J. C. (1998). *Women's sexuality across the lifespan: Challenging myths, creating meanings.* New York, NY: Guilford Press.

DeLamater, J., & Koepsel, E. (2015). Relationships and sexual expression in later life: A biopsychosocial perspective. *Sexual and Relationship Therapy, 30*(1), 37–59. https://doi.org/10.1080/14681994.2014.939506

DeLamater, J., & Sill, M. (2005). Sexual desire in later life. *Journal of Sex Research, 42*(2), 138–150.

Dennis, A. C., & Wood, J. T. (2012). "We're not going to have this conversation, but you get it": Black mother-daughter communication about sexual relations. *Women's Studies in Communication, 35*(2), 204–223. https://doi.org/10.1080/07491409.2012.724525

Dinapoli, E., Breland, G., & Allen, R. (2013). Staff knowledge and perceptions of sexuality and dementia in older adults in nursing homes. *Journal of Aging and Health, 25*(7), 1087–1105. https://doi.org/10.1177/0898264313494802

Donorfio, L., & Sheehan, N. (2001). Relationship dynamics between aging mothers and caregiving daughters: Filial expectations and responsibilities. *Journal of Adult Development, 8*(1), 39–49. https://doi.org/10.1023/A:1026497721126

Faulkner, S. L. (1999). *Good girl or flirt girl: Understanding the process and implications of sexual talk for Latinas* (Doctoral dissertation). Retrieved from ProQuest (9960580).

Faulkner, S. L. (2003). Good girl or flirt girl: Latinas' definitions and meanings of sex and sexual relationships. *Hispanic Journal of Behavioral Sciences, 25*(2), 174–200. https://doi.org/10.1177/0739986303253803

Faulkner, S. L. (2017a). MotherWork collage (A queer scrapbook). *QED: A Journal in GLBTQ Worldmaking, 4*(1), 166–179. https://doi.org/10.14321/qed.4.1.0166

Faulkner, S. L. (2017b). Poetic Inquiry: Poetry as/in/for Social Research. In P. Leavy (Ed.), *The handbook of arts-based research* (pp. 208–230). New York, NY: Guilford Press.

Faulkner, S. L. (2018). Queering sexuality education in family and school. In A. M. Harris, S. Holman Jones, S. L. Faulkner, & E. D. Brook (Eds.), *Queering families, schooling publics: Keywords* (pp. 23–41). New York, NY: Routledge.

Faulkner, S. L., & Mansfield, P. K. (2002). Reconciling messages: The process of sexual talk for Latinas. *Qualitative Health Research, 12*(3), 310–328. https://doi.org/10.1177/104973202129119919

Fingerman, K. (2000). "We had a nice little chat": Age and generational differences in mothers' and daughters' descriptions of enjoyable visits. *Journal of Gerontology: Psychological Sciences, 55B*(2), 95–106. https://doi.org/10.1093/geronb/55.2.P95

Flores, D., & Barroso, J. (2017). 21st century parent-child sex communication in the United States: A process review. *The Journal of Sex Research, 54*(4–5), 532–548. https://doi.org/10.1080/00224499.2016.1267693

Gott, M., & Hinchliff, S. (2003). How important is sex in later life? The views of older people. *Social Science & Medicine, 56*(8), 1617–1628. https://doi.org/10.1016/S0277-9536(02)00180-6

Gott, M., Hinchliff, S., & Galena, E. (2004). General practitioner attitudes to discussing sexual health issues with older people. *Social Science & Medicine, 58*(11), 2093–2103. https://doi.org/10.1016/j.socscimed.2003.08.025

Grigorovich, A. (2016). The meaning of quality of care in home care settings: Older lesbian and bisexual women's perspectives. *Scandinavian Journal of Caring Sciences, 30*(1), 108–116. https://doi.org/10.1111/scs.12228

Heisler, J. M. (2005). Family communication about sex: Parents and college-aged offspring recall discussions topics, satisfaction, and parental involvement. *The Journal of Family Communication, 5*(4), 295–312. https://doi.org/10.1207/s15327698jfc0504_4

Hillman, J. (2017). The sexuality and sexual health of LGBT elders. *Annual Review of Gerontology & Geriatrics, 37*(1), 13–26. https://doi.org/10.1891/0198-8794.37.13

Hinchliff, S., & Gott, M. (2011). Seeking medical help for sexual concerns in mid- and later life: A review of the literature. *Journal of Sex Research, 48*(2–3), 106–117. https://doi.org/10.1080/00224499.2010.548610

Hite, S. (1994). *Women as revolutionary agents of change: The Hite reports and beyond.* Madison: The University of Wisconsin Press.

Hughes, A. K., & Lewinson, T. D. W. (2015). Facilitating communication about sexual health between aging women and their health care providers. *Qualitative Health Research, 25*(4), 540–550. https://doi.org/10.1177/1049732314551062

Hurd-Clarke, L. (2006). Older women and sexuality: Experiences in marital relationships across the life course. *Canadian Journal on Aging, 25*(2), 129–140. https://doi.org/10.1353/cja.2006.0034

Jen, S. (2017). Older women and sexuality: Narratives of gender, age, and living environment. *Journal of Women & Aging, 29*(1), 87–97. http://doi.org/10.1080/08952841.2015.1065147

Kelly, A., & Macready, D. (2009). Why disclosing to a confidant can be so good (or bad) for us. In T. D. Afifi & W. A. Afifi (Eds.), *Uncertainty, information management, and disclosure: Decisions, theories and applications* (pp. 384–401). New York, NY: Routledge.

Koch, P. B., Moglia, R., & Fitzpatrick, M. (2003, August). *Family influences on adolescent sexual and contraceptive behavior: Sample college lesson plan using the Journal of sex research.* Retrieved from http://sexscience.org/

Lefkowitz, E., & Fingerman, K. (2003). Positive and negative emotional feelings and behaviors in mother-daughter ties in late life. *Journal of Family Psychology, 17*(4), 607–617. https://doi.org/10.1037/0893-3200.17.4.607

Lindau, S., Schumm, L., Laumann, E., Levinson, W., O'Muircheataigh, C., & Waite, L. (2007). A study of sexuality and health among older adults in the United States. *The New England Journal of Medicine, 357*(8), 762–774. https://doi.org/10.1056/NEJMoa067423

Lodge, A., & Umberson, D. (2012). All shook up: Sexuality of mid- to later life married couples. *Journal of Marriage and Family, 74*(3), 428–443. https://doi.org/10.1111/j.1741-3737.2012.00969.x

MacDonald, J., Lorimer, K., Knussen, C., & Flowers, P. (2016). Interventions to increase condom use among middle-aged and older adults: A systematic review of theoretical bases, behaviour change techniques, modes of delivery and treatment fidelity. *Journal of Health Psychology, 21*(11), 2477–2492. https://doi.org/10.1177/1359105315580462

Makimoto, K., Kang, H., Yamakawa, M., & Konno, R. (2015). An integrated literature on sexuality of elderly nursing home residents with dementia. *International Journal of Nursing Practice, 21*(S2), 80–90. https://doi.org/10.1111/ijn.12317

McKee, M. D., & Karasz, D. (2006). You have to give her that confidence: Conversations about sex in Hispanic mother-daughter dyads. *Journal of Adolescent Research, 21*(2), 158–184. doi: 10.1177/0743558405285493

McParland, J., & Camic, P. (2016). Psychosocial factors and ageing in older lesbian, gay and bisexual people: A systematic review of the literature. *Journal of Clinical Nursing, 25*(23–24), 3415–3437. https://doi.org/10.1111/jocn.13251

Meneses, L. M., Orrell-Valente, J. K., Guendelman, S. R., Oman, D., & Irwin, Jr., C. E. (2006). Racial/Ethnic differences in mother-daughter communication about sex. *Journal of Adolescent Health, 39*(1), 128–131. https://doi.org/10.1016/j.jadohealth.2005.08.005

Montemurro, B., & Siefken, J. (2014). Cougars on the prowl? New perceptions of older women's sexuality. *Journal of Aging Studies, 28*, 35–43. http://doi.org/10.1016/j.jaging.2013.11.004

Petronio, S. (2002). *Boundaries of privacy: Dialectics of disclosure.* New York, NY: State University of New York Press.

Radosh, A., & Simkin, L. (2016). Acknowledging sexual bereavement: A path out of disenfranchised grief. *Reproductive Health Matters, 24*(48), 25–33. https://doi.org/10.1016/j.rhm.2016.11.005

Reingold, D., & Burros, N. (2004). Sexuality in the nursing home. *Journal of Gerontological Social Work, 43*(2–3), 175–186. https://doi.org/10.1300/ J083v43n02_12

Roelofs, T., Luijkx, K., & Embregts, P. (2014). Intimacy and sexuality of nursing home residents with dementia: A systematic review. *International Psychogeriatrics, 27*(3), 367–384. https://doi.org/10.1017/S1041610214002373

Rosenthal, D., Senserrick, T., & Feldman, S. (2001). A typology approach to describing parents as communicators about sexuality. *Archives of Sexual Behavior, 30*(5), 463–482.

Santos-Iglesias, P., Byers, E. S., & Moglia, R. (2016). Sexual well-being of older men and women. *The Canadian Journal of Human Sexuality, 25*(2), 86–98. https://doi.org/10.3138/cjhs.252-A4

Sheehan, N., & Donorfio, L. (1999). Efforts to create meaning in the relationship between aging mothers and their caregiving daughters: A qualitative study of caregiving. *Journal of Aging Studies, 13*(2), 161–176.

Sneed, C. D., Somoza, C. G., Jones, T., & Alfaro, S. (2013). Topics discussed with mothers and fathers for parent-child sex communication among African American adolescents. *Sex Education, 13*(4), 450–458. https://doi.org/10.1080/14681811.2012.757548

Spring, L. (2015). Older women and sexuality—are we still just talking lube? *Sexual and Relationship Therapy, 30*(1), 4–9. https://doi.org/10.1080/14681994.2014.920617

Thomas, H., Hess, R., & Thurston, R. (2015). Correlates of sexual activity and satisfaction in midlife and older women. *Annals of Family Medicine, 13*(4), 336–342. https://doi.org/10.1370/afm.1820

Thorpe, R., Fileborn, B., Hawkes, G., Pitts, M., & Minichiello, V. (2015). Old and desirable: Older women's accounts of ageing bodies in intimate relationships. *Sexual and Relationship Therapy, 30*(1), 156–166. https://doi.org/10.1080/14681994.2014.959307

Usher-Seriki, K. K., Bynum, M. S., & Callands, T. A. (2008). Mother-daughter communication about sex and sexual intercourse among middle- to upper-class African American girls. *Journal of Family Issues, 29*(7), 901–917. https://doi.org/10.1177/0192513X07311951

van den hoonaard, D. (2002). Attitudes of older widows and widowers in New Brunswick, Canada towards new partnerships. *Ageing International, 27*(4), 79–92.

Waite, L., Iveniuk, J., Laumann, E., & McClintock, M. (2017). Sexuality in older couples: Individual and dyadic characteristics. *Archives of Sexual Behavior, 46*(2), 605–618. https://doi.org/10.1007/s10508-015-0651-9

Walker, A., Shin, H., & Bird, D. (1990). Perceptions of relationship change and caregiver satisfaction. *Family Relations, 39*(2), 147–152.

Watson, W., Stelle, C., & Bell, N. (2017). Older women in new romantic relationships: Understanding the meaning and important of sex in later life. *The International Journal of Aging and Human Development, 85*, 33–43. https://doi.org/10.1177/0091415016680067

Westwood, S. (2016). "We see it as being heterosexualised, being put into a care home": Gender, sexuality and housing/care preferences among older LGB individuals in the UK. *Health & Social Care in the Community, 24*(6), e155–e163. https://doi.org/10.1111/HSC.12265

Wolf, N. (1997). *Promiscuities: The secret struggle for womanhood.* New York, NY: Fawcett.

CHAPTER NINE

Mother-Daughter Communication About HPV Vaccination

SUELLEN HOPFER,* HUONG DUONG,† AND SAMANTHA GARCIA‡

One of our neighbors is a girl who recently turned 11-years-old and got her three recommended adolescent vaccinations, including the human papillomavirus (HPV) vaccine. She hates—and is terrified of—shots. She and her mom went to the pediatrician for her annual well visit and the pediatrician talked to her about how these shots, especially the HPV vaccine, are recommended to protect her against infections and cancer. The pediatrician explained to her that the shots would protect her and so she agreed to be vaccinated. On the drive home, the daughter turned to her mom and thanked her. Her mother asked why she was thanking her and she answered, "For loving me enough to want to protect me from those terrible things."

This illustration shows a mother-daughter communication scenario related to decision-making about the HPV vaccine. There are many other possible ways this scene could go. We begin this chapter asking each reader the following questions: Did you get the series of HPV vaccinations? What was your experience when deciding to get the HPV vaccination (if you did)? Were you younger or older than my neighbor? Do you remember your mother talking with you about the HPV vaccination? If so, what did she say? How was it presented to you and what prompted the discussion?

* Suellen Hopfer, assistant professor, University of California, Irvine, shopfer@uci.edu.
† Huong Duong, University of California, Irvine.
‡ Samantha Garcia, University of California, Irvine.

I (Suellen) always thought it was a no brainer that you should get vaccinated against cancer. Not that it's great getting a shot but it beats worrying about maybe having a sexually transmitted infection (STI) or a cancer of your reproductive parts. I became interested in vaccine communication professionally as a communication scholar because, while it seemed straightforward at first, it became clear when talking with other people that they perceived the HPV vaccination in a wide range of ways. While some women say, "Of course, why wouldn't people vaccinate when it's an anticancer vaccine," others believe the vaccine unnecessary. These women often interpret the HPV vaccine first and foremost as a vaccine against STIs and all the stigma that accompanies an STI vaccine. Furthermore, there were many young adult women who simply didn't know about the HPV vaccine. Beyond a lack of awareness, the way clinicians present and talk about HPV vaccination with patients sets the tone for how HPV vaccination is understood and how parents, adolescents and young adults react.

This chapter is intended to provide a review of the current research on mother-daughter communication about HPV vaccination. We start with a brief history of the vaccine and then review the literature on mother-daughter communication about HPV and the vaccine.

BACKGROUND ON HPV AND THE HPV VACCINE

HPV stands for human papillomavirus (HPV) and is the most common sexually transmitted infection in the U. S. affecting approximately one in four Americans throughout their lifetime (Brianti, De Flammineis & Mercuri, 2017; Centers for Disease Control and Prevention, 2015). HPV is transmitted through skin-to-skin or mucosa-to-mucosa contact and through oral, anal, or vaginal sex. There are often no signs or symptoms and over 100 types of the virus. Some HPV virus types are associated with cancer (16 and 18) while other types are associated with genital warts (6 and 11). Though most HPV infections typically resolve on their own, persistent infection of oncogenic HPV types like 16 or 18 may progress to cervical, anal or oropharyngeal cancers (Committee on Infectious Diseases, 2012; Munoz, Castellsague, Gonzalez, & Gissman, 2006).

The HPV vaccine was first approved by the US Food and Drug Administration (FDA) and made available to the public in 2006 but only for girls initially (*HPV vaccine safety*, 2018). The vaccine was subsequently licensed for boys in 2009 and routinely recommended for them in 2011 (Markowitz et al., 2014). One of the first anticancer vaccines, HPV vaccination (also known as Gardasil 9 in the US) effectively protects against 9 common HPV types (16, 18, 6, 11, 31, 33, 45, 52, 58) (Crowe et al., 2014; Lu, Kumar, Castellsague, & Giuliano, 2011; Markowitz, Hariri, Lin, Dunne, Steinau, McQuillan, & Unger, 2013; Markowitz et al., 2016).

Adolescent girls and boys ages 11–12 are recommended to receive this vaccine as part of the routine adolescent immunization schedule (Centers for Disease Control and Prevention, 2016; Committee on Infectious Diseases, 2012). Catch up HPV vaccination is recommended for women and men ages 13–26 who have not received the vaccine during adolescence (Centers for Disease Control and Prevention, 2010; Zimmerman, 2007).

As of 2016, the National Immunization Survey-Teen indicated that only 43% of teens have completed the recommended 2 shot series (Walker et al., 2017). Since November 2016, for those who vaccinated before age 15, only two (rather than 3) HPV vaccine shots are needed (Meites, Kempe, & Markowitz, 2016). Among women and men aged 15–26 years, 3 shots are still required for receiving full immunity benefits. It is estimated that about 40% of young adult women have received the HPV vaccine (Williams et al., 2016). Within the young adult age group, vaccination rates vary by ethnicity. In 2014, the Surveillance of Vaccination Coverage among Adult Populations indicated that Hispanics and Asian women (28.1% and 22.8%) had lower vaccination initiation compared to Whites and African American populations (46.3% and 37.46%) (Williams et al., 2016).

Among the several predictors of HPV vaccination, mother-daughter conversations play an important role. There are a number of factors that shape mother-daughter HPV vaccine talk including (a) awareness and knowledge about the HPV vaccine (b) how a clinician discusses HPV vaccination, (c) age of daughter, (d) parenting communication style, and (e) family cultural values. These factors influence how mothers and daughters communicate about HPV, related sexual health, and HPV vaccination.

LOW KNOWLEDGE HINDERS MOTHER-DAUGHTER COMMUNICATION ABOUT HPV

While many mothers and daughters have heard of HPV vaccination, their knowledge about the subject is often quite low (Lechuga, Vera-Cala, & Martinez-Donate, 2016; Niccolai, Hansen, Credle, & Shapiro, 2016). Awareness and knowledge are important precursors for quality mother-daughter conversations (Griffioen et al., 2012). Mothers and daughters with low HPV knowledge often may turn to the Internet for answers and subsequently are exposed to negative and or inaccurate information about HPV vaccination expressing concern about HPV vaccine safety, distrust with science, and unknown substances in the vaccine (Gollust, LoRusso, Nagler, & Franklin, 2016; Rendle & Leskinen, 2017; Tangherlini et al., 2016). Accurate understanding about HPV and the vaccine are important given that negative personal beliefs about HPV vaccine safety can lower intentions to vaccinate (Lechuga et al., 2016).

Some mothers have concerns that HPV vaccination could lead daughters to become more promiscuous, and being less careful in protecting themselves despite research showing this is not the case (Bair, Mays, Sturm, & Zimet, 2008; Morales-Campos, Markham, Peskin, & Fernandez, 2013). Low HPV knowledge, confusion over purpose of the vaccine, confusion over recommended age to vaccinate, concern about side effects, and concerns of increased sexual activity include reasons why some mothers avoid mother-daughter discussions around HPV vaccination (Moran, Murphy, Chatterjee, Amezola de Herrera & Baezconde-Garbanati, 2014). In many cases, mothers rely on practitioners to explain the benefits of HPV immunization and to initiate conversations (Hopfer, Ray, et al., 2017; Joseph et al., 2014; Thompson, Arnold, & Notaro, 2012).

TOPICS ADDRESSED IN HPV DISCUSSIONS

When mothers and daughters talk—whether mother-initiated or daughter-initiated—topics around HPV vaccination may include cancer prevention, genital warts prevention, support for daughters being vaccinated, STI prevention, and what the practitioner has said about vaccinating (Griffioen et al., 2012; McRee, Reiter, Gottlieb, & Brewer, 2011; Mullins et al., 2013). Depending on the mother, communication with a daughter may additionally include discussion about getting periods, having sex for the first time, the relationship between sex and moral/cultural/religious values, and prevention of sexually transmitted infections (STIs). Discussions about these topics between mother and daughter have been positively associated with HPV vaccination uptake among college-age women (Roberts, Gerrard, Reimer, & Gibbons, 2010).

Adolescent girls indicate that they prefer not to discuss sexual health with their mothers in the context of HPV vaccination, but mothers note the importance of discussing sexual health education in the context of HPV vaccination (Mullins et al., 2013). Both girls and mothers seem to agree that clinicians and parents are the most important source to communicate vaccine information. Although mothers and clinicians are the most important sources, adolescent girls also learn about HPV through school health classes, informal social networks of peers, cousins, siblings, and online (Hopfer & Clippard, 2011; Hopfer, Garcia, Duong, Russo, & Tanjasiri, 2017).

MOTHER-DAUGHTER COMMUNICATION ABOUT HPV VACCINATION IN YOUNG ADULTHOOD

During young adulthood women transition into a new stage of independence yet many health decisions are still made at home by mothers or parents. In the case of HPV vaccination, mothers' perceived approval often plays an important role (Hopfer & Clippard, 2010; Miller-Ott & Durham, 2011; Romo, Cruz, & Neilands, 2011). In fact, mothers' approval even among college-aged women remains one of the most important predictors of vaccinating against HPV in this age group (Hopfer & Clippard, 2011; Roberts, Gerrard, Reimer, & Gibbons, 2010). A mother's approval may be important for a range of reasons.

Mothers' approval for HPV vaccination may be important to young adult women for practical health insurance coverage reasons—that young adult women may still have coverage under a parent's health insurance. But young adult women may also simply value the support of their mother pertaining to social family norms—wanting to know that their mother is in agreement that her daughter should vaccinate, that she thinks it's a good thing to do and the right thing to do to protect her health. Supportive vaccination messages from mothers may be expressed explicitly or implicitly in several ways: financially paying for vaccination, logistically making the medical appointment and driving daughters to their appointment, mothers stating that vaccinating is a good idea (positive norms), and/or mothers sending newspaper or magazine articles about HPV vaccination to daughters at college (Hopfer & Clippard, 2011). By contrast, unsupportive messages from mothers may include mothers saying that vaccination is not necessary, not safe, that a daughter can vaccinate when she is older (not realizing that vaccination is not available after age 26), that if a daughter is smart about sex she doesn't need to vaccinate (a falsehood), or that vaccinating will encourage a daughter to be promiscuous (Hopfer & Clippard, 2011).

By young adulthood, most women have some knowledge about HPV having learned about it at school or through a family member such as a sibling, cousin, aunt or mother (Hopfer, Garcia, et al., 2017). A proportion of young women who did not receive HPV vaccination as an adolescent seek vaccination on their own in later years. Approximately 75% of women are aware of HPV vaccination, but only estimated 40% have received the HPV vaccine following the 2010 provision of the Affordable Care Act (ACA), which required insurance plans to cover dependent costs for preventive services among 19 to 25-year-olds (Lipton & Decker, 2015). Even with costs covered for many after the ACA provision, the social implications of obtaining the HPV vaccine still affect women's perceived social approval and likelihood of vaccinating.

Costs of vaccination can impact mother-daughter communication especially among young adult women whose insurance is still covered by parents. Daughters may need to discuss vaccination with their mothers to receive financial assistance or logistical support (ride to the doctor's office; paying for vaccination through parents' health insurance plan) (Hopfer & Clippard, 2011; Krieger, Kam, Katz, & Roberto, 2010). Cost of the vaccine has been a barrier in some cases due to young adult women fearing judgement from mothers or parents about vaccinating based on erroneous associations between HPV vaccination and sexual activity (Hopfer & Clippard, 2010; Krieger et al., 2010). Women also have expressed fear that their parents would receive the bill following vaccination, which would trigger questions from parents about sexual initiation (Hopfer & Clippard, 2010). There have been many stories in fact even memes about mothers opening mail of young adult daughters still living at home with their parents. Stories of mothers opening mail about bills for birth control or bills about HPV vaccination can prompt mother-daughter discussions.

Young adult women still seek the approval of their mothers and are more likely to vaccinate if they have support and open communication about sexual health with their mothers prior to vaccination (Dempsey, Abraham, Dalton, & Ruffin, 2009; Hopfer & Clippard, 2011).

PARENTING STYLE IN COMMUNICATING ABOUT HPV

A mother's parenting style can influence when and how she discusses HPV vaccination with her daughter(s) (Askelson, Campo, & Smith, 2012). Parenting styles may be characterized by the degree of social control mothers assert and their responsiveness to daughter's needs. In addition, mothers' parenting style may vary by the degree to which they treat HPV vaccination as cancer prevention versus a topic related to sexual health, and the degree to which they then explicitly or implicitly discuss HPV vaccination. For mothers who treat HPV vaccination as part of discussions about female reproductive health, they may either directly talk with daughters about related sexual health or indirectly communicate with daughters. For example, mothers may give daughters books to read about becoming a teenager and growing up as a girl (See *A Mighty Girl*: https://www.amightygirl.com) or mothers may give their daughters a journal to write about their questions and thoughts about various topics. Mothers may then communicate about sensitive topics indirectly by having the daughter give her mother the diary and then the mom answers questions in turn in the diary. Authoritative mothers, who are characterized as highly demanding and highly responsive to daughters, were more likely to discuss sex and HPV vaccination (Askelson et al., 2012; Rosenthal et al., 2008).

A smaller number of mothers who associate HPV vaccination with sexual activity delay having daughters vaccinated based on the belief that their daughters are too young for the vaccine and conversation (Askelson et al., 2012; Rendle & Leskinen, 2017). Mothers who decide not to communicate with their daughters about HPV during adolescence tend to believe HPV vaccination is unnecessary because their daughters are not sexually active. In a national study, nearly half (47%) of mothers incorrectly reported that their child was not sexually experienced or underestimated their daughters' sexual debut. Mothers tend to underestimate

their adolescent's sexual debut, which becomes a missed occasion for early protection (Liddon, Michael, Dittus, & Markowitz, 2013). In recognizing parenting
style trends, it is also important to understand that parenting style may equally be
shaped by cultural and family norms.

MOTHER-DAUGHTER COMMUNICATION BY CULTURAL VALUES: HPV AS A CULTURALLY TABOO TOPIC

Mothers who are not comfortable discussing sexual health with their daughters
focus HPV vaccine discussions on cancer protection or avoid discussing the topic
altogether (McRee et al., 2012). Many Hispanic and Asian mothers do not discuss sexual health topics with daughters (Hopfer, Garcia, et al., 2017). The topic
of HPV vaccination and sexual health is simply taboo and not discussed at home
(Hopfer, Garcia, et al., 2017). Several studies indicate that open communication
between mother and daughter about sex leads to a decrease in adolescent daughter's likelihood to engage in risky sexual behavior and perceptions of risk (Askelson
et al., 2012; Askelson et al., 2011; Mullins et al., 2013). Additionally, a positive
association has been found between parents who discussed sexual health and HPV
vaccination (Gross, Laz, Rahman, & Berenson, 2015).

A mother's communication about HPV can be crucial to her daughter's
HPV vaccination status. Familial support may be a better predictor of HPV
vaccine completion than a doctor's communication highlighting the need for a
mother's acceptance (Fiks et al., 2013; Ylitalo, Lee, & Meta, 2013). However,
many factors can hinder adequate mother-daughter HPV communication. For
example, although Hispanic mothers and daughters have reported value in communication about women's reproductive health, mothers' traditional upbringings
may result in lack of communication about important health issues (McKee &
Karasz, 2006). Hispanic mothers are more likely to report discomfort discussing
issues related to sex compared to other race/ ethnicities (Meneses, Orrell-Valente,
Guendelman, Oman & Irwin, 2006). Hispanic daughters, often sensing their
mothers' reluctance to speak about reproductive health, also avoid discussions
with their mothers (McRee et al., 2011). Hispanic women have unique cultural
and traditional values some based in conservative Catholicism that influence
whether mother-daughter discussion about HPV takes place (Hopfer, Garcia,
et al., 2017b ; McKee & Karasz, 2006). Indirect communication may be a more
common communication approach among Hispanic mothers and daughters.

Parent-child communication about sex and sexual health among many Asian
American and Pacific Islanders (AAPI) families are similar to Hispanic culture and
typically seen as taboo subjects, resulting in topic avoidance (Kim & Ward, 2007).
Consequently, little to no communication research describes HPV communication

between mothers and daughters in Asian families. In a study comparing college women's confidence in communicating about HPV, AAPI women reported lower levels of perceived openness in past general communication and less reproductive health topic discussions with their mothers, which led to less confidence to discuss HPV with their healthcare providers (Romo et al., 2011). Among Asian mothers, the most common reason for rejecting HPV vaccination for their daughters was low knowledge and awareness of the HPV vaccine and its cancer prevention benefits (Chow et al., 2010; Marlow, Wardle, Forster, & Waller, 2009; Nguyen, Leader, & Hung, 2009). South Asian mothers tend to reject HPV vaccination on the basis that it encourages their daughters to engage in risky behavior and pre-marital sex (Gelman, Nikolajski, Schwarz, & Borrero, 2011). Nevertheless, other studies have indicated that Cambodian and Vietnamese mothers reported that they would accept the vaccination for their daughters if explicitly recommended by a health care provider (Taylor et al., 2014; Yi, Anderson, Le, Escobar-Chaves, & Reyes-Gibby, 2013).

Interestingly, differences in attitudes toward sexual health conversations exist among Asian subgroups. A study of Cambodian mothers reflects the struggle for mothers to communicate with their daughters about HPV. Despite this, mothers still had a strong desire to protect their daughters although they lacked understanding of how different their daughters' behaviors were compared to their own (Burke et al., 2015). Intergenerational differences in parenting and openness about sexual health persist. South Asian mothers have found it difficult to accept sexual education as a component of school in America, believing that these topics were meant to be discussed in the privacy of their homes (Maiter & George, 2003).

EARLY AND OPEN MOTHER-DAUGHTER COMMUNICATION ABOUT HPV VACCINATION AND SEXUAL HEALTH

African-American mother-daughter HPV communication is particularly important given that HPV related cervical cancer mortality rates are highest among African-American women compared to Hispanic and non-Hispanic Whites in the U.S. and have the second highest cervical cancer incidence rates following Hispanic women (Beavis, Gravitt, & Rositch, 2017). This is coupled with the fact that African-American HPV vaccination rates are lowest relative to all other ethnicities (Dempsey, Cohn, Dalton, & Ruffin, 2011; Reagan-Steiner et al., 2015).

Mother-daughter communication about HPV among African-American mothers has been shown to influence HPV vaccine decision-making as much as practitioner recommendation (Galbraith-Gyan et al., 2017; Hamlish, Clarke, & Alexander, 2012; Miller et al., 2009). While African-American mothers' comfort in discussing HPV vaccination may vary depending on the community and local culture (e.g., urban/rural/suburban, Muslim/Christian, Caribbean, African-American), African American mothers have generally been more likely to discuss sexual health topics with their daughters and discuss at an earlier age compared to Hispanic, Asian, and White mothers (Joseph et al., 2014; Meneses et al., 2006). Cues to talking about sex included "because daughter asked about it," "daughters' friends are having sex/talking about it," "something in the media," or "something else" (McRee, Reiter, Gottlieb, & Brewer, 2011).

As with other ethnicities, African American mothers indicate that their decision about HPV is frequently initiated at the doctor's office (Hull et al., 2014). Daughter's level of involvement increased with age (Hull et al., 2014). Several studies suggest that African-American mothers' history of cervical disease was a strong motivator to vaccinate daughters with about one third of mothers having had personal experiences with an abnormal Pap smear and reporting a strong desire to protect daughters (Hamlish et al., 2012; Hull et al., 2014; Joseph et al., 2014; Pluhar & Kuriloff, 2004). Mother narratives expressed a "strong sense of maternal obligation and authority to protect daughters from the unintended consequences of sexual activity; daughters acknowledged and accepted this authority" (Hamlish et al., 2012, p. 12). In sum, African American mothers are more likely to discuss sexual health explicitly with their daughters and discuss it earlier in daughter's age compared with other ethnicities.

WHAT DOES ALL THIS MEAN?

The purpose of this chapter was to provide a review of the current research on mother-daughter communication about HPV vaccination. You should now be aware of some different contexts in which mother-daughter communication about HPV occurs, and how mother-daughter communication about HPV may vary depending on awareness, knowledge, cultural understanding, age of daughter, parenting style, and how a clinician presents HPV vaccination.

In some geographic and cultural communities, particularly Asian and Hispanic as well as Catholic and Muslim communities, mothers may talk much less or not at all about sexual health with daughters. Sexual health communication is taboo in more socially conservative cultures, and is often simply not discussed or left to discuss with daughters when they are adults, already married, and passed the age when they can benefit from vaccinating against HPV. When HPV vaccination is not discussed at home, education that takes place at school, at a clinician visit, or online plays an increasingly important role in raising awareness and educating adolescent girls and young adult women about reproductive and sexual health.

Mother-daughter communication about HPV vaccination may be validated when mothers and daughters receive information about HPV vaccination from multiple communication channels. Hearing about the importance of vaccination from many sources reinforces the message, credibility, and normalization about HPV vaccination. Receiving positive and supportive messages that vaccinating is protective from multiple channels—a clinician, a mother, school, a peer friend, a friend's mother, or the media—these channels have the potential to contribute to positive evaluations and approval of HPV vaccination among mothers and daughters (Galbraith-Gyan et al., 2017; Hull et al., 2014; Scarinci, Garces-Palacio, & Partridge, 2007).

WHAT DO WE STILL NEED TO KNOW?

- It is important to learn more about how to best educate and reach conservative or isolated cultural communities who may be more insular and receive less prevention messages.
- We need to understand more about how mother-daughter communication about important cancer prevention efforts like HPV vaccination can be communicated in families where it is culturally taboo to approach any topic related to sexual health.
- More information is needed on how to encourage clinicians to interact and communicate with families about the importance of HPV vaccination effectively.

HOW DOES THIS WORK IN REAL LIFE?

- Mother-daughter relationship quality, history, and context shape how conversations about health unfold, what topics are discussed, and whether these conversations have positive outcomes.
- When mothers and daughters discuss HPV and vaccination, these conversations are shaped by whether or not mothers have knowledge about HPV and the vaccination, encourage vaccination, express their support for vaccination, and are comfortable in talking about sexual health.

CLASSROOM ACTIVITIES

- Discuss the following questions as a group or assign as a written paper:
  - Can you think of contexts in which your mother raised the issue of HPV vaccination?
  - How was the topic raised?

○ Did your mother use the opportunity to talk about sexual health?

○ How old were you when these discussions took place?

○ How did you feel about it? (Comforted that your mother was trying to protect you or resentful that you had to vaccinate, embarrassed …)

○ For those who received the vaccination: Did you talk about HPV again anytime afterward?

REFERENCES

Askelson, N. M., Campo, S., & Smith, S. (2012). Mother-daughter communication about sex: The influence of authoritative parenting style. *Health Communication, 27*(5), 439–448. doi: 10.1080/10410236.2011.606526

Askelson, N. M., Campo, S., Smith, S., Lowe, J. B., Dennis, L. K., & Andsager, J. L. (2011). The birds, the bees, and the HPVs: What drives mothers' intentions to use the HPV vaccination as a chance to talk about sex? *Journal of Pediatric Health Care, 25*(3), 162–170. doi: 10.1016/j.pedhc.2010.01.001

Bair, R., Mays, R. M., Sturm, L. A., & Zimet, G. D. (2008). Acceptability of the human papillomavirus vaccine among Latina mothers. *Journal of Pediatric Adolescent Gynecology, 21*(6), 329–334. doi: 10.1016/j.jpag.2008.02.007

Beavis, A. L., Gravitt, P. E., & Rositch, A. F. (2017). Hysterectomy-corrected cervical cancer mortality rates reveal a larger racial disparity in the United States. *Cancer, 123*(6), 1044–1050. doi: 10.1002/cncr.30507

Brianti, P., De Flammineis, E., & Mercuri, S. R. (2017). Review of HPV-related diseases and cancers. *New Microbiology, 40*(2), 80–85.

Burke, N. J., Do, H. H., Talbot, J., Sos, C., Ros, S., & Taylor, V. M. (2015). Protecting our Khmer daughters: Ghosts of the past, uncertain futures, and the human papillomavirus vaccine. *Ethnicity & Health, 20*(4), 376–390. doi: 10.1080/13557858.2014.921895

Centers for Disease Control and Prevention. (2010). FDA licensure of bivalent human papillomavirus vaccine (HPV2, Cervarix) for use in females and updated HPV vaccination recommendations from the Advisory Committee on Immunization Practices (ACIP). *Morbidity and Mortality Weekly Report, 59*(20), 626–629. Retrieved from https://www.cdc.gov/mmwr/preview/mmwrhtml/mm5920a4.htm

Centers for Disease Control and Prevention. (2015). *Inside knowledge: Get the facts about gynecologic cancer.* Atlanta, GA: CDC. Retrieved from https://www.cdc.gov/cancer/knowledge/

Centers for Disease Control and Prevention. (2016). *Human papillomavirus (HPV) ACIP vaccine recommendations.* Atlanta, GA: CDC. Retreived from https://www.cdc.gov/vaccines/hcp/acip-recs/vacc-specific/hpv.html

Centers for Disease Control and Prevention. (2018). *HPV vaccine safety.* Atlanta, GA: CDC. Retrieved from https://www.cdc.gov/hpv/parents/vaccinesafety.html

Chow, S. N., Soon, R., Park, J. S., Pancharoen, C., Qiao, Y. L., Basu, P., & Ngan, H. Y. (2010). Knowledge, attitudes, and communication around human papillomavirus (HPV) vaccination amongst urban Asian mothers and physicians. *Vaccine, 28*(22), 3809–3817. doi: 10.1016/j.vaccine.2010.03.027

Committee on Infectious Diseases. (2012). HPV vaccine recommendations. *Pediatrics, 129*(3), 602–605. doi: 10.1542/peds.2011-3865

Crowe, E., Pandeya, N., Brotherton, J. M., Dobson, A. J., Kisely, S., Lambert, S. B., & Whiteman, D. C. (2014). Effectiveness of quadrivalent human papillomavirus vaccine for the prevention of cervical abnormalities: Case-control study nested within a population based screening programme in Australia. *British Medical Journal, 348*, 1458. doi: 10.1136/bmj.g1458

Dempsey, A., Cohn, L., Dalton, V., & Ruffin, M. (2011). Worsening disparities in HPV vaccine utilization among 19–26 year old women. *Vaccine, 29*(3), 528–534. doi: 10.1016/j.vaccine/2010.10.051

Dempsey, A. F., Abraham, L. M., Dalton, V., & Ruffin, M. (2009). Understanding the reasons why mothers do or do not have their adolescent daughters vaccinated against human papillomavirus. *Annals of Epidemiology, 19*(8), 531–538.

Fiks, A. G., Grundmeier, R. W., Mayne, S., Song, L., Feemster, K., Karavite, D., … Localio, A. R. (2013). Effectiveness of decision support for families, clinicians, or both on HPV vaccine receipt. *Pediatrics, 131*(6), 1114–1124. doi: 10.1542/peds.2012-3122

Galbraith-Gyan, K. V., Lechuga, J., Jenerette, C. M., Palmer, M. H., Moore, A. D., & Hamilton, J. B. (2017). HPV vaccine acceptance among African-American mothers and their daughters: An inquiry grounded in culture. *Ethnicity & Health, 29*, 1–18. doi: 10.1080/13557858.2017.1332758

Gelman, A., Nikolajski, C., Schwarz, E. B., & Borrero, S. (2011). Racial disparities in awareness of the human papillomavirus. *Journal of Women's Health (Larchmt), 20*(8), 1165–1173. doi: 10.1089/jwh.2010.2617

Gollust, S. E., LoRusso, S. M., Nagler, R. H., & Franklin, E. (2016). Understanding the role of the news media in HPV vaccine uptake in the United States: Synthesis and commentary. *Human Vaccine & Immunotherapeutics, 12*(6), 1430–1434. doi: 10.1080/21645515.2015.1109169

Griffioen, A. M., Glynn, S., Mullins, T. K., Zimet, G. D., Rosenthal, S. L., Fortenberry, J. D., & Kahn, J. A. (2012). Perspectives on decision making about human papillomavirus vaccination among 11- to 12-year-old girls and their mothers. *Clinical Pediatrics (Phila), 51*(6), 560–568. doi: 10.1177/0009922812443732

Gross, T. T., Laz, T. H., Rahman, M., & Berenson, A. B. (2015). Association between mother-child sexual communication and HPV vaccine uptake. *Preventive Medicine, 74*, 63–66. doi: 10.1016/j.ypmed.2015.03.004

Hamlish, T., Clarke, L., & Alexander, K. A. (2012). Barriers to HPV immunization for African American adolescent females. *Vaccine, 30*(45), 6472–6476. doi: 10.1016/j.vaccine.2012.07.085

Hopfer, S., & Clippard, J. R. (2011). College women's HPV vaccine decision narratives. *Qualitative Health Research, 21*(2), 262–277. doi: 10.1177/1049732310383868

Hopfer, S., Garcia, S., Duong, H. T., Russo, J. A., & Tanjasiri, S. P. (2017). A narrative engagement framework to understand HPV vaccination among Latina and Vietnamese women in a Planned Parenthood setting. *Health Education & Behavior, 44*(5), 738–747. doi:10.1177/1090198117728761

Hopfer, S., Ray, A. E., Hecht, M. L., Miller-Day, M., Belue, R., Zimet, G., … McKee, F. X. (2017). Taking an HPV vaccine research tested intervention to scale in a clinical setting. *Translational Behavioral Medicine, 8*(5), 745–752. doi:10.1093/tbm/ibx066

Hull, P. C., Williams, E. A., Khabele, D., Dean, C., Bond, B., & Sanderson, M. (2014). HPV vaccine use among African-American girls: Qualitative formative research using a participatory social marketing approach. *Gynecologic Oncology, 132*(1), S13–S20. doi:10.1016/j.ygyno.2014.01.046

Joseph, N. P., Clark, J. A., Mercilus, G., Wilbur, M., Figaro, J., & Perkins, R. (2014). Racial and ethnic differences in HPV knowledge, attitudes, and vaccination rates among low-income African-American, Haitian, Latina, and Caucasian young adult women. *Pediatric Adolescent Gynecology, 27*(2), 83–92. doi:10.1016/j.jpag.2013.08.011

Kim, J. L., & Ward, L. M. (2007). Silence speaks volumes: Parental sexual communication among Asian American emerging adults. *Journal of Adolescent Research, 22*(1), 3–31. doi:10.1177/0743558406294916

Krieger, J. L., Kam, J., Katz, M. L., & Roberto, A. J. (2010). Does mother know best? An actor-partner model of college-age women's human papillomavirus vaccination behavior. *Human Communication Research, 37*(1), 107–124. doi: 10.1111/j.1468-2958.2010.01395.x

Lechuga, J., Vera-Cala, L., & Martinez-Donate, A. (2016). HPV vaccine awareness, barriers, intentions, and uptake in Latina women. *Journal of Immigrant and Minority Health, 18*(1), 173–178. doi: 10.1007/s10903-014-0139-z

Liddon, N., Michael, S. L., Dittus, P., & Markowitz, L. E. (2013). Maternal underestimation of child's sexual experience: Suggested implications for HPV vaccine uptake at recommended ages. *Journal of Adolescent Health, 53*(5), 674–676. doi: 10.1016/j.jadohealth.2013.07.026

Lipton, B. J., & Decker, S. L. (2015). ACA provisions associated with increase in percentage of young adult women initiating and completing the HPV vaccine. *Health Affairs (Millwood), 34*(5), 757–764. doi: 10.1377/hlthaff.2014.1302

Lu, B., Kumar, A., Castellsague, X., & Giuliano, A. R. (2011). Efficacy and safety of prophylactic vaccines against cervical HPV infection and diseases among women: A systematic review and meta-analysis. *BMC Infectious Diseases, 11*(1), 13–29. doi:10.1186/1471-2334-11-13

Maiter, S., & George, U. (2003). Understanding context and culture in the parenting approaches of immigrant South Asian mothers. *Affilia, 18*(4), 411–428. doi: 10.1177/0886109903257589

Markowitz, L., Dunne, E. F., Saraiya, M., Chesson, H. W., Curtis, C. R., Gee, J., … Unger, E. R. (2014). Human papillomavirus vaccination: Recommendations of the advisory committee on immunization (ACIP). *Morbity and Mortality Weekly Report, 63*(5), 1–30.

Markowitz, L. E., Hariri, S., Lin, C., Dunne, E. F., Steinau, M., McQuillan, G., & Unger, E. R. (2013). Reduction in human papillomavirus (HPV) prevalence among young women following HPV vaccine introduction in the United States, National Health and Nutrition Examination Surveys, 2003–2010. *Journal of Infectious Disease, 208*(3), 385–393. doi:10.1093/infdis/jit192

Markowitz, L. E., Liu, G., Hariri, S., Steinau, M., Dunne, E. F., & Unger, E. R. (2016). Prevalence of HPV after introduction of the vaccination program in the United States. *Pediatrics, 137*(3), 1–19. doi: 10.1542/peds.2015-1968

Marlow, L. A., Wardle, J., Forster, A. S., & Waller, J. (2009). Ethnic differences in human papillomavirus awareness and vaccine acceptability. *Journal of Epidemiology and Community Health, 63*(12), 1010–1015. doi: 10.1136/jech.2008.085886

McKee, M. D., & Karasz, A. (2006). You have to give her that confidence: Conversations about sex in hispanic mother-daughter dyads. *Journal of Adolescent Research, 21*(2), 158–184. doi: 10.1177/0743558405285493

McRee, A. L., Gottlieb, S. L., Reiter, P. L., Dittus, P. J., Halpern, C. T., & Brewer, N. T. (2012). HPV vaccine discussions: An opportunity for mothers to talk with their daughters about sexual health. *Sexually Transmitted Diseases, 39*(5), 394–401. doi: 10.1097/OLQ.0b013e318248aaa0

McRee, A. L., Reiter, P. L., Gottlieb, S. L., & Brewer, N. T. (2011). Mother-daughter communication about HPV vaccine. *Journal of Adolescent Health, 48*(3), 314–317. doi: 10.1016/j.jadohealth.2010.07.006

Meites, E., Kempe, A., & Markowitz, L. (2016). Use of a 2-dose schedule for human papillomavirus vaccination—Updated recommendations of the advisory committee on immunization practices. *Morbity and Mortality Weekly Report, 65*(49), 1405–1408. doi: 10.15585/mmwr.mm6549a5

Meneses, L. M., Orrell-Valente, J. K., Guendelman, S. R., Oman, D., & Irwin, C. E. (2006). Racial/ethnic differences in mother-daughter communication about sex. *Journal of Adolescent Health, 39*(1), 128–131. doi: 10.1016/j.jadohealth.2005.08.005

Miller, K. S., Fasula, A. M., Dittus, P., Wiegand, R. E., Wyckoff, S. C., & McNair, L. (2009). Barriers and facilitators to maternal communication with preadolescents about age-relevant sexual topics. *AIDS and Behavior, 13*(2), 365–374. doi: 10.1007/s10461-007-9324-6

Miller-Ott, A. E., & Durham, W. T. (2011). The role of social support in young women's communication about the Genital HPV vaccine. *Women's Studies in Communication, 34*(2), 183–201. doi: 10.1080/07491409.2011.618239

Morales-Campos, D. Y., Markham, C. M., Peskin, M. F., & Fernandez, M. E. (2013). Hispanic mothers' and high school girls' perceptions of cervical cancer, human papillomavirus, and the human papillomavirus vaccine. *Journal of Adolescent Health, 52*(5), S69–S75. doi: 10.1016/j.jadohealth.2012.09.020

Moran, M. B., Murphy, S. T., Chatterjee, J. S., Amezola de Herrera, P., & Baezconde-Garbanati, L. (2014). Mexican-american mother's perceptions regarding vaccinating their daughters against HPV and recommended strategies to promote vaccine uptake. *Women's Reproductive Health, 1*(2), 106–119. doi: 10.1080/2393691.2014.966033

Mullins, T. L., Griffioen, A. M., Glynn, S., Zimet, G. D., Rosenthal, S. L., Fortenberry, J. D., & Kahn, J. A. (2013). Human papillomavirus vaccine communication: Perspectives of 11–12 year-old girls, mothers, and clinicians. *Vaccine, 31*(42), 4894–4901. doi: 10.1016/j.vaccine.2013.07.033

Munoz, N., Castellsague, X., Gonzalez, A. B. d., & Gissman, L. (2006). HPV in etiology of human cancer. *Vaccine, 24*(S3), S1–S10. doi: 10.1016/j.vaccine.2006.05.115

Nguyen, G. T., Leader, A. E., & Hung, W. L. (2009). Awareness of anticancer vaccines among Asian American women with limited english proficiency: An opportunity for improved public health communication. *Journal of Cancer Education, 24*(4), 280–283. doi: 10.1080/08858190902973127

Niccolai, L. M., Hansen, C. E., Credle, M., & Shapiro, E. D. (2016). Parents' recall and reflections on experiences related to HPV vaccination for their children. *Qualitative Health Research, 26*(6), 842–850. doi: 10.1177/1049732315575712

Pluhar, E. I., & Kuriloff, P. (2004). What really matters in family communication about sexuality? A qualitative analysis of affect and style among African American mothers and adolescent daughters. *Sex Education, 4*(3), 303–321. doi: 10.1080/1468181042000243376

Reagan-Steiner, S., Pierre-Joseph, N., Jeyarajah, J., Elam-Evans, L., Singleton, J. A., Curtis, C. R., ... Stokley, S. (2015). National, regional, state, and selected local area vaccination coverage among adolescents aged 13–17 years—United States, 2014. *Morbidity and Mortality Weekly Report, 64*(29), 784–792.

Rendle, K. A., & Leskinen, E. A. (2017). Timing is everything: Exploring parental decisions to delay HPV vaccination. *Qualitative Health Research, 27*(9), 1380–1390. doi: 10.1177/1049732316664499

Roberts, M. E., Gerrard, M., Reimer, R., & Gibbons, F. X. (2010). Mother-daughter communication and human papillomavirus vaccine uptake by college students. *Pediatrics, 125*(5), 982–989. doi: 10.1542/peds.2009-2888

Romo, L. F., Cruz, M. E., & Neilands, T. B. (2011). Mother-daughter communication and college women's confidence to communicate with family members and doctors about the human papillomavirus and sexual health. *Journal of Pediatric and Adolescent Gynecology, 24*(5), 256–262. doi: 10.1016/j.jpag.2011.02.006

Rosenthal, S. L., Rupp, R., Zimet, G. D., Meza, H. M., Loza, M. L., Short, M. B., & Succop, P. A. (2008). Uptake of HPV vaccine: Demographics, sexual history and values, parenting style, and vaccine attitudes. *Journal of Adolescent Health, 43*(3), 239–245. doi: 10.1016/j.jadohealth.2008.06.009

Scarinci, I. C., Garces-Palacio, I. C., & Partridge, E. E. (2007). An examination of acceptability of HPV vaccination among African American women and Latina immigrants. *Journal of Women's Health, 16*(8), 1224–1233. doi: 10.1089/jwh.2006.0175

Tangherlini, T. R., Roychowdhury, V., Glenn, B., Crespi, C., Bandari, R., Wadia, A., … Bastani, R. (2016). Mommy blogs and the vaccination exemption narrative: Results from a machine-learning approach for story aggregation on parenting social media sites. *Journal of Medical Internet Research, 2*(2), e166. doi: 10.2196/publichealth.6586

Taylor, V. M., Burke, N. J., Ko, L. K., Sos, C., Liu, Q., Do, H. H., … Bastani, R. (2014). Understanding HPV vaccine uptake among Cambodian American girls. *Journal of Community Health, 39*(5), 857–862. doi: 10.1007/s10900-014-9844-8

Thompson, V. L. S., Arnold, L. D., & Notaro, S. R. (2012). African American parents' HPV vaccination intent and concerns. *Journal of Health Care for the Poor and Underserved, 23*, 290–301. doi: 10.1353/hpu.2012.0007

Walker, T. Y., Elam-Evans, L., Singleton, J. A., Yankey, D., Markowitz, L., Fredua, B., … Stokely, S. (2017). National, regional, state, and selected local area vaccination coverage among adolescents aged 13–17 years—United States, 2016. *Morbidity and Mortality Weekly Report, 66*(33), 874–882. doi: http://dx.doi.org/10.15585/mmwr.mm6633a2

Williams, W. W., Lu, P.-J., O'Halloran, A., Kim, D. K., Grohskopf, L. A., Pilishvili, T., … Bridges, C. B. (2016). Surveillance of Vaccination Coverage Among Adult Populations—United States, 2014. *Morbidity and Mortality Weekly Report, 65*(1), 1–36. doi: http://dx.doi.org/10.15585/mmwr.ss6501a1

Yi, J. K., Anderson, K. O., Le, Y. C., Escobar-Chaves, S. L., & Reyes-Gibby, C. C. (2013). English proficiency, knowledge, and receipt of HPV vaccine in Vietnamese-American women. *Journal of Community Health, 38*(5), 805–811. doi: 10.1007/s10900-013-9680-2

Ylitalo, K. R., Lee, H., & Meta, N. K. (2013). Health care provider recommendation, human papillomavirus vaccination, and race/ethnicity in the US national immunization survey. *American Journal of Public Health, 103*(1), 164–169. doi: 10.2105/AJPH.2011.300600

Zimmerman, R. K. (2007). HPV vaccine and its recommendations, 2007. *Journal of Family Practice, 56*(2 Suppl Vaccines), S1–5, C1.

CHAPTER TEN

"A Different Closeness"

Emerging Adult Daughters' Depictions of Their Relational Changes with Their Mothers

MEGAN MEADOWS* AND MEREDITH MARKO HARRIGAN†

We are very close I'm just secret about some things

—SAMANTHA

We don't battle about everyday things like chores

—AMELIA

I have to call my mom every single day, it's her rule

—NORA

Relationships change over time as people enter new life stages and begin new experiences. The comments that begin this chapter describe some daughters' experiences with their mothers during one life stage—*emerging adulthood*, the topic to which we now turn. Do these comments sound familiar? Have you heard yourself thinking similar thoughts?

As you have read throughout this book, the mother-daughter relationship is argued to be one of the most important relationships within the family system (Furman & Buhrmester, 1992) and daughters view mothers among the most meaningful relational partners they will have in their life (Fisher & Miller-Day,

* Megan Meadows, State University of New York College and Geneseo.
† Meredith Marko Harrigan, Associate Professor, State University of New York College and Geneseo, harrigan@geneseo.edu.

2006). In this chapter, we take into consideration the evolutionary nature of the relationship by exploring how it changes over time, particularly during daughters' transition to adulthood, a time that has been labeled *emerging adulthood* (Arnett, 2005). Relationships and communication change with—and adapt to—new life stages and experiences; therefore, as daughters grow and change, so too will their relationships with their mothers. As daughters mature and move into adulthood and begin to live away from their mothers, communication with their mothers may increase or decrease in frequency and/or in openness, tone, or occur through new and different channels. In the coming pages, we will discuss some of the changes that take place during emerging adulthood and explore how daughters who geographically move away from their mothers during this life stage adjust their communication with their mothers, including how they manage privacy and disclosure and what role technology plays as a tool in this process.

THE MOTHER-DAUGHTER RELATIONSHIP DURING EMERGING ADULTHOOD

All relationships are dynamic and influenced, in part, by the members' life stages (David-Barrett et al., 2016). As daughters mature, both mothers and daughters, as communicative and relational partners, influence and change the relationship, including the patterns of interaction (Balsam & Fischer, 2006, p. 59).

One particularly noteworthy life stage and the focus of the present chapter is emerging adulthood (Arnett, 2005). Psychologist Jeffrey Arnett (2005) used the term "emerging adult" to describe the time in life when adolescents transition into adults. Emerging adulthood is a label that is typically used to describe people between the ages of 18–25 years old and has been characterized as a life stage involving identity exploration, self-focus, and perceived new possibilities as well as feelings of instability and being "in-between" adolescence and adulthood (Arnett, 2005, p. 235). For example, daughters want more freedom, yet still rely on their mothers in various ways such as for financial assistance, help with school, or with new tasks in their lives including cooking and cleaning. Reader, we ask you to consider how living away from your mother has impacted or will impact your relationship. Do some of these topics resonate with you? It is during this transition to adulthood that daughters may leave home for the first time to pursue higher education or start careers.

The increased geographic distance between mothers and daughters combined with the daughters' developmental changes during this stage—such as her maturity and identity exploration—may affect the mother-daughter relationship, making it feel strained or different. It is during this time that mothers and daughters often seek to manage the newfound physical and emotional distance between them by adjusting communication processes or creating new rules for their relationships. These long-distance relationships can require more work to maintain relational closeness.

Because mothers and children often share a close bond during infancy, mothers impact their children's development more than any other relational member, including their attachment behavior and mental health (Bowlby, 1998). But what might this look like during daughters' emerging adulthood life stage? Well, we are not quite sure yet. We know that daughters often discuss a variety of topics with their mothers. Daughters often choose their mothers to discuss a wide breath of topics with and view their mothers as their "preferred conversational partner for important topics" (Miller-Day, 2002, p. 610), more so than their fathers (Hetherington & Stanley-Hagan, 1995). But do daughters continue to turn to their mothers during emerging adulthood when they are living apart and trying to establish independence? Again, the research in this area has been unclear. Lastly, we know that the mother-daughter relationship often involves high emotional connection and interdependence when compared to other intergenerational relationships (Fischer, 1981). But do the qualities associated with emerging adulthood impact the degree of emotional connection between daughters and mothers? Does the newfound physical distance between them impact their relational closeness? These are some of the questions that guide our discussion in this chapter.

Managing Physical and Relational Distance

One important point to consider when examining the mother-daughter relationship during this life stage is how physical distance impacts relational closeness. *Intimacy* is a term often used to describe the feeling of closeness that exists between relational parties, in this case between mothers and daughters. Because many daughters choose to attend residential colleges or move away from their mothers to establish a career, the mother-daughter relationship often becomes long-distance during emerging adulthood. Long-distance relationships often require increased effort to maintain intimacy (Stahlstein, 2004). You may have experienced this in your relationships as you moved away to college. When you moved away from home, how did the physical distance impact the relational closeness you have with your mother?

Geographic location can also be a stressor in the mother-daughter relationship and require renegotiation and added effort. For example, Cameron and Ross (2007) and Miller-Day (2004) explained that separation may result in attachment threat, relational uncertainty, and even psychological distress. Thus, daughters and mothers need to consider how to renegotiate their relationship to maintain closeness and prevent personal and/or relational stress. When we, the authors, were away at college, there were so many changes in our mother-daughter relationships, beginning with not telling our mothers everything about our lives like we used to, which we know was hard for our mothers. Although there are difficulties like this one, Kolozsvari (2015) explained, in long-distance relationships "partners stretch temporal and spatial limitations and demonstrate how togetherness and belonging can be achieved … creating ways in possible unconventional spaces" (p. 113). Fortunately, the mother-daughter relationship is believed to be more able to withstand geographic location than other relationships because of familial ties and periodic visits for important events (Stahlstein, 2004). Has your relationship with your mother endured stress since becoming long-distance? What steps did you take to enable a relationship that can withstand stressors?

One important communicative process related to intimacy is *disclosure*. Disclosure refers to the "interplay of granting or denying access to information that is defined as private" (Petronio, 2002, p. 3). People make the decision to disclose information with various factors in mind including context, motivation, and the risks or benefits coming from the possible disclosure (Petronio, 2002). Disclosure has relational benefits; it has been linked to relational satisfaction, especially in instances where it is reciprocal. As Stafford and Reske (1990) argued, "frequent communication and high levels of self-disclosure are equated with relationship development and intimacy … [and] communication leads to accuracy and understanding, which, in turn, produces relational satisfaction" (pp. 274–275). In the case of the mother-daughter relationship, frequent communication between mothers and their daughters can lead to increased intimacy and relational closeness, despite differing geographic settings.

Yet, there are also risks associated with disclosure, such as giving up one's sense of control (Petronio, 2002). By sharing private information with others, people may feel vulnerable. If daughters share private information with their mothers, for example, the information then becomes co-owned, allowing their mothers to do what they wish with it. There may be a feeling of vulnerability for daughters due to the uncertainty of how their mothers will handle and use the information. In her theory called Communication Privacy Management (CPM), Petronio (2002) explained various ways that relational members manage their private information, including how they build and negotiate personal boundaries in order to meet their personal and relational needs. When people are "allowed into a privacy boundary, [they] have responsibilities to fulfill the disclosers' expectations about how their private information will be treated" (Petronio, Helft, & Child, 2013, p. 176). For example, if a daughter shares private information with her mother and asks her mother to maintain her privacy, the mother has a responsibility to keep that information private. Petronio, Helft, and Child (2013) explained that people use several criteria to determine whether or not to disclose private information. These include cultural guidelines (e.g., does your cultural context value privacy or openness?), gender-related norms (e.g., are men and women socialized to be open or private?), contextual factors (e.g., what situational factors influence openness or privacy?), motivational reasons (e.g., are there benefits tied to disclosure or privacy?), and the result of a risk-benefit assessment (e.g., what are the pros and cons of disclosure and privacy in this situation?).

One specific aspect of the relationship that we suspect changes during emerging adulthood is the degree of information, especially *private information*, daughters disclose to their mothers. Fischer (1981) described the strong bond between mothers and daughters as "a 'life-cycle,' which is marked by several periods of transition" (p. 613). Thus, it seems logical to expect adjustments in information sharing as a daughter becomes more independent. As we noted earlier, daughters often talk to their mothers about a wide variety of important issues (Miller-Day, 2002). However, discussion of a wide range of topics may be a result of proximity, with daughters frequently see their mothers when sharing a residence. In contrast, when living apart from their mothers, daughters might be more likely to share private information with individuals who live in close geographic proximity to their new environment such as roommates, friends, professors, or mentors.

Additionally, emerging adulthood comes with increased freedom and exploration due to having fewer rules and less guidance from mothers (Arnett, 2005). It is during this time that daughters might participate in behaviors that may be deemed risky such as drinking alcohol, using drugs, or engaging in sexual activity (Bearak, 2014). Out of fear of disapproval or criticism, daughters sometimes withhold those experiences from their mothers. As Kennedy-Lightsey, Martin, Thompson, Himes, and Clingerman (2012) noted, decisions to maintain privacy may be "out of fear of being rejected by others, creating a negative impression, losing autonomy, and/or losing influence in a relationship" (p. 666). And, as Arnett (2005) explained, during this period of increased freedom and identity exploration, "many emerging adults want to have a wide range of experiences before they settle into adult life" (p. 240), even ones their mothers previously prohibited. Thus, it is not surprising that daughters might become more private about the details of their lives, especially in interactions with their mothers. After reading about disclosure, consider, for a moment, what changes you have made to your own disclosures. Do you talk about the same number of topics since moving away from your mother? Do you share the same amount of information with your mother as you did when living together? For you, what are the benefits and drawbacks of disclosure? In addition to understanding what daughters talk with their mothers about during emerging adulthood and how the newfound physical distance between them might influence their choices, it is important to understand *how* daughters manage private information with their mothers.

Managing Private Information with Technology

As we have discussed, sharing private information is both beneficial and risky for relationships. Both the amount and type of information that daughters disclose with their mothers could impact their level of intimacy. During emerging adulthood, daughters will likely seek independence and, in doing so, withhold information to create a sense of personal control. Moreover, because of their likelihood to experiment with new experiences, including some of which their mothers might disapprove, daughters may be hesitant to share private information with their mothers so as to minimize relational risks like negative perceptions or disappointment. Yet, disclosure can help maintain intimacy between mothers and daughters.

One potentially important tool in allowing mothers and daughters to share information and remain close while being long distance is *technology*. Through various electronic tools, including social media, mothers and daughters can bridge physical distance and stay relationally connected. Emerging adult daughters who are living away from their mothers may use various synchronous (in real time) and asynchronous (across time) technologies to stay in touch and maintain their relationships. Among the most common technologies emerging adults use for relational purposes are cell phones, computers, and tablets (Swanson & Walker, 2015). Emerging adults are frequent users of social media, as you are probably aware. In fact, recent statistics show that 90% of American emerging adults use Facebook, Twitter, Instagram and/or Snapchat to communicate (Lenhart, 2015). However, while technology is a helpful tool for achieving closeness through communicating while apart, daughters may want to control how much and what type of private information their mothers have access to, especially on social media. van den Broeck, Poels, and Walrave (2015) highlight that emerging adults frequently use privacy settings in their social media platforms to manage personal and collective boundaries within their relationships, including the mother-daughter relationship. Even with set boundaries, many long-distance relational partners will use technology to communicate in order to maintain their relationships.

Advances in these synchronous and asynchronous technologies have enabled long-distance relationships to function and maintain intimacy (Stahlstein, 2004). Frequent use of various technologies may enable regular communication between long-distanced mothers and daughters (Stahlstein, 2004) and the degree to which mothers and daughters enjoy this type of communication may have a positive influence on the relationship. In previous studies, scholars found a positive association between phone satisfaction and relationship satisfaction as well as between frequency of cell phone interaction and relational closeness (Miller-Ott, Kelly, & Duran, 2014).

As you can see, daughters' transition from adolescence into emerging adulthood is often marked by significant changes, including changes to their living arrangements and behaviors, and these changes might influence the tools they use when they interact with their mothers (Arnett, 2005; Bearak, 2014; Reid & Carey, 2015). Through these many changes, daughters often experience increased independence, which may impact their communication with their mothers, including the degree of information they share and the means through which they stay connected. Knowing that this time in life is often associated with experimentation (Arnett, 2005), understanding these changes could shed important insight about the mother-daughter relationship during this underexplored life stage and highlight potential implications related to daughters' well-being.

Given all this knowledge, we were curious both about how adult daughters who live away from their mothers manage private information with mothers and what role technology plays in information management and thus we conducted a study to investigate these topics.

THE STUDY

What Were We Interested in Learning?

We were interested in learning about some of the specific ways the mother-daughter relationship changes when the daughter is in the emerging adult life stage. *We were particularly interested in understanding what emerging adult daughters share or do not share with their mothers and the technological tools they use when managing their private information.* We believe technology will play a large factor in maintaining the closeness of the relationship and hoped to learn more about the technological channels daughters use as well as the rules daughters (or mothers) place on communication.

How Did We Go About Learning This Information?

To deepen our understanding about daughter's disclosures and technology, we interviewed and surveyed emerging adult daughters about how they manage private information in their mother-daughter relationship while living apart and how they use technology as a tool to employ their privacy strategies and meet their privacy needs.

Through conducting semi-structured qualitative interviews, we collected the experiences of 32 daughters who were between the ages of 19 and 25 and lived apart from their mothers for at least three months (but no longer than 5 years). These daughters varied in how far they lived from their mothers with the distance ranging between a 30-minute and 8-hour drive. While some daughters saw their mothers each week, others saw them much less frequently.

We asked daughters a variety of questions about their communication with their mothers including: (a) what communication channels do you use most often with your mother?; (b) how, if at all, is your relationship with your mother similar to or different from the relationship you had with her when you lived in the same household?; (c) how, if at all, have you adjusted your privacy settings on social media since moving away?; (d) what impact have those privacy adjustments had on your relationship with your mother?, (e) what topics do you talk with your mother about that you previously had not?; and, (f) in what ways do you believe your relationship with your mother has benefited and/or been hurt by the physical distance between you? Take a moment and consider how *you* might answer these questions. Given our desire to understand the details of daughters' relational and communication experiences, we analyzed the answers to these questions qualitatively, generating descriptive results and an in-depth understanding of participants' experiences. Specifically, we conducted and transcribed the interviews, closely examined, and compared participant comments to ultimately provide a description of emerging adult daughters' experiences of information sharing, privacy management, use of technology, and the mother-daughter relationship.

What Did We Learn?

Types of Information and Frequency of Disclosure

Our study provided interesting insight into the mother-daughter relationship during daughters' emerging adulthood. Findings from our analysis indicate that emerging adult daughters decreased the amount of everyday small talk with their mothers but added new "mature" topics to their range of topics, adding more depth to mother-daughter conversations. We are using the term *everyday small talk* to refer to sharing daily happenings, such as what they did that day, how classes are going, who they saw—all the little details of the day. The reduction of everyday small talk with their mothers is due, in part, to the fact that daughters share these details with people who are currently in their immediate circle like their roommates, classmates, and/or friends. Because they live away from their families, their mothers are no longer part of that circle. Daughters explained that engaging in everyday small talk with their mother would be repetitive and feel burdensome. As Brooke said, "I'll have to tell it again."

Daughters noted that in high school (before entering emerging adulthood), the topics of mothers and daughters' everyday small talk centered on a *shared* social circle, which in emerging adulthood is absent. In high school, for example, mothers were familiar with the daughters' friends and her school-related experiences. Once daughters lived apart from their mothers, their social circle changes and, as a result, mothers became unfamiliar with their daughters' friends and daily activities. Katie pointed out, "we don't know everything the other is doing" and Renee said that she does not share information about her friends because her mother has never met these new friends. Additionally, Harper added, "when I lived with her I told her almost everything. Now it's more things that feel relevant to our phone calls." Samantha shared a similar example. She noted, "In high school it was, like, written on our calendar on our fridge that I had a test and stuff and, like, now she doesn't know." Mothers were once woven into the daily life of the daughter, yet the newfound geographic location between them has reduced the mothers' awareness of her daughters' everyday experiences. Rather than the daughter taking the time to share the information with her and bring her up-to-speed, daughters reported avoiding these sorts of conversations and meeting their need to share everyday life details by discussing them with someone in close proximity.

Although daughters reported participating less frequently in everyday small talk with their mothers, they described discussing *new topics* with them since moving away. Many daughters introduced talk about "adult" topics with their mothers, such as graduate school, cleaning, and—perhaps most frequently—food preparation! Samantha noted that she now talks to her mother about "real things, like people things, like how to cook." Similarly, Nora explained that, "we talk a lot more about real life situations and I'll ask her like about how to cook things or what does a good zucchini look like?" Some daughters, like Mary, also mentioned being even more open with their mothers about risky behaviors, such as "drugs, sex, or alcohol." Daughters perceive that adding these topics to mother-daughter conversations adds increased depth and personal connection to the relationship.

Daughters' conversations with their mothers seemed to become more purposeful, switching from casual small talk to more serious topics. Renee described the topics she discusses with her mother as "more relevant," providing the example of "getting a job." Daughters reported looking to their mothers for advice and information about similar personal experiences. Leah pointed out that "we talk more about her past. Because she has a lot of anecdotes that are applicable to my own life ... you know, things that weren't relevant when I was 18, but are now that I'm 20." Jessie and her mother talk about money management since she now has the responsibility of paying her bills. Not surprisingly, daughters often talk to their mothers about advanced education and careers, which were not part of their previous range of topics. As we can see, while daughters were striving to be their own autonomous adults, they simultaneously looked to their mothers to guide them on important decisions.

As noted previously, although daughters engage in less frequent everyday small talk with their mothers, they have integrated new topics into their interactions. Their conversations now focus on more mature topics such as their responsibilities and their futures. What we found interesting (and a point we believe is important for people to know) is that daughters attributed the reduction of everyday small talk to a decrease in the amount of conflict they have with their mothers. Katie noted, "we only talk about good things, as opposed to fighting over stupid stuff at home." Daughters explained that their everyday small talk was often centered on conflict-inducing topics such as chores and school tasks. Daughters reported less bickering with their mothers and associated this change with a decrease in conflict. As Nora explained, "we don't talk about the clothes that I have to put away in my room since she can't see the pile" and Olivia agreed "we don't battle about everyday things like chores." This decrease in conflict is consistent with the findings of other studies about emerging adult children and their parents. For example, Morton and Markey (2009) found, parent-child emerging adult relationships had less "conflict and more positive interactions," which they connected to having similar goals (p. 915). The fact that the mothers and daughters are living apart seems especially impactful to the frequency of conflict because geographic distance reduces conflicts about topics such as chores or curfew, as they are no longer applicable topics of discussion (Lindell & Campione-Barr, 2017). When mothers·no longer give daily demands or make their daughters the recipients of "nagging," as Olivia called it, emerging adult daughters experience less conflict with their mothers. Victoria summarized this change nicely when she said, "I don't really come into conflict with her when we're apart because there is nothing really to fight about." Yet, it is important to note that some daughters discussed an increase in conflict upon their return home for visits or breaks. When daughters are away from home, they are able to make their own decisions, but when they return home, they are again under their parents' jurisdiction. Mary explained, "it is different when we are apart as we have less disagreements over chores but when we are together there are the same type of arguments that you have when you live in such constant proximity to someone." Importantly, however, although daughters described less frequent conflict, they also noted that when conflict does occur while apart, it is more difficult for them to manage because of the geographic location between them. Brooke hypothesized, "I guess they're harder to resolve since you have to call them and you can't see their face." Geographic distance appears to reduce conflict in general, but sometimes the duration of conflict is extended. As Madeline noted, "fights can last much longer when we're apart" and Nora explained, "it's easier for me to hide when I get angry at something that she says." Daughters across our study reported having less frequent, though sometimes more drawn out, conflicts with their mothers since moving away.

In summary, daughters' transition from adolescence to emerging adulthood and the move from living *with* to living *away* from their mothers is perceived by daughters to be associated with both communicative and relational changes. Daughters describe having less frequent everyday small talk with their mothers but more frequent conversations about adult-like topics, many of which involve advice-seeking. Of these two changes, daughters see the reduction of everyday talk as being more impactful to their relationships with their mothers because they attribute it to a decrease in conflict between them.

In addition to understanding the *topics* of conversation that change, we were also curious how their *methods* of communicating might change as daughters enter this new life stage. We turn to the topic of communication methods now and explore how technology can be a useful tool for maintaining mother-daughter relationship connection.

Communicating with Technology

Studies have suggested that technology use such as computers and smart phones allows family members to increase closeness (Boneva, Kraut, & Frohlich, 2001) and we expected the same to be true for the mothers and daughters in our study. We found that emerging adult daughters learn to adapt their use of technology to their mothers' skillset and wishes while still meeting their own needs. Mothers and daughters frequently share images both as a way to stay connected and for daughters to show off their new adult-like skills. We elaborate on these points in the following section.

Daughters choose technology based on their mothers' technological literacy, which results in them using phone calls, texting, or video conferencing most often. Daughters, like Leah, frequently reported that their mothers are "not that great with the technology." As Samantha put it, "texting [my mother] is a nightmare and she like doesn't get it … so I like to talk to her on the phone." Olivia often chooses to call her mother because, as she notes, "some of the [text] messages I send her she doesn't understand." Victoria attributed this challenge with technology to the "generation gap." Daughters also choose technology based on their mothers' wishes. For example, Grace uses FaceTime because, as she noted, her mom "likes to see me" and Renee calls her mother because "that is what she appreciates." Some daughters reported that their mothers established actual rules on when and how interactions would occur: Nora shared, "I have to call my mom every single day, it's her rule."

In addition to mothers' needs and wishes, daughters choose technology with their own needs in mind. For example, this life stage is very busy for daughters, therefore, daughters, often rely on texting or phone calls because they are fast and can be done while accomplishing other tasks like "walking to class," as Katie said. The phone call seemed to be the easiest method for daughters as it is quick and portable. In contrast, video chatting is chosen when closeness or intimacy matters to daughters, as it is often not done in conjunction with other activities. Daughters appear to consider FaceTime to be the most intimate channel. As Maggie noted, it is the "closest thing you can have to really talking to somebody." And, in stressful situations, daughters often choose to talk on the phone to discuss the stress-inducing issues. Voice calling seems to allow daughters to resolve issues quicker and more effectively than through other channels such as texting, because, as Sarah noted, they can "talk through the issue."

Regardless of which form of technology daughters chose, they highlighted the importance of *image sharing* to their relationship. Images are sent by many daughters and mothers in their attempt to feel close and to share special events with each other. Images are also used by daughters to "show off" their new skills, especially culinary skills. First, image and video sharing allow daughters to feel like they are in close proximity to home. Daughters discussed being upset about missing special events and how their mothers would share images to make them feel like they were present. Daughters described many images that were important to them because they made them feel as though they were with their families during important moments, such as when Julia's sister was "getting ready for homecoming," or Kelly wanted to be present at a high school concert. Some daughters, like Nicole, even reported the importance of receiving pictures of her dog. Daughters wanted to see the events happening in order to feel like they were not missing out on as much. Olivia described this as staying "in the loop" and Elizabeth noted, "it made it better." Daughters shared images with their mothers to feel close to them. Julia stated she remains close with her mother through images because, "it feels like you're still home and for her it makes her feel like I'm remembering to think of her." Here, technology is a tool that allows the daughters to feel less geographically separated from their mothers.

In addition to helping daughters and mothers sustain closeness, image sharing allowed daughters to display their new "adult" skills. Theresa discussed sending pictures of her doing mature things such as domestic labor. She said, I "send them pictures of things like my vacuum or a new soap." Here too, food-related accomplishments were often captured by daughters and shared with their mothers. Julia commented, "when I cook things and I'm proud of them I'll send her some pictures … [which is] definitely better than if we just got to send texts and just words." Technology is a tool that allows daughters to lessen the burden of geographically separation from their mothers, and likewise lessen emotional distance by promoting communication and intimacy.

WHAT DOES ALL THIS MEAN?

This chapter centered on the mother-daughter relationship during daughters' emerging adulthood. In our quest to understand how daughters' relationships with their mother evolve during emerging adulthood, we learned that topic management and technology play central roles. Given the newfound distance between them, this period marks a transition for the mother-daughter relationship because daughters can now manage autonomy and relational closeness through the topics they discuss. Although daughters reduce everyday small talk with their mothers because their mothers are no longer part of their immediate social circles, they now talk about new topics that they perceive add depth to their relationship. Additionally, daughters rely on technology to share private information and manage their relationship with their mother, especially placing value on image sharing because it allows daughters to stay relationally connected when they are physically separated. Maybe you have experienced the benefits of technology while being away from friends or family and can see how helpful technology can be in staying emotionally close to those we care about.

As we conclude, we think it is important to stress that most daughters described their relationships with their mothers as remaining intimate despite the geographic distance and increased desire for privacy and autonomy that comes with emerging adulthood, with some even stating that it had become closer. Many daughters described their relationship as more mature and qualitatively richer than before. Using Colleen's words, "she's more of my friend now" and for many emerging adult daughters and mothers, it is just "a different closeness."

WHAT DO WE STILL NEED TO KNOW?

While we learned a lot about the mother-daughter emerging adult relationship, there is still much more to learn on the topic. Below are some points for future direction:

- We see value in studying this relationship from the mother's perspective to understand how, if at all, she changes what information, including private information, she shares with her daughter and how she uses technology as a tool to accomplish her goals.
- In the coming years, how will the mother-daughter relationship change with new technologies?

HOW DOES THIS WORK IN REAL LIFE?

We're hoping that this study provided some insight into the mother-daughter relationship for daughters in the emerging adult life stage. Below are some tips for mothers and daughters using technology to stay connected.

Mothers

- Understand that your daughters are creating and sustaining new relationships through everyday small talk. Thus, they might not want to talk about all the details of their day.
- Disclosure is often about the context and with whom they cross paths, not specifically the mother-daughter relationship. Consider what new topics

you might want to bring to your conversations to maintain a connection with your daughter.

- Send images of key events that happen at home to allow daughters to feel connected to the family.

Daughters

- Understand that there may be technology barriers between you and your mother. While one form of technology may be easy and beneficial for you, it might not be for your mother. Take some time to understand which channels she feels comfortable using.
- Try to share images with your mother. Just as images of events at home help you feel connected, your mother might enjoy seeing what you are doing. Photos and videos allow mothers to feel connected to your life.

CLASSROOM ACTIVITIES

- For one week, keep a diary, noting every instance you communicate with your mother. This will be across all channels, not limited to: calling, texting, video chatting, "liking" or "commenting" on social media. Also add in a few words on how you felt after each interaction (ex: happy, close to her, annoyed …). After one week, make a chart of how often you communicated, what topics you discussed, and what channels you used most often. Consider what this tells you about your relationship with your mother and mother-daughter relationships in general.
- Write down one technology you would like for your mom to learn. This may be a new feature of an app she already uses or an entirely new system. Think of two good reasons why you would like for her to learn to use it. Brainstorm ways to ask her to adopt this technological feature or method, then give it a whirl: ask your mom to communicate with you in a brand new way. Explore the benefits and detractions to using a new method. Is it better to use a well-known tool with a lower quality or to use a tool that is challenging to adopt, but offers the potential for a qualitatively rich interaction?

REFERENCES

Arnett, J. J. (2005). The developmental context of substance use in emerging adulthood. *Journal of Drug Issues, 35*(2), 235–254. doi: 10.1177/002204260503500202

Balsam, R. H., & Fischer, R. S. (2006). *Mothers and daughters II.* New York, NY: Routledge.

Bearak, J. M. (2014). Casual contraception in casual sex: Life-cycle change in undergraduates' sexual behavior in hookups. *Social Forces, 93*(2), 483–513. doi: 10.1093/sf/sou091

Boneva, B., Kraut, R., & Frohlich, D. (2001). Using e-mail for personal relationships: The difference gender makes. *American Behavioral Scientist, 45*(3), 530–549. doi: 10.1177/00027640121957204

Bowlby, J. (1988). *A secure base: Parent-child attachment and healthy human development.* New York, NY: Basic Books.

Cameron, J. J., & Ross, M. (2007). In times of uncertainty: Predicting the survival of long-distance relationships. *Journal of Social Psychology, 147*(6), 581–606. doi: 10.3200/SOCP.147.6.581-606

David-Barrett, T., Kertesz, J., Rotkirch, A., Ghosh, A., Bhattacharya, K., Monsivais, D., & Kaski, K. (2016). Communication with family and friends across the life course. *PLoS One, 11*(11), 1–15. doi: 10.1371/journal.pone.0165687

Fischer, L. R. (1981). Transitions in the mother-daughter relationship. *Journal of Marriage and Family, 43*(3), 613–622. doi: 10.2307/351762.

Fisher, C., & Miller-Day, M. (2006). Communicating over the life span: The mother-adult daughter relationship. In K. Floyd & M. Mormon (Eds.), *Widening the family circle: New research on family communication* (pp. 3–19). Thousand Oaks, CA: Sage Publications.

Furman, W., & Buhrmester, D. (1992). Age and sex differences in perceptions of networks of personal relationships. *Child Development, 63*(1), 103–115. doi: 10.2307/1130905

Hetherington, E. M., & Stanley-Hagan, M. M. (1995). Parenting in divorced and remarried families. In M. Bornstein (Ed.), *Handbook of parenting: Status and social conditions of parenting,* vol. 3 (pp. 233–254). Hillsdale, NJ: Lawrence Erlbaum.

Kennedy-Lightsey, C. D., Martin, M. M., Thompson, M., Himes, K. L., & Clingerman, B. Z. (2012). Communication privacy management theory: Exploring coordination and ownership between friends. *Communication Quarterly, 60*(5), 665–680. doi: 10.1080/01463373.2012.725004

Kolozsvari, O. (2015). "Physically we are apart, mentally we are not." Creating a shared space and sense of belonging in long-distance relationships. *Qualitative Sociology Review, 11*(4), 102–113.

Lenhart, A. (2015). Teens, social media & technology overview 2015 [Online article]. Retrieved from http://www.pewinternet.org/2015/04/09/teens-social-media-technology-2015/

Lindell, A. K., & Campione-Barr, N. (2017). Continuity and change in the family system across the transition from adolescence to emerging adulthood. *Marriage & Family Review, 53*(4), 388–416. doi: 10.1080/01494929.2016.1184212

Miller-Day, M. (2002). Parent-adolescent communication about alcohol, tobacco, and other drug use. *Journal of Adolescent Research, 17*(6), 604–613. doi: 10.1177/074355802237466

Miller-Day, M. (2004). *Communication among grandmothers, mothers, and adult daughters: A qualitative study of maternal relationships.* Mahwah, NJ: Lawrence Erlbaum.

Miller-Ott, A. E., Kelly, L., & Duran, R. L. (2014). Cell phone usage expectations, closeness, and relationship satisfaction between parents and their emerging adults in college. *Emerging Adulthood, 2*(4), 313–323. doi: 10.1177/2167696814550195

Morton, L. C., & Markey, P. M. (2009). Goal agreement and relationship quality among college students and their parents. *Personality and Individual Differences, 47*(8), 912–916. doi: 10.1016/j.paid.2009.07.015

Petronio, S. (2002). *Boundaries of privacy: Dialectics of disclosure.* Albany, NY: State University of New York Press.

Petronio, S., Helft, P. R., Child, J. (2013). A case of error disclosure: A communication privacy management analysis. *Journal of Public Health Research, 2*(3), 175–181. doi: 10.4081/jphr.2013.e30

Reid, A. E., & Carey, K. B. (2015). Interventions to reduce college student drinking: State of the evidence for mechanisms of behavior change. *Clinical Psychology Review, 40*, 213–224. doi: 10.1016/j.cpr.2015.06.006

Stafford, L., & Reske, J. R. (1990). Idealization and communication in long-distance premarital relationships. *Family Relations, 39*(3), 274–279. doi: 10.2307/584871

Stahlstein, E. M. (2004). Relating at a distance: Negotiating being together and being apart in long-distance relationships. *Journal of Social and Personal Relationships, 21*(5), 689–710. doi: 10.1177/0265407504046115

Swanson, J. A., & Walker, E. (2015). Academic versus non-academic emerging adult college student technology use. *Technology, Knowledge and Learning, 20*(2), 147–158. doi: 10.1007/s10758-015-9258-4

van den Broeck, E., Poels, K., & Walrave, M. (2015). Older and wiser? Facebook use, privacy concern, and private protection in the life stages of emerging, young, and middle adulthood. *Social Media and Society, 1*(2), 1–11. doi: 10.1177/2056305115616149

CHAPTER ELEVEN

"We Talk Like Friends"

Openness and Closedness in the Mother/Married Daughter Relationship

AIMEE E. MILLER-OTT[*]

Mothers and daughters tend to report higher closeness than the other family dyads (e.g., Fisher & Miller-Day, 2006). However, their closeness typically changes over time. Daughters often report feeling more distant from mothers during their adolescence, often because they are trying to establish their independence (Parker, Ludtke, Trautwein, & Roberts, 2012). Likewise, during emerging adulthood (the time that most traditional colleges students are experiencing right now), children also struggle with wanting to be more independent from their parents (Arnett, 2000). As I look back to my relationship with my own mother, my closeness with her definitely decreased during my adolescence. I thought I knew everything, and when she disagreed with me, I (as she likes to remind me as I now raise my own young daughter) would storm up the stairs, stomping into my bedroom, slamming the door behind me. After high school, as I went away to college, I gained a new sense of independence from but also closeness to my mom. I was on my own (the independence) but also liked keeping in touch and sharing with her stories about school and asking for her support and help when I needed it (the closeness).

Mothers and daughters experience changes in their closeness during significant life events (Petronio, 2002), for instance when moving away for the first time, when having a baby, and when getting married. I was married seven years ago and the closeness between my mom and me has definitely changed during that time.

---

[*] Aimee E. Miller-Ott, associate professor, Illinois State University, aeott@ilstu.edu.

The biggest change in our closeness has been how much I tell my mom about my life. As some of you reading this may relate, I was once an open book, but now I am very selective in what I tell her about my marriage, my husband, and my kids for many reasons (I will get to those later!). In this chapter, I chose to focus on the life event of marriage and the impact of daughters' marriage on openness in the mother-daughter relationship.

MOTHER-DAUGHTER CLOSENESS

In my study with another family communication scholar (Harrigan & Miller-Ott, 2013), we looked at the relationship between college daughters and their mothers. In this study, we found that daughters tend to feel closer to mothers and begin to see their mothers as a friend as they transition to college, especially when mothers do things that a friend might do, like supporting them in times of need. Daughters in college also tend to feel distance when mothers express negative emotions, reveal what daughters consider to be inappropriate information (like problems they are having with their husbands/the daughters' fathers) and when mothers enact too much control. It appears that as daughters age, they experience a tension between having a friendship and a parent-child relationship with mothers. When mothers try to cross into the "friend zone" with daughters, and share information daughters feel is inappropriate or too friend-like, daughters report more distance. This finding brings up an important question of whether friendships with mothers are different from friendships with peers. Bradbury and Karney (2010) argue that friendships differ from other intimate relationships because they are voluntary and reciprocal, and friends share equal status. We concluded in our study that the "girlfriend" relationship that daughters want with mothers is opposite to the "mother-as-parent" relationship they also want, and that daughters expect mothers to take on both roles. They want to be friends as long as "mothers remain emotionally contained and behaviorally appropriate" (Harrigan & Miller-Ott, 2013, p. 127). So are mother-daughter friendships voluntary? The switch from parent-child to friend may be voluntary, but are these relationships reciprocal if daughters have limits of what mothers can share but not what they share with mothers? Finally, are they equal if daughters still want mothers to take on the "mother" role while also being a friend? If mothers and daughters don't technically have a friendship (as it is defined), then what do we call the relationship that transcends the traditional parent-child one?

Physical distance also impacts closeness and openness in the mother-daughter relationship. However, the exact influence that distance has on the relationship varies. Harrigan and Miller-Ott (2013) found that daughters feel more relational distance when physically separated from their mothers. But other scholars (e.g., Schwarz, Trommsdorff, Albert, & Mayer, 2005) have found that mothers and daughters feel more supported by one another the further apart they live. In another of my studies on mothers and daughters (see chapter 12, this volume), we found that mothers and daughters rely on technology to "bridge the distance" when physical space separates them—technology allows them to share, talk, and connect more. However, daughters become frustrated when mothers contact them too much, expect immediate responses, and/or pry into their lives.

This research indicates that aging daughters like to connect with their mothers as friends. They appreciate a relationship that allows for openness and equal treatment but clearly have expectations for how much contact, connection, guidance, and openness is appropriate. As daughters age, they tend to feel closer to mothers, but significant life events can impact their closeness and also how open they are with each other.

CHANGES IN MOTHER-DAUGHTER RELATIONSHIPS AFTER MARRIAGE

Married couples often belong to three families simultaneously: the family they create together and the two families in which they were raised (often referred to as someone's "family of origin") (Bryant, Conger, & Meehan, 2001). Married children's families-of-origin can affect their marriage, and mothers are particularly influential in daughters' marriages (Bryant et al., 2001). This is likely because daughters tend to maintain close ties with their mothers after marriage (Prentice, 2009).

People's social networks also play important roles in their romantic relationships (Jin & Oh, 2010). Many studies of parents' and friends' support of romantic relationships do not separate mother-daughter relationships from other parent-child dyads although women more often participate in these studies than men do (e.g., Mikucki-Enyart, 2011; Prentice, 2009). Overall the research shows that if your social network supports and approves of your romantic relationship, then you are more likely to have higher relationship satisfaction, relational quality, and commitment, and are more likely to stay together than people whose networks do not approve (e.g. Felmlee, 2001; Felmlee, Sprecher, & Bassin, 1990; Sprecher & Felmlee, 1992). Sprecher and Felmlee (1992) found that men perceived more approval by their families of their romantic relationships than women did. Leslie, Huston, and Johnson (1986) found that daughters were slightly more likely to try to persuade their mothers to like their dating partners than sons were; however, daughters were also less likely to gain approval of their dating partners from mothers. A study looking specifically at the uncertainty that parents-in-law feel about their child's new husband or wife uncovered that parents are uncertain about the husband or wife as a person, spouse, and future parent, and often worry that the new husband or wife will interfere with the relationship they have with their child (Mikucki-Enyart, 2011). On the other hand, children-in-law (that is, the husbands or wives of the parents' children) are concerned with the parents-in-law meddling and providing unsolicited advice (Mikucki-Enyart, Caughlin, & Rittenour, 2015). Mikucki-Enyart and colleagues did not find sex differences in experiences of uncertainty concerning parents-in-law.

Openness between parents and children can shift throughout the lifespan (e.g., Plander, 2013). Scholars have acknowledged that parent-child openness changes after marriage. In her study of relational dialectics in in-law relationships, Prentice (2009) argued that married children experience a "knot of contradiction" related to issues of loyalty, closeness, and openness. Married children experience tension pertaining to how much they and their spouses can be a separate entity and to what extent they need to include each other's family of origin. Additionally, she found that within the tension of revelation/concealment, couples feel expected to share details of their married life with their families but desire to keep some of their lives private. In her study of same-sex couples, Lannutti (2013) found that marriage leads to some couples becoming more direct and open when communicating with family members and social networks. Spouses also begin maintaining privacy about details of their relationship but also acknowledge that marriage means sacrificing some control of their private marital information.

THE STUDY

What Was I Interested in Learning?

My interest in openness in mother-daughter relationships led me to conduct a study to examine if and how openness between mothers and daughters change after daughters get married. I didn't know what I would find, but since daughters have their own relationships with mothers but also add a third-party (the spouse) to the family, I suspected that their openness and decisions about sharing would change and perhaps even become more complicated. The theory that I used to investigate this topic was Communication Privacy Management Theory (Petronio, 2002). I thought this theory would be most helpful in the study because the main idea is that people feel the right to own their private information (in this context, daughters may think that they have the right to share or not share personal information with mothers). When someone chooses to share private information with another person (referred to in this theory as a "boundary insider"), a collective boundary forms between the discloser and insider. Together, both people develop and enact rules/expectations for how to manage the shared information (for instance, is the insider expected to keep the information to him/herself or can he/she share the information with others?). If the process goes smoothly and both parties manage information as intended/agreed up, then successful boundary coordination has occurred. If they don't, for instance, if the boundary insider shares the information on social media or tells his/her best friend, boundary turbulence has occurred. We often create rules about privacy management based on different criteria, including our sex, cultural background, the context/relationship, our motivations for disclosing, and our perceptions of how risky and/or beneficial sharing may be.

Based on the main ideas of this theory and the literature I consulted before the study, I created the following questions to guide my research:

RQ1: *What changes, if any, do daughters perceive in their openness with mothers after they get married?*

RQ2: *What factors influence daughters' decisions about openness with mothers after marriage?*

RQ3: *How likely are married daughters to discuss certain topics (i.e., money, sex, family planning, relationship with spouse, their day-to-day experiences, spouse's family, and health) with mothers?*

RQ4: *Is married daughters' reported closeness and satisfaction with mothers and spouses related to their likelihood to disclose the topics to mothers?*

RQ5: *What factors predict whether daughters disclose to mothers about certain topics (money, sex, family planning, relationship with spouse, their day, spouse's family, and health)?*

How Did I Go about Learning This Information?

To answer these questions, I conducted interviews with married daughters and also had married daughters complete online surveys. This study received approval from the university IRB committee. Each participant read an informed consent document and agreed to participate before starting the interview or survey. To locate participants, I posted announcements about the interviews and survey on an online research pool website at my university and on social media. Participants had to be female, 18 to 35, married for ten years or fewer, and have a living mother with whom they communicated regularly.

First, I, along with one of my graduate students, conducted interviews with 11 married daughters.. The eleven daughters who participated in the interviews were between 21 to 34 years old, with the average age of 28. They were all married to men. They had been married between two months and eight years (average length of marriage was four years). Seven did not have any children, and the other four had at least one child. Their mothers' ages ranged from 42 to 65 (average age was 55.5). Nine mothers were married to participants' fathers, and two mothers were remarried.

The purpose of the interviews was to figure out how open the daughters were with mothers regarding specific issues related to marriage and what factors influenced their decisions to talk about certain information with mothers. We asked daughters questions about the nature of the relationship with mothers (for instance, "How would you characterize the relationship you have with your mom?" and "How often do you talk to your mom?") and the content of communication with mothers (for instance, "What do you and your mom talk about, and why are these things you discuss?" and "Are there any topics that are off limits between you two and if so, why are they off limits? Has that changed since getting married?"). The interviews gave me some ideas about the topics daughters tended to talk about and avoid with mothers and why they chose to share some information and not others.

From the interviews, I developed a survey to figure out what factors influence daughters' openness about specific topics and whether how close and satisfied they felt in their mother-daughter relationship affected sharing certain information with mothers after marriage.

One hundred twenty-one married daughters completed the online survey. Their ages ranged from 18 to 35 (average age was 27). One hundred and six daughters were married to men, 13 to women, and two did not indicate the sex of their spouse. They had been married, on average, 47.5 months, ranging from 1 to 144 months. Most (72) did not have children, 44 had at least one child, and five did not indicate if they had children. Most mothers (96) were currently married, 12 were divorced, 5 were single, 3 were widowed, 2 were engaged, 1 was involved with someone but not married, and 2 daughters did not report this information.

In the online survey, they first answered some demographic questions like their age, sexual orientation, and length of the marriage. They then responded to questions about specific topics (money, sex, family planning, day-to-day experiences, relationship with spouse, spouse's family, and daughter's health issues) that daughters talked about discussing and/or avoiding with mothers in the interviews.

Also based on the interview data, I created six semantic-differential-type items (for instance, "The information I share is part of me/not part of me" and "I am not at all likely to share/I am very likely to share") and ten 5-point Likert-type items (for instance, "I ask my mom for advice/feedback about this topic," My partner would be/is upset that I share this information with my mother," "I expect that my mother will share my information with others") to measure factors that might influence daughters' openness with mothers about these topics. Participants responded to the same items for each topic. See Table 11.1 for the averages and standard deviations for each item/topic and the appendix for a list of the items.

To measure daughters' relationship satisfaction with their spouses and with their mothers, I used a version of the Marital Opinion Questionnaire (Huston, McHale, & Crouter, 1986). The 7-item, 5-point semantic differential scale consisted of bi-polar adjectives such as "unhappy-happy," "content-not content," and

Table 11.1. Descriptive Statistics for Predictors of Married Daughters' Openness with Mothers.

Items*	Topic M (SD)						
	Money	Sex	Family Planning	Daughter's Day-to-Day Experiences	Daughter's Marriage	Spouse's Family	Daughter's Health
1	3.51 (1.25)	1.92 (1.17)	3.63 (1.12)	4.35 (1.01)	3.41 (1.23)	3.93 (1.04)	4.20 (.90)
2	3.40 (.84)	3.33 (.85)	3.60 (.85)	3.57 (.82)	3.48 (.84)	2.93 (.93)	3.11 (.83)
3	3.55 (1.01)	3.63 (1.11)	4.01 (.95)	3.76 (1.11)	3.99 (.93)	3.10 (1.15)	3.93 (1.06)
4	3.47 (1.03)	3.21 (1.12)	3.96 (.93)	3.49 (.99)	3.71 (.94)	3.40 (.83)	3.90 (.91)
5	3.21 (1.12)	3.16 (1.06)	3.83 (1.00)	3.59 (1.05)	3.79 (1.03)	2.85 (1.07)	3.63 (1.10)
6	3.43 (1.15)	1.77 (1.05)	3.48 (1.32)	4.38 (.98)	3.28 (1.14)	3.95 (1.12)	3.87 (1.10)
7	3.17 (1.09)	3.91 (1.15)	3.78 (1.16)	3.88 (1.06)	3.83 (1.09)	3.29 (1.14)	4.16 (1.05)
8	4.24 (.84)	4.33 (.91)	4.36 (.88)	3.13 (1.17)	4.27 (.85)	3.87 (1.06)	3.44 (1.20)
9	1.83 (1.07)	1.36 (.78)	2.17 (1.19)	3.23 (1.21)	1.90 (1.14)	1.98 (1.04)	2.10 (1.12)
10	3.35 (1.24)	1.79 (1.11)	3.35 (1.26)	3.57 (1.11)	3.24 (1.31)	3.26 (1.28)	3.64 (1.10)
11	3.13 (1.15)	1.88 (1.20)	3.24 (1.34)	3.50 (1.13)	3.18 (1.23)	3.07 (1.25)	3.60 (1.08)
12	2.10 (1.22)	2.95 (1.45)	2.38 (1.29)	3.10 (1.14)	2.10 (1.14)	2.13 (1.17)	2.30 (1.22)
13	3.21 (1.16)	3.73 (1.22)	3.21 (1.29)	3.15 (1.30)	3.34 (1.25)	3.35 (1.26)	3.29 (1.24)
14	2.61 (1.10)	3.73 (1.22)	2.49 (1.04)	2.03 (1.13)	3.16 (1.03)	3.10 (1.11)	2.01 (.94)
15	2.69 (1.20)	1.74 (1.06)	3.12 (1.34)	4.07 (.86)	3.21 (1.21)	3.23 (1.17)	3.63 (1.05)
16	3.60 (1.06)	2.40 (1.24)	3.42 (1.18)	3.81 (.83)	3.39 (1.14)	3.48 (1.05)	3.73 (1.00)

*See Appendix for numbered list of items.
Source: Author.

"rewarding-disappointing" and included an assessment of global satisfaction. A higher score indicated greater relationship satisfaction. The average satisfaction with spouse was 4.36 (SD = .74), α = .95. The average satisfaction with mothers was 4.04 (SD = .87), α = .95.

To measure daughters' closeness with their spouses and with their mothers, I used the Parent-Child Closeness Scale (Buchanan, Maccoby, & Dornbusch, 1991). I reworded items to reflect the specific relationship. The scale consists of 10 items (e.g., "How close do you feel to your spouse/mother?" "How often does your spouse/mother express affection or liking for you?"). Response options range from 1 (not at all) to 5 (very). Alpha reliabilities were .95 for spouses and .91 for mothers. The average closeness with a spouse was 4.33 (SD = .83). The average closeness with mothers was 3.98 (SD = .86).

What Did I Learn?

Daughters reported in interviews that the most significant change in openness after marriage was that their mothers became their friends. As Becky (*note: I changed all names to pseudonyms*) recalled:

> When I was just out of high school, and college, engaged, it was weird 'cause that's when I was living with her, and that's when I felt the most distant from her. But when I moved out after I got married, I felt a lot closer to her, and I started actually enjoying her as a person and more of a friendship level value.

Jennifer said that "I learned that she's more of a friend, you know, we're at that stage now where we talk like friends, versus she's just my mom, you know" (8, 93–94). Along with this friendship, according to many daughters, came the ability to, as Nicole explained, "talk to her about anything."

Although the mother-daughter relationship may transition into more of a friendship after marriage, daughters explained that their spouse became their confidant, which influences openness with mothers. As Julie said:

> With the transition of me being married… it never led to more actual distance or us not talking. It was just more conflict. It was just her adjusting to not being the number one person in my life anymore.

Halle shared a similar idea: "A lot of time I would talk to her about, I think I was seeking emotional support from her, and I don't really do that anymore 'cuz I get that from my husband." As Molly explained:

> Both of my parents I count as some of my best friends, so I called them, or talked to them, or saw them frequently to ask, you know, advice and to tell them about my day or what I was learning [when she was in high school and college]. Then once I met my partner and as

we started, you know, creating our family, then it changed. So, more of that talking I would do with him instead of my parents, and so I would still say that I am close with my mom, but I would say that the relationship maybe necessarily changed.

Daughters also shared three common factors that influence their decisions about being open with their mothers: mothers' anticipated reactions, whether mothers have experience with the topic, and how openness may impact mothers' perceptions of the spouses.

Anticipated Reactions of Mothers

First, daughters are very concerned with mothers' reactions to the shared information. Daughters consider whether the information will hurt or put stress on mothers. As Jennifer explained about sharing family planning with her mother:

The whole baby planning thing I think is also private, only a couple of my close friends know about it, but I don't think I want to let my parents get too excited. I just want to keep it a surprise for when it does happen. So that's why I didn't tell her that. And again, if I know it's something that she's gonna get stressed out about I don't try to talk about it.

Natalie also explained that "I don't feel I can talk to my mom about not wanting to be a stay at home mom. I don't think that she's able to have that conversation without taking it as a personal threat to her."

In addition to hurting mothers' feelings, daughters also consider whether mothers will offer helpful or unhelpful advice/feedback. As Nicole explained, "I think it's just about like whether I want to hear her feedback on it or not. And most of the time I know that her feedback isn't going to be that helpful." Mothers' unsolicited advice was another concern for most daughters. As Molly stated:

So talking to her about, um some of the decisions we made. We co-sleep with our daughter and my mom, I remember her telling me this, probably uh six months ago anyway of, that I surprised her as a mom that she said something like, "I knew you would be a good mom, but some of your decisions, I just thought you would never make." And I said, "Like what?" and she said, "Like co-sleeping. I just can't believe you would do that. That just doesn't seem like something you'd be interested in." and then she had also said something about like, "I knew you would love your daughter, but I just didn't know you would love her this much."

Nicole also recalled:

My mom kind of expects marriages to be that way 'cause that's how they work in our family, so sometimes I'll be like, "Me and Ryan were arguing about doing this," and she'll be like, "Why don't you just tell him that's the way it's going to be?" And I'm like, "Because that's like not how we work."

Christina also explained:

> Sometimes I'll probably vent to her about that [money issues with husband], and sometimes I get frustrated that I told her because then she'll bring it up or be like, "you really need to have your own bank account." And then it's like, ugh I wish I wouldn't even have told her about that incident because then it wouldn't be an issue right now.

Mothers' Experiences

Daughters are more likely to share if mothers have had common experiences. Shared experiences seem to center on work and marriage. Christina and her mother work in the same field. She shared:

> So I generally like—if I have like a work concern or if I want somebody's opinion on something she would be the person I would turn to because you know my husband doesn't really understand the field as well. So, she'd probably be the one and only person I would turn to with like work-related, professional advice.

However, it appears that if Christina's husband did have similar work experiences, she might have relied on her husband instead.

Daughters are more likely to talk to mothers about their marriage if they believe mothers can relate. Samantha recalled being open with her mother about a relational problem that her mother had also experienced. She explained:

> My husband has had issues with drinking in the past, and it got horrible right after we got married. And, you know, my parents had just spent a bunch of money on our wedding. I was really hesitant to talk to my mom about it, but she's like, "Whatever, we had a party for relatives, like if you ever need to get out, not that I'm telling you to get out of it, but like, I don't know what to tell you to do, I don't know what it's like, but I've been married to an alcoholic for 30, or whatever, so if you need out, get out now, better now than later."

As Molly also indicated:

> Having been through that or some sort of relationship and whether it's having advice or just being a sounding board and being able to offer some of that validation. I think can be really important, especially if you get married and feel like you're kind of alone in that. I think sometimes if you don't have your partner to talk to, you're mad at your partner then it can be very lonely if you don't have anyone else to talk to.

Impact of Disclosure on Mothers' Perceptions of Spouses

Lastly, daughters expressed concern that sharing information about their marriage and/or spouse might affect mothers' perceptions of the spouse. The daughters tend to censor information that will make mothers judge or look poorly on their spouses. As Nicole said:

I mean like I—I don't talk to her about like relationship problems with Ryan like I already said 'cause I try and handle that with—between me and him. Because when you get like your family involved I think like that—I don't want to change her perception of him if it's something I know I'm going to get over. Like little things like that are okay, but I think if it's like a big issue I would advise against it because like I said if it's something you know you're eventually going to get over and forgive like if you take it to your parents or especially even your mom she might not forgive and forget. She might hold a grudge and then look at your partner differently.

Likewise, as Molly explained:

I am very protective of Bob. He's more effeminate than my family. When he came into the family, he didn't drink, and he wrote poetry. I'm the one fixing cars and toilets and you know, but I'm also trying a little to cook and bake a pie or something, so it's, we've got a different kind of relationship than what my mom expected for me I think, or even I expected for me, and so I try to protect him by kind of censoring out some of that information.

These factors highlight the interconnected nature of the mother-daughter relationship and the marriage. It appears that daughters experience a push and pull between their friendship with and concerns for mothers and loyalties to and friendships with their spouses. They want to be open and maintain a close bond with mothers but also see spouses as confidants and seriously consider how any information they share can negatively impact mothers' perceptions of the spouse.

Through the online surveys, I found that daughters overall were most likely to talk to mothers about their day-to-day experiences, followed by their health, their spouse's family, family planning, money, and their relationship with their spouses. Daughters were not very likely to talk about sex with mothers.

Daughters who reported high closeness with mothers were more likely to talk about money, their day-to-day experiences, their relationships with spouses, family planning, their health, and their spouses' families. Closeness did not influence how likely they were to talk about sex.

Daughters who reported being relationally satisfied with mothers were more likely to talk about money, their relationships with spouses, their day-to-day activities, family planning, their health, and sex. How satisfied they were did not influence how likely they were to talk about their spouses' families.

Daughters who reported closeness to spouses were more likely to talk to their mothers about family planning, day-to-day experiences, and the spouse's family, but daughters who had more closeness with spouses were less likely to speak to mothers about sex. Closeness with spouses did not influence how likely they were to talk to mothers about money, their relationships with spouses, and their health.

Daughters who reported being relationally satisfied with spouses were more likely to talk to mothers about their day-to-day experiences, family planning, and their spouses' family. Their satisfaction with their spouse did not influence how likely they were to talk to mothers about money, sex, relationship with spouse, or their health.

I also discovered many factors that predicted how likely the daughters were to talk about each topic with mothers. Daughters were more likely to talk about money with mothers if they want advice, appreciate their mother's feedback, and see money as part of their identity. Daughters were less like to talk about money with mothers if they believe mothers might share their information with other people. Daughters were more likely to talk to mothers about sex if they want advice, see this information as part of themselves, and if their mothers also share this type of information with them; they were less likely to talk about sex if they think the mothers will share this information with others and if spouses will be upset if daughters talk to mothers about sex. Daughters were more likely to talk to mothers about family planning if they want advice, see family planning as part of themselves, if mothers initiate conversations about family planning, and if the information they have to share is positive. Daughters are less likely to talk about family planning with mothers if their spouses will be upset with them for doing so. Daughters were more likely to talk to mothers about day-to-day experiences if the information is a part of them, if mothers reciprocate the same type of information, and if daughters want advice. Daughters are less likely to share their day-to-day experiences if their spouses would be upset with them for sharing. Daughters were more likely to talk to mothers about their relationships if they want advice and if the information is part of their identities but are less likely to talk about their relationships if spouses will be upset with them for sharing. (As you can tell by now, it seems that whether spouses would be upset with wives for sharing plays a significant role in deciding what to share with moms!) Daughters were more likely to talk to mothers about their spouses' families if they appreciate the feedback mothers give about the topic, if the information is significant, and if mothers reciprocate similar information. Daughters were more likely to talk to mothers about health if they want advice and see the information as part of their identities but were less likely to talk to mothers about health if they think mothers will share this information with others.

WHAT DOES ALL THIS MEAN?

In support of other research (e.g., Harrigan & Miller-Ott, 2013), daughters who participated in interviews tended to describe their adult relationship with mothers as friendships and consider themselves to be open when communicating with moms. However, the interviews and surveys revealed more complexity when it comes to their openness. There are topics that daughters do not want to share with mothers, and many factors impact daughters' approaches toward openness and their likelihood to share certain information with mothers. The finding that daughters were more likely to talk about almost all of the topics if they were more satisfied with and closer to mothers reflects that often, closeness equals openness.

Also emerging from this study is that the mother/daughter/son-in-law relationships are quite interconnected. Spouses play a significant role in changes in openness after marriage, in that spouses often replace mothers as confidants. Daughters expressed concern that sharing certain information may influence mothers' perceptions of their spouses. They also worry that spouses will be upset with them if they share certain information with their moms. Despite the large role that spouses play, daughters still rely on mothers. They continue to see mothers as part of their support network and are more likely to share information with mothers if they need support and believe mothers' advice will be helpful. In fact, daughters are more likely to talk to mothers about all the topics in the study if they want and/or appreciate advice from moms. They also seek support from mothers about their relationship if they think mothers have similar experiences. Previous research indicates that support from mothers can help daughters cope with stressors related to life transitions (e.g., Ge, Conger, Lorenz, & Simons, 1994). The data here seem to suggest that mothers' support during daughters' marriage must be helpful, solicited, not encroaching on the marriage, coming from mothers' experiences, and not critical of the spouse, to be positive and impactful. If the support deviates in any way from these characteristics, or if the mothers provide unsolicited advice, daughters will often respond by limiting their openness, similar to unmarried college daughters who increase distance when mothers enact controlling behaviors (Harrigan & Miller-Ott, 2013).

However, while there are expectations for the ways mothers should support daughters, there seems to be fewer restrictions on the content of what daughters and mothers can share in this married sample of women, contrary to the Harrigan and Miller-Ott's (2013) study of college women who were not accepting of mothers sharing anything too personal or risky. Daughters are more likely to talk to mothers about their day-to-day activities, sex, and their spouse's family if mothers reciprocate the same type of information. As a relational maintenance strategy, it makes sense that daughters would engage in joint-sharing about their daily lives; however, it is surprising that they also talk about sex and in-laws and their mothers do the same. Harrigan and Miller-Ott (2013) found that daughters felt distance when mothers revealed what they considered to be too intimate of information, including sex. Our sample in the 2013 study was comprised of unmarried college-aged women. It may be that older daughters who are also married may experience an increase in acceptable topics of conversation. Their friendships may become reciprocal and egalitarian, thus fitting into the definition of friendship shared earlier (Bradbury & Karney, 2010).

Two factors influence the likelihood of sharing the most. First, daughters are less likely to talk about sex, money, and health if they think mothers will share the information with other people. Second, daughters are less likely to talk about sex, family planning, day-to-day experiences, and their relationship with spouses if doing so will upset the spouses. These two factors tie into the CPM concepts of boundary coordination (i.e., managing the collectively held privacy boundaries once someone shares private information with a boundary insider) and turbulence (i.e., obstacles to maintaining collective boundaries) and highlights the intricacies of appropriate disclosure when taking into consideration the spouse. As Bryant et al. (2001) argued, married couples belong to their own marital family but also to their families of origin. Both factors seem to reflect violations of two sets of intersecting boundaries, that of mother-daughter and daughter-spouse. Daughters' experiences reflect the challenge in maintaining a relationship and being open with mothers while also trying to honor the privacy expectations in the marriage and possible face loss when revealing something to mothers that makes a spouse look bad. Mothers who share daughters' information with others violate daughters' expectations that their information will remain private. Also, wives and their spouses have a set of privacy boundaries that daughters may violate if choosing to share something with mothers that spouses wish to remain private.

Further reflecting boundary issues, daughters' likelihood to talk about certain topics also seems to decrease when they consider the information jointly owned by themselves and their spouses. Daughters in the study were most likely to talk about their *own* day-to-day experiences and their *own* health. They were less likely to talk about their in-laws, money, family planning, and relationship with their spouses, and even less likely to talk about sex—all reflecting jointly-held private information. This again highlights the intricate web of openness in which daughters operate as they manage private information with their mothers and spouses that perhaps did not exist to this extent before marriage.

Previous research shows that the mother-daughter relationship is often characterized by a lot of openness in what they consider a friendship. But what happens when the daughter meets a spouse and gets married? How does that change openness and what factors influence those changes? At the beginning of this chapter, I explained that my own privacy boundaries with my mom changed after I got married. My own experiences support what I found through interviews and surveys. I often worry about what my mom will think of my husband if I share particular information with her, but my bigger concern is whether she will violate my privacy and tell other people what I tell her. Unfortunately, boundary turbulence has happened before, and so we have had to go back and revisit/rework our privacy expectations, and it seems to be an ongoing process of trial and error. Perhaps you can relate to this. I'm not sure that process ever stops, even as we get older. We don't want people to think poorly of our romantic partners, and we don't want our private information shared with other people. What I found in this study was that as we add more people to our lives, we develop expectations of privacy with them, so we have to figure out the best way to maintain these relationships and respect the privacy we have established with each person. What I also learned, and what I hope you take away from this, is when we say that "my mom is my friend," we should probably think more about what that means. Are we being fair to our moms by saying that we're best friends with them but then putting conditions on what we can talk or not talk about and what we expect from them? Do we have different, and perhaps even unfair, expectations of mothers as friends compared to women who are our same ages?

WHAT DO WE STILL NEED TO KNOW?

- How do mothers perceive their daughters' changes in openness after marriage?
- How might daughters' openness change with fathers after marriage?
- How might sons' openness change with mothers and fathers after marriage?
- How do daughters and their romantic partners talk about daughters' privacy management with mothers?
- What does the process of mother-daughter boundary negotiation after turbulence look like?

HOW DOES THIS WORK IN REAL LIFE?

- Talk about privacy boundaries with your mom, especially when it comes to what you feel comfortable or uncomfortable sharing with her. It is better to have that conversation now before boundary turbulence occurs and you then have to go back and talk about what went wrong.
- To avoid uncertainty and hurt feelings, be upfront with mothers about what you are going to share with her once you start your new romantic relationship.
- Respect the privacy expectations of your romantic partner. If there is something that you feel you need to talk to your mom about, assess whether the benefits are worth the risks of violating your partner's expectations.
- Think about how you maintain your friendship with your mom. Is it equal? Is it voluntary? Is it reciprocal? Are there ways to have your friendships fulfill these criteria, without having to share what you don't want to share with

her? Are there ways to feel close to her without having to violate privacy expectations of your romantic partner?

CLASSROOM ACTIVITIES

For your assignment, interview a friend who has a romantic partner and a mom. Below are some of the questions from my interviews. Use this interview guide (and feel free to add questions of your own!) to see how the responses you get compare to what I found. What topics do they share and not share? How has that changed over time? What does your friend share about her romantic relationship with her mom? Then bring your responses to class and share with your classmates. How do your interview responses compare to those of your classmates?

- First, how would you characterize the relationship you have with your mom?
- How often do you talk to your mom? What is the most common way that you talk to your mom? (for instance, face-to-face, texting, phone calls, video chatting)
- On a scale of 1–5, 5 being the closest and 1 being not close at all, how would you rate your current closeness with your mother? Has this changed over time?
- In general, what do you and your mom talk about? Why are these the things you discuss?
- Are there any topics that are off limits between you two? If so, why are they off limits?
- Has that changed since you started your romantic relationship? If so, how?
- How do you decide what to share with your mom and what to keep private from her?
- Has that changed since getting married? If so, how?
- Would you say that your mom knows a lot, a little, nothing, or an average amount about your romantic relationship? Are you happy that she knows that amount? Why/why not?
- What about her marriage or romantic relationship do you know? Are you happy that you know that amount? Why/why not?
- Did/does your mom ever ask you questions about your romantic relationship? If so, what types of questions does she ask? How do you typically respond to her questions?
- Can you think of a time when you told your mom something about your romantic relationship that she didn't handle like you wanted her to (for instance, she responded negatively or told other people what you told her)? If so, what information did she share, and how did you respond to her behavior?

APPENDIX

Semantic-Differential Items

1. How likely are you to share information about this?
   Not at all likely (1) – Very likely (5)
2. How positive or negative is the information you share or would share with your mother about this?
   Very negative (1) – Very positive (5)
3. How much of a part of you is the information you share/would share with your mother about this topic?
   Not part of me at all (1) – Completely part of me (5)
4. How significant is the information you share/would share with your mother about this topic?
   Completely insignificant (1) – Completely significant (5)
5. How much a part of your identity is the information you share/would share with your mother about this topic?
   Not at all essential to my identity (1) – Very essential to my identity (5)
6. How likely is it that your mother does/would share information about the same topic with you?
   Not at all likely (1) – Very likely (5)

Likert Items (Answer options ranged from 1 = Strongly disagree to 5 = Strongly agree)

7. I feel like I own this information myself.
8. I feel like my spouse and I both own this information.
9. I feel like my mother has the right to share this information with others.
10. I ask my mom for advice/feedback about this topic.
11. My mom offers advice/feedback on this topic without being asked.
12. I expect that my mother will share my information with others.
13. I tell my mom whether she can or cannot share with others.
14. My spouse would be/is upset that I share this information with my mother.
15. My mom initiates conversations/asks questions to me about this topic.
16. I appreciate the advice/feedback my mom gives me about this topic.

NOTE

1. The author would like to thank Danielle Shermulis for her assistance conducting interviews.

REFERENCES

Arnett, J. (2000). Emerging adulthood: A theory of development from the late teens through the twenties. *American Psychologist, 55*(5), 469–480. https://doi.org/10.1037//0003-066X.55.5.469

Bradbury, T. N., & Karney, B. R. (2010). *Intimate relationships.* New York, NY: W. W. Norton.

Bryant, C. M., Conger, R. D., & Meehan, J. M. (2001). The influence of in-laws on change in marital success. *Journal of Marriage and Family, 63*(3), 614–626. https://doi.org/10.1111/j.1741-3737.2001.00614.x

Buchanan, C. M., Maccoby, E. E., & Dornbusch, S. M. (1991). Caught between parents: Adolescents' experience in divorced homes. *Child Development, 62*(5), 1008–1029. https://doi.org/10.1111/j.1467-8624.1991.tb01586.x

Felmlee, D. (2001). No couple is an island: A social network perspective on dyadic stability. *Social Forces, 79*(4), 1259–1287. https://doi.org/10.1353/sof.2001.0039

Felmlee, D. H., Sprecher, S., & Bassin, E. (1990). The dissolution of intimate relationships: A hazard model. *Social Psychology Quarterly, 53*, 13–30. https://doi.org/10.2307/2786866

Fisher, C., & Miller-Day, M. (2006). Communication over the lifespan: The mother-adult daughter relationship. In K. Floyd & M. T. Morman (Eds.), *Widening the family circle: New research on family communication* (pp. 3–19). Thousand Oaks, CA: Sage.

Ge, X., Conger, R. D., Lorenz, F. O., & Simons, R. L. (1994). Parents' stressful life events and adolescent depressed mood. *Journal of Health and Social Behavior, 35*, 28–44. https://doi.org/10.2307/2137333

Harrigan, M. M., & Miller-Ott, A. E. (2013). The multivocality of meaning making: An exploration of the discourses college-aged daughters voice in talk about their mothers. *Journal of Family Communication, 13*(2), 1–18. https://doi.org/10.1080/15267431.2013.768249

Huston, T. L., McHale, S. M., & Crouter, A. C. (1986). When the honeymoon's over: Changes in the marriage relationship over the first year. In R. Gilmore & S. Duck (Eds.), *The emerging field of personal relationships* (pp. 109–132). Hillsdale, NJ: Lawrence Erlbaum.

Jin, B., & Oh, S. (2010). Cultural differences of social network influence on romantic relationships: A comparison of the United States and South Korea. *Communication Studies, 61*(2), 156–171. https://doi.org/10.1080/10510971003604042

Lannutti, P. J. (2013). Same-sex marriage and privacy management: Examining couples' communication with family members . *Journal of Family Communication, 13*, 60–75. https://doi.org/10.1080/15267431.2012.742088

Leslie, L. A., Huston, T. L., & Johnson, M. P. (1986). Parental reactions to dating relationships: Do they make a difference? *Journal of Marriage and Family, 48*, 57–66. https://doi.org/10.2307/352228

Mikucki-Enyart, S. L. (2011). Parent-in-law privacy management: An examination of the links among relational uncertainty, topic avoidance, in-group status, and in-law satisfaction. *Journal of Family Communication, 11*(4), 237–263. https://doi.org/10.1080/15267431.2010.544633

Mikucki-Enyart, S. L., Caughlin, J. P., & Rittenour, C. E. (2015). Content and relational implications of children-in-law's relational uncertainty within the in-law dyad during the transition to extended family. *Communication Quarterly, 63*(3), 286–309. https://doi.org/10.1080/01463373.2015.1039714

Parker, P. D., Ludtke, O., Trautwein, U., & Roberts, B. W. (2012). Personality and relationship quality during the transition from high school to early adulthood. *Journal of Personality, 80*(4), 1061–1089. https://doi.org/10.1111/j.1467-6494.2012.00766.x

Petronio, S. (2002). *Boundaries of privacy: Dialectics of disclosure.* New York, NY: State University of New York Press.

Plander, K. L. (2013). Checking accounts: Communication privacy management in familial financial caregiving. *Journal of Family Communication, 13*, 17–31. https://doi.org/10.1080/15267431.201 2.742090

Prentice, C. (2009). Relational dialectics among in-laws. *Journal of Family Communication, 9*(2), 67–89. https://doi.org/10.1080/15267430802561667

Schwarz, B., Trommsdorff, G., Albert, I., & Mayer, B. (2005). Adult parent-child relationships: Relationship quality, support, and reciprocity. *Applied Psychology: An International Review, 54*(3), 396–417. https://doi.org/10.1111/j.1464-0597.2005.00217.x

Sprecher, S., & Felmlee, D. (1992). The influence of parents and friends on the quality and stability of romantic relationships: A three-wave longitudinal investigation. *Journal of Marriage and Family, 54*(4), 888–900. https://doi.org/10.2307/353170

CHAPTER TWELVE

Connection OR Intrusion?

Mother-Daughter Communication Through Technology

AIMEE E. MILLER-OTT[*] AND LYNNE KELLY[†]

When we talk to our students about communication technology, we hear comments like "I call my mother every day," "My mother takes forever to respond to my texts," "I feel close to my mother because we text all the time," and "I wish my mother would stop commenting on my Facebook posts—it's embarrassing." The more our students talk, the clearer it becomes that they have a love-hate relationship with technology when using it with their mothers. One of us has an adult daughter, and it has been a challenge over the years figuring out what medium to use, when, about what, and how often. The technology has kept us close but has also caused conflicts. The other author's mother frequently texts her and will start sending "Are you alive? I haven't heard back from you" messages when texts go unanswered. On a few occasions, this mother has also posted on Facebook something said to her in confidence. No doubt you have also had positive and negative experiences with using technology to communicate with your mother. It is also likely that your experiences have changed over time and will continue to do so. Existing technologies will be modified and new ones created, and our mother-daughter relationships are also dynamic and change over time. Mediated communication may be the most common way you communicate with your mother now that you are in college. As you may have already discovered, how well you and she are able to use technology to stay connected affects the quality of your relationship.

[*] Aimee Miller-Ott, associate professor, Illinois State University, aeott@ilstu.edu.

[†] Lynne Kelly, professor, University of Hartford, kelly@hartford.edu.

Mothers and daughters tend to characterize their relationships as bonded, interdependent, and emotionally connected (Fischer, 1991) while simultaneously also highly conflictual (Penington, 2004), particularly during certain developmental periods (e.g., adolescence). Mothers and daughters often report ups-and-downs over time (Miller-Day, 2004; Penington, 2004). In a study exploring the tension between closeness and distance that mothers and college daughters experience through the lens of relational dialectics theory, Harrigan and Miller-Ott (2013) found that three discourses of closeness (i.e., friendship, parenthood, and independence), and three discourses of distance (i.e., containment, impropriety, and separation) characterized this relationship type. Daughters discussed wanting to be close but also feeling burdened by mothers who tried to limit their independence or became judgmental when they made poor choices. Likewise, daughters were happy to know their mothers on a personal level but also were uncomfortable when mothers disclosed what daughters considered inappropriate thoughts or behaviors.

Unfortunately, scholars know little about technology usage specific to mothers and daughters. Given that mothers and daughters are the closest family dyad (e.g., Fisher & Miller-Day, 2006) and that technology allows for connection even without shared physical space (e.g., Miller-Ott, Kelly, & Duran, 2014), it is important to understand how mothers and daughters use technology and issues they experience from its use. In this chapter, we discuss the limited relevant research on technology and parent-child relationships, and then present a study of daughters and mothers designed to understand the media they use and the perceived benefits and problems of technology in their relationship.

PARENT-CHILD COMMUNICATION AND TECHNOLOGY

Technology use and misuse is a topic discussed by parents and children at many times during their childhood. Most of the research on technology between parents and children does not explain differences between the various family dyads (i.e., mother/daughter, mother/son, father/daughter, father/son), but instead lumps all family relationships together. As you undoubtedly know, communication patterns can be quite different with mothers vs. fathers. Existing research has focused mainly on cell phone use by young children and college students (e.g., Miller-Ott et al., 2014). Young people, overall, report positive attitudes about cell phone communication with their parents (e.g., Chen & Katz, 2009). Parents report many reasons for using cell phones with children including ensuring their safety (Green, 2007), supervising and monitoring them (e.g., Devitt & Roker, 2009), and communicating love and support (e.g., Chen & Katz, 2009).

Young people report struggles with freedom and control related to cell phone usage with parents (Green, 2007; Ling & Yttri, 2002). The constant tie between parents and emerging adults via cell phones, referred to as a "type of umbilical cord between parent and child" (Ling, 2004, p. 100), can hinder their adult children's autonomy and social development. For instance, technology use can worsen "helicopter parenting" tendencies (Kelly, Duran, & Miller-Ott, 2017). On the one hand, new communication technologies create opportunities for intensified connection between parents and children, but this can also lead to parent-child boundary violations (Caughlin & Petronio, 2004). One author vividly remembers trying to call her teenaged daughter when she was out with friends, only to hear the call go to voicemail. This produced the dilemma of how long to wait for a return call, whether to call again, whether to send a text, or do nothing. From my daughter's point of view, she was simply with friends and didn't need to be monitored. The cell phone was supposed to enable more freedom precisely because it allowed more connection, but instead it sometimes created tension.

There is some research on other forms of parent-child technology usage, particularly Facebook. Forty-seven percent of parents are friends with their children on Facebook (Duggan, Lenhart, Lampe, & Ellison, 2015). Mothers are particularly heavy users of social media. Kanter, Afifi, and Robbins (2012) found that children who accepted Facebook friend requests from parents reported decreased conflict in their relationship. In fact, children who reported high conflict prior to the parent joining Facebook reported higher closeness after becoming Facebook friends. Whether becoming Facebook friends has this positive effect may depend, in part, on the nature of the family communication patterns established. Rudi, Walkner, and Dworkin (2015), in a study of adolescents, found that families with a conversation orientation pattern engage in more frequent use of texting and email than conformity-oriented families.

Technology highlights issues of children wanting to be connected to but also independent (i.e., autonomous) from their parents. Mothers and daughters often struggle with connection and autonomy issues over time, so it is important to explore how they use technology to maintain their relational ties while also experiencing struggles.

MOTHER-DAUGHTER TECHNOLOGY USAGE

Some research has separated the family dyads, giving us more indication of how children communicate with their mothers specifically. One study showed that children tend to have more cell phone contact with mothers than with fathers (Chen & Katz, 2009; Rudi et al., 2015). In another of our studies, we found college-aged children feel closer when communicating via cell phone more frequently with mothers as well as are more relationally satisfied when their cell phone usage with moms is satisfying (Miller-Ott et al., 2014). We also found that the more these young adults perceived that mothers should always be available to them via the cell phone and that there are no limits to what they can discuss via phone, the more they were satisfied with cell phone usage. These young adult children were also more relationally satisfied if they had rules that mothers should always be available to them via cell phone but that there are certain times of the day when they cannot call or text each other. Believing that they should always be available to each other via phone was linked to greater feelings of closeness to mothers.

It is clear from our discussion so far that existing research provides a starting point but is insufficient for giving a full understanding of mother-daughter use of the complete range of communication technologies. Since the research on these topics is limited, we set out to conduct a study to explore many aspects of mother-daughter communication via technology.

THE STUDY

What Were We Interested in Learning?

Because the existing research has not looked at all communication technologies, we were curious about which media mothers and daughters use and how often. For instance, do they use video chat such as Skype or Facetime? Beyond that, we wondered if daughters and mothers are satisfied with their use of communication technologies with each other. Finally, we wanted to know what they saw as the benefits and problems of communication technologies. Thus, we attempted to address these research questions:

> RQ1: *How often, if at all, do daughters/mothers use email, cell phone calls, texting/messaging, video chat, and social media to communicate with each other?*

> RQ2: *What problems do daughters/mothers perceive in their use of communication technology and what, if anything, do they do to try to alleviate those problems?*

> RQ3: *What benefits do daughters/mothers perceive in their use of communication technologies?*

> RQ4: *How satisfied are daughters and mothers with their usage of communication technology with one another?*

How Did We Go About Learning This Information?

We constructed two versions of a survey, one for daughters and one for mothers. We administered the anonymous survey online and recruited participants in several ways, including through an online research announcement board at one of our universities. Students who were enrolled in communication courses earned extra or course credit for completing the survey. We recruited mothers primarily through word-of-mouth and social media posts. This study received approval from the university IRB committee. Each participant read an informed consent document and agreed to participate before starting the survey.

The versions of the survey were identical except for wording referencing mothers or daughters. In addition to the demographic questions, we asked about communication technology use and had sections on email, cell phone calls, texting/ messaging, social media, video chat, and face-to-face communication. We asked how often they used each medium to communicate with their mother/daughter. We also asked about their satisfaction with communication technology use with their mother/daughter. Finally, using open-ended questions, we asked what participants considered the "biggest source of problems you have using technology to communicate with your daughter/mother," and if there is anything they or their daughter/mother do "to try to alleviate that problem." Finally, we asked what they considered "the biggest benefit of using technology to communicate with your daughter/mother."

Who responded to our survey? There were 408 daughters, ages 18–57, with an average age of 22.53, and whose mothers' average age was 52.43, ranging from 29–80. Most of the daughters were white (80.7%) and single (85.2%). Most of their mothers were married (74.6%), and about two-thirds of the daughters reported that they did not live with their mothers at the time of the survey. There were also 91 mothers, ages 40–75, with an average age of 59.09, whose daughters ranged in age from 8–50, with an average of 27.96. Nearly all mothers were white (96.7%), and most were married (73.6%). Nearly two-thirds of their daughters were single, and most of the mothers (86.8%) reported that they did not live with their daughters.

What Did We Learn?

Regarding communication technologies daughters and mothers use and how often they use them, texting is the most frequently used means of communication. Most of the daughters (89%) text with mothers several times a week to multiple times per day as do most (89.3%) of the mothers. The next most popular means of communication is phone calls. Most daughters (76.9%) have phone conversations with their mothers from several times a week to multiple times a day, as do most mothers (64%), although it is interesting that a smaller percentage of mothers have frequent phone conversations with daughters. Less than half of daughters and mothers use email, video chat, and social media. For instance, just under half of the daughters do not use email with their mothers, 41.2% do not use video chat, and 39% do not use social media to interact with their mothers. Of those who do use social media, under a third (28.6%) use it daily or multiple times a day. Mothers gave very similar responses. Nearly half do not use video chat, and a third do not use social media to communicate with daughters. Mothers' responses differed from daughters regarding email, with twenty percent saying they do not use it compared to about half of daughters. Finally, concerning face-to-face communication, most daughters (82.3%) indicated that they talk to their mothers one to two times a month or less, and 72.8% of mothers talk face-to-face with daughters one to two times a month or less. Overall, it is clear that most mothers and daughters use texting and calling with each other and these are the most frequent means of mother-daughter communication.

Responses to open-ended questions provided insight into mothers' and daughters' perceptions of the benefits and challenges of using technology in their relationships and some strategies they used to overcome the limitations. The data reveal that technology enables connection for both parties but causes annoyance, problems, and miscommunication and can make some people, especially daughters, feel suffocated and frustrated.

Both parties love the idea of using technology to communicate and provide positive comments about its use. Mothers and daughters like that they can stay in quick and convenient contact. One daughter wrote, "I wouldn't be able to see my mom's face or have quick and unimportant convos [sic] with her if she didn't have a cellphone" [Note: All quotes from participants are exactly as they wrote them on the survey]. Highlighting the tension between autonomy and connection another daughter wrote that a benefit is that "[technology] allows us to live our lives individually while still staying connected." One mother explained, "Sometimes we both don't have the time or in situations where we can pick up the phone and talk so texting becomes a convenient way to relay something quickly to each other."

Technology also helps them compensate for physical distance, as most daughters in our sample lived far from mothers (median distance was 138 miles). One daughter wrote, "It [technology] closes the gap between us," and a mother noted, "It allows me to stay connected to her in ways I can't because we are so physically far apart."

Technology also helps them maintain closeness. One daughter who has lived far from her mother since high school wrote, "Without technology, we wouldn't be nearly as close. As technology has improved, we have gotten closer, because we have had opportunities to talk more frequently, to share more, to connect more." Another commented:

> Since I am away at college, it is a nice way to still feel connected with my mom. In high school, I was very close with my mom and told her everything, and I was nervous I would lose that when I went away to college, but I didn't because of technology.

A mother also explained that "This [technology] keeps us connected in a way we would not be otherwise. Big matters need phone calls or visits, but texts keep us knowing and liking each other, and have improved and increased our contact and our relationship."

Technology (particularly social media, photos/videos, and video chatting) allows parties to be able to "see" each other over a distance. One daughter explained, "I can see what my family and friends are up to through social media. Overall, technology keeps me connected to the people I care about at home." A mother wrote, "I can send her photos/videos of the snow storm out our window or the new baby cousin. Instant!"

Daughters described that they can get support, love, and advice from mothers over a distance. A daughter remarked, "I consider my mom one of my best friends, and I am able to talk to her and have her support even though I do not get to see her in person." One mother indicated that "being able to talk on the phone to alleviate stress, provide comfort, and solve problems is very beneficial."

Technology, however, is not without challenges. Of all open-ended questions, both parties expanded most in their responses to the question about problems using technology. One of the biggest struggles for both parties was mothers' incorrect or inappropriate technology use, which appeared to be very frustrating for mothers but more so for daughters. In some instances, it was mothers' inability to use the device (e.g., cell phone, tablet) and the programs and software (e.g., Facebook, FaceTime) correctly, or poor cell reception or internet connectivity. One daughter wrote, "Technology troubles are the largest issue because either the Wi-Fi connection is bad for myself or my mom, or my mom does not understand all the functions on Skype." Another daughter commented:

> We like to FaceTime a lot and have problems with the connection. We get frustrated with each other when FaceTime freezes or doesn't work, but it really isn't the other person's fault, just the technology. I get annoyed because I cannot simply talk to her like I would like to.

The technology issues appear to annoy daughters but also influence their ability to communicate with mothers as they would like. One daughter wrote:

> There are times when my mom doesn't know how to work her phone/whatever and needs help to figure it out how to fix her technology issue, so she can't reply to me until she figures out what she's doing or has to get back to me through a more inconvenient way.

Many mothers admitted to these issues impacting communication. For instance, one mother noted: "[My daughter's] far more advanced with technology and I sometimes worry I'll click the wrong button or not be able to keep up with her in general. She has to re-explain things to me frequently."

Another major issue for daughters was mothers' inability to follow technology etiquette or expectations. Many daughters explained that mothers often did not answer their phones or did so at inappropriate times, which caused annoyance and frustration. One daughter explained, "When she is at home she never has her phone near her so if I need to get ahold of her I have to call my dad and ask to talk to her." Another daughter explained:

> Sometimes I call, and she doesn't answer, she calls me back and tells me she's busy. I find it annoying because she could either wait until she's not busy or send me a text saying she's busy instead of calling back and giving me only 2 minutes to tell her whatever it is I need to.

Beyond issues around answering or not answering, daughters also shared that the content of mothers' communication through technology can be inappropriate. One daughter provided an example of her mother's inappropriate texting: "Instead of calling me when my dad had heart problems and had to go to the ER, she texted my boyfriend and me, like she didn't want to bother us." Another daughter explained:

> She forwards/sends me chain letters, funny photo emails, or advice articles unsolicited. I don't have time for them, they are often not funny, unsolicited advice, esp. when it's on topics I have already explored/discussed/checked is frustrating. Sometimes it feels like she doesn't know email etiquette.

Mothers' writing style in text messages can also cause issues. One daughter wrote, "My mother doesn't type out everything when she's texting. It makes her hard to understand and a lot of miscommunication happens." Daughters classified mothers' misuse of texting lingo, acronyms, punctuation, and abbreviations as other writing style issues that caused them frustration and annoyance and impacted the ease with which they could communicate.

To overcome mothers' technology problems, daughters' wrote about teaching mothers how to use technology (e.g., "I try to teach her new technology things in person, and leave her with step by step instructions on how to complete common tasks with that technology"), relying on technology that mothers know how to use (e.g., "She will ask me to call her if I have time rather than text"), asking mothers to change their behaviors (e.g., "I ask her to charge her phone more or keep track of her phone more often so I can reach her better"), and doing nothing (e.g., "She will never get better at it and we just stick to phone calls"). Mothers' responses focused on daughters teaching them proper technology usage (e.g., "She tries to teach me new things"). Mothers did not report adapting their own communication behaviors.

While mothers did not express the same frustration with their daughters' technology usage, they did write about the difficulties of understanding the message tone that led to miscommunication. One mother wrote, "Sometimes it's hard to read the tone of a text or email. I can't always tell the emotion that's associated with what's being said, and sometimes that can cause misunderstandings." Another mother echoed this feeling:

> The biggest issue I have is when we text. Sometimes I misunderstand her feelings. You cannot always tell how a person feels in a text. I might respond in a way that she might think I am being mean when that is not the case at all.

Although less frequently, some daughters acknowledged miscommunication due to message tone. One daughter wrote, "When she thinks I'm mad, nothing I say can convince her otherwise because my 'tone' shows her that I am indeed mad as she suspected. Sigh." Neither party offered many solutions to challenges to understanding tone and emotion through technology.

The tension between autonomy and connection was evident in the differing perspectives on the benefits of constant contact. The biggest advantage of technology for many mothers is being able to contact daughters at any time without disrupting their lives. One mother wrote that a benefit is "staying in touch 24 seven—she is a very busy working mom so this allows us to stay connected anytime day or night." Similarly, another mother wrote, "I can text her at any time without disturbing what she is doing." However, daughters believed that mothers' constant contact affected their independence. One daughter wrote that "Some days my mom literally is trying to communicate with me on some form of technology all day. It can get annoying if I'm busy and don't have time to respond to her." One daughter explained, "Texting every day can be exhausting." Therefore, mothers considered constant contact a benefit while it was a major problem for daughters.

Particularly problematic for daughters was that mothers use technology to check on their well-being throughout the day. One mother wrote, "[Technology] lessens my worry about her because she is available at a moment's notice to ease my worries about her well-being." Another mother admitted that her daughter "does not always answer texts very quickly. Since I use text primarily to check in on her, this can be problematic." However, daughters wrote that a major problem is their mothers expected quick responses and assumed the worst when they did not respond immediately. As one daughter reflected, "Mothers today seem to think your [sic] dead if you don't respond within an hour. And that causes anxiety on both ends. I get being cautious, but I don't always need to have my phone with me or answer it right away."

Daughters shared many instances of mothers getting upset when they did not respond to texts immediately. One daughter wrote that "when I'm in class, my phone is on do not disturb, and when I'm working out or writing assignments, my phone is not by my side. This tends to annoy her because she expects to be answered immediately." Similarly, another daughter wrote, "My mother tends to call me at a time that is not convenient for me which is the biggest problem/issue. For example, she will call me during a class and when I can't answer, she texts me angrily."

Daughters also reported that mothers used technology to pry into their lives, typically through social media. One daughter wrote:

> She tries to pry into my life a lot and almost try to catch me doing or saying bad things on my Twitter or Instagram, for instance. It bothers me very much when she does that because it makes me feel less like an adult and that my personal life is being manipulated.

While daughters voiced frustration that mothers expected immediate contact, daughters often expressed frustration with having opposite schedules from mothers and not being able to contact them. One daughter commented that:

> I guess the only issues I sometimes have is when I have a quick question that I ask her over text message that I need her to respond to in a good amount of time, but then ends up not responding for a really long time is sometimes frustrating but I understand she's busy sometimes just like I am.

To overcome scheduling issues, both parties shared examples of using technology to coordinate schedules. As one daughter wrote, "We usually text back and forth to find out what our schedules look like that day, and then we plan a time to talk on the phone." They also relied on short text messages throughout the day to explain why they did not answer the phone or to give a heads-up of when they would be calling next. They also set expectations about talk time. One mother wrote, "We talk M-F briefly by phone to check in with each other, and have deeper conversations by phone on the weekend."

As this analysis reveals, both mothers and daughters identified problems and benefits of communication technology. We were also interested in whether daughters and mothers are satisfied with technology as a means of mother-daughter communication. In general, daughters are moderately satisfied, scoring an average of 3.91 on a 5-point scale, as are mothers, who averaged 3.95. Even though, overall, mothers and daughters were moderately satisfied with using technology, not all participants in our study were satisfied. So, we wondered if mothers and daughters who were very satisfied with their technology use gave different answers to the open-ended questions than those who were not satisfied. Specifically, we compared their responses to the questions about the benefits and problems of technology use and how they manage the problems.

Surprisingly, both groups of daughters identified the same benefits and problems of communication technology use with their mothers. They cited the convenience, speed, ease, and ability to feel close and connected as key benefits of technology. At the same time, they noted problems such as miscommunication, availability and response time issues, technical difficulties, and mothers' lack of competency with the technology. Where the two groups seemed to differ was in how they addressed the problems they experience and in the degree of negativity they expressed about mothers' lack of experience and expertise with technology. Daughters in the high satisfaction group, for instance, seemed to find constructive ways to overcome problems, writing "Try and schedule a time to talk via technology that we are both available," "I just continue to remind her when I have class and the best time to call me," "I use emojis to express my emotions," and "I try to explain how to use it [the technology] and show her examples." The dissatisfied daughters seemed less able to find solutions to address technology-related problems and just seemed to accept them. For example, they offered comments such as, "No, she [her mother] will never get better at it and we just stick to phone calls," "I just live with it and move on with life," "I try to visit more often but I also doubt the social media posts will ever stop," and "I just tell her to stop trying to communicate with me via Facebook." A few wrote that they explained the technology to their mothers or tried to arrange schedules, but the majority provided no solutions and/or gave comments suggesting frustration and inability to solve the problems.

Comparing mothers in the high and low satisfaction with technology use groups revealed agreement on benefits such as being able to stay in touch regularly, feeling connected to their daughters, immediacy and convenience, and the ability of platforms like Skype to let them see daughters. For the most part, they perceived similar problems including difficulty understanding tone/misunderstandings, technical issues, and the feeling that that technology use replaces calling and prevents extended conversations. Dissatisfied mothers also suggested they and their daughters have different preferences when it comes to means of communication. Similar to daughters, mothers in the high satisfaction group reported constructive ways to alleviate problems such as their daughters teach them how to use technology, they schedule conversations, and they switch platforms to accommodate one another. Few mothers in the low satisfaction group offered any solutions, but one wrote that she uses emoticons or asks directly about tone, and another noted that they arrange to have more in-depth conversations on weekends. There were not many mothers who were highly satisfied and few who were very dissatisfied, meaning the mothers' responses were mostly in the middle; therefore, it was hard to compare highly satisfied to dissatisfied mothers.

WHAT DOES ALL THIS MEAN?

Autonomy vs. connection is a useful way of trying to understand how daughters and mothers interpret technology use with each other. The original version of relational dialectics theory (Baxter & Montgomery, 1996) best helps us to understand the tension between autonomy and connection. Baxter and Montgomery (1996) argued that interpersonal partners simultaneously experience competing tensions or oppositional forces. These competing forces interact to create meaning in the relationship (Baxter, 2011), and thus, partners aim to manage the tensions rather than eliminate them (Baxter, 1990). Autonomy (independence) and connection (interdependence) is the central set of dialectical tensions in this theory (Baxter, 1990). Past research has indicated that partners experience autonomy and connection tensions when using technology to interact (e.g., Duran, Kelly, & Rotaru,

2011; Katz & Aakhus, 2002; Miller-Ott & Kelly, 2016). Mothers and daughters seem to have a love-hate relationship with using technology to communicate with one other, and these opposing feelings seem to relate to autonomy and connection. In this section, we are going to talk about their relationship with technology and other majors themes in the research.

First, it is important to address the "what" and "how often" of mother-daughter technology use. Mothers and daughters prefer texting and phone calls to communicate. They supplement texting and calling with some combination of email, video chat, and social media. Due to the physical distance that is typical between adult mothers and daughters (in college and beyond), they have less face-to-face interaction and rely instead on frequent (often daily) technologically-mediated interactions (Chen & Katz, 2009; Kelly et al., 2017; Lee, Meszaros, & Colvin, 2009; Miller-Ott et al., 2014).

The key benefit of communication technology is staying connected to one another. Technology helps overcome physical distance and busy schedules and enables sharing the small, mundane happenings of daily life to maintain closeness. Daily, routine interactions help daughters and mothers maintain the close bond that generally characterizes mother-daughter relationships (Lawton, Silverstein, & Bengtson, 1994) and enable the provision of emotional and other types of support that mothers and daughters exchange (Eaton & Bradley, 2008; Schwarz et al., 2006). Communication technologies help daughters and mothers stay close by keeping them interconnected in daily life. The ability to share photos and spontaneous thoughts and to check in on one another helps them to maintain a closeness that would likely not be possible without the technology.

Frequent communication and closeness, however, can create tension in mother-daughter relationships if daughters feel their independence is threatened (Harrigan & Miller-Ott, 2013). Technology, especially cell phones, can act like an "umbilical cord between parent and child" (Ling, 2004, p. 100) and can increase helicopter parenting (Kelly et al., 2017). This constant contact can result in daughters feeling suffocated and experiencing threats to their autonomy. A major take-away from the research in this area is: *While mothers and daughters share the view of technology as enabling close connection, daughters tend to experience tension associated with too much connection.* To them, the 24/7 instantaneous quality of text messaging, in particular, is a double-edged sword. They are particularly bothered by mothers assuming something terrible has happened to them if their responses are not immediate.

People generally accept as a given that youth are more technologically savvy than older people since they grew up with technology. Thus, it may not be too surprising that the issue of mothers' technological literacy is a problem in mother-daughter technology use. Our female students often complain that their mothers don't know how to use their phones or don't know how to text correctly. Our research supports our students' experiences. In this chapter, we talked about mothers and daughters who expressed feelings ranging from mild annoyance to frustration with mothers' ineffective use of technology such as not knowing how to operate hardware or software and not having the phone on hand and charged. Mothers seem to misinterpret text messages. Daughters are frustrated that mothers don't follow technology norms that daughters follow, especially when daughters are dissatisfied with how they use technology with mothers. Hall, Baym, and Miltner's (2014) study found that in friendships and romantic relationships, partners who thought that they had the same norms for cell phone use reported more liking and commitment and less sense of mobile relationship interference, suggesting that daughters might have greater technology satisfaction if they develop norms with their mothers. Autonomy and connection tensions emerge when mothers do not respond in a timely fashion. On the one hand, daughters can feel suffocated by texts from mothers, but on the other, they expect mothers to be available and respond when they need their mothers, as Miller-Ott et al. (2014) found.

Given that there often are differences in the technological competency of mothers and daughters, and daughters are more aware of usage norms, how do and should daughters handle this issue? It seems that a lot of how mothers and daughters handle issues with technology relates to how satisfied they are with their relationship with mothers. Highly satisfied daughters use constructive ways to deal with problems, such as having more patience, teaching their mothers multiple times if needed, arranging schedules to overcome availability issues, and finding ways to accommodate each other's preferences. Less satisfied daughters accept problems and are less willing to develop solutions. In looking at all of the research in this area, we suggest that daughters and mothers mutually arrive at ways to overcome these problems and try to use the strategies that more satisfied daughters use.

WHAT DO WE STILL NEED TO KNOW?

- How do daughters' experiences with mothers compare to daughters' experiences using technology to communicate with their fathers?
- What rules do daughters and mothers follow when using technology to communicate? How do these rules develop?
- How might daughters and mothers increase their satisfaction with using technology to communicate?
- How might our findings differ based on ethnic identity, socioeconomic status, region of the country families reside, parents' or daughters' marital status, and/or age of the mothers and daughters?

HOW DOES THIS WORK IN REAL LIFE?

Suggestions for successful technology use with mothers:

- Set rules for communicating through technology—determine a time to talk, decide what you want to use technology for (sharing news, catching up, sending photos, etc.), and determine how frequently you will communicate using technology.
- Be sure that your mom knows how to use the specific technology you wish to use. And if she doesn't, then show her! She will likely appreciate the knowledge and being able to communicate in a way that you prefer.
- If availability is a concern, share schedules, so your mom knows when you are in class, at work, etc. and when you can't respond right away (without giving up too much of your independence!).
- If you're not satisfied with the way you are using technology to communicate with your mom, talk to her to figure out what's not working. Then try to adapt/fix the issues. Don't get into a pattern where your communication through technology isn't satisfying or helping you to feel close to your mom.

CLASSROOM ACTIVITIES

Diary/Reflection

For the next week, record the number of times you communicate with your mom (or if your mother is unavailable, then select your female caregiver or important female figure in your life) using the technology we discussed in our chapter: email, cell phone calls, texting/messaging, social media, video chat, and face-to-face communication. At the end of the week, compare your numbers to what we found. Do you use texting more than any other technology? If so, reflect on what it is about texting that leads you to use it most. If you didn't use texting the most, which did you use and why? Be ready to share with your class how your own experiences compare to what we found in our study.

Conversation

Write down three things you would like for your mom to know about your preferences for communicating via technology. Ask her to write down three things she wants you to know. Talk to each other about these requests and develop some rules for your future communication that will help enhance relationship satisfaction and decrease conflict.

REFERENCES

Baxter, L. A. (1990). Dialectical contradictions in relationship development. *Journal of Social and Personal Relationships, 7,* 69–88. doi:10.1177/0265407590071004

Baxter, L. A. (2011). *Voicing relationships: A dialogic perspective.* Los Angeles, CA: Sage.

Baxter, L. A., & Montgomery, B. M. (1996). *Relating: Dialogues and dialectics.* New York, NY: Guilford.

Caughlin, J. P., & Petronio, S. (2004). Privacy in families. In A. L. Vangelisti (Ed.), *Handbook of family communication* (pp. 379–412). Mahwah, NJ: Lawrence Erlbaum.

Chen, Y., & Katz, J. E. (2009). Extending family to school life: College students' use of the mobile phone. *International Journal of Human-Computer Studies, 67*(2), 179–191. doi:10.1016/j.ijhcs.2008.09.002

Devitt, K., & Roker, D. (2009). The role of mobile phones in family communication. *Children and Society, 23*(3), 189–202. doi:10.1111/j.1099-0860.2008.00166.x

Duggan, M., Lenhart, A., Lampe, C., & Ellison, N. B. (2015). *Parents and social media.* Retrieved from http://www.pewinternet.org/2015/07/16/parents-and-social-media/

Duran, R. L., Kelly, L., & Rotaru, T. (2011). Mobile phones in romantic relationships and the dialectic of autonomy versus connection. *Communication Quarterly, 59,* 19–36. doi:10.1080/01463373.2011.541336

Eaton, R. J., & Bradley, G. (2008). The role of gender and negative affectivity in stressor appraisal and coping selection. *International Journal of Stress Management, 15,* 94–115. doi:10.1037/1072-5245.15.1.94

Fischer, L. R. (1991). Between mothers and daughters. *Marriage and Family Review, 16*(3–4), 237–248. doi:10.1300/J002v16n03_02

Fisher, C., & Miller-Day, M. (2006). Communication over the lifespan: The mother-adult daughter relationship. In K. Floyd & M. T. Morman (Eds.), *Widening the family circle: New research on family communication* (pp. 3–19). Thousand Oaks, CA: Sage.

Green, K. M. (2007). *Understanding college students' and parents' perceptions of cell phone communication in family relationships: A grounded theory approach* (Dissertation). University of Minnesota, Minnesota.

Hall, J. A., Baym, N. K., & Miltner, K. M. (2014). Put down that phone and talk to me: Understanding the roles of mobile phone norm adherence and similarity in relationships. *Mobile Media & Communication, 2*(2), 134–153. doi: 10.1177/2050157913517684

Harrigan, M. M., & Miller-Ott, A. E. (2013). The multivocality of meaning-making: An exploration of the discourses college-aged daughters voice in talk about their mothers. *Journal of Family Communication, 13*(2), 114–131. doi:10.1080/15267431.2013.768249

Kanter, M., Afifi, T., & Robbins, S. (2012). The impact of parents "friending" their young adult child on Facebook on perceptions of parental privacy invasions and parent-child relationship quality. *Journal of Communication, 62*(5), 900–917. doi:10.1111/j.1460-2466.2012.01669.x

Katz, J. E., & Aakhus, M. A. (2002). Conclusion: Making meaning of mobiles—A theory of Apparatgeist. In J. Katz & M. Aakhus (Eds.), *Perpetual contact: Mobile communication, private talk, public performance* (pp. 301–320). Cambridge, UK: Cambridge University Press.

Kelly, L., Duran, R. L., & Miller-Ott, A. E. (2017). Helicopter parenting and cell phone contact between parents and children in college. *Southern Communication Journal, 82*(2), 102–114. doi:10.1080/1041794X.2017.1310286

Lawton, L., Silverstein, M., & Bengtson, V. (1994). Affection, social contact, and geographic distance between adult children and their parents. *Journal of Marriage and Family, 56*, 57–68. Retrieved from http://www.jstor.org/stable/352701

Lee, S., Meszaros, P. S., & Colvin, J. (2009). Cutting the wireless cord: College student cell phone use and attachment to parents. *Marriage & Family Review, 45*(6–8), 717–739. doi: 10.1080/01494920903224277

Ling, R. (2004). *The mobile connection: The cell phone's impact on society.* San Francisco, CA: Morgan Kaufmann.

Ling, R., & Yttri, B. (2002). Hyper-coordination via mobile phones in Norway. In J. E. Katz & M. Aakhus (Eds.), *Perpetual contact: Mobile communication, private talk, public performance* (pp. 139–169). Cambridge, UK: Cambridge University Press.

Miller, A. E., & Harrigan, M. M. (2009, November). *A typology of turning points and trajectories: An exploration of mother-young adult daughter communication.* Paper presented to the Family Communication Division of the National Communication Association, Chicago, IL.

Miller-Day, M. A. (2004). *Communication among grandmothers, mothers, and adult daughters: A qualitative study of maternal relationships.* Mahwah, NJ: Lawrence Erlbaum Associates.

Miller-Ott, A. E., & Kelly, L. (2016). Competing discourses and meaning-making in talk about romantic partners' cell-phone contact with non-present others. *Communication Studies, 67*, 58–76. doi:10.1080/10510974.2015.1088876

Miller-Ott, A. E., Kelly, L., & Duran, R. L. (2014). Cell phone usage expectations, closeness, and relationship satisfaction between parents and their emerging adults in college. *Emerging Adulthood, 2*(4), 1–11. doi:10.1177/2167696814550195

Penington, B. A. (2004). The communicative management of connection and autonomy in African American and European American mother-daughter relationships. *Journal of Family Communication, 4*, 3–34. doi:10.1207/s15327698jfc0401_2

Rudi, J. H., Walkner, A., & Dworkin, J. (2015). Adolescent-parent communication in a digital world: Differences by family communication patterns. *Youth & Society, 47*(6), 811–828. doi:10.1177/004418X14560334

Schwarz, B., Trommsdorff, G., Kim, U., & Park, Y. (2006). Intergenerational support: Psychological and cultural analyses of Korean and German women. *Current Sociology, 54*(2), 315–340. doi:10.1177/0011392106056748

Steinberg, L. S., & Silk, J. J. (2002). Parenting adolescents. In M. Bornstein (Ed.), *Handbook of Parenting* (2nd ed., pp.103–133). Mahwah, NJ: Lawrence Erlbaum.

CHAPTER THIRTEEN

Storying Love

Retrospective Storytelling Between Mothers and Daughters

JODY KOENIG KELLAS,* AMANDA HOLMAN,† AND ELIZABETH FLOOD-GRADY‡

Storytelling is at the center of everyday interpersonal life. Think about how many stories you have already told today. Maybe you told your classmate the story of commuting into campus or texted your sister a quick version of the story of the party you went to last night or posted on Facebook about the awkward moment you had with a customer at your coffee shop job. Telling stories is one of the primary ways we make sense of our lives.

Storytelling is also at the heart of families and the mother-daughter relationship. Families tell stories to socialize one another to the beliefs, values, and norms that come to guide daily life, and women are often known as the kinkeepers of those family stories (Stone, 2004). Stories shared between mothers and daughters are like meaning-making maps across this important relational context. The stories that daughters recall hearing from their mothers provide insight into the messages that endure and that guide the complexities of life, including the development and maintenance of romantic relationships and marriage (e.g., Gilchrist-Petty & Reynolds, 2015). In the current chapter, we talk about the stories daughters recall hearing from their mothers about romantic relationships and how those stories have a lasting impact on daughters' adult relationships and lives. We use Communicated

* Jody Koenig Kellas, Professor, University of Nebraska-Lincoln.
† Amanda Holman, Associate Professor, Creighton University.
‡ Elizabeth Flood-Grady, University of Florida.

Narrative Sense-Making (CNSM) Theory (Koenig Kellas, 2018; Koenig Kellas & Kranstuber Horstman, 2015)—a theory designed to test the links between family storytelling and individual and relational health—to gain insight into how mothers' stories of love and romance help to form their daughters' own views and stories of romantic relationships. By the end of the chapter, you should have a sense of why storytelling matters in the mother-daughter relationship, especially when it comes to stories of romance and love.

MOTHER-DAUGHTER STORYTELLING

> The best kind of love is with the most unexpected person at the most unexpected moment.
> —JANE OLSON, AMANDA'S MOM

This quote is the first thought that surfaces when I think of the stories my mom told me about the love she found with my dad. When she was in her twenties, my mom had just started her career as an occupational therapist in a rural elementary school. One of her students at the time had mild Spina bifida and was in need of a standing frame table that would help improve his small motor skills and movements. As my mom searched for a professional who could build the table, a colleague of hers strongly recommended a shop teacher at the high school. About a week later she walked into his classroom. The shop teacher was a tall, gruff, and stern man. He was obnoxiously arrogant, rarely smiled, and this "highly" recommended shop teacher talked more than he listened during the negotiations of the table designs. She felt pity for this abrasive man's wife. At the end of their first encounter, she thanked him for his willingness to build the table and said she would come and pick it up when it was ready. Two weeks later she walked back into his office to pick up the table and this time he greeted her with an unexpected smile and a request to get pizza and a beer for building the table. This made it clear to her that this man had no wife for her to pity. And even though she was hesitant to spend any more time with this "big-headed" man, she agreed. That very next Friday night she ate pizza, talked, and laughed at his sarcastic (at times even slightly risqué) jokes. She started to fall in love with this man who was turning out to be much more than his rigid exterior. They continued to date for a few months and were married less than a year later. According to my mom, it was simple: she met an unexpected man at the most unexpected moment and it changed her life forever—in the best way possible.

Stories told in the family serve a number of functions. They help us understand who we are as a family (e.g., the story of what it means to be a Flood), who we are as individuals in that family (e.g., Jody's mom describes herself essentially as a subordinate in a family of bosses), help us make sense of and cope with difficulty (e.g., telling fond stories of loved ones when they pass), and they socialize family members by teaching lessons, values, and how to behave in the world (Koenig Kellas & Trees, 2013). For example, Amanda's story about how her mother met and fell in love with her father ends with the enduring lesson that love might be unexpected. As the keeper of family stories and key socializing agents (Stone, 2004), mothers may be the most important storytellers in the family and, for this reason, the messages and meanings they convey in their storytelling deserve more attention.

The stories moms tell daughters and the ways they tell them have a lasting impact. For example, research shows that the style through which mothers tell stories to their children (e.g., elaboration) predicts child's own storytelling style and autobiographical consistency. In other words, the ways mothers tell stories influences how their children tell stories. Mothers engage in casual conversations or reminisce with their children as a way to achieve goals (Bohanek, Marin, & Fivush, 2008) and share family narratives that "become a scrapbook of family history resulting from a process of meaning-making in the family" (Fiese & Sameroff, 1999, p. 3). These stories offer us insight into how our families socialize each other and how these processes affect and reflect family and other relational functioning. Our family stories are the foundation of how we view relationships and even love.

Storytelling also helps to explain how we feel in and about relationships. Research supports the importance of parent-child storytelling for understanding its effects on current relationship functioning (e.g., Fiese & Sameroff, 1999), future relationship functioning (e.g., marital satisfaction, Gilchrist-Petty & Reynolds 2015), and gender socialization (e.g., Fiese & Skillman, 2000). For example, Fiese and Skillman found that fathers tell, and sons hear, stories with stronger themes of autonomy than mothers tell or daughters hear, suggesting that the combination of parent and child characteristics have a bearing on child socialization. Peterson and Roberts (2003) found significant similarity between older daughters' (ages 8–13) and mothers' narrative style across length, elaboration, coherence, context, and cohesion when they each separately recounted a shared stressful family event. The similarity in storytelling style between mothers and daughters was not present between fathers and sons or fathers and daughters, reinforcing the importance of the mother-daughter relational storytelling context and the idea that mothers and daughters may tell stories together more often than other parent-child dyads. In a study on birth stories, mothers and daughters often told similar versions of the daughters' birth stories, and the positivity of the mothers' narratives predicted daughters' higher self-esteem (Hayden, Singer, & Chrisler, 2006). Also, how often and how much (i.e., frequency) mothers give daughters advice about marriage and the extent to which daughters followed their mother's advice predicted how satisfied daughters were in their marital relationships later in life (Gilchrist-Petty & Reynolds, 2015).

Thus, research tells us that mother-daughter storytelling may affect and/or reflect daughters' identity, gender socialization (Fiese & Skillman, 2000) and well-being (Hayden et al., 2006). Preliminary findings also indicate that mother-daughter storytelling relates to the mother-daughter relationship (i.e., relational functioning, Fiese & Sameroff, 1999) and the relationships that daughters engage in later in life (e.g., marriage, Gilchrist-Petty & Reynolds, 2015).

In this chapter, we set out to further explore the nature of mother-daughter storytelling, particularly stories about love and romance to understand the lasting impact mothers' stories might have on daughters. We based our investigation on Communicated Narrative Sense-making theory (CNSM, Koenig Kellas, 2018) because it puts storytelling at the center of understanding communicated meaning-making in the family.

Communicated Narrative Sense-making (CNSM)

CNSM theory presumes and tests the links between (family) storytelling and individual and relational health and well-being (Koenig Kellas, 2018). CNSM focuses on storytelling and its functions, including constructing individual and family identity, socializing family members to values, beliefs, and norms, and coping and making sense of difficulty. CNSM is guided by three frameworks, called heuristics, including retrospective storytelling (i.e., a focus on content), interactional storytelling (i.e., a focus on process), and translational storytelling (i.e., a focus on application and intervention) (Koenig Kellas, 2018; Koenig Kellas & Kranstuber Horstman, 2015).

Retrospective storytelling is about the stories we hear and tell in families and the lasting impact of those stories. For example, the story Amanda shared at the beginning of the chapter is a story that stuck with her and had a lasting impact on how she viewed her potential partner and how she now thinks about love within her own marriage to her husband, Will. Proposition 1 of CNSM theory suggests that the stories we hear and tell in the family help us build a sense of who we are and how we should act inside and outside the family. It says: *The content of retrospective storytelling reveals individual, relational, and intergenerational meaning-making, values, and beliefs.* CNSM's retrospective storytelling heuristic focuses centrally on the theme, meaning, and content of the stories we hear and tell. We were interested in understanding the kinds of meanings, values, and beliefs mothers pass onto their daughters about relationships and love in the stories they tell.

Previous research has focused on the meanings mothers pass onto daughters about romantic relationships in the form of memorable messages about romantic relationships (Koenig Kellas, 2010) and advice about marriage (Gillchrist-Petty & Reynolds, 2015). For example, Koenig Kellas identified four supra-types of messages in which mothers communicated lessons about romantic relationships to daughters, including *value self, characteristics of a good relationship, warnings,* and *value the sanctity of love.* Gillchrist-Petty and Reynolds found nine themes in mothers' messages to daughters about marriage, such as *women are the main care-givers and homemakers* and *marriage is a compromise and partnership*. Although not specific to mothers and daughters, Kranstuber Horstman (2013) examined court-ship narratives and found that adult children gleaned various meanings about love from their parents' courtship stories, including *love is patient, love is following your heart*, and *love isn't always good*, to name a few. This research got us thinking about what retrospective storytelling about romantic relationships, in general, revealed about meaning-making between mothers and daughters and how these meanings add to the tapestry that previous research has begun to weave about the messages and stories passed from mothers to daughters about love and romance.

THE STUDY

What Were We Interested in Learning?

In this study we set out to ask the following question: *What kinds of meanings, val-ues, and beliefs did mothers pass onto their daughters through storytelling about romantic relationships?*

We also wanted to know more about how the stories daughters recall hearing from their mothers help to provide a window into the mother-daughter relation-ship. Previous research suggests that stories serve as a small package for explain-ing larger relational culture. In other words, the way we frame our stories also reflects how we feel about our family relationships. For example, Koenig Kellas et al. (2014) analyzed the themes of adult stepchildren's stepfamily origin stories and found that those who told *idealized* family stories were significantly more satisfied (in survey measures) with their stepfamilies than those who told stories with *dark-sided* or *sudden* themes. In a separate study, families who told often-told family stories with themes of *stress* were much less satisfied, adaptable, and cohe-sive than families who told stories with themes of *accomplishment and appreciation* (Koenig Kellas, 2005). Thus, stories whose themes are more positive and hopeful also predicted higher levels of relational functioning within the family.

Others have examined the affective, or emotional, tone of narratives in order to understand the relationship between stories and well-being. For example, McAdams (1993) establishes affective tone as a central element to understanding individuals' life stories in his theory of narrative identity. He and his colleagues (McAdams, Reynolds, Lewis, Patten, & Bowman, 2001) examined young and middle-aged adults life narratives for redemptive (i.e., when something bad turns to something good) and contaminated (i.e., when something good turns to some-thing bad) imagery and found that redemption sequences predicted higher levels of generativity in midlife adults and better well-being in young adults; contamination sequences were related to lower levels of generativity and well-being in midlife adults. In other words, redemptive stories were related to higher well-being and contaminated life stories were related to lower levels of well-being. In the context of mother-daughter storytelling, Kranstuber Horstman and colleagues (2016) found that mothers helped daughters to make sense of difficulty in storytelling conversations, further suggesting that the mother-daughter relationship is an important context for understanding the benefits of storytelling. In short, extant research shows that people who frame their narratives more positively, also report higher levels of individual and relational well-being. This matches CNSM's Proposition 2: *Storytelling content that is framed positively will be positively related to individual and relational health and well-being.*

We were also interested in how stories daughters recall being told by their mothers about romantic relationships would explain relational functioning in the mother-daughter relationship. Koenig Kellas and Trees (2013) argue that stories tell us a lot about our families and help to explain what our families view as important. Thus, we expected that the stories daughters recall being told would provide a barometer for the functioning in the mother-daughter relationship. Thus, using story theme and story tone as markers of meaning-making in retrospective storytelling, we expected to find the following: *When daughters heard positively themed stories that were redemptive in tone, they would be more satisfied with their relationship with their mother than if the stories were negatively framed.*

How Did We Go About Learning This Information?

To address our overall questions and predictions, we asked college-aged women to fill out questionnaires in which they wrote down stories they remember hearing from their mothers about love and romance. We also asked them to fill out measures of mother-daughter satisfaction. In total, we collected stories from 146 women ranging in age from 19 to 49 (*average age* = 21.60). Most of the women who participated in our study were white (*n* = 137, 93.8%), heterosexual (*n* = 143, 97.9%), and reported on mothers who were still living (*n* = 142, 97.3%). All the women were currently involved in a romantic relationship.

To participate in the study, the women completed a paper-pencil survey that included demographic questions (e.g., age, ethnicity), scales (e.g., relationship satisfaction) and open-ended (e.g., stories) items. To gather data on stories their mother had told them participants were instructed to: "Please provide any memorable story that your mother shared with you about romantic relationships or love below; be as specific and detailed as possible." They were given an unlimited amount of paper, and after writing the story, they also answered a series of questions about why they thought their mother shared the story and whether or not and why they would pass the story on to their own daughter (if and when they had one). Finally, the women completed scales about their satisfaction with their relationship with their mother.

To identify what meaning-making, values, and beliefs emerge from mother-daughter stories about romantic relationships, the open-ended narrative data, as well as the open-ended responses in which daughters shared the reasons they believed their mothers shared the stories with them, were coded and examined for themes across the responses (Bulmer, 1979; Owen, 1984). Through this process five themes emerged across the reported stories. These themes included *don't rush or settle, choose wisely, love is complicated, you'll know when you find the right one,* and *be open to love.* Also, when coding the stories, we coded for positive or negative feelings or tone. Three of the themes—don't rush or settle, choose wisely, and love is complicated—were characterized by both positive and negative feelings. The other two themes—you'll know when you find the right one and be open to love—were almost exclusively positive in feelings or tone. We further explain these themes in the following section of this chapter.

What Did We Learn?

Storytelling Meaning, Values, and Beliefs

Our overall question asked what individual, relational, and intergenerational meaning-making, values, and beliefs emerge in mother-daughter storytelling about romantic relationships. Through our thematic analysis, we discovered five common themes in the stories that daughters recalled hearing from their mothers about love and romance. We describe each of these below and talk about how each theme was framed either positively, negatively, or in both ways.

Don't Rush or Settle

The first theme that emerged from the stories focused on maternal encouragement for daughters to be patient. These stories encouraged patience in finding the right person, marriage, and/or engaging in sexual behavior. These stories also highlighted the importance of prioritizing personal goals (e.g., college, career) before romantic relationships. The "don't rush or settle" stories that daughters reported were framed both positively and negatively. For example, one daughter wrote:

> My mom tells me the story about her high school boyfriend, Dick. They had been dating for three years and when she graduated, she really wanted to go to college. But he was very against the idea. She said that they fought all the time until finally she decided that because he was not supportive of her goals, they needed a break up. She said it was a huge shock to Dick because they had talked about getting married, but school was just too important to her to stay with him. She ended up going to Iowa State and meeting my dad who encouraged her to go on and get her masters and then go to law school. She said she is thankful that she

broke up with Dick and instead reach her goals. I think she told me because she wanted me to know that a boy should not influence your decisions in life and education is very important.

"Don't rush or settle" stories were not always seen in a positive light, as illustrated in the comments of the following daughter:

> My mom always tells me not to get tied down with kids. Be smart about your choices so you can keep your options open. Don't let a "puppy love" turn into something more by accident. There is no need in getting married at a young age. You have your whole life to live, so live. I know my mother has told me all this so that I will be cautious of who I date and get involved with. She would never want this to happen to me [be stuck in a bad marriage that resulted in stalking when her mom tried to leave] and wants me to know what can happen if I got into a relationship right felt trapped.

In short, moms encouraged their daughters to be patient and to be cautious about rushing into love. Daughters sometimes found these stories to be positive lessons and sometimes experienced them more negatively as warnings.

Choose Wisely

The second category of stories daughters reported hearing from their mothers focused on daughters finding a good relationship that is respectful, honest, loving, and/or fun. These stories also highlighted the importance of finding someone that will be there through life's ups and downs. For example, one daughter wrote:

> My mother told me about how she dated several boys from her high school and that [she met] my father on a blind date. She talks about how most of the boys expected some sort of "repayment" for taking her out and how frustrated she would get because my father was the only boy that "didn't get handsy" and still wanted a second date. I asked her how she knew my father was "the one" she laughed and said that their first kiss was thankfully not an indicator. Then she told me about all of the different dates they went on and the progression of their relationship. She said she knew he was the one because her cheeks hurt every time he dropped her off: "He made me laugh and we always had a great time. Most of all though, he respected me and was always a gentleman." She then told me that if I'm dating someone who doesn't make me laugh that I ought to consider why: "Your father and I couldn't have survived 35 years of marriage without laughter. Life can get tough and if you can't keep your sense of humor, it will seem much harder." Humor is a big source of communication in my family. My mother can be very anal and intense at times and my father's ability to make her laugh complements their relationship. She wants me to be with someone who will make me want to be a better person and who will be my "cheerleader" like my father always has been for her.

Similar to the "don't rush or settle" stories, "choose wisely" stories were not always seen as positive. One daughter shared the following:

> Growing up my mom would always tell me about how my biological father would go out hunting and was never home. She said it made her feel unimportant. She said that it was

important to find someone who shared similar interest and spent time [with you] together. She was unhappy with her marriage and did not want me to have the same fate.

"Choose wisely" stories were about looking out for and prioritizing good qualities in a potential mate (e.g., sense of humor) and avoiding partners that didn't have those qualities or exhibited negative qualities that might harm the relationship (e.g., self-centeredness).

Love Is Complicated

The third category that emerged from stories daughters reported hearing from their mothers were stories that that expressed how love and relationships are not always perfect or easy. These stories highlighted that relationships can be challenging and how love takes sacrifice, hard work, and compromise from both people. Daughters told *love is complicated* stories that were both positive and negative in tone. As one daughter explained:

> I always remember her telling me about when dad and her got married right out of high school. She would travel four hours every weekend just to come back home from college to see him. Also when my dad went into the military, she went everywhere with him. My dad was stationed in South Korea for a while and my mom gave up all the modern US luxuries to go over there and live with him. There wasn't running water, fresh meat, and the place was unsanitary. All in all, she really doesn't complain about what she went through for him. They've been married 39 years now. She's a stay at home farm wife and he farms, dozes, fences, and welds.

Although the previous story lauds the benefits of embracing the complexity of love, the "love is complicated" stories are not always presented positively. The following excerpt illustrates the difficulties of marriage:

> My mother told me about a hard time in my parents' marriage. She told me the time early in their marriage when things weren't looking good. Divorce looked good at the time … my parents' relationship was strained. They ended up talking things out and my mom discovered that my dad was not feeling appreciated by her, so he turned to someone else who did appreciate him … She told me their relationship grew stronger because of it.

The "love is complicated" stories reveal that mothers seek to be honest with their daughters about how hard love and marriage can be. Sometimes daughters learned positive lessons from these stories, but other times, the tone was more negative.

Unlike the categories mentioned above, the following stories, "you'll know when you find the right one" and "be open to love" were always framed positively.

You'll Know When you Find the Right One

This fourth category of stories daughters reported hearing from their mothers were stories that love is something a daughter will know or feel once she meets the right person. These stories highlighted "love at first sight" and falling in love quickly. One daughter's story illustrated this category:

> My mom told me one time how when she met my dad, she was dating another guy when she met my dad. However, right after she met my dad through a mutual friend, she went home and broke up with her boyfriend because she knew my dad was the one. My mom said it felt like a whirlwind rushed through her when she met [my dad] because the second she met eyes with him they just "clicked."

All of the stories in this category were positively or redemptively framed. Finding the "right one" was seen as a happy experience for moms and by the daughters reporting the stories.

Be Open to Love

The fifth and final category of stories daughters reported hearing from their mothers that encouraged daughters to be open to finding love and keeping their heart open. These stories highlighted how love is unpredictable and unexpected and they should be willing to be open to the process. For example, one daughter wrote:

> My mom was working as a waitress in college, and my dad had moved to the same town to go to college. They met the night my mom was throwing out some kids who are causing trouble dad just happened to be sitting at another table my mom was his waitress. They dated a month and then my dad proposed engagement that lasted two years, but they were finally married.

In general, the stories daughters recalled being told by their mothers conveyed values and lessons that were prescriptive about love and the intentionality that should be involved in developing and maintaining romantic relationships (e.g., don't rush, be open, and choose wisely). Daughters also recalled being told stories about the reality of love once it was established (e.g., love is complicated). Stories were framed both positively and negatively.

Links Between Storytelling and Relational Health

We expected that daughters who heard more positively themed stories (i.e., those that were redemptive in tone), would be more satisfied with their relationships with their mother than stories that were negatively framed (CNSM's Proposition 2). To test this, we conducted some statistical tests with story theme as the independent variable and mother-daughter satisfaction as the dependent variable. Positively valenced themes included "don't rush" (positive), "choose wisely" (positive), "love is complicated" (positive), "you'll know when you find the right one," and "be open to love" stories. Negatively valenced themes included "don't rush" (negative), "choose wisely" (negative), and "love is complicated" (negative) stories. The results of our study indicates that story theme tends to help explain mother-daughter satisfaction. Specifically, we found that daughters who told "choose wisely" (negative) stories (M = 5.28) were less satisfied than daughters who told all other story types including "choose wisely"[positive] (M = 6.19), "love is complicated" [positive] (M = 6.26), "don't rush"[positive] (M = 6.31), "you'll know when you find the right one" (M = 5.99), "be open to love" (M = 6.23), "love is complicated" [negative] (M = 6.21), and "don't rush" [negative] (M = 6.08). As you can see from the mean or average levels of satisfaction, daughters who recalled "don't rush" stories that were positive in tone were the most satisfied with their mother-daughter relationship.

We also tested whether the tone of the stories daughters recalled (redemptive, ambivalent, contaminated) helped to explain mother-daughter satisfaction. Results of this analysis reveals that daughters who told stories characterized by redemption sequences (M = 6.23) were significantly more satisfied with the mother-daughter relationship than were those who told stories characterized by contaminated sequences (M = 5.70).

WHAT DOES ALL THIS MEAN?

Storytelling between mothers and daughters was memorable to the daughters in our study and was significant to their meaning-making about love. CNSM theory helped guide our analysis of what kinds of meanings, values, and beliefs mothers pass onto their daughters through storytelling about romantic relationships and the potential lasting effects of these messages. The findings of the current study reveal both positive and negatively valenced lessons that daughters recall mothers passing onto them through retrospective storytelling about romantic relationships. Those themes were both prescriptive and descriptive about love and relationships. As expected, negatively valenced themes and contaminated sequences predicted lower levels of mother-daughter relationship satisfaction than did positive and redemptive stories. We present our interpretations of these findings as well as some ideas for future research in the sections that follow.

Support for CNSM Propositions

Daughters recalled a wide range of stories from their mothers about love, several of which overlap with the stories children (i.e., daughters and sons) reported hearing about their parent's courtship (i.e., the story of how parents met, fell in love, and got married) (Kranstuber Horstman, 2013) and stories daughters recalled hearing from their mothers about marriage (Gillchrist-Petty & Reynolds, 2015) in previous research. For example, mother-daughter stories about love reflecting the themes, *you'll know when you find the right one*, *don't settle/rush*, and *be open to love*, which highlighted the unexpected nature of love and stressed the importance of being open to the process, are akin to the themes and lessons, *love is following your heart, love is patient*, and *love can be unexpected* that emerged from children's reports of their parent's courtship narratives (Kranstuber Horstman). The stories in our study also emphasized that love is complicated and that marriage and relationships can be challenging at times. These conclusions are similar to Gillchrist-Petty and Reynolds' (2015) findings which revealed themes such as *marriage is work* and *good and bad times* in mother-daughter advice about marriage and Kranstuber's (2013) courtship story themes including *tainted, overcoming adversity*, and lessons such as *love isn't always good* and *love is work*. Combining our findings with the small body of extant research on mother-daughter storytelling themes reveals mounting evidence for the cultural values and beliefs about love and relationships transmitted across generations from mothers to daughters in 21st century America. The overlap between our findings and Kranstuber's showcase a narrative inheritance (Goodall, 2005) in parent-child storytelling emphasizing values of *openness, honesty, choice, fate*, and *realism* in approaching future relationships. Retrospective storytelling focused on the negative or difficult aspects of love, relationships, and marriage are—perhaps not surprisingly—in the minority. Kranstuber's participants reported on the lessons "love is work" and "love isn't always good" a combined 21.3% of the time in her data set. In our study, negatively valenced (and a combination of contaminated and ambivalent toned) stories represented approximately 36% of the stories reported. Thus, it seems a majority of stories that daughters recall as significant and meaningful are positive, but a sizeable minority are negative, fraught with warnings, or honest in their depiction about the struggles of marriage. If, as CNSM and decades of other research contends, storytelling socializes, understanding the themes of retrospective storytelling is important. Girls who do not hear stories about the difficulties of romantic relationships may—between family communication and media portrayals—develop an unrealistic and overly romantic sense of love and marriage. On the flip side, girls who only hear warning stories or about the negative aspects of love and marriage may have a jaded view of romance and may not feel as close to their mothers than if they heard more positive stories.

The developing master narrative of mother-daughter retrospective storytelling presented here must be interpreted carefully, however, based on regional, racial, ethnic, and religious differences, to name a few. Interestingly, for example, the most common theme emerging from this data, *don't rush/settle*, is inconsistent with the most commonly reported theme, *women are the main caregivers and home-maker*, identified by Gillchrist-Petty and Reynolds's (2015) in their research on mother-daughter communication about marriage. *Don't rush/settle*, which highlighted the importance of prioritizing personal goals (e.g., career) before romantic relationships, differs, unequivocally, from *women are the main caregivers and home-maker*, which explained that women's role as caretakers and that women should be submissive to men. Indeed, another theme in Gillchrist-Petty and Reynold's study was *man is the head of the household*. This difference in the prevalence of each story theme could be explained by sample differences. In the current study, daughters were younger ($M = 21.60$) and the majority ($n = 117$, 80.1%) were in non-married, romantic relationships as compared to Gillchrist-Petty and Reynolds's (2015) study where daughters were older ($M = 40.1$), and the majority ($n = 107$, 84.9%) were married. Moreover, whereas their sample was primarily southern, ours was primarily Midwestern, as was Kranstuber's. Thus regional, racial, and religious values likely play an important role in narrative inheritance and retrospective storytelling. These differences in story themes likely underscore the changes in intergenerational meaning-making that occur over time and reveal how family communication captures cultural shifts through storytelling.

We also found support for CNSM's Proposition 2 on the links between mother-daughter storytelling and mother-daughter relational satisfaction. This supports the notion that stories provide a window into relationships (Stone, 2004). Importantly, these themes are not overtly Pollyanna. Instead, mothers tell stories about their negative experiences. These, however, predicted less mother-daughter satisfaction, suggesting the framing matters. Daughters who heard negatively valenced, *choose wisely* stories tended to interpret them as warnings not to make the mistakes in love that their mothers made. These stories seemed more detrimental than other negatively valenced stories. For example, girls who heard negatively valenced *love is complicated* stories were highly satisfied in their relationship with their mothers. As the example in the results illustrates, such stories were often redemptive, suggesting that the way story themes are framed are important to understanding relational outcomes. Indeed, redemption sequences positively predicted mother-daughter satisfaction. It could be that positively told stories predict relational health or that when daughters are happy and satisfied in their relationships with their mothers, daughters recall happier stories. Regardless, this finding further supports the CNSM proposition that storytelling is reflective of relational health and well-being, but suggests the need to specify further how researchers measure positive framing.

Future research should examine what daughters "do" with the stories they hear. Recent research (Gillchrist-Petty & Reynolds, 2015) shows that whether daughters *followed* the advice they received in their mothers' stories was related to current marital satisfaction. It may be that daughters' intentions for following—or passing on—the advice they received helps to explain their own experience of romantic relationships. It would be interesting to know how the stories daughters hear affect the way they choose or relate to romantic partners. For example, Jody's mom always told her stories that encouraged her to marry someone with whom she had a lot in common. That theme always served as a measuring stick for how Jody thought about her serious boyfriends and whether she thought the relationship would last. Future researchers should ask daughters how their mothers' stories affect the ways they think about and behave in adult relationships.

Overall, grounded in CNSM, our study extends the literature on mother-daughter storytelling about romantic relationships and suggests that mother-daughter relational satisfaction is linked to daughters' recollection of happier, more redemptive stories about love. In general, we found that daughters felt closer to their moms when they heard stories that were positive and hopeful about love. In particular, girls whose mothers told them stories that encouraged them not to rush into love, but instead to take time for their education, careers, and/or wait for the right person to come along also reported being the most satisfied with their relationship with their mothers. This was in contrast with daughters who heard stories that were negatively framed about the need to choose wisely. These stories seemed to be more like warnings. Moreover, these stories were often about negative experiences mothers had with the daughters' own fathers (see also Koenig Kellas, 2010). These negative stories, then, might signify even more complexities in the mother-daughter relationship such as loyalty conflicts if the daughters feel caught in the middle (Amato & Afifi, 2006) of their parents' marital struggles. Ultimately, results of this study shed light on the importance of mother-daughter stories about romantic relationships as foundational to daughters' expectations of meanings surrounding love and romance and as indicators of the strength of the mother-daughter relationship. They also tell us something about the values of love and marriage at this moment in time for a Midwestern sample of women. The story themes uncovered here convey that mothers tried to pass on valued of independence, thoughtfulness, selectivity, openness, and intuition in finding love. Importantly, it also shows that mothers were realistic about love—framing love as complicated and not always sunny. Overall, the stories told by daughters in this study suggest an ethic that encourages daughters to put themselves first, find love on their own terms, and choose wisely, but also recognize the inevitable ups and downs of love and relationships.

WHAT DO WE STILL NEED TO KNOW?

- Do mothers with different religious backgrounds, from different regional areas of the United States, of different ages and races share the same types of stories about love and relationships with their daughters?
- How do mother-daughter stories about love and romance change from daughters' childhood into adulthood?
- How do mothers and daughters tell stories about love and romantic relationships jointly/together?
- Are daughters willing to pass their mother's stories to their own daughters (if they have their own daughter)?

HOW DOES THIS WORK IN REAL LIFE?

For many of us, storytelling is not something we think about it's something we simply do. We hope this chapter makes you more aware and mindful of the stories that pepper your daily life. We also hope it might help you reach out to your mothers or other family members to hear the stories that teach values, lessons, and give you ideas about how to navigate our complicated world.

- If you are a daughter, try to recall the stories you have heard from your mother. How do they compare or contrast with the stories we told you about in this chapter? How, if at all, do they help you think about your relationship with your mother or a romantic relationship you are or have been in previously?
- If you are a son, think about what stories you have heard from your mother about romantic relationships. How are they different or the same as what you read about in this chapter?
- Do you think there are sex differences in family storytelling?
- Do dads tell stories about relationships? How are they similar to or different from mothers' stories?
- If you have only (or mostly) heard negatively framed stories from your mothers (or parents), consider asking them to tell you a positive story about love.

We also hope this chapter might help you think about how you frame your own stories and how you might frame them when you have children. If you think about it, even though we do not have control of many things in life, we do get to tell our own stories. Even if we experience adversity, we can always think about what we learned of value and/or how we have grown or changed for the better as a result of these experiences. Because CNSM and other narrative research demonstrates positive health benefits (both individual and relational) to positive framing:

- Think about how you can frame your stories in redemptive terms (McAdams et al., 2001.
- Also, pay attention to the commonalities across your family stories: they will give you clues into what your family values and how that fits with the way you see the world.
- If you do not know many family stories, use this chapter as a good excuse to ask for them. Stories connect us in ways that endure over time.
- Make sure to know the stories that animate your family, ask yourself about the stories you like and do not like, think about how those stories shape who you are, and be mindful about the stories you tell and how you want to write your individual and relational stories into the future.

- Finally, remember, stories are at the center of who we are, and they emerge collaboratively in communication with others. How we tell them matters.

CLASSROOM ACTIVITIES

A Love Story

For this activity get into small groups and share a story your mom (or another family member—dad, grandparent, sibling) told you about love. Be detailed as you share your story and make sure to include a beginning, middle, and end. Once each group member has shared your stories, answer the following discussion questions:

- How, if at all has this story shaped how you think of relationships, dating, and/or marriage? How has the story made you think positively or negatively about love, romance, or relationships?
- What is your relationship like with the person who told you the story? Do you think the framing of the story helps to explain that relationship as it did in the chapter?
- Would you share this story with your own children one day? If so, what parts will you highlight or focus on in this story?
- Do you think the sex of the person (mom or dad, family member) who told the story plays a role in how you think about love, romance, and relationships?

Family Storytelling

Interview your mother (or another family member) about important family stories. Ask for at least three stories that tell you something about the family. Look across all of the stories and see if there are any common themes. If so, what are they? What do these stories tell you about what your family values? What about these stories do you embrace? Want to change? Why?

REFERENCES

Amato, P. R., & Afifi, T. D. (2006). Feeling caught between parents: Adult children's relations with parents and subjective well-being. *Journal of Marriage and Family, 68*(1), 222–235. https://doi.org/10.1111/j.1741-3737.2006.00243.x

Bohanek, J. G., Marin, K. A., & Fivush, R. (2008). Family narratives, self, and gender in early adolescence. *Journal of Early Adolescence, 28*(1), 153–176. https://doi.org/10.1177/0272431607308673

Bulmer, M. (1979). Concepts in the analysis of qualitative data. *Sociological Review, 27*(4), 651–677. https://doi.org/10.1111/j.1467-954X.1979.tb00354.x

Fiese, B. H., & Sameroff, A. J. (1999). The family narrative consortium: A multidimensional approach to narratives. *Monographs of the Society for Research in Child Development, 64*(2), 1–36. https://doi.org/10.1111/1540-5834.00017

Fiese, B. H., & Skillman, G. (2000). Gender differences in family stories: Moderating influence of parent gender role and child gender. *Sex Roles, 43*(5), 267–283. https://doi.org/10.1023/A:1026630824421

Gilchrist-Petty, E. S., & Reynolds, N. (2015). Momma's embedded advice: The relationship between mother–daughter marriage narratives and daughters' marital satisfaction. *Southern Communication Journal, 80*(4), 293–310. https://doi.org/10.1080/1041794X.2015.1052151

Goodall, H. L., Jr. (2005). Narrative inheritance: A nuclear family with toxic secrets. *Qualitative Inquiry, 11*(4), 492–513. https://doi.org/10.1177/1077800405276769

Hayden, J. M., Singer, J. A., & Chrisler, J. C. (2006). The transmission of birth stories from mother to daughter: Self-esteem and mother-daughter attachment. *Sex Roles, 55*(5), 373–383. https://doi.org/10.1007/s11199-006-9090-3

Koenig Kellas, J. (2005). Family ties: Communicating identity through jointly told family stories. *Communication Monographs, 72*(4), 365–389. https://doi.org/10.1080/03637750500322453

Koenig Kellas, J. (2010). Transmitting relational world views: The relationship between mother-daughter memorable messages and adult daughters' romantic relationship schemata. *Communication Quarterly, 58*(4), 458–479. https://doi.org/10.1080/01463373.2010.525700

Koenig Kellas, J. (2018). Communicated narrative sense-making theory: Linking storytelling and health. In D. O. Braithwaite, E. Suter, & K. Floyd (Eds.), *Engaging theories in family communication* (2nd ed., pp. 62–74). New York, NY: Routledge.

Koenig Kellas, J., Baxter, L., LeClair-Underberg, C., Thatcher, M., Routsong, T, & Normand, E. L. (2014). Telling the story of stepfamily beginnings: The relationship between young-adult stepchildren's stepfamily origin stories and their satisfaction with the stepfamily. *Journal of Family Communication, 14*(2), 149–166.

Koenig Kellas, J., & Kranstuber Horstman, H. (2015). Communicated narrative sense-making: Understanding family narratives, storytelling, and the construction of meaning through a communicative lens. In L. Turner & R. West (Eds.), *Sage handbook of family communication* (pp. 76–90). Thousand Oaks, CA: Sage.

Koenig Kellas, J., & Trees, A. (2013). Family stories and storytelling: Windows into the family soul. In A. L. Vangelisti (Ed.), *Handbook of family communication* (2nd ed., pp. 391–406). Mahwah, NJ: Lawrence Erlbaum.

Kranstuber Horstman, H. K. (2013). "Love stories aren't always like the movies": The relational implications of inheriting parent's courtship stories. In J. Koenig Kellas (Ed.), *Family storytelling: Negotiating identities, teaching lessons, and making meaning* (pp. 31–53). New York, NY: Routledge.

Kranstuber Horstman, H. K., Maliski, R., Hays, A., Cox, J., Enderle, A., & Nelson, L. R. (2016). Unfolding narrative meaning over time: The contributions of mother–daughter conversations of difficulty on daughter narrative sense-making and well-being. *Communication Monographs, 83*(3), 326–348. https://doi.org/10.1080/03637751.2015.1068945

McAdams, D. P. (1993). *The stories we live by: Personal myths and the making of the self.* New York, NY: Guilford Press.

McAdams, D. P., Reynolds, J., Lewis, M., Patten, A. H., & Bowman, P. J. (2001). When bad things turn good and good things turn bad: Sequences of redemption and contamination in life narrative and their relation to psychosocial adaptation in midlife adults and in students. *Personality and Social Psychology Bulletin, 27*(4), 474–485. http://dx.doi.org/10.1177/0146167201274008

Owen, W. F. (1984). Interpretive themes in relational communication. *Quarterly Journal of Speech, 70*(3), 274–287. https://doi.org/10.1080/00335638409383697

Peterson, C., & Roberts, C. (2003). Like mother, like daughter: Similarities in narrative style. *Developmental Psychology, 39*(3), 551–562. http://dx.doi.org/10.1037/0012-1649.39.3.551

Stone, E. (2004). *Black sheep and kissing cousins: How our family stories shape us.* London, UK: Transaction.

CHAPTER FOURTEEN

Busy Squirrels, Well-Oiled Machines, AND Warm Bread

Adult Daughters' Discursive Constructions of Their Full-Time Working Mothers

MEREDITH MARKO HARRIGAN,* ANGELA M. HOSEK,[†] AND SEUNGJI YANG[‡]

She did it all and she did it really well

—(KRISTEN)

She is a wonder-woman because she attempts to do every work without complaining or showing any stressed-out faces. Also, her image of trying her best regardless of outcomes gives me an impression of [a] hero and an admiration to be like her when I become a mother

—(EUN-YOUNG)

The quotes above, although spoken by daughters from different cultural backgrounds (Kristen is American and Eun-young is South Korean), depict perceptions of *successful* working mothers. Why do these daughters evaluate success in the same way? What other meanings do daughters from these cultures voice when they talk about their mothers, especially full-time working mothers? And, to what degree does daughters' discourse about their mothers cross cultural lines, especially for American and South Korean daughters? Given the authors' cultural backgrounds (two Americans and one South Korean) and our roles as mothers and daughters (or both!), these questions make us curious.

* Meredith Marko Harrigan, State University of New York at Geneseo.
[†] Angela M. Hosek, Ohio University.
[‡] Seungji Yang, Daegu, South Korea.

When we communicate, we create expectations that shape and reflect how we make sense of and evaluate our relational partners, including our mothers. Ideas about motherhood in general and about *effective mothering,* in particular, are socially constructed through discourse (Elvin-Nowak & Thomsson, 2001). The present chapter centers on daughters' involvement in evaluating their mothers, and the differences in these evaluations through cultural lenses. We believe this topic is important not only because of the close relationship daughters and mothers often share, but also because daughters may become mothers and, in turn, be impacted by their own discourse.

The mother-daughter relationship is argued to be highly significant in many cultures; yet, we know little about daughters' perceptions of mothering in various parts of the world (Rastogi & Wampler, 1999). Thoughts, interpretations, and expectations about motherhood may be shared across cultural lines, or they may vary from culture to culture. It is these possibilities that are the topic of this chapter.

As discussed in previous chapters, discursive constructions of motherhood—meanings of motherhood that are constructed through our language—take place in both the *macro-context,* such as in popular culture and the media (Kirby, Riforgiate, Anderson, Lahman, & Lietzenmayer, 2016), and the *micro-context,* such as in family relationships (Heisler & Ellis, 2008). As Buzzanell and Liu (2005) explained, what social and personal discourse says (or doesn't say) may create or alter meanings, in this case about motherhood. This perspective positions communication not merely as the process of transmitting information but as a *formative process* of constructing social realties, including identities (Leeds-Hurwitz, 2006). The present chapter centers on the construction of one particular identity—that of the *full-time working mother*—and explores how adult daughters make sense of and discursively construct that identity in both the U.S. and South Korea. This follows the explanation from Miller-Day (2004), who explained, "a speaker's talk situates his or her partner in a certain identity" (p. 173). So, through talk we can begin to understand how the "motherhood" identity is perceived by daughters. Tracy and Robles (2013) expand our understanding of *identity-work* by noting that individuals often ascribe characteristics to people or "cast" them into identities through the way they interact with or about them. This view of the self is rooted, in part, in the notion of the looking-glass self, explained by Cooley (1983) that "in imagination we perceive in another's mind some thought of our appearance, manners, aims, deeds, character, friends, and so on, and are variously affected by it" (p. 184). We form this imagination—these perceptions, these identities—through interacting with others in various contexts. Let's explore how this relates to mothers and daughters.

MOTHERS AND DAUGHTERS

As you have read throughout this book, the mother-daughter dyad is argued to be one of the closest relationships in the family system (Fisher & Miller-Day,

2006; Steinberg & Silk, 2002) and central to young women's lives (Jordan, 1993). Mothers are often sources of support and encouragement for daughters, particularly during important life transitions (e.g., Eaton & Bradley, 2008). Despite what we know about mothers' role in daughters' lives, we know less about the role daughters might play in mothers' lives and/or how their experiences of being a daughter might influence their role as a potential future mother. Given the importance of the mother-daughter relationship for many women, and what we know about communication in identity-work, we can assume that the perceptions daughters hold of their mothers are impactful to mothers' sense of self as well as to their role evaluation. In other words, how daughters see their mothers might influence how mothers see themselves and how they evaluate themselves as mothers. Thus, daughters' perceptions of their mothers could provide important information that shapes the experience of motherhood for their mothers. As Miller-Day (2004) reminded us "how we talk and act towards others casts them in a role and serves to write their story for them" (p. 173). In addition, and central to this chapter, how daughters make sense of and evaluate their mothers could affect how the daughters enact the role of a mother, when they become mothers.

For many women, being a "good" mother is an important goal and one that motivates their behavior (Guendouzi, 2005). Contrary to what some people believe, good mothering is not innate to women (Cowdery & Knudson-Martin, 2005), nor do people always agree on what counts as good mothering (See chapter 3, this text, on motherhood). Rather, role expectations—appropriate behaviors associated with roles—are communicatively constructed and may differ across time, place, and culture. For example, Guendouzi conducted an ethnographic study about "good" mothering and found that British women associated good mothering with being protective, nurturing, caring, organized, proud of their children, and capable of instilling appropriate values in their children (2005).

Images of so-called good mothers abound in American media (Guendouzi, 2005). Kirby and colleagues (2016) explained that these mediated messages form "ideals/ideologies of who one should be" and serve as "resources for identity construction" (p. 79). What television or movie characters have you come to associate with good mothers? What qualities do the characters' display? (For more on this, see chapter 4 on motherhood in the media, this volume).

At the micro or relational level, women may learn the expectations associated with good mothering from members of their family of origin or through other direct interactions (Heisler & Ellis, 2008). Take a moment to consider this question—What messages have you received about effective or ineffective mothering from those with whom you have developed close personal relationships? Heisler and Ellis (2008) explained, some messages become memorable and part of that person's identity. Role expectations are important to understand because, in addition to influencing behavior, they may provide a benchmark for evaluating role effectiveness and, in turn, might serve as an impetus for role negotiation if the evaluation is negative (Turner & West, 2013).

Full-Time Working Motherhood

The experience of motherhood has changed over time, as has the notion of the typical or traditional mother (Guendouzi, 2005). However, it is important to consider how *expectations* tied to effective mothering have shifted with the changes. For example, women's participation in the paid workforce has nearly doubled over the last 70 years resulting in a high number of dual earning families (Sweet, 2014). Specifically, as of 2014, 60.2% of married couples in families with children were dual earning families, meaning both partners chose to engage in paid work or had a financial need to work (Bureau of Labor Statistics, 2015). Despite the increase in the number of dual earning families, responsibility for domestic labor, including child-related labor and invisible labor, often still rests on mothers. Hochschild and Machung (1989) refer to this workload as the "second-shift" and it often results in perceived (or real) gender inequality.

Working mothers often face demands unlike those experienced by working fathers. Kirby and colleagues (2016) wrote, "there is no parallel term of a good working father; since discourses of work-family/life issues often reflect gendered role expectations of work and private responsibilities, the personification of 'balance' seems more targeted at working mothers" (p. 77). As we are sure you can imagine, coordinating one's work and family roles has increased in difficulty as more women engage in paid work and because expectations for both work and family have become more demanding (Craig & Powell, 2012). For example, today mothers are expected to be more heavily involved in their children's lives than in the past (Craig & Powell, 2012; Sweet, 2014). This experience is often referred to as "intensive mothering" (Gunderson & Barrett, 2017). In their discussion about working mothers, Kirby and colleagues (2016) argued, macro-contextual messages of mothers, such as those in film, create and sustain "cultural ideologies of being an ideal worker, a true domestic woman, and an intensive mother" (p. 77). How do you envision working motherhood? How does this vision affect your view of your mother? It is a valuable exercise to imagine how our own thoughts are shaped by the messages on working motherhood that we receive from those around us. Moreover, it is important to know that these thoughts about our mothers are shaping how we will parent our children and frame ourselves as working parents. What types of expectations do you envision for yourself as a potential future working mother? How has your culture influenced your views and expectations on work and parenting?

The Role of Culture

Expectations and talk about motherhood may differ among cultural groups. Although *culture* can be defined in various ways, in a general sense, it refers to the attitudes, values, beliefs, and practices that are shared by a group of individuals. Anthropologists and social psychologists have described a variety of cultural value orientations that influence perception and communication. Anthropologist Geert Hofstede (see Hofstede, Hofstede, & Minkov, 2010) put some of the most often discussed forward. Hofstede's typology includes individualism and collectivism (the degree to which people emphasize I or We), low and high power distance (the attitudes people hold about power differences), masculinity and femininity (motivation tied to being the best or enjoying activities), low and high uncertainty avoidance (the degree to which we approach the future's unpredictability), long and short-term orientation (views regarding the linking of the past to the future), and indulgence (the degree to which people control desires). As you can see, culture can have a large impact on our values and expectations.

THE STUDY

What Were We Interested in Learning?

With all of this in mind, *we wanted to begin to understand how daughters in both the U.S. and South Korea make sense of their full-time working mothers* through a close analysis of their discourse, since, as you read, discourse helps constitute social realities (Buzzanell & Liu, 2005). We wanted to understand what daughters actually say about their full-time working mothers. In addition, given our backgrounds (two American and one South Korean authors) *we were curious how, if at all, daughters in the U.S. and South Korea differ in their sense-making*. Therefore, we designed a study to address these questions.

How Did We Go About Learning This Information?

Our study is an example of *interpretive research*. This approach is used when researchers are interested in understanding "how particular social realities are produced and maintained though everyday practices of individuals" (Baxter & Braithwaite, 2006, p. 5). We were specifically interested in *daughters'* discursive practices regarding their full-time working mothers. We used a process called *purposive sampling* to locate participants. Purposive sampling involves searching for participants who have experiences that match the project's goals (Baxter & Babbie, 2004). Specifically, we sought daughters who: (a) were at least 18 years old,

(b) were living in the United States or South Korea and identified as members of those cultures, and (c) were raised by two full-time working parents, with at least one of them being a mother. We asked participants to list and describe the first five words that came to their minds when they thought of their working mothers and to choose a metaphor that described their working mothers. A total of 76 daughters participated, 52 were from the U.S. and 24 were from South Korea.

To make sense of the data, we focused on specific terms and phrases that daughters used to describe their working mothers. This process resulted in 474 descriptive terms or phrases by American daughters (an average of 8.6 per participant) and 197 descriptive terms and phrases by South Korean daughters (an average of 8.2 per participant). We then categorized the descriptive terms or phrases, which resulted in ten categories of discursive constructions.

What Did We Learn?

We assessed if the ten categories of discursive constructions captured the descriptive terms expressed by both American daughters and South Korean daughters and discovered that they did. This suggests similar perceptions about successful working mothers across both cultures. The findings from our study showed us that not only do American and South Korean daughters talk about their working mothers in similar ways, they share an overwhelmingly positive perception of them. In the following paragraphs, we explain the categories of discursive constructions. These categories reflect the descriptive language used when discussing working mothers. These categories include: *driven, omnipresent, kind, competent, essential, busy, challenged, resilient, superhuman, and inspirational.*

Driven

In this first category of descriptors, daughters discussed their mothers as *driven*: women who "always wanted more" (Katie[?]) and who are highly motivated and determined to excel in both their professional and parental roles. Daughters, like Christa, frequently commented that their mothers displayed an admirable work ethic and put tremendous effort into everything they did, making them some of the hardest working people they know. As Keisha wrote about her mother, "she put her all into everything she did." Similarly, Hope expressed that her mother "always gave her very best." Gabrielle concurred noting her mother "never did anything half-way." Sasha even described her mother as a "work horse" and Jung-min used an ant as a metaphor noting, "my mom is like an ant who always works hard." Daughters characterized their mothers as people who are goal-oriented, ambitious, and determined to meet their goals. Jillian highlighted her mother's determination when she said that her mother, "never gives up when her mind is on something." Despite the demands of their professional work, daughters described their mothers as constantly present in their lives and in the lives of their families.

Omnipresent

In the second category, daughters offer descriptions of committed mothers who were physically and emotionally *omnipresent* in their lives and the lives of their families, despite the demanding nature of their professional jobs. Daughters, like Jasmine, described their mothers as attentive and involved, noting they "always made time for us no matter what." Ha-eun similarly noted that her mother "did not stop keeping [her] eyes on her children." Megan said her mother "worked a full day and then would still find time to bring me to the park and hang out with me." Bridget shared a similar experience, noting that her mother "always went to certain school events and kept up on my life and my sister's life." As daughters spoke about their mothers and voiced a discourse of presence, they framed their mothers as dependable and capable of effectively meeting their many needs. Sasha commented, "no matter how many hours she worked or how few hours she slept, my siblings and I always had food to eat and clean laundry." Carissa added to her list of her mother's accomplishments, helping her prepare for school. Carissa wrote, "even after a long day of work, she would still sit down and go over homework with me, making sure I was prepared for the next day of school." Not only were mothers described as being physically and emotionally present in their daughters' lives, they were constructed as kind while interacting with their daughters.

Kind

The third category of descriptions included discussion of mothers with *kind* hearts, good-natured demeanors, generosity, and abundant love for their families. Daughters described their mothers as supportive, compassionate, and caring. Emily even compared her mother to "an angel." Seo-yun chose "bread" as her metaphor and explained the comparison this way: "she is very warm and soft just like the bread we eat in the morning." Francesca shared that her mother "always made it obvious how much she cared for each member of our family" and Young-eun shared, "I always feel like my mom loves me." Perhaps this positive demeanor was best captured by Megan who called her mom a "ray of sunshine" and Vanessa who noted her mom is "always brightening the day."

Daughters also described their mothers as generous and selfless, or as Seo-hyeon framed them, as women who sacrificed "so many things for family," including their personal time, to fulfill the needs of others. Laura commented that her mother "gave most of her time to make sure we were still able to do what we wanted." Keisha's experience was similar noting that her mother was "always putting us first over herself." Morgan went as far as to say, "everything my mom does is for her family." Showcasing her awareness of the extra steps her mother took, Eun-bee referred to her mother as a "friendly dad" explaining "she was just like my dad who stayed busy working every day, but she always spared her time to be there for her children." Mothers' omnipresence and kindness, combined with their strong drive are reflected in the fourth construction, which describes their competence.

Competent

The fourth category of descriptors reflected daughters' discussions of their mothers as *competent*, or good at what they do. They are effective mothers, successful professionals, and skilled working mothers. Kristen summarized this nicely when she wrote, "she did it all and she did it really well." Su-min went as far as to say that her mother "did both her work in and out of the house perfectly."

In terms of their parental role, daughters, like Carissa, often chose the word "great" to describe the type of mother they have. Participants listed a variety of factors that made their mothers great. For example, Gabrielle described her mom as "fun" and bragged about the fact that she always came up with enjoyable "activities for my siblings to do after we finished our homework." Da-eun's mother's greatness was situated in her endless knowledge. Da-eun explained, "whenever we ask questions to her, she always answered every question." Isabella's mother "excelled at problem solving." Daughters also commented on their mothers' professional success. For example, Jasmine's noted that her mom "really knew how to do her job well." Some daughters even spoke about their mothers' skill managing full-time work and motherhood. Rachel called her mother "productive" because she "balanced things successfully." Daughters often attributed their mothers' success managing their professional and parental roles to their organizational skills. Bethany even described her mother akin to "a bear preparing for hibernation" and Bridget chose a "well-oiled machine" to showcase their masterful organization. Mothers' strong organizational skills connect to the fifth construction, essential.

Essential

In this fifth category, daughters provide descriptions recognizing the *essential* and important role their mothers play in their lives and in the lives of their families. Daughters framed their mothers as linchpins who were vital to the successful functioning of the family. Jessica called her mother the "backbone" of her family and Brianna noted that her mother "kept the whole family going." Isabella shared a similar perception, even highlighting her mother's radiating influence when she wrote that her mother "kept the family together even when she was away."

Daughters also recognized the important role their mothers played in their personal lives by working full-time. Da-eun explained that without her mother's support, she would "not have been able to do both economically and mentally that I desire."

The essential role mothers played for their daughters and their families in combination with their work demands help illustrate the sixth construction, which is busy.

Busy

The sixth category of descriptors, and perhaps most frequently noted description by daughters, was the characteristic of busyness; that is, how *busy* their mothers always seemed to be. Daughters, like Carissa and Hope, framed their mothers' demands as endless, which led them to be seen as "constantly moving" and working "non-stop." Sasha wrote, "my mom never stops working. She works at her [office] during the week, in her garden when it's warm, and in the house when it's cold." Daughters often commented about their mothers' abilities to multitask or, as Haley said, "do a million things at once." To convey the extent of how busy their mothers are, daughters drew on a number of interesting metaphors. These included squirrels, who, as Sam noted were "always busy, running around"; cars, as Jillian commented, "never stopped running"; and even bees that, according to Haley, were "pollinating every flower in the world." Some daughters illustrated how busy their moms were by comparing their mothers to their fathers. For example, Kaily noted, "my mom did a lot more at work than my dad did" and Da-som wrote her mother "cleaned everything by herself." Daughters acknowledged the many demands their mothers faced both at work and at home, including what Da-som described as the "invisible work she had to do." What is important to note is that daughters attribute their mothers' busy lives to the professional and parental roles, rather to personal hobbies or endeavors. As described, daughters depicted their mothers as needing to be continuously moving to meet the many demands they faced, both at work and at home. This need is connected to daughters' perceptions of their mothers as challenged, the seventh construction.

Challenged

In the eighth category of descriptors, daughters discuss the *challenge* of what Seo-yun described as the "heavy burden" of managing both their professional and parental roles. As Ha-yoon noted, "managing full-time work and family is a difficult thing to do" and Su-min hypothesized, "all this work cannot be done without getting a certain amount of stress." Seo-yun even framed her mother as a "shaking wild flower," especially during hard times. Daughters described their mothers as overworked and tired and, at times, overwhelmed and stressed. For example, Christa noted that her mother "was always falling asleep on the couch" and Young-eun commented that her mother "was overwhelmed by her duties and felt lonely that no one was there to relieve her of her burden." Addressing the stressful nature of being a full-time working mother, Min-ji described her mother as having "a knot in her shoulder and back." Displaying a different form of *challenge*, some daughters perceived their mothers as emotionally conflicted over their status as working mothers. As Nicole expressed, "I know my mom struggled sometimes to choose between family responsibilities and work responsibilities."

Despite the presence of these challenges, daughters noted that their mothers rarely complained about their struggles or expressed negative emotions. Framing these as strengths, Ji-woo wrote, "It is not easy to manage work from both house and profession, but she kept her benevolent and kind mother image even after work." Su-min agreed and elaborated noting that her mother "never said she is tired, rather, she said she enjoys everything even about work and house." Seo-hyeon perceives that her mother masks her stress in order "not to burden her family." She even went as far as to say, "I respect highly of her for managing it without complaining." Not only did daughters perceive their mothers to withhold negative commentary and/or emotion tied to the stress they face managing full-time work and motherhood; they also framed their mothers as capable of "pushing through" the challenges. We used the term resilient to describe this quality.

Resilient

The responses included in this eighth category, reveal that daughters view their mothers as *resilient*: capable of pushing through hard times and overcoming challenges they face managing full-time work and motherhood. Here too, daughters often used the word *strong* when describing their mothers. Seo-yun noted that her mother "faced hardships but she went through those difficult times with a strong mind and strength" and Danielle commented that her mom "endures a lot" but "powers through." Metaphorically, Hope framed her mother as a "warrior" and others described their mothers as tough as nails, bricks, and rubies. As Courtney noted, her mother "didn't let anything stand in her way" and Alexandra said her mother "never wanted to take defeat." Nicole elaborated explaining that her mother "worked through guilt and exhaustion to be a good mom and teacher." All the aforementioned discourses culminate in the final two constructions: superhuman and inspirational.

Superhuman

The ninth category includes daughters' descriptions of their mothers as being *superhuman* and extraordinary in what they can do. Daughters used words like "amazing," "incredible," "awesome," and "unbelievable" and metaphors like "wonder woman," "machines," and "robots" to characterize their mothers. Daughters' general sentiment was that their mothers were "capable of so many things," as Kyung-hee expressed. On top of being able to do everything and anything, daughters commented that their mothers could do it with little sleep. Suggesting the machine-like quality of her mother, Carissa noted that her mom "only needs a few hours to recharge." This perception of their mothers needing only little sleep highlights their perceived ability to function beyond of an average human. Distinguishing her mother from others, Kyung-hee expressed "not everyone could do what she does."

Some daughters said they could not imagine being able to do what their mothers can do. As Seo-hyeon shared, "If I were her, I do not think I could do [everything] like her." Bethany similarly expressed, "I don't know how she did it all." Daughters' descriptions of their mothers as superhuman makes sense given the range of other positive attributes they ascribed to them in the categories of descriptors detailed above. This superhuman identity appears to serve as a model and source of inspiration for many daughters.

Inspirational

Mothers' superhuman abilities—or their ability to function in ways beyond what is viewed as typical of a human being—were an *inspiration* to many participants. As Olivia noted, her mother "inspired me more than anyone." Rachel even said her mother "made me want to be a working mom." Daughters, including Eun-young and Bridget, described respecting and admiring their mothers and, in doing so, framed them as "heroes" and as positive role models they "can look up to." Amanda even commented that she looks at her mother "in awe."

As we have described, American and South Korean daughters' discourse about their full-time working mothers is overwhelmingly positive and similar in content. Although daughters see their mothers as constantly busy because of and challenged by both their professional and parental demands, they affirmed their mothers' competence and the effective management of both. Daughters describe their mothers as driven and resilient as well as kind, physically and emotionally present in the lives of their children and families, and essential to their families. Together these qualities paint a picture of their mothers who are superhuman and capable of doing amazing things, which left many daughters inspired, but left other daughters questioning their own abilities to function well as potential future mothers. In the following section, we consider the positive and negative implications these findings might have for daughters as potential future mothers.

WHAT DOES ALL THIS MEAN?

After stopping to consider what all of this means, we realize that daughters' discourse is powerful. How daughters talk about working mothers may reflect and even reinforce certain expectations for motherhood. These expectations, in turn, could have consequences for current and future mothers. Understanding this process as well as the specific content of daughters' talk raises some important questions about quality-of-life and culture. Our study, for example, suggests that daughters from different cultural contexts make sense of and talk about their full-time working mothers in similar (and overly positive) ways. Although daughters acknowledge the intensive workload their mothers experience and the possible toll the workload has on them, they are impressed and inspired by their mothers' abilities to persevere without complaining. In turn, daughters see their mothers as role models and the kind of mother they wish to become.

Role Modeling and Quality-of-Life

As we discussed, daughters describe a positive and inspiring model. However, a close examination of implicit messages highlights areas for potential concern. For example, daughters' ultra-positive talk about their mothers seems to support Quindlen's (2005) notion of the "uber-mom" (p. 50) which is a mom that "bounces from soccer field to school fair to play date until she falls into bed at the end of the day, exhausted, her life somewhere between the Stations of the Cross and a decathlon" (p. 50). In our study, this hyperactive style of mothering applied to their professional, parental, *and* domestic-related activities. Given the high demands of paid and unpaid labor expectations, we would expect that certain tasks would need to go unfulfilled (how can one do *every*thing?). However, our work makes us wonder if, instead, daughters think their mothers are fulfilling *all* of their responsibilities at home and at work in a manner that is extraordinary and impressive. What we did not hear in daughters' talk is a value for the self, including one's health and well-being. This is concerning because daughters who replicate what they perceive as impressive models of motherhood could face consequences tied to *quality-of-life*, which is the "overall satisfaction with one's work experience in the context of other life experiences, constraints, and aspirations" (Eisenberg, Trethewey, LeGreco, & Goodall, 2018). Scholars have used the term *work-life conflict* to refer to the experience of being unable to balance their work and personal life and frame it as a barrier to quality-of-life. This is potentially worrisome since work-life conflict has been associated with various negative outcomes including psychological distress (Frone, 2003), stress (Tomazevic, Kozjek, & Stare, 2014), family-related and work-related absenteeism (Frone, 2003), and risky behaviors such as heavy alcohol and cigarette use (Frone, Barnes, & Farrell, 1994). Thus, might daughters' positive commentary about their working mothers create a framework of expectations that could have negative future consequences for themselves? Likewise, daughters' commentary about their mothers' omnipresence, or what scholars have referred to as "intensive mothering" (Gunderson & Barrett, 2017, p. 993) is likely to interfere with the demands of their professional role and create a double-bind. As Hays (1996) explained, the logic of intensive mothering is often in contrast with the expectations of the marketplace. Although Buzzanell et al. (2005) found that working mothers often *reframe* the "good mother" role into a "good working mother" role, our research suggests that daughters *combine* qualities associated with a "good worker" and "good mother." This layering of identities appears to create an unrealistic expectation that daughters themselves acknowledged when they described their mothers as superhuman and capable of amazing things that they personally do not feel they can accomplish. This apparent compliment—of being superhuman—could be modeled by daughters in their future mother role and negatively impact their quality-of-life.

Understanding daughters' discourse might also teach us something important about *emotion labor*, a term that refers to the process of adjusting feelings and expressing emotions in a manner necessary for a job (Hochschild & Machung, 1989). Daughters spoke positively about how their mother rarely complained. Daughters may try to model this process of emotion regulation. However, scholars have provided warnings about the impact of emotion labor on quality-of-life. For example, Researchers Noor and Zainuddin (2011) found a connection between surface acting and emotional exhaustion. They explained:

> There is a discrepancy or dissonance between felt and displayed emotions (e.g. a teacher feeling angry with the student but has to fake and not express the anger as part of the work role), and this emotional dissonance has been shown to be associated with burnout and other negative psychological outcomes. (Noor & Zainuddin, 2011, p. 289)

We believe it is important to ask if full-time working mothers' infrequent complaining and expression of negative emotion exemplifies emotion dissonance and, if so, the implications these behaviors may have for mental and physical health, well-being, and overall quality-of-life so daughters do not replicate unhealthy models.

Before we close this section, we must say something about the positive lessons daughters might be learning about resilience from their full-time working mothers. *Resilience* includes "the capacity of individuals and families to bounce back, reintegrate, or develop positive identities and life courses" (Lucas & Buzzanell, 2012, p. 191). Mothers might be teaching daughters how to push through difficult times in order to maintain a positive working mother identity! The information provided in this chapter also raises interesting questions about the role of culture in daughterhood and motherhood.

The Role of Culture in Mothering

As you have read in this chapter, American and South Korean daughters talk about their full-time working mothers in similar ways. However, an example of cultural variation was also evident, which raises important questions about the role of culture in perceptions of motherhood. When talking about the challenges that working mothers face, South Korean daughters integrated more *empathic* messages than American daughters did. This might be tied to how much each culture values collectivism and masculinity. According to Hofstede Insight's (2018) country comparison, the United States culture is more individualistic and masculine than South Korean culture. A *collectivist orientation* involves shared long-term commitment to and responsibility for members of the group, in this case the family, and a value for face maintenance (Hofstede Insights, 2018). Common in collective cultures is the practice of facework, behaving in ways that maintain one's own or others' preferred self-image or *face* (Goffman, 1967). Thus, South Korean mothers may be masking negative emotion in their effort to maintain their face and the face of their family members. Likewise, South Korean daughters' expressions of empathy and concern for their mothers might be tied to this same collectivistic value. Hofstede Insights (2018) adds that a high score in *masculinity* (the United States scored a 62 compared to South Korea, which scored a 39) indicates that the culture values "competition, achievement and success" whereas a lower score displays a value for "caring for others and quality of life" (para. 6–7). Thus, culture often shapes perception and, as a result, could have important personal and relational implications for daughters, especially those who become mothers.

As we conclude the chapter, we hope you have given new thought to how you, as daughters, think and talk about full-time working mothers and that you will be willing to engage in critical thought about the implications those processes have for current and future mothers. We also hope this information generated important new questions about mothers, daughters, quality-of-life, and culture.

WHAT DO WE STILL NEED TO KNOW?

- How, do daughters challenge their mothers' role modeling when they become mothers, either through divergent behaviors or discussions with their mother?
- How do mothers challenge daughters' positive discourse about motherhood, rejecting it as hyperbole?
- In what ways do mothers and daughters communicatively negotiate expectations for motherhood? Do we see evolving discourses about motherhood?
- How is working motherhood framed in the media in the United States, South Korea, and across the globe?
- When cultural value orientations are taken into consideration, how do these influence daughters' expectations and evaluations of their mothers across the globe?

HOW DOES THIS WORK IN REAL LIFE?

- When daughters comment about their working moms' performance (as a mom, as a worker), this talk contributes to mothers' understanding of their identity. Daughters should know that the things they say to moms and to other daughters really does impact how a mom thinks and feels about herself. It may even change how her mother behaves.

- This talk can also influence how daughters will act when they are moms, working or not. When a daughter becomes a mother, she will think back to her own working mom and may use these perceptions to help form her own identity as a working mother. Through many role changes over a lifespan, mothers and daughters are connected even in their identity constructions!

- Though culture uniquely influences how mothers and daughters interact, we found that both American and South Korean daughters evaluate their moms' ability to work and mother simultaneously very positively. This means that daughters most notice the good aspects of their mother as a worker instead of feeling slighted by her working outside of the home, even in different countries halfway across the world from one another.

CLASSROOM ACTIVITIES

- Discuss the various levels of cultural diversity that exist in your classroom. How do the cultural differences influence children's perceptions of motherhood and the mother-daughter relationship? Use Hofstede's Cultural Comparison tool available at https://www.hofstede-insights.com/product/compare-countries/ What cultural values seem most impactful?

- As a class, brainstorm 5 hit television shows that depict a relationship between a daughter and working mother. How do these relationships depict effective mothering?

- Spend an entire day shadowing your own (or another) working mother. What was most surprising about the experience? What was most satisfying about the experience? What was most difficult about the experience?

- Follow the steps the research participants in our studied took. First, list the first five words that come to mind when thinking about your working mother. Second, choose a metaphor that describes your working mother. Talk to your mother about your choices and discuss how your perceptions of working motherhood are similar or different from her perceptions.

NOTE

1. Each name is a pseudonym. We chose common American and South Korean women's names to distinguish the samples. All South Korean participant names contain a hyphen between syllables, which is commonplace.

REFERENCES

Baxter, L. A., & Babbie, E. (2004). *The basics of communication research*. Belmont, CA: Wadsworth.

Baxter, L. A., & Braithwaite, D. O. (2006). Introduction: Meta-theory and theory in family communication research. In D. O. Braithwaite & L. A. Baxter (Eds.), *Engaging theories in family communication: Multiple perspectives* (pp. 1–15). Thousand Oaks, CA: Sage.

Bureau of Labor Statistics. (2015). Employment characteristics of family summary. Available at http://www.bls.gov/news.release/famee.nr0.htm

Buzzanell, P. M., & Liu, M. (2005). Struggling with maternity leave policies and practices: A poststructuralist feminist analysis of gendered organizing. *Journal of Applied Communication Research, 33*(1), 1–25. https://doi.org/10.1080/0090988042000318495

Buzzanell, P. M., Meisenbach, R., Remke, R., Liu, M., Bowers, V., & Conn, C. (2005). The good working mother: Managerial women's sensemaking and feelings about work-family issues. *Communication Studies, 56*(3), 261–285. https://doi.org/10.1080/10510970500181389

Cooley, C. H. (1983). *Human nature and the social order*. New Brunswick, NJ: Transaction Books.

Cowdery, R. S., & Knudson-Martin, C. (2005). The construction of motherhood: Tasks, relational connection, and gender equality. *Family Relations, 54*(3), 335–345. https://doi.org/10.1111/j.1741-3729.2005.00321.x

Craig, L., & Powell, A. (2012). Dual-earner parents' work-family time: The effects of a typical work patterns and non-parental childcare. *Journal of Popular Research, 29*(3), 229–247. https://doi.org/10.1007/s12546-012-9086-5

Eaton, R. J., & Bradley, G. (2008). The role of gender and negative affectivity in stressor appraisal and coping selection. *International Journal of Stress Management, 15*(1), 94–115. https://doi.org/10.1037/1072-5245.15.1.94

Eisenberg, E. M., Trethewey, A., LeGreco, M., & Goodall, H. L. (2018). *Organizational communication: Balancing creativity and constraint* (8th ed.). New York, NY: Bedford/ St. Martin's.

Elvin-Nowak, Y. (1999). The meaning of guilt: A phenomenological description employed by mothers' experiences of guilt. *Scandinavian Journal of Psychology, 40*(1), 73–83. https://doi.org/10.1111/1467-9450.00100

Elvin-Nowak, Y., & Thomsson, H. (2001). Motherhood as idea and practice: A discursive understanding of employed mothers in Sweden. *Gender & Society, 15*(3), 407–428. https://doi.org/10.1177/089124301015003005

Fisher, C., & Miller-Day, M. (2006). Communication over the life span: The mother-adult daughter relationship. In K. Floyd & M. T. Morman (Eds.), *Widening the family circle: New research on family communication* (pp. 3–19). Thousand Oaks, CA: Sage.

Frone, M. R. (2003). Work-family balance. In J. C. Quick & L. E. Tetrick (Eds.), *Handbook of occupational health psychology* (pp. 143–162). Washington, D.C.: American Psychological Association.

Frone, M. R., Barnes, G. M., & Farrell, M. P. (1994). Relationship of work-family conflict to substance use among employed mothers: The role of negative effect. *Journal of Marriage and Family, 56*(4), 1019–1030. https://doi.org/10.2307/353610

Goffman, E. (1967). *Interaction ritual: Essays on face-to-face behavior*. New York, NY: Pantheon Books.

Guendouzi, J. (2005). "I feel quite organized this morning": How mothering is achieved through talk. *Sexualities, Evolution & Gender, 7*(1), 17–35. doi: 10.1080/14616660500111107

Gunderson, J., & Barrett, A. E. (2017). Emotional cost of emotional support? The association between intensive mothering and psychological well-being in midlife. *Journal of Family Issues, 38*(7), 992–1009. https://doi.org/10.1177/0192513X15579502

Hays, S. (1996). *The cultural contradictions of motherhood*. New Haven, CT: Yale University Press.

Heisler, J. M., & Ellis, J. B. (2008). Motherhood and the construction of "mommy identity": Messages about motherhood and face negotiation. *Communication Quarterly, 56*(4), 445–467. https://doi.org/10.1080/01463370802448246

Hochschild, A., & Machung, A. (1989). *The second shift: Working families and the revolution at home*. New York, NY: Viking Press.

Hofstede, G., Hofstede, G. J., & Minkov, M. (2010). *Cultures and organizations: Software of the mind* (3rd ed.). Boston, MA: McGraw-Hill.

Hofstede Insights. (2018). Country comparison. Available at https://www.hofstede-insights.com/country-comparison/south-korea,the-usa/

Johnston, D. D., & Swanson, D. H. (2006). Constructing the "good mother": The experience of mothering ideologies by work status. *Sex Roles, 54*(7–8), 509–519. https://doi.org/10.1007/s11199-006-9021-3

Jordan, J. (1993). The relational self: A model of women's development. In J. van Mens-Verhulst, J. Schreurs, & L. Woertman (Eds.), *Daughtering and mothering: Female subjectivity reanalyzed* (pp. 135–144). New York, NY: Routledge.

Kirby, E. L., Riforgiate, S. E., Anderson, I. K., Lahman, M. P., & Lietzenmayer, A. M. (2016). Good working mothers as jugglers: A critical look at two work-family balance films. *Journal of Family Communication, 16*(1), 76–93. https://doi.org/10.1080/15267431.2015.1111216

Leeds-Hurwitz, W. (2006). Social theories: Social constructionism and symbolic interactionism. In D. O. Braithwaite & L. A. Baxter (Eds.), *Engaging theories in family communication: Multiple perspectives* (pp. 229–242). Thousand Oaks, CA: Sage.

Lucas, K., & Buzzanell, P. M. (2012). Memorable messages of hard times: Constructing short- and long-term resiliencies through family communication. *Journal of Family Communication, 12*(3), 189–208. https://doi.org/10.1080/15267431.2012.687196

Miller-Day, M. (2004). *Communication among grandmothers, mothers, and adult daughters: A qualitative study of maternal relationships*. Mahwah, NJ: Erlbaum.

Noor, N. M., & Zainuddin, M. (2011). Emotional labor and burnout among female teachers: Work-family conflict as mediator. *Asian Journal of Social Psychology, 14*(4), 283–293. https://doi.org/10.1111/j.1467-839X.2011.01349.x

Quindlen, A. (2005, February 21). The good enough mother. *Newsweek Magazine, 145*, 50–51.

Rastogi, M., & Wampler, K. S. (1999). Adult daughters' perceptions of the mother-daughter relationship: A cross-cultural comparison. *Family Relations, 48*(3), 327–336. https://doi.org/10.2307/585643

Sweet, S. (2014). *Work-life interface: An introduction*. Los Angeles, CA: Sage.

Steinberg, L. S., & Silk, J. J. (2002). *Parenting adolescents*. In M. Bornstein (Ed.), *Handbook of parenting* (2nd ed., pp. 103–133). Mahwah, NJ: Lawrence Erlbaum.

Tomazevic, N., Kozjek, T., & Stare, J. (2014). The consequences of a work-family (im)balance: From the point of view of employers and employees. *International Business Research, 7*(8), 83–91. https://doi.org/10.5539/ibr.v7n8p83

Tracy, K., & Robles, J. (2013). *Everyday talk: Building and reflecting identities* (2nd ed.). New York, NY: Guilford Press.

Turner, L. H., & West, R. (2013). *Perspectives of family communication* (4th ed.). New York, NY: McGraw Hill.

CHAPTER FIFTEEN

It's Not That Easy

Challenges of Motherhood

CHRISTINE E. RITTENOUR[*] AND KELLY G. ODENWELLER[†]

Both of us are mothers. But our paths to motherhood were very different. Always desiring motherhood, Christy remembers a nametag she made in second grade that, as instructed, reflected her interests and goals. Her bubble-lettered name was surrounded by a stick figure touting an enormous belly, and several tiny drawings of music notes, smiley faces, and hearts. The bellied self-portrait was, of course, just a symbol of motherhood (like most kids, she knew early that carrying a baby was not the only way to become a mother), and it was probably most inspired by the love her parents showed in raising her and her brother. The dream of motherhood never ceased and was rarely rivaled. In fact, it wasn't until her college mentor, a man, said "*Of course* you can be a mother *and* a professor!" that this second professional dream came close in the ranks. After joining an incredibly family-friendly department at her university, she soon "leaned in" alongside Kelly whose honesty and perseverance as a mother refreshed and inspired Christy.

Kelly's desire to become a mother was always present in her heart, but her academic and career aspirations were far more pronounced. The female role models in her early life made the combination of mothering and career success seem unlikely—or full of mediocrity, guilt, and exhaustion. When asked what she "wanted to be when she grew up," Kelly always answered "teacher," never "mother" as that role didn't seem like a role for which you aspired, rather one that would

[*] Christine E. Rittenour, West Virginia University.

[†] Kelly G. Odenweller, Iowa State University.

eventually choose (or not choose) you. It wasn't until she was pregnant with her first child that she even started thinking (and worrying) about what it would feel like to be a mother, how to be a good mother, and if she could "do it all." Despite having a linear plan for her life, Kelly became a mother of two while working on her graduate degrees. With the support of her mentor (Christy!), Kelly realized that being a mother *and* a professional was not only achievable but worth all the challenges.

Now, we are mothers studying mothers! In this chapter we address some challenges of motherhood including societal expectations of mothers, socializing daughters to embrace a feminist identity, and mothers undermining other mothers.

EXPECTATIONS OF MOTHERS

Motherhood is one of the most challenging—but also the most rewarding—roles a woman can have. When it comes to expectations about motherhood, the bar is set pretty high! Mothers are expected to raise children selflessly and to love every minute of it. Because of its iconic status, Buchanan boldly asserts that "mother" is a god-term that somehow washes away the sins of the devil-term "woman" (2013). Well, after you take a moment to bristle at the ugly truth that much of the world still sees women as "less than" and unwelcomed, you might get resentful about this other extreme. Moms aren't gods, they are humans! And setting us up to be heavenly creatures is bound to create feelings of failure.

Family life is expected to be perfect too, which we often hear about through people's everyday use of the term "normal" to really describe what is set as a high and impossible standard for actual life. (We think you'll agree that the only thing truly normal for families is to feel like they are *not* normal.) We put high standards on family members' communication with each other. Members are supposed to be open, affectionate, and supportive; have fun and celebrate rituals together; and even to do impossible things like read each other's minds to figure out what they're feeling, thinking, and needing (Caughlin, 2003). As discussed in more detail in chapter 4 (this volume), the media plays a large role in creating unrealistic expectations for mothers. For example, American media discourse propagating the "Mommy Wars" argues that there are two main types of mothers: the working supermom and the traditional stay-at-home mom (Hays, 1996). Cultural expectations of motherhood foster tense relationships between mothers that are fraught with unproductive social comparisons, competition, and conflicts. As mothers evaluate their own ability to perform intensive mothering, they simultaneously compare themselves to other mothers in their social networks, including comparisons to their own daughters (Carr, 2004), or to celebrity mothers (Chae, 2015). These social comparisons influence mothers to label and stereotype other mothers (e.g., the lazy stay-at-home mother, the busy and overextended working mother; Odenweller & Rittenour, 2017) and to cling to their "mom ingroups" for support (Johnston & Swanson, 2004; Rubin & Wooten, 2007), while excluding "mom outgroups" who have dissimilar characteristics and lifestyles. As a result, divisions among (sub)groups of mothers are formed. We agree with Dillaway and Paré's (2008) commentary on the problem of women being isolated into "full time mothers" or "working mothers" spheres. There seems to be a public assumption that women either pick mothering *or* pick work. Truly, every mother is a working mother, and every worker can feel a strong mothering identity.

This dichotomous representation of motherhood is not just happening in the U.S. Korean mothers who are exposed images of intensive mothering via Korean celebrity mothers and online news sources are more likely to compare themselves to unrealistic standards of motherhood and compete against other mothers for the "best mom" award (Chae, 2015). Pop culture can detract from women's empowerment by setting too many unrealistic standards and stimulating mother-to-mother competition.

Across these decades until today, the media proclaims motherhood as a fundamental part of femininity, which places the burden of caregiving on women despite the fact that today's fathers are more involved in childrearing than they were in previous generations (Xue, Shorey, Wang, & He, 2018) and not all women want to be mothers. Further, in pitting mothers against one another based on their parenting choices, the media engulfs mothers in a battle over the "best way to mother." As a result, women are distracted from serious social issues affecting women and families (e.g., homelessness, healthcare, wage gap, p/maternity leave policies; Zimmerman, Aberle, Krafchick, & Harvey, 2008).

Although media and societal expectations exert powerful influence on mothers' perceptions of motherhood (and themselves as women), mothers ultimately decide for themselves who they are and who they want to be. Mothers construct complex "mommy identities" through their communication with family members and friends. These co-constructed identities shape mothers' choices and behaviors. For some, this involves highlighting the importance of their mother role, describing things that "good" mothers do, and identifying the stresses *and* successes of motherhood (Heisler & Ellis, 2008). For others, the "mommy identity" consists of working outside the home and involves "cognitive acrobatics" to manage the tensions between intensive mothering standards and career aspirations (Buzzanell et al., 2005; Johnston & Swanson, 2006; Medved & Kirby, 2005). Although some mothers consider mothering and employment as an "either-or" based on their religious teachings or mothers' working experiences (Colaner & Giles, 2008; Korman, 1983), others successfully construct a "good working mother identity" by relinquishing unrealistic expectations of intensive mothering (Johnston & Swanson, 2006), ignoring commentary that suggests working mothers are less committed to mothering and more selfish than unemployed mothers (Gorman & Fritzsche, 2002), or reframing previously stigmatized choices (e.g., stay-at-home fathers) into empowering social change positions (e.g., breadwinning mothers; Duckworth & Buzzanell, 2009). These empowering ideas are not created in a "mothers only" vacuum. Women and men are socialized from an early age to adopt gendered expectations about the role of mother and influenced by the feminist identities of their own mothers.

FEMINIST IDENTITIES

Despite women gaining impressive ground regarding increased number of positions and pay in the workplace (Women's Bureau, 2017), personal beliefs and behaviors of mothers about gender equality have a significant impact on daughters' choices about career and motherhood (e.g., Barber, 2000). A *feminist identity* is the belief that gender inequality exists, is unjust, and seeing oneself as behaving in ways that improve gender inequality (hooks, 2000). Previous research shows feminist mothers are embracing feminist identities and enacting activism through their parenting, as they teach their daughters to fight against social injustice and carry the torch of activism (Colaner & Giles, 2008). When asked how they talk to their daughters about feminism, mothers often talk about their desires to instill confidence and appreciation for education (Rittenour, Colaner, & Odenweller, 2014). These women believe that serving as models of womanhood is an effective means of transmitting feminism. Yet, some women believe there is no need for instilling feminist identities in their daughters (Rittenour et al., 2014). Even though some mothers see feminism as "everything" (Green, 2005), our findings suggest that most mothers integrate feminism subtly into their everyday parenting. When mothers believe in the ability of women to achieve, succeed, and contribute, they tend to communicate this to daughters outside of talking directly about feminism. Instead, many mothers support daughters' education efforts, encouraging them to help in various tasks around the home, and nurture their interest in behaviors both within and outside of their gendered box (Rittenour et al., 2014).

Related research on mother/daughter communication about work and family suggests that a broader value—generativity—is an important impetus for socialization (Colaner & Rittenour, 2015). *Generativity* is the altruistic orientation targeted at the next generation. Mothers rated high in generativity were those most likely to encourage rather than discourage their daughters' enactment of *both* stereotypically feminine and stereotypically masculine behaviors. The predictive power of generativity identity is even greater than that of feminist identity when it comes to mothers' parenting behaviors, suggesting that encouraging rather than limiting daughters stems from mothers' deep desires to ensure a bright future for their daughters (Colaner & Rittenour, 2015). Put differently, among this sample of American women, it wasn't being a loyal mother that made a difference in this realm of parenting (many loyal moms only want their daughters to do "girl things") and it wasn't the degree to which these mother upheld feminist principles, it was the degree to which mothers were focused on the next generation, specifically how much they wanted to leave a lasting impression and to actively make lives better for the next and future generations of young(er) people, that made the difference in daughters! Strong presence of generativity was the best indicator of which mothers would help their daughters think and act toward a broad range of goals in the work and family spheres (Colaner & Rittenour, 2015).

Mothers' feminist identity and gender socialization behaviors ignite daughters' heightened career aspirations and result in heightened self- and relationship satisfaction (Colaner & Rittenour, 2015) and daughters' reported sexual satisfaction in adulthood (Rudman & Phelan, 2007). Mothers who cultivate a feminist identity in daughters heighten their daughters' career aspirations (Fingeret & Gleaves, 2004). Cultivating a feminist identity does not necessarily exclude the socialization of traditional feminine activities. There is beauty in supporting "girly" things in young women, but in conjunction with the support of "non-girly" things (Colaner & Rittenour, 2015), a trend that adds complexity to the differential "boys versus girls" small but significant cross-cultural gendered trends of years passed (Lytton & Romney, 1991). These studies on feminist identities, mothering, and daughters' career aspirations reveal that mothers who encourage daughters to explore and engage in masculine *and* feminine behaviors feel better about their own lives *and* are more likely to raise daughters high in self-esteem and with strong aspirations for career *and* family.

MOMMY WARS

As Nancy Friday proclaims in the bestselling book *My Mother, My Self*, it is in our relationships with other girls that women first venture out from their mothers (1977), but these relationships are also often characterized as highly negative, perpetuating the "Mommy Wars" and the stereotypes that undermine feminist identities and daughters' pursuits. Research on closeness among adolescent girls teaches us that young women are shaped heavily by their same-sexed peers—sometimes building each other up and sometimes tearing down each other (see Willer & Cupach, 2011 for overview). When we converse with other moms about what we study, they tell us that it is difficult to make and build friendships, with extra difficulty forming friendships that are not centered fully around mothering/the children. The priority placed on the "mommy identity" (Heisler & Ellis, 2008) leads mothers that we know to say "I only know her as 'Micah's mom' or 'Viola's mom'" rather than addressing women by their first names. Yet, meaningful friendships with other women can really help mothers feel valued and important as individuals, help them cope with the stressors of caregiving (e.g., Bradbury, Fincham, & Beach, 2000), and support their children's self-esteem (Bost, Cox, Burchinal, & Payne, 2002).

When we examined the role stereotypes play in mother-mother communication, we found that stay at home mom's (SAHMs) were stereotyped as busy and overworked, lazy and lost, ideal mothers, and executives of their homes; whereas working mothers (WMs) were stereotyped as overextended with no free time, supermoms, hardworking and determined, and flexible and family-oriented (Odenweller & Rittenour, 2017). Although these stereotypes highlight some positive characteristics, they are largely consistent with negative media portrayals of mothers and society's attitudes about mothers. We also found that when outgroup mothers encounter each other (e.g., when SAHMs and WMs run into each other in the carpool line at their children's school), they have a tendency to filter each other through these stereotypes and—regardless if they label each other in terms of the more positive (e.g., ideal mother, supermom) or negative (e.g., lazy, overextended) stereotypes—they feel unfavorably toward each other (Odenweller et al., 2016). These unfavorable attitudes then elicit negative emotions such as envy, pity, or anxiety and those negative emotions lead to outgroup mothers avoiding, verbally attacking, and excluding each other (Odenweller et al., 2016).

You might be thinking how historical tensions between races, hate speech about nationalities, hate crimes and other "outgrouping" problems are far more serious than what these mothers are doing to each other. But, when you think about the prominence placed on mothering and the effect "combative mothering" can have on families (Moore & Abetz, 2016), communities, and feminism, it is important to consider the impact of outgrouping among women. Imagine a community full of mothers who don't support or help each other or, worse, judge and criticize each other. It is not difficult to imagine, and reality television is full of these kinds of representations. Not only does combative mothering make it difficult for mothers to build friendships "across group lines" (Johnston & Swanson, 2004), it can consume mothers and distract them from their quality family time, career aspirations, or personal interests. Combative mothering is also incredibly detrimental to non-mothering women as mothers fighting against other mothers makes the large group of women more susceptible to patriarchal discrimination (Douglas & Michaels, 2005; Zimmerman et al., 2008). How can we expect organizations and government officials to take our requests for equal rights, pay, and treatment seriously if we are more focused on arguing about the best way to swaddle our newborns?

In another study we investigated the role communication plays in making "mom peace" so mothers can become more unified and develop strong support networks (Odenweller & Rittenour, 2017). Our findings show that mothers can build commonalities by having a few low-risk conversations focusing on similarities in experience rather than differences. Mothers who participate in this kind of communication will likely have less anxiety about interacting with an out-group mother and will be more willing to do so. Once a friendship is developed, deeper discussions about different parenting choices tends not to elicit as harsh of reactions because mothers can cognitively separate favorable attitudes about their friend with any differing viewpoints they might hold as outgroup members (Odenweller & Rittenour, 2017).

WHAT DOES ALL THIS MEAN?

Motherhood is probably as challenging as it is fulfilling. High standards for motherhood, and for family life in general, create unrealistic ideals that can make mothers feel inadequate. This inadequacy coincides with glances to mothers on the left and right, leaving mothers to compare and compete. Despite the divisiveness that can occur, many women use communication to co-create healthy, empowering identities. Early communication with women's own mothers can be one of the most effective ways of instilling positive messages about being a woman.

Among the many standards (what women *should* be) and expectations (what women *will* be) surrounding motherhood, there is increasing importance placed on helping daughters to be all that they can be. As "being all you can be" is at the heart of feminism, successful feminist socialization occurs by many mothers, even those reluctant to broadcast their identification with this term (that's a lot of women, by the way) (Toller, Suter, & Trautman, 2004). When mothers communicate the importance of self-worth, and display behavior that emphasize doing for the next generation *over* serving oneself, they communicate messages that empower daughters (Rittenour & Colaner, 2012), and daughters ultimately form greater aspirations about work *and* family life (Colaner & Rittenour, 2015).

Women "learn womanhood" by watching the women around them, and peer groups are incredibly influential in constructing positive and/or negative ideas about being a woman, being a working woman, and being a mother. As our own and others' work have shown, the ways that we talk about other women is most uplifting when we focus on what makes each woman unique *and* what makes her similar to other women. Our hope is that supportive communication rises to the top of the list of those traits that are shared among all women, and we place scholarship on family communication at the forefront of making this hope a reality!

WHAT DO WE STILL NEED TO KNOW?

- *What happens when the person mothering is not female or not a mother?* In her daughtering chapter, Alford points out that the term "mothering" is used in place of the word "caregiving," and thus can be placed upon males, females, and any human who engages in this act for another person who is usually presumed to be younger than themselves and (often assumed to be) biologically related. It is so hard for us to separate women from this role that some consider it a compliment to call a man "Mr. Mom" when he is a strong caregiver (See Vavrus, 2002 for a critique that is still relevant). Although this is somewhat insulting to men (men/dads can receive high praise and still be called "dads," can't they?), this term shows the powerful, persistent placement of women as the optimum providers of care in the family. Still, men's influence as parents is also highly demonstrated, whether in co-parenting roles with women, or with other men, and all that we know about mothering would be more wholly understood if we looked at it alongside this growing body of research on fatherhood and fathering (See Floyd and Morman, 2005 for a review on the "changing culture of fatherhood").

- *Why is so much research still just focused on biological mothers?* Many activists have fought long and hard to show other researchers and society that being a mother does not always mean that you gave birth to your daughter or son. Biological relationships are just one of many types of mother/child relationship, and yet they still receive the most attention. As is covered in other chapters, adoptive mothers, birth mothers without legal guardianship of their children, step-mothers, lesbian co-parenting mothers, custodial grandmothers who are raising their grandchildren, aunts and big sisters, and adolescent mothers who are mothering while still children themselves, have similar *and* unique communication patterns, opportunities, and challenges. It is important to continue exploring motherhood through all women's voices in order to expand the narrow definitions and deconstruct the unrealistic standards placed on this role (See Horstman, Colaner, Nelson, Bish, & Hays, 2018 for a discussion or parenting in an open adoption).

- *Mothers help their children bloom, but who is helping mother to grow?* We believe that the answers to this are not "just" society, grandmothers, mothers, and older male family figures, but also a mother's children! As we discussed above, mothers grow from other mothers, from their own mothers, and from society, but we are sure most of you will agree that mothering dynamics don't just happen "from" the older to the younger family member, they can also move from the younger to the older family member. Alford (Chapter 2, this volume) told us about the power of daughters to influence or act upon mothers, and we also encourage you to think about this phenomenon what we call *upward socialization* regarding all of mothers' relationships to their children. An obvious example of this is the daughter who takes on a mothering role by caring for her aging, ill mother. There is much research about the strain and stress of caregiving for a older family member (Kang, 2016), but researchers have been closed-minded in their pursuit of mostly negative research trends. Perhaps all of our hypotheses surround the downside of caregiving (and we call it that instead of mothering), because we think that mothering should only happen from old to young. But that's an absurd assumption! The joys and fulfillment of caring for one's mother are often just as beautiful as those experienced by a new mother for her young child (e.g., Koerner, Kenyon, & Shirai, 2009) and we imagine them carrying the added benefit of reciprocity. Is there anything more profound and honorable than providing assistance to the very person who first assisted you? We need to widen the breadth and depth of our understanding about this type of mothering, as well as the daily acts of upward socialization that occur over relationship lifespans. Of course, the diverse examples of mothering described here are only a few of those that exist.

HOW DOES THIS WORK IN REAL LIFE?

Below is a bulleted list of how we seen these expectations about motherhood, feminist identities in mothering, and mommy wars playing out in everyday life and what we can do about it.

- Although we have all used stereotyping to make sense of someone at some point in our lives, it's important that mothers become aware of how their biases toward other mothers/women influence their interactions. Putting mothers in mental boxes (e.g., "helicopter parent" or "stay-at-home mother") based on a few superficial observations (e.g., clothing, freshly polished nails, number of children in tow) can make it difficult to perceive information that counters pre-existing stereotypes of those groups. But, if we take time to process information more carefully, we will probably realize that mothers are too complex to be labeled by just one social identity and, as our stereotypes unravel, we can let go of the biases that are associated with those stereotypes and feel more comfortable asking open-ended questions will help us get to know other mothers as individual people.
- Media portrayals of motherhood make it seem as if mothers are quick to go to war with each other. Most Americans are probably smart enough to know that spectacled female disagreements (i.e., catfights) among the "Real Housewives" or the working women on "Celebrity Apprentice" are

just that … spectacles. Still, there are *many* mediated messages about women being at war with each other (see the *Huffington Post's* online news section devoted to the mommy wars), and these messages might fuel our misperceptions that women are inclined to compete more than they are to collaborate.

- Women take matters into their own hands by using social media to broadcast the supportive side of womanhood and mothering. As the most common users of social media (Duggan, Lenhart, Lampe, & Ellison, 2015), mothers have been making motherhood more public on Facebook (e.g., Comma Mommas) and blogs (www.ctworkingmoms.com) by sharing photos of breastfeeding, exchanging advice about co-sleeping, and posting childcare resources for working mothers. These are everyday ways that mothers might reduce stigma surrounding mothers' choices, celebrate their similarities *and* differences, and build a cohesive ingroup of moms.
- We are not the first, nor the last, to have written that feminism begins at home. While we still hold this to be true, we also assert that feminism continues in the schoolyard and in the workplace. When adolescent girls talk about STEM classes *and* their love of babies, they are engaging in communication that makes motherhood stronger. This type of behavior probably lends itself to more working women explicitly saying "I support you" to their female coworkers, employees, and bosses. Even better, this type of support is demonstrated through active listening and a mutual exchange of everyday behaviors meant to assist rather than compete (e.g., swapping shifts so that a mother can stay home with her sick child, telling the boss about an achievement for which another female employee is too humble to self-disclose).

CLASSROOM ACTIVITIES

- Before reading this chapter, describe your version of an ideal mother. Bring your descriptions to class on the day this chapter is assigned. Then, when discussing the chapter in class, students will be asked to compare/contrast their descriptions with the research trends.
- Invite mothers with diverse backgrounds, lifestyles, and identities to visit your class and share their stories. Provide a list of suggested topics (e.g., birth stories, work-life balance, parenting choices) but allow these visitors to share their mom triumphs and tribulations in any way they feel comfortable. Allow time for students to ask questions during the session. Then, ask students to write a 1–2 page reaction paper to share their thoughts, feelings, and curiosities following the mothers' visit.

- Interview your mother (or grandmother) about their role as a mother. Ask them about the pressures they perceive as a woman/mother. Was being a mother what they expected? What was the positive and the negative (and perhaps the ambiguous!) feedback they've received about their mothering? Compare their responses to the literature discussed in the chapter (explain inconsistencies).
- Critique a movie with a mother, daughter and/or son, and romantic partner (or father) characters. What is useful and empowering in these films? What is debilitating? What is missing from these social constructions of motherhood? Some timeless and recent choices are Steel Magnolias, Stepmom, and Bad Moms. Provide evidence of the societal expectations of motherhood, deviant mothers, or "mommy wars." Should we work against or toward these societal expectations? How can we do so?

REFERENCES

Barber, J. S. (2000). Intergenerational influences on the entry into parenthood: Mothers' preferences for family and nonfamily behavior. *Social Forces, 79*, 319–348.

Bost, K. K., Cox, M. J., Burchinal, M. R., & Payne, C. (2002). Structural and supportive changes in couples' family and friendship networks across the transition to parenthood. *Journal of Marriage and Family, 64*(2), 517–531.

Bradbury, T. N., Fincham, F. D., & Beach, S. R. (2000). Research on the nature and determinants of marital satisfaction: A decade in review. *Journal of Marriage and Family, 62*(4), 964–980.

Buchanan, L. (2013). *Rhetorics of motherhood (Studies in rhetorics and feminisms)*. Carbondale, IL: Southern Illinios Univeristy Press.

Buzzanell, P. M., Meisenbach, R., Remke, R., Liu, M., Bowers, V., & Conn, C. (2005). The good *working* mother: Managerial women's sensemaking and feelings about work-family issues. *Communication Studies, 56*(3), 261–285.

Carr, D. (2004). "My daughter has a career; I just raised babies": The psychological consequences of women's intergenerational social comparisons. *Social Psychologyl Quarterly, 67*(2), 132–154. https://doi.org/10.1177/019027250406700202

Caughlin, J. P. (2003). Family communication standards: What counts as excellent family communication and how are such standards associated with family satisfaction? *Human Communication Research, 29*, 5–40. https://doi.org/10.1111/j.1468-2958.2003.tb00830.x

Chae, J. (2015). "Am I a Better Mother Than You?": Media and 21st-century motherhood in the context of the social comparison theory. *Communication Research, 42*(4), 503–525. https://doi.org/10.1177/0093650214534969

Colaner, C. W., & Giles, S. M. (2008). The baby blanket or the briefcase: The impact of evangelical gender role ideologies on career and mothering aspirations of female evangelical college students. *Sex Roles, 58*(7–8), 526–534.

Colaner, C. W., & Rittenour, C. E. (2015). "Feminism begins at home": The influence of mother-daughter gender socialization on daughter career and motherhood aspirations as channeled through daughter feminist identification. *Communication Quarterly, 63*, 81–98. https://doi.org/10.1080/01463373.2014.965839

Dillaway, H., & Paré, E. (2008). Locating mothers: How cultural debates about stay-at-home versus working mothers define women and home. *Journal of Family Issues, 29*(4), 437–464. https://doi.org/10.1177/0192513x07310309

Douglas, S., & Michaels, M. (2005). *The mommy myth: The idealization of motherhood and how it has undermined all women.* New York, NY: Free Press.

Duckworth, J. D., & Buzzanell, P. M. (2009). Constructing work-life balance and fatherhood: Men's framing of the meanings of both work and family. *Communication Studies, 60*(5), 558–573.

Duggan, M., Lenhart, A., Lampe, C., & Ellison, N. B. (2015). *Parents and Social Media: Mothers are especially likely to give and receive support on social media.* Pew Research Center: Internet and Technology. www.pewinternet.org/2015/07/16/parents-and-social-media/

Fingeret, M. C., & Gleaves, D. H. (2004). Sociocultural, feminist, and psychological influences on women's body satisfaction: A structural modeling analysis. *Psychology of Women Quarterly, 28*(4), 370–380.

Floyd, K., & Morman, M. T. (2005). Fathers' and sons' reports of fathers' affectionate communicatoin: Implicatons of a naive theory of affection. *Journal of Social and Personal Relationships, 22,* 99–109.

Friday, N. (1977). *My mother/my self: The daughter's search for identity.* New York, NY: Delacorte Press.

Gorman, K. A., & Fritzsche, B. A. (2002). The good-mother stereotype: Stay at home (or wish that you did!). *Journal of Applied Social Psychology, 32*(10), 2190–2201.

Green, F. J. (2005). Feminist mothering: Challenging gender inequality by resisting the institution of motherhood and raising children to be critical agents of social change. *Socialist Studies, 1,* 83–99.

Hays, S. (1996). *The cultural contradictions of motherhood.* New Haven, CT: Yale University Press.

Heisler, J. M., & Ellis, J. B. (2008). Motherhood and the construction of "mommy identity": Messages about motherhood and face negotiation. *Communication Quarterly, 56*(4), 445–467. https://doi.org/10.1080/01463370802448246

hooks, b. (2000). *Feminism is for everybody: Passionate politics.* Cambridge, MA: South End Press.

Horstman, H. K., Colaner, C. W., Nelson, L. R., Bish, A., & Hays, A. (2018). Communicatively constructing the birth parent relationship in open adoptive families: Naming, connecting, and relational functioning. *Journal of Family Communication, 18*(2), 138–152. https://doi.org/10.1080/15267431.2018.1429444

Johnston, D. D., & Swanson, D. H. (2004). Moms hating moms: The internalization of mother war rhetoric. *Sex Roles, 51*(9–10), 497–509.

Johnston, D. D., & Swanson, D. H. (2006). Constructing the "good mother": The experience of mothering ideologies by work status. *Sex Roles, 54*(7–8), 509–519.

Kang, S.-Y. (2016). Perceived overload as a predictor of physical strain among spousal and adult child caregivers of frail elders in the community. *Journal of Human Behavior in the Social Environment, 26*(7–8), 636–647. https://doi.org/10.1080/10911359.2016.1241201

Koerner, S. S., Kenyon, D. B., & Shirai, Y. (2009). Caregiving for elder relatives: Which caregivers experience personal benefits/gains? *Archives of Gerontology and Geriatrics, 48*(2), 238–245. https://doi.org/10.1016/j.archger.2008.01.015

Korman, S. K. (1983). The feminist: Familial influences on adherence to ideology and commitment to a self-perception. *Family Relations, 32,* 431–439.

Lytton, H., & Romney, D. M. (1991). Parents' differential socialization of boys and girls: A meta-analysis. *Psychological Bulletin, 109*(2), 267–296.

Medved, C. E., & Kirby, E. L. (2005). Family CEOs: A feminist analysis of corporate mothering discourses. *Management Communication Quarterly, 18*(4), 435–478.

Moore, J., & Abetz, J. (2016). "Uh Oh. Cue the [new] mommy wars": The ideology of combative mothering in popular U.S. newspaper articles about attachment parenting. *Southern Communication Journal, 81*(1), 49–62. https://doi.org/10.1080/1041794X.2015.1076026

Odenweller, K. G., & Rittenour, C. E. (2017). Stereotypes of stay-at-home and working mothers. *Southern Communication Journal, 82*(2), 57–72. https://doi.org/10.1080/1041794X.2017.1287214

Odenweller, K. G., Rittenour, C. E., Dillow, M. R., Metzger, A., Myers, S. A., & Weber, K. (2016). *Communicated stereotypes among stay-at-home and working mothers: An intergroup communication perspective of the "mommy wars."* Paper presented at the Annual Convention of the National Communication Association, Philadelphia, PA.

Rittenour, C. E., & Colaner, C. W. (2012). Finding female fulfillment: Intersecting role-based and morality-based identities of motherhood, feminism, and generativity as predictors of women's self satisfaction and life satisfaction. *Sex Roles, 67*(5–6), 351–362. https://doi.org/10.1007/s11199-012-0186-7

Rittenour, C. E., Colaner, C. W., & Odenweller, K. G. (2014). Mothers' identities and gender socialization of daughters. *Southern Communicatiion Journal, 79*(3), 215–234. https://doi.org/10.1080/1041794X.2014.895408

Rubin, S. E. & Wooten, R. (2007) Highly educated stay-at-home mothers: A study of commitment and conflict. *The Family Journal, 15*(4), 336–345. https://doi.org/10.1177/1066480707304945

Rudman, L. A., & Phelan, J. E. (2007). The interpersonal power of feminism for romantic relationships. *Sex Roles, 57*(11–12), 787–799. https://doi.org/10.1007/s11199-007-9319-9

Toller, P. W., Suter, E. A., & Trautman, T. C. (2004). Gender role identity and attitudes toward feminism. *Sex Roles, 51*(1–2), 85–90. https://doi.org/10.1023/B:SERS.0000032316.71165.45

Vavrus, M. D. (2002). Domesticating patriarchy: Hegemonic masculinity and television's "Mr. Mom." *Criticial Studies in Media Communication, 19*(3), 352–375.

Willer, E. K., & Cupach, W. R. (2011). The *meaning* of girls' social aggression: Nasty or mastery? In W. R. Cupach & B. H. Spitzberg (Eds.), *The dark side of close relationships* (pp. 297–326). New York, NY: Routledge.

Women's Bureau, U.S. Dept. of Labor. (Producer). (2017). Working Mothers Issue Brief. *Issue Brief.* https://www.dol.gov/wb/resources/wb_workingmothers_508_finaljune13.pdf

Xue, W. L., Shorey, S., Wang, W., & He, H.-G. (2018). Fathers' involvement during pregnancy and childbirth: An integrative literature review. *Midwifery, 62*, 135–145. https://doi.org/https://doi.org/10.1016/j.midw.2018.04.013

Zimmerman, T. S., Aberle, J. T., Krafchick, J. L., & Harvey, A. M. (2008). Deconstructing the "mommy wars": The battle over the best mom. *Journal of Feminist Family Therapy, 20*(3), 203–219.

CHAPTER SIXTEEN

Understanding Mother-Daughter Communication AND Health Through A Discourse OF "Responsible Womanhood"

CARLA L. FISHER[*] AND BIANCA M. WOLF[†]

Selflessness potentially undermines a woman's capacity to fully define and convey her needs to others, and ... well-meaning people within a woman's primary sphere of relationships may not know what is needed or how to provide it.

—SULIK (2007A, P. 871)

For many years, we have talked with women and their families about their experiences with breast cancer. We talked about how they dealt with cancer and if they coped together to understand better how women communicate with their spouses, children, siblings, and parents as they all navigate breast cancer, side by side. However, one relationship is especially interesting to us, and it stands out to us concerning how women and families experience a life-threatening illness like cancer—the mother-daughter relationship.

The influence mothers and daughters have on each other is profound. Their connection can function as a lifeline in the face of crisis. They impact each other's mental, physical, and relational well-being playing a prominent role in their health from birth until death. Mothers and daughters also influence and socialize one another, shaping each other's attitudes, behavior and habits, decision making, and relational expectations. In the face of health and illness, their connection can set

[*] Carla L. Fisher, Associate Professor, University of Florida, carlalfisher@ufl.edu.

[†] Bianca M. Wolf, Associate Professor, University of Puget Sound, bwolf@pugetsound.edu.

the tone becoming a critical component to the entire family's ability to cope and emerge resilient, both on a day-to-day basis and across the entirety of their lives.

Although mother-daughter communication can contribute to good health, it is not a relationship that is without struggle. Mothers and daughters want to be there for one another. At the same time, this desire can compete with and even silence each woman's individual needs. To better understand this complexity, it is essential to consider how women are socialized in our world. For instance, what roles do we expect women to play? How are women characterized in the family? Also, with these answers in mind, what societal messages do we hear or perpetuate that help shape what we expect of mothers and daughters?

In this chapter, we unpack these questions a bit further by exploring mother-daughter communication and health, specifically within the experience of breast cancer. We attempt to understand this experience by examining how it is informed by a social discourse or script labeled *"responsible womanhood"* (RW). Wolf (2015) first identified RW in her work on how families communally cope with breast cancer or how they view the diagnosis as a family issue by uniting to cope together. She interviewed not only patients but multiple family members to understand better their shared coping and, in doing so, identified a script that informed how they communicated with each other while coping with breast cancer. This script of "responsible womanhood" represents a blend of social discourses that inform family members' expectations of the "right" way for mothers to cope after diagnosis. In other words, RW comprises the social "voices" that we (and mothers and daughters) hear through various societal channels that ultimately influence how we respond to and behave in the midst of a health change or crisis. These are the voices that tell us that *breast cancer is a woman's disease, moms should not get sick,* and *women should always prioritize their families first.*

In the pages that follow we strive to take a closer look at what RW conveys and how it plays a role in the mother-daughter bond and health experiences like breast cancer. We begin by looking at research broadly to illustrate the striking interconnection between mothers, daughters, and their health across the life span. Then, we pull from our programs of research on family communication and breast cancer coping to illustrate the enactment of RW. In the end, we address what this all means to us and what we can do next, particularly regarding improving mother-daughter breast cancer coping.

CONNECTING MOTHER-DAUGHTER COMMUNICATION AND HEALTH ACROSS THE LIFE SPAN

Mother-daughter communication is a critical component of girls' and women's health. Research using a life-span perspective of communication has helped to illustrate this. A life-span perspective of interaction is grounded in the idea that "the interpersonal communication that fuels our social world is as essential to our survival as any biological or physical process that keeps us alive" (Hummert, Nussbaum, & Wiemann, 1994, p. 3). *Lifespan communication* scholars argue that:

> Communication is a primary skill to be mastered … [and] is best viewed as a flow of events across time rather than a static occurrence … impacted by a wide range of individual factors. … An individual's capacity to communicate must continuously develop for that individual to master his or her environment and to interact effectively throughout the transitions, adaptations, and new challenges that arise over the life span. (Pecchioni, Wright, & Nussbaum, 2005, pp. 10–11)

In other words, mothers and daughters can develop communication skills as they mature and encounter diverse experiences. Moreover, these communication competencies are central to both mothers' and daughters' well-being.

In the face of change or transition, some research has shown that certain communicative behaviors (or skills) can either promote healthy outcomes or contribute to unhealthy outcomes. Mother-daughter communication that encourages autonomy, support, openness, and warmth are all linked with better health whereas other forms of communication (e.g., conflict, control, critical communication, expressing hostility) can contribute to poorer health outcomes (Berg et al., 2007; Beveridge & Berg, 2007; Rosland, Heisler, & Piette, 2012; Segrin & Flora, 2011). Some of these communication skills are complicated, however. Take for instance—openness. Typically, we associate being open with better health. For example, we know that when breast cancer patients have a more open mother-daughter relationship, they also tend to have less cancer-related symptoms like pain or fatigue (Fisher, Wolf, Fowler, & Canzona, 2016). However, at times, being open can contribute to unhealthy outcomes. For example, when mothers disclose to their daughters about their divorce, daughters can develop anxiety (Koerner, Wallace, Lehman, & Raymond, 2002).

While these communication patterns or behaviors certainly impact how mothers and daughters cope with changes they encounter, their communication also has long-term health implications. For instance, mothers and daughters who use power or control to restrict each other's autonomy are at an increased risk for mental health disorders including disordered eating behavior, addiction, suicidality, and schizophrenia (Levy et al., 2010; Miller-Day, 2004; Miller-Day & Fisher, 2008). At the same time, how they communicate can impact their long-term health physically. For example, daughters learn healthy (or unhealthy) habits related to exercise, weight, and nutrition from their mothers, which can also impact their body image (Shenaar-Golan & Walter, 2015). Maternal and daughter's advice affects daughters' and mothers' risk-reducing behavior (e.g., medical screening for breast and cervical cancer) (Kratzke, Vilchis, & Amatya, 2013; Mosavel, 2012; Sinicrope et al., 2009).

Ultimately, both mothers and daughters describe each other as critical sources of emotional, instrumental, and informational support across the life span. They can fulfill this supportive and caregiving role on a day-to-day basis and during acute (i.e., severe or sudden) health crises and chronic (i.e., long-developing) health conditions (e.g., diagnosis of breast cancer; living with dementia; managing diabetes) (Alemán & Helfrich, 2013; Cooke-Jackson, 2011; Fisher, 2014; Pecchioni & Nussbaum, 2000). This is particularly true when women face breast cancer.

Mothers, Daughters, and Breast Cancer

Fisher (2014) is the only evidence-based book on how breast cancer is inherently a mother-daughter experience socially, psychologically, and even physiologically. This research takes a life-span perspective by capturing patients' and their mothers/daughters' coping experiences during various phases of the life span (emerging/young adulthood, midlife, and later life). While mother-daughter communication is central to both patients' and their mother/daughter's disease coping regardless of age, their needs differ based on age and generation (Fisher, 2010, 2011, 2014). Even though mothers and daughters want to "be there" for each other (e.g., by going to appointments, managing treatment effects, listening), they also struggle in this role, not always knowing what to say or do to be supportive or behaving in ways they think are supportive but actually are not health-promoting (Fisher, 2014). They also struggle with being open—they need each other's support but also want to protect one another from distress which can often create a paradox of "to be or not to be open" about breast cancer-related experiences (Fisher, 2010; Fisher et al., 2017).

Mothers' and daughters' coping behavior during health transitions like breast cancer and their attempts to fulfill supportive or caregiving roles is informed by what they, their families, and society deem are the "right" things to do. These expectations are informed by larger societal ideologies that contribute to messages suggesting how mothers and daughters "should" behave or communicate. One social narrative or discourse that is particularly insightful in understanding mother-daughter communication during health crises is what Wolf (2015) has described as "responsible womanhood" (RW).

"RESPONSIBLE WOMANHOOD" IN HEALTH

To fully understand how the social discourse of what is considered "*responsible womanhood*" (RW) and how it operates and impacts mother-daughter experiences, it is first necessary to recognize how broader interconnected ideologies such as gender (identity/roles/scripts), Western individualism, and scientific bio-medicine inform RW (Wolf, 2015). These larger discourses operate in concert to define, constrain, and empower women to behave as "responsible" women when it comes to their health and their families' well-being.

Gender discourses inform women's health behavior in significant ways. A primary role of women in society is as "carer"—the nurturer in society and kinkeeper of families (Gilligan, 1982; Hays 1996). These gendered discourses construct women to be "by nature" the better parent, and "good" mothering is associated with emotional involvement with children requiring the mother to self-sacrifice and care for others (Bell, 2004; Fisher & O'Connor, 2012; Hays, 1996; Rizzo, Schiffrin, & Liss, 2013). As such, women are expected to maintain "care work" in the family, often becoming the person responsible for influencing (and prioritizing) others' health behavior, outcomes, and decision making (Gilligan, 1982; Mackenzie, 2014).

This gendered role expectation of "carer" or "care work" prioritizes the relational other's well-being over the health of the woman. In other words, womanhood is defined and depicted as done and done *well* to the extent that women privilege their relational partner's well-being over their own individual needs. Sulik (2007a) notes that "the feminization of care places care work within women's realm of responsibility and expertise while it simultaneously denies care work for the self" (p. 868). Thus, to do the role of woman correctly, women often suppress their own needs, sacrificing personal well-being to instead behave selflessly (i.e., "responsibly") by prioritizing the needs of others. If women fail to perform their gendered role as expected and instead put themselves first, they are deemed deviant and selfish (Bell, 2004).

Societal discourses of Western individualism further complicate this self-sacrificing "carer" role of women—what it means to be a healthy (and "responsible") individual—a western biomedical "ideology of healthism" (Crabb & LeCouteur, 2006; Crawford, 1980; Lorber, 1997). For instance, in our culture, we are held individually responsible for self-surveillance, prevention, and rectification of health problems (Crawford, 1980; Gibson, Lee, & Crabb, 2015). Upholding individuals to be "good" members of society means that health is only done right when individuals proactively take charge of it. However, while we expect women to be responsible for their health, we bind them in a paradox; their health is only prioritized insomuch as they can fulfill their aforementioned carer or kinkeeper responsibilities (Norberg et al., 2015; Sulik, 2007a, 2007b; Sweeney, 2012). Furthermore, these gendered behaviors are rhetorically naturalized and rendered invisible, part and parcel with a woman's "responsibility" in her role as mother/kinkeeper/carer. Women themselves help to reinforce and model these behaviors to their offspring, as do other family members, thereby perpetuating gendered health knowledge and behavior across generations.

All of these "voices" of gender, health, and individualism in society speak to us, telling us how we should behave during health crises as well as how mothers (and daughters) should behave. To illustrate this, we turn now to a more in-depth exploration of how RW operates in mother-daughter communication during their experiences with breast cancer.

"Responsible Womanhood" in Women's Breast Cancer Experiences

"Responsible womanhood" informs how a diagnosed woman and her mother/ daughter should behave to "do" illness, womanhood, motherhood/daughterhood, and family "right." In her cancer research, Wolf (2015) interviewed consenting family members and found that members invoked gendered ideas when they explained how they prioritized individual coping over communal coping (coping together as a family) (Lyons, Mickelson, Sullivan, & Coyne, 1998). Overall, the patient's (i.e., mother's) needs—most often in the form of social support—took a back seat to her family's needs. This finding led to a deeper conceptualization of the discourse of "responsible womanhood." Wolf (2015) noted that women's (and their family members') narratives of coping with breast cancer put into conversation women's relevant social roles as *patients, breast cancer survivors*, and *wives/ mothers*. Each role worked independently as well as conjointly to support women in primarily denying aspects of self-care and receipt of social support.

Only after close linguistic analyses, was it clear that while talk associated with those roles often seemed at odds with one another on the surface (i.e., patient/ survivor role = self-care versus mother = carer for others), that still, by and large, women's overarching reliance on gender as the primary way to frame those discourses only further reinforced RW. In essence, this meant that a discourse of RW influenced women's (and their families') prioritization of (1) the woman's role as carer/mother versus that of a patient and (2) the well-being of others/her family (i.e., self-sacrifice) versus her own well-being as a patient. Even when women and family members seemed to privilege the patient role (and, thus, self-care), they did so in ways that always highlighted the fact that the patient was a woman and that female patients are, in the end, held to different sick role expectations.

For instance, in interviews with a family, Wolf (2015) found that both the husband and daughter of a diagnosed woman each made it clear that they offered their opinions with regards to treatment but that their wife/mother had to ultimately make decisions alone and live with those consequences. They stripped themselves of responsibility in their articulation of her care and left her as the sole authority to decide/cope alone, as "responsible patient" and "responsible woman." Patient accounts like these were associated with a discourse of "normality" which made it clear that diagnosed women were to handle both the patient role and mother role simultaneously to maintain a "normal" family life.

Take, for instance, the following case extracted from Wolf's research. Tammy,[1] the daughter of a diagnosed woman, shared how pleased she and her family members were that her mother was able to still attend her brother's soccer game following a lumpectomy: "It was kind of a relief, like she was going through all this but she was still doing everything normal and still acting like herself and nothing was changing." As this excerpt helps to highlight, diagnosed mothers were constructed according to their gender role first. Gender discourse always trumped their patient/survivor status.

It is also notable here that gender not only frames expectations regarding both illness and familial roles, but these are reinforced by a broader social discourse—the social movement and culture of breast cancer (Sulik, 2011; Sweeney, 2012). Breast cancer culture (a.k.a. Pink Ribbon Culture) has depicted the disease as primarily a woman's cancer, one that only other female cancer patients fully understand (Crabb & LeCouteur, 2006; Sulik, 2011). In framing breast cancer (or any illness) as chiefly a woman's experience, women are further subject to the gendered ideologies that infiltrate their experiences as patient/survivor. Accordingly, when individuals construct breast cancer according to an embodied patient role and in concert with breast cancer survivorship, they are always inherently circling back to those overarching gendered ideologies that socialize females in our culture to *care for others first, as they care for themselves.* This construction of reality, ingrained in multiple gendered ideologies for women, positions women to act as good patients/survivors, women, and relational partners, simultaneously requiring that they deny themselves priority in their care work. Paradoxically, if they are to fulfill those roles, they must also undermine them (by genuinely prioritizing their own health) if they are to survive their cancer.

Every time women in Wolf's study (2015) invoked the discourse of RW, apparent in phrases like, "I kind of wanted to go through it alone, to be honest with you. I didn't want to burden anybody else," they effectively prioritized their ongoing motherly/wifely duty as a carer and sacrificed their own needs as a patient for the betterment of others. Their linguistic ambivalence tied to the unburdening of others (i.e., "kind of") and their behavioral accounts that restricted their family member's involvement (e.g., made treatment decisions autonomously, withheld information or went to medical visits alone) demonstrate how women's gendered health behaviors can effectively work to undermine their personal needs.

THE STUDY

What Were We Interested in Learning?

While most of the diagnosed women in our studies have been mothers, we have also observed RW in the accounts and behaviors of daughters (both diagnosed and healthy), fathers, husbands, and sons. In this present study, *we wanted to better understand how RW could be ingrained in the broader fabric of family culture and examine its impact on coping with breast cancer.*

How Did We Go About Learning This Information?

To accomplish this, we examined previous interview transcripts from studies receiving institutional review board approval and participant consent. We examined these transcripts for examples of RW enactments by any family member. Collectively our breast cancer coping scholarship includes 142 individual in-depth interviews (more than 4,300 single-spaced pages of transcribed data) with multiple adult family members (aged 18–83). These include 68 patients/survivors (53 mothers and 15 daughters) as well as 74 of their healthy family members (41 daughters, 9 mothers, 19 husbands, and 5 sons) (Fisher, 2010, 2011, 2014; Fisher & Wolf, 2015; Fisher, Wolf, Fowler, & Canzona, 2016; Wolf, 2015). Using Wolf's conceptualization of RW, we found numerous enactments of RW not only in mother-daughter communication but also in the discourse of other family members. We found that RW has significant implications not only for how mothers and daughters cope but also how their collective family copes. This chapter now turns to providing exemplar RW illustrations according to family relationship in an effort to illustrate how (1) the woman's role as carer takes precedence over her role as patient and (2) the family's well-being takes precedence over the patient's well-being.

What Did We Learn?

Mothers and Daughters

Mothers and their daughters both described how they prioritized the role of carer in their coping approaches, mainly when the mother was the patient. This enactment of RW was typically performed by diagnosed moms to buffer daughters from stress (especially younger daughters in their teens and twenties).

> *Karen:* I tended to just gloss over things. I did not want [my daughters] worrying about it … I just wouldn't say anything because I didn't want them to be concerned. I didn't tell them much because they were already going through enough and they were both going back to school. … I didn't want them worrying about me.
>
> *Cally:* She does not want to make me feel bad about it or something like that. … It would kind of bother me a little bit that she did [that]. … She would try and hide it. And sometimes she could, but sometimes she was not good at it.

As Cally indicates in this interview excerpt, daughters were not always comfortable with moms prioritizing their carer role (and daughter's health) as opposed to their mother/patient's needs. Daughters described not liking their mothers' secrecy stating that this made it "scary" and so they sought out their fathers for information. Daughters of diagnosed moms also wanted to enact the carer role themselves (which was often the first time they had encountered an opportunity for a role reversal), and if mom was hiding things, this inhibited daughter's ability to fulfill that role.

At times, a daughters' behavior did not reflect care or interest and seemed tied to societal "norms" of what it means to be a self-focused adolescent, a period in which individual development is privileged but also a crucial phase of human development. Moms recalled that younger adolescent daughters seemed aloof, uninterested, or withdrawn. They interpreted this behavior in various ways (e.g., she's a teen—selfishness is characteristic of that age period; she's young and overwhelmed and withdrew to cope). Daughters similarly described their behavior. These moms embedded their experience within the RW dilemma of patient/individual needs versus the mother/carer role. Ultimately, they perpetuated RW by continuing to self-sacrifice, while still wanting someone to care for them.

> *Evelyn:*   I didn't want her more upset than me. The fact that you worry about your daughter when you are going through this ... You worry about the effects [on her]. ... But it's funny. I mean if they weren't upset you felt like they didn't care. ... I think, a little bit, you needed to know this affected [her].

In dyads in which the daughter was the patient, the "carer" role was privileged by both daughter and mother. Meghan, a diagnosed daughter, said the following about her mother, "She set the standard [of care] for everyone else." Mothers with diagnosed daughters described the need (and desire) to perform that role of carer, indicating it helped them cope with their daughter's illness. They needed to "be there" in that way. Diagnosed daughters with their own children seemed understanding of their mother's needs to fulfill the "carer" role, whereas diagnosed daughters without children found this more challenging. Addie, a single woman diagnosed in her twenties with no children, described this saying: "[Mom] always calls and checks up on me ... If she doesn't reach me ... she'll start calling my friends. It was a little excessive."

Although less common, young-adult daughters of diagnosed mothers would enact RW in their own selfless "carer" behavior. Mothers would invoke RW when describing their daughter's behavior. For example:

> *Laura:*   [My daughter] dropped everything she was doing and came home, which I didn't anticipate her doing that, but it was great for me. She gave up everything. She gave things up. She was there all the way. ... I was glad she was here because you do need that.

Likewise, daughters also described enacting RW in their "responsible" daughter role as a carer for their sick mom. Like mothers of diagnosed women, these daughters felt that the carer role helped them cope with their mom's illness. They also asserted that no one in the family could fulfill that role better:

> *Brittney:* There's a huge emotional draw for me to be there supporting her because I know that that level of support, number one, she's only going to get from me. And number two, she definitely counts on it.

It was abundantly evident to us that both mothers and daughters employ, accept, and perpetuate the RW script in how they narratively construct their experiences of coping. Interestingly, their approaches to coping, informed by RW, seemed to be both health-promoting and inhibiting.

Wives and Husbands

RW also emerged in the discourse of women's coping experiences with husbands. Being the "good wife" also meant sacrificing one's own needs to maintain the role of carer and protect the husband's well-being. As is illustrated below, mothers' enactment of RW informed husbands' breast cancer coping behavior, which at times (like daughters) limited the spouse's ability to become involved. The following excerpts help illustrate this:

> *Betty:* I was kind of um, stubborn, and I really didn't want to bother [my husband] about what I was thinking about. But we um, it was our problem, and he kept assuring me he didn't marry me for that, and you know, that kind of stuff. He was there for me. He really wanted to be more active in all these appointments and stuff, and I kept saying, "It's not that big a deal. Let me just do it." ... I don't know why I did that. ... I thought of that you don't really involve more people than you have to, even though he was my husband. I didn't want to him to get in trouble from say work and stuff like that.
>
> *Carl:* As things progress closer to the surgery date, I felt like I was left out more and more ... because she's taking her friends to her checkups ... I had to go to work. I wasn't allowed to go. To me, it felt like that was my choice. ... I think she didn't want me to worry, is what she said. Okay, well, that was, that—to me, it felt like that was my choice.

Interestingly, when asked about his "choice" Carl's answer suggests it was more of a collective choice driven by his wife's behavior:

> *Interviewer:* You felt like she was taking that away from you?
>
> *Carl:* Yeah.

Although spouses like Carl noted their felt disempowerment resulting from a lack of participation in the cancer experience, none attempted to alter their exclusion. Rather, they highlighted their wives' autonomous coping. Beyond mentioning discussions with their wives about it, husbands did not describe trying to change it. Women were still coping primarily alone, albeit often self-induced though relationally reinforced.

Mothers and Sons

Sons' accounts further demonstrated RW. Most sons seemed especially separated from their mothers' breast cancer experiences (be it geographically, communicatively, etc.) and reported little involvement, as well as little negative impact on their well-being as a result of any exclusion, all which was deemed appropriate and expected under the discourse of RW. One son explained:

> *Brian*: I didn't feel like I needed to deal with it [cancer]. It was already dealt with. It was dealt with before I got there. It was like, "Hey, I broke a glass in the kitchen. And I swept it up."

Brian's narrative demonstrates how mothers, in particular, did the expected work to "clean up" their cancer so that their sons (and others) did not have to deal with it. Women were appraised as having performed their role responsibly by simply dealing with it as they would any other type of women's work (e.g., housework, childcare, etc.)—a carer role recognized, prioritized, and reaffirmed narratively by their sons.

WHAT DOES ALL THIS MEAN?

It is important to step away and consider now, what does this mean for mothers and daughters? Ultimately, the way in which mothers and daughters face breast cancer is inherently tied to larger social expectations of what it means to be a woman and, therefore, a mother or daughter. The "responsible womanhood" narrative helps us understand the gendered expectations we have of mothers/daughters, even in the midst of coping with a health crisis like breast cancer. All family members can perpetuate these gendered scripts. One of the most critical considerations to walk away with is that the gendered experience of "responsible womanhood" can contribute to both healthy and unhealthy communication. With this in mind, we believe this scholarship highlights areas in which we could intervene to enhance mother-daughter communication to promote better adjustment to breast cancer.

In other words, women and their family members could benefit from psychosocial health interventions that offer education about gendered ideologies that influence how they respond to health crises like breast cancer. If women (and their family members) are more cognizant of their enactments of RW, they might be more aware of how they can communicate in ways that prioritize the diagnosed woman's (e.g., mother's) well-being, first and foremost. In related research, this reprioritization of patient role (as opposed to carer) has been associated with better health. When women with breast cancer reported that they set and maintained boundaries with their relational partners to prioritize self-care, in spite of felt pressure to attend to others' need before their own, they reported empowerment to maintain such boundaries and framed this behavior as optimal to their health (Mackenzie, 2014; Norberg et al., 2015; Sulik, 2007a). Sulik (2007a) reiterates this point:

> The balancing act [self-care vs. care for others] is both a process of resocialization and a problem-focused strategy that, if successful, is capable of increasing women's sense of control in coping with the uncertainty of illness and engaging in care work for the self. However, it requires women to relinquish (to some extent) the dominant cultural scripts that construct women's identities in terms of care work for others. (p. 875)

It is our hope that by intervening in this way, both patients and their family members will experience better, health-promoting coping for the entire family system. Interventions could teach the following takeaway lessons.

Lesson 1

When mothers/daughters exhibit strong adherence to a discourse of RW, while they may believe they are prioritizing the health of others (and acting selflessly), two problematic outcomes can occur: (1) they risk inhibiting their own well-being, and (2) they may restrict family members from communicating in ways that promote their own (and the patient's) health. The obvious irony of RW is that when one is not healthy themselves, they are not ideally positioned to care for others. Within our own data, we noted that when mothers/daughters lacked social support and openness as a potential function of RW their self-reports of health were not as positive as those who did report more open and supportive familial bonds (e.g., Fisher et al., 2017). This observation is consistent with research linking social capital, social support, and health outcomes (Reis, 1984; Ryff & Singer, 2001; Segrin, 2006). Our findings held true for both mothers and daughters in our data. Daughters reported struggling with their own and/or their mothers' diagnosis resulting in diminished well-being, but denied themselves the support needed to properly cope, ultimately resulting in compromised or full inability to support their mothers at various times throughout the cancer trajectory.

While coping behaviors are malleable, family members, especially women, are likely unaware their coping approach may actually function maladaptively by inhibiting their own and others' health. As a potential area of intervention, health care practice could prioritize teaching families healthy communication approaches. Psychosocially focused resources could not only enhance communication aptitude in coping with illnesses but educate women (and their families) about gendered health behaviors.

Lesson 2

Women alone cannot combat and change traditional gender scripts, nor are they alone in their (re)production of such discourses. It is clear that RW gender scripts can/are employed and reinforced by all family members. Ultimately, what we suggest is that interventions adopt a familial approach to educating members as to how they might support women/patients (both mothers and daughters) during health crises. In doing so, several things are accomplished. Women (and their family) have the opportunity to adopt more flexible gendered behaviors, whereby they prioritize their health when ill (without guilt, reservation, or sabotage), and in so doing, women (and mother-daughter communication) begins a process of reconstructing "normative" gendered discourses that ideally, result in better health outcomes.

WHAT DO WE STILL NEED TO KNOW?

- How do enactments of RW contribute to both healthy and unhealthy experiences? Some may believe that traditional gender ideologies (like RW) are preferred and that efforts to "fix" this ideology and behavior is offensive and unnecessary.
- Future research could tease out if there are any significant differences between perceptions or appraisals of gender role scripts (valued positively/negatively) and their subsequent health outcomes (positive/negative). It may be the appraisals themselves that impact health outcomes if deemed problematic or wrong and not the actual behavior itself.

HOW DOES THIS WORK IN REAL LIFE?

- On a daily basis we are challenged with balancing multiple roles. Mothers and daughters find themselves having to make choices about prioritizing the role of carer versus patient (or vice versa) or personal health versus the mother/daughter's health. Balancing our needs with our mother/daughter's is not an easy feat and indeed, one that takes self-awareness and practice. Work on recognizing the "responsible womanhood" script in your own life.
- It is important to take care of yourself. For us, "responsible" womanhood is remembering that *"You can't pour from an empty cup."*

CLASSROOM ACTIVITIES

Recall Two Memories

- Recall a time when your mother was ill (it can be a common illness like the flu or a more severe diagnosis like cancer).
  - Reflect on what you learned about RW and how this script played a role in her behavior, your behavior, and your family members' response to her not being in good health.
  - Knowing what you do now, would you have changed your behavior or interacted with her differently?
- Recall a time when you were ill or going through a health change.
  - Ask yourself the same questions. How did your mother behave? Did RW inform her behavior? Your behavior?
  - Knowing what you do now, would you have wanted your mother to change her behavior or interacted with you differently?

NOTE

1. All participant names are pseudonyms.

REFERENCES

Alemán, M. W., & Helfrich, K. W. (2013). Inheriting the narratives of dementia: A collaborative tale of a daughter and mother. In J. K. Kellas (Ed.), *Family storytelling: Negotiating identities, teaching lessons, and making meaning* (pp. 125–142). New York, NY: Routledge.

Bell, S. E. (2004). Intensive performances of mothering: A sociological perspective. *Qualitative Research, 4*(1), 45–75. https://doi.org/10.1177/1468794104041107

Berg, C. A., Wiebe, D. J., Beveridge, R. M., Palmer, D. L., Korbel, C. D., Upchurch, R., … Donaldson, D. L. (2007). Mother-child appraised involvement in coping with diabetes stressors and emotional adjustment. *Journal of Pediatric Psychology, 32*(8), 995–1005. https://doi.org/10.1093/jpepsy/jsm043

Beveridge, R. M., & Berg, C. A. (2007). Parent-adolescent collaboration: An interpersonal model for understanding optimal interactions. *Clinical Child and Family Psychology Review, 10*(1), 25–52. https://doi.org/10.1007/s10567-006-0015-z

Cooke-Jackson, A. F. (2011). A world of difference: Unraveling the conversations African American mothers have with their adult daughters to negotiate diabetes. *Journal of Intercultural Communication Research, 40*(3), 237–258. https://doi.org/10.1080/17475759.2011.618843

Crabb, S., & LeCouteur, A. (2006). "Fiona farewells her breasts": A popular magazine account of breast cancer prevention. *Critical Public Health, 16*(1), 5–18. https://doi.org/10.1080/09581590600601957

Crawford, R. (1980). Healthism and the medicalization of everyday life. *International Journal of Health Services, 10*(3), 365–388. https://doi.org/10.1111/j31467-9566.2009.01198.x

Fisher, C., & O'Connor, M. (2012). "Motherhood" in the context of living with breast cancer. *Cancer Nursing, 35*(2), 157–163. https://doi.org/10.1097/NCC.0b013e31821cadde

Fisher, C. L. (2010). Coping with breast cancer across adulthood: Emotional support communication in the mother-daughter bond. *Journal of Applied Communication Research, 38*(4), 386–411. https://doi.org/10.1080/00909882.2010.513996

Fisher, C. L. (2011). "Her pain was my pain": Mothers and daughters sharing the breast cancer journey. In M. Miller-Day (Ed.), *Family communication, connections, and health transitions: Going through this together* (pp. 57–76). New York, NY: Peter Lang.

Fisher, C. L. (2014). *Coping together, side by side: Enriching mother-daughter communication across the breast cancer journey.* New York, NY: Hampton Press.

Fisher, C. L., & Wolf, B. (2015). Morality and family communication at the end of life. In V. Waldron & D. Kelley (Eds.), *Moral talk across the lifespan: Creating good relationships* (pp. 95–114). New York, NY: Peter Lang.

Fisher, C. L., Wolf, B., Fowler, C., & Canzona, M. R. (2016). Experiences of "openness" between mothers and daughters during breast cancer: Implications on coping and health outcomes. *Psycho-oncology, 26*(11), 1872–1880. https://doi.org/10.1002/pon.4253

Gibson, A. F., Lee, C., & Crabb, S. (2015). "Take ownership of your condition": Australian women's health and risk talk in relation to their experiences of breast cancer. *Health, Risk & Society, 17*(2), 132–148. https://doi.org/10.1080/13698575.2015.1032215

Gilligan, C. (1982). *In a different voice: Psychological theory and women's development.* Cambridge, MA: Harvard University Press.

Hays, S. (1996). *The cultural contradictions of motherhood.* New Haven, CT: Yale University Press.

Hummert, M. L., Nussbaum, J. F., & Wiemann, J. (1994). Interpersonal communication and older adulthood: An introduction. In M. L. Hummert, J. M. Wiemann, & J. F. Nussbaum (Eds.), *Interpersonal communication in older adulthood: Interdisciplinary theory and research* (pp. 1–14). Thousand Oaks, CA: Sage.

Koerner, S. S., Wallace, S., Lehman, S. J., & Raymond, M. (2002). Mother-to-daughter disclosure after divorce: Are there costs and benefits? *Journal of Child and Family Studies, 11*(4), 469–483. https://doi.org/10.1023/A:1020987509405

Kratzke, C., Vilchis, H., & Amatya, A. (2013). Breast cancer prevention knowledge, attitudes, and behaviors among college women and mother-daughter communication. *Journal of Community Health, 38*(3), 560–568. https://doi.org/10.1007/s10900-013-9651-7

Levy, D. L., Coleman, M. J., Sung, H., Ji, F., Matthysse, S., Mendell, N. R., & Titone, D. (2010). The genetic basis of thought disorder and language and communication disturbances in schizophrenia. *Journal of Neurolinguistics, 23*(3), 176–192. https://doi.org/10.1016/j.jneuroling.2009.08.003

Lorber, J. (1997). *Gender and the social construction of illness.* Thousand Oaks, CA: Sage.

Lyons, R. F., Mickelson, K. D., Sullivan, M. J. L., & Coyne, J. C. (1998). Coping as a communal process. *Journal of Personal and Social Relationships, 15*(5), 579–605. https://doi.org/10.1177/0265407598155001

Mackenzie, C. R. (2014). "It is hard for mums to put themselves first": How mothers diagnosed with breast cancer manage the sociological boundaries between paid work, family and caring for the self. *Social Science & Medicine, 117*, 96–106. https://doi.org/10.1016/j.socscimed.2014.07.043

Miller-Day, M. A. (2004). *Communication among grandmothers, mothers, and adult daughters: A qualitative study of maternal relationships.* New York, NY: Routledge.

Miller-Day, M. A., & Fisher, C. L. (2008). Parent-emerging adult child communication and disordered eating patterns. In J. N. Fuchs (Ed.), *Eating disorders in adult women* (pp. 1–19). New York, NY: Nova Science.

Mosavel, M. (2012). Health promotion and cervical cancer in South Africa: Why adolescent daughters can teach their mothers about early detection. *Health Promotional International, 27*(2), 157–166. https://doi.org/10.1093/heapro/dar014

Norberg, M., Magnusson, E., Thyme, K. E., Åström, S., Lindh, J., & Öster, I. (2015). Breast cancer survivorship—Intersecting gendered discourses in a 5-year follow-up study. *Health Care for Women International, 36*(5), 617–633. https://doi.org/10.1080/07399332.2015.1017640

Pecchioni, L. L., & Nussbaum, J. F. (2000). The influence of autonomy and paternalism on communicative behaviors in mother-daughter relationships prior to dependency. *Health Communication, 12*(4), 317–338. https://doi.org/10.1207/S15327027HC1204_1

Pecchioni, L. L., Wright, K. B., & Nussbaum, J. F. (2005). *Life-span communication.* New York, NY: Routledge.

Reis, H. (1984). Social interaction and well-being. In S. Duck (Ed.) *Personal relationships: Repairing personal relationships* (pp. 21–45). London, UK: Academic Press.

Rizzo, K. M., Schiffrin, H. H., & Liss, M. (2013). Insight into the parenthood paradox: Mental health outcomes of intensive mothering. *Journal of Child and Family Studies, 22*(5), 614–620. https://doi.org/10.1007/s10826-012-9615-z

Rosland, A. M., Heisler, M., & Piette, J. D. (2012). The impact of family behaviors and communication patterns on chronic illness outcomes: A systematic review. *Journal of Behavioral Medicine, 35*(2), 221–239. https://doi.org/10.1007/s10865-011-9354-4

Ryff, C. D., & Singer, B. H. (2001). *Emotion, social relationships, and health.* New York, NY: Oxford Press.

Segrin, C. (2006). Family interactions and well-being: Integrative perspectives. *The Journal of Family Communication, 6*(1), 3–21. https://doi.org/10.1207/s15327698jfc0601_2

Segrin, C., & Flora J. (2011). *Family communication.* New York, NY: Routledge.

Shenaar-Golan, V., & Walter, O. (2015). Mother-daughter relationship and daughter's body image. *Health, 7*(5), 547–559. https://doi.org/10.4236/health.2015.75065

Sinicrope, P. S., Patten, C. A., Clark, L. P., Brockman, T. A., Frost, M. H., Petersen, L. R., … Sellers, T. A. (2009). Adult daughters' reports of breast cancer risk reduction and early detection advice received from their mothers: An exploratory study. *Psycho-oncology, 18*(2), 169–178. https://doi.org/10.1002/pon.1393

Sulik, G. A. (2011). *Pink ribbon blues: How breast cancer culture undermines women's health.* New York, NY: Oxford University Press.

Sulik, G. A. (2007a). The balancing act: Care work for the self and coping with breast cancer. *Gender & Society, 21*(6), 857–877. https://doi.org/10.1177/0891243207309898

Sulik, G. A. (2007b). On the receiving end: Women, caring, and breast cancer. *Qualitative Sociology, 30*(3), 297–314. https://doi.org/10.1007/s11133-007-9057-x

Sweeney, E. (2012). Tracing the role of gender in the history of breast cancer social movements. *Women's Health & Urban Life, 11*(1), 76–93.

Wolf, B. M. (2015). Do families cope communally with breast cancer, or is it just talk? *Qualitative Health Research, 25*(3), 320–335. https://doi.org/10.1177/1049732314549605

CHAPTER SEVENTEEN

Communicating About Mental Health IN THE Mother-Daughter Dyad

LEAH M. SEURER*

"Do you think it's time that you went and talked to someone?"
I shifted my gaze from my kitchen window to my mother. "Talk to someone? Like who?"
"Like your primary physician maybe? You haven't been yourself for months."
"I'm not going on meds, mom." I sighed, "I'm not depressed. I'm stressed and I'm sad."
"Well depressed or not, you could at least go talk to someone about this. You don't have to figure it out by yourself."

Despite months of struggles, it was the first time my mother had voiced the need for me to see someone about my mental health. I had recently uprooted my life for my job and had been dealing with chronic health issues that had prevented me from working. It made sense to me why I was, in my opinion, not myself most days.

"I can't complicate this situation any more than it already is, mom. I know that I'm not ok, but we also can't say that it's mental illness. I don't want to put any other medications on board. And what is a therapist going to tell me that I don't already know?"

"I know you think that honey, but we can't ignore how you've been this entire year even before the physical health problems. You've been stressed before but not like this. This isn't stress Leah. And your family history might be playing a part in this. Dad, his sisters, your cousins, you know it runs in our family. If you would just talk to your primary doctor about options, I would feel better," she paused and followed my gaze out the window as I quietly nodded in agreement.

---

* Leah M. Seurer, Assistant Professor, The University of South Dakota, lseurer@gmail.com.

* * *

I begin this chapter with a snapshot of my own story to demonstrate the immense complexities and subtleties of communicating about mental health within the mother-daughter dyad. Questions of whether I had a mental illness (i.e., medical illness or stress), its causes (i.e., genetic or environmental/situational) and how to best treat it (i.e., medication or non-medication treatments) all permeated this small, everyday exchange. Similarly, as this chapter will discuss, understanding the line between illness and personality is a unique challenge both for individuals with mental illnesses and their loved ones. Was I depressed or simply stressed? Was my mother right in noting that this was different than the "stressed Leah" or did she not understand what I was like when I truly was just stressed? Finally, though much of the research discussed in this chapter looks at mother-daughter communication in response to a mother's illness, this story is a reminder that dialogue about mental health can also be in response to a daughter's illness or in response to a mother-daughter relationship in with both individuals have a mental illness.

Mental health is a term broadly defined as a state of mental, emotional, and behavioral wellbeing (NIMH, 2018). Mental illness, conversely, is a term defined as any number of mental, emotional, and behavioral disorders that range from mild to severe impairment (NIMH). Mental illness is an overarching term for many more specific diagnoses such as depression, post-traumatic stress disorder (PTSD), eating disorders, bipolar disorder, anxiety, or obsessive-compulsive disorder (OCD), to name a few. As of 2016, approximately 18.3% of U.S. adults had a mental illness (NIMH, 2018). These numbers are higher for women and young adults, with 21.7% of women and 22.1% of young adults reporting a mental illness within the last year (NIMH). With approximately one in five women and one in five young adults experiencing a mental illness, it is essential to understand how mental health and mental illness is addressed within the mother-daughter dyad.

This chapter explores mother-daughter communication surrounding mental health and illness. To begin, I provide a brief overview of the literature on mental illness in the family with specific attention paid to what we know about the mother-daughter relationship. Next, I share the results of a study I conducted examining how daughters of mothers with depression come to understand the meaning of depression and subsequently the meaning of motherhood. Finally, I suggest potential directions for future work in the field of mother-daughter communication about mental illness and provide suggestions for navigating mental illness in the mother-daughter dyad.

MENTAL HEALTH WITHIN THE FAMILY

Historically, the assumption that family environments contributed to mental illness ran throughout psychiatric models of why individuals developed mental illnesses (Jones, 2002). Today, understandings of the causation of mental illness are believed to be more multidimensional wherein both genetics and environmental factors may contribute to mental illness; an understanding of mental illness that still in part implicates the biological family. While current literature continues to include the family environment as a potential contributor to mental illness, a family environment may also serve to buffer stressors and protect against mental illness. In the same way that adverse family environments and dynamics may hinder one's mental health, positive and supportive ones may help in preventing mental health issues or in navigating them more successfully. Broadly, research on mental illness in the family covers three major areas: (1) effects of family dynamics on an individual member's mental illness, (2) effects of a family member's mental illness on his or her family, and (3) perceived burdens of care for well family members.

In examining prior research on the effects of family dynamics on a member's mental health, many studies explore the presence or absence of maternal communication about mental health and the results of that communication. For example, Prescott and Le Poire (2009) found that a mother's inconsistent communication tactics surrounding a daughter's eating disorder could inadvertently reinforce her problematic eating behaviors. In their study on communication dominance, Miller-Day, Dorros, and Day (2016) examined if dominant parent-offspring communication (i.e., communication that seeks to control, discourages independent thinking and expression, and punishes noncompliance) increased children's negative self-talk, suicidality, or depression. Results indicated that dominant communication from a mother did increase the likelihood of a child engaging in negative self-talk and depression.

It is important to note that mothers' communication also has the potential to safeguard daughters from the transmission and/or development of mental health problems. Recent work notes that the risk for transmission of depression between mothers and daughters can be buffered by high-quality communication (Manczak, Donenberg, & Emerson, 2018). Similarly, having a supportive mother-daughter relationship has been noted as playing a positive role in a mother's recovery from major depression (Mesidor & Maru, 2015) and is associated with lower depressive symptoms in children (Shin, Lee, & Miller-Day, 2013). Similar to research on family environments at large, these studies demonstrate that the mother-daughter relationship, and specifically the communication within the mother-daughter relationship, can serve to hinder or help mental health outcomes.

The second body of work on mental health in the family examines the effect of a family member's mental illness on the family. In the mother-daughter dyad, the majority of this research focuses on the impact of a mother's mental illness on her child(ren). Mothers with a mental illness often note negative or reduced parenting behaviors (Lovejoy, Graczyk, O'Hare, & Neuman, 2000), and daughters may experience a number of negative physiological, psychological, and physical health outcomes (for full review see Lampard, Franckle, & Davison, 2014). More recently, Arroyo,

Segrin, and Curran (2018) found that children of mothers with higher psychosocial problems reported receiving less care and had higher levels of psychosocial problems.

The third body of work on mental health in the family explores daughters' experiences of providing care for mothers with mental illness. A common finding in this work is daughters' experience of *parentification*. Parentification is essentially a role reversal wherein children take on traditional roles of parents both in independently caring for themselves and caring for their parents. Types of care that children report giving include emotional (e.g., handling their own and their parents' negative emotions), instrumental (e.g., doing chores or helping with younger siblings), and supportive (e.g., comforting and taking care of a parent) (Champion et al., 2009).

In the mother-daughter dyad, how daughters frame parentification experiences has important impacts on the mother-daughter relationship overall (Van Parys, Smith, & Rober, 2014). While some daughters frame the ability to provide care for mothers as positive for themselves and their relationship with their mothers, daughters who feel obligated to provide care report lower quality relationships overall (Petrowski & Stein, 2016). Caregiving is associated with increased anxiety-depression symptoms in daughters, lower levels of affection between mothers and daughters, lower levels of future caregiving intent, and daughters' increased fear of developing mental illnesses (Abraham & Stein, 2012; Champion et al., 2009; Kadish, 2016).

Caring for mothers unable to fulfill their normative social roles is a challenging experience for daughters in that it is vastly different from cultural expectations of the mother-daughter relationship. Regardless of daughters' attitudes towards caregiving, all daughters must make sense of the fact that they provide care to the person that culture tells them should be the primary caregiver for them. If your culture says that your mother should be your main provider of care and support, but you find yourself being that provider for her, how might you reconcile what mothering and motherhood mean? How might you come to understand her illness?

THE STUDY

What Was I Interested in Learning?

My interest in learning about daughters' sense-making processes led me to design a study examining how daughters talk about and make sense of depression and motherhood. More specifically, *I wanted to understand how daughters who were raised with a mother with depression communicatively (i.e., through their talk) made sense of their mother's illness and her role as a mother.* I reasoned that the experience of mental illness in mother-daughter relationships required a (re)negotiation of what depression and motherhood meant, but what did this (re)negotiation look like?

How Did I Go About Learning This Information?

I used relational dialectics theory (hereafter RDT) to explore my questions and a common RDT analysis method, contrapuntal analysis, to understand my data. RDT examines how language use creates and defines our individual and relational identities. RDT argues that these meaning-making processes occur in our everyday talk through our voicing of *discourses*, or generally understood systems of meaning (Baxter, 2011). For example, if I were to say that my family is "traditional," you might assume that I have a mother, father, and perhaps a sibling or two. This "traditional family" discourse is one that you were never taught but absorbed merely by living in a culture where the commonly understood meaning of a traditional family is as I have described.

Central to the premise of RDT is the understanding that these discourses carry with them differential amounts of power or legitimation within a culture. Some discourses are *centripetal discourses* or common and legitimized viewpoints. An excellent example of a centripetal discourse is our "traditional family" example. Other discourses that we voice are *centrifugal discourses*, or marginalized viewpoints (Baxter, 2011). Perhaps you are estranged from your family of origin and you say that family is not whom you are related to but whom you choose to call family. While this view is certainly a worthwhile discourse of family, the discourse of "chosen family" is a *less* accepted discourse in U.S. culture, and you might find yourself having to justify this statement more than you would if you had a "traditional" family. Moreover, you might grapple with your situation not because it is wrong, but because it does not line up with what culture told you a family was going to be in your life. In conversations with others and/or yourself, you might challenge the centripetal discourse of family with your centrifugal discourse (e.g., "I may not have a traditional family, but I have a real and happy one, and I don't need a traditional one!"). You might allow that centripetal discourse to maintain its predominant position (e.g., "I don't have a traditional family, and I'm learning to be ok with that."). Or, you might give both discourses equal footing (e.g., "Traditional and chosen families are equally real and wonderful. It just depends on what you need."). With this in mind, I began my study by examining centripetal discourses of motherhood and depression in current U.S. culture to better understand which discourses currently have the most legitimation in our culture and which discourses daughters might voice in communicating about their experiences of being raised by a mother with depression.

Centripetal Discourses of Importance

Motherhood is a familial role fashioned by our culture (Hequembourg, 2013), and the idea of what a "good mother" is comes from expectations of that culture (Arendell,

2000). The predominant (or centripetal) discourse of motherhood in current U.S. culture is that of *intensive mothering*. This discourse of mothering began to emerge in the 1990s and defines motherhood as a parental role requiring extensive time and energy (Hays, 1996). A mother is completely centered on her children's needs and is expected to: "devote her entire physical, physiological, emotional, and intellectual being, 24/7, to her children" (Douglas & Michaels, 2005, p. 4; Hays, 1996). Despite its demanding and arguably unattainable expectations, this discourse of intensive mothering remains the dominant model of motherhood in contemporary culture (Liss, Shiffron, Mackintosh, Miles-McLean, & Eachull, 2013).

The other centripetal discourse of particular importance in this study is the discourse surrounding *depression*. Most cultural discourses of depression surround understandings of depression's causes. In professional contexts, the dominant discourse of depression is the *biomedical discourse* (Hirshbein, 2009). In the biomedical discourse, depression is linked to biochemical and neurological conditions, stems from genetic or neurobiological issues, and is diagnosed and treated best by modern medicine (Miller, 2010). Among the general public or lay contexts, the dominant discourse of depression is the *psychosocial discourse* of depression (Schomerus, Matschinger, & Angermeyer, 2006). This discourse of depression circulating rests on the assumption that the causes of depression stem not from biological discrepancies but instead many internal cognitive factors and/or external environmental factors (Ainsworth, 2000). Depression is viewed as an illness to be treated through various behavioral methods as opposed to explicit medical ones.

After obtaining this broad understanding of current cultural beliefs of motherhood and depression, I was ready to explore if and how daughters used similar discourses in talking through their experiences and beliefs of motherhood and depression. To investigate my research questions, I conducted 30 interviews with emerging adult women (ages 18–26) who reported being raised by a mother with depression. Each of the interviews was examined to identify what commonly understood meanings of motherhood and depression, if any, were expressed. I then examined the data to see how these discourses either aligned with or diverged from currently privileged cultural understandings of motherhood and depression.

WHAT DID I LEARN?

Despite the conceptual separation between motherhood and depression, participants did not narrate their understandings surrounding the two in isolation. Instead, their stories moved amidst and amongst them as they described their experiences. Overall, I identified two common communicative struggles, or instances when two different discourses were present, within daughters' talk about motherhood and depression. The first involved meanings of motherhood. The second involved a struggle not about the cause of depression as expected (and reviewed above) but rather the struggle to locate depression as a real illness versus a part of their mother. Below, I explain these two struggles and their implications.

Struggle One: The Meaning of Motherhood

While daughters may not have realized it in their interviews, the way that they spoke about their mothers demonstrated a continued struggle between two different discourses of motherhood (named by me): the *discourse of ideal motherhood* and the *discourse of real motherhood*. These discourses of motherhood were each comprised of two primary, oppositional beliefs. The *discourse of ideal motherhood* (hereafter the DIM) is articulated through two main ideas: (1) mothers enact a cultural script of motherhood, and (2) mothers provide full care and support. In opposition to the DIM is the *discourse of real motherhood* (hereafter the DRM). The DRM is articulated through two primary beliefs that sit in response to the assumptions of the DIM: (1) mothers are individuals, (2) mothers provide what they can. In the following section, I explore each at length.

The Discourse of Ideal Motherhood (DIM)

Daughters voicing the DIM called upon specific scripts of motherhood circulating within the U.S. culture at large that align with the dominant ideology of *intensive mothering*. The DIM describes motherhood as a set of culturally specific scripts (e.g., "moms bake cookies") in addition to a role requiring a mother to provide full daily care and emotional support for children. Participants often described their mothers as doing "mom things." Without the need to unpack and/or elaborate further what the phrase "mom things" meant, these participant statements operated on the assumption that I, as a member of U.S. culture, understood exactly what mom things were. In describing mothers as those expected to provide full care and emotional support for children, the DIM echoes the discourse of intensive motherhood by positioning mothers as those who are wholly and selflessly devoted to all of their children's needs. Daughters described mothers not only as those that should provide the daily care required (e.g., "picking you up from every sports practice") but also their full emotional support for to their children (e.g., "supporting 110 percent in everything").

The Discourse of Real Mother (DRM)

In contrast with the DIM, the DRM is centered on individuality, and the lived reality of being a woman with depression while trying also to be a mother. By positioning individuality as paramount to motherhood, daughters describing motherhood through the DRM discussed motherhood as a role occupied by a unique, multi-dimensional individual with an identity and life experience stretching beyond that of mother. In voicing the DRM, daughters described mothers as unique people (e.g., "I felt like she was her own person"). Similarly, daughters describing motherhood using the DRM rejected the DIM's description of providing total support and instead talked about support as a mutual interdependence between mother and child (e.g., "So I only expect what I think she's capable of giving"). Overall, the DRM dismisses the expectations set forth by culture as narrated in the DIM and instead foregrounds expectations of motherhood contextually. Motherhood is one part of a woman doing what she can and not the entirety of her being.

Daughters took on several different positions regarding motherhood using the DIM and the DRM. A typical experience for some daughters was a renegotiation of their understanding of motherhood or a shift from privileging the DIM to privileging the DRM. This shift towards privileging the DRM was attributed to growing older and more mature and understanding that their mothers were doing the best they could while handling their depression. Most pointed to late high school and early college as the time frame when they began to understand motherhood in different or new ways. Participants often expressed guilt, and in some cases embarrassment, for coming to these new understandings later in their relationships with their mothers. Remaining participants firmly maintained the DIM and noted that depression had essentially robbed them of the experience of having a mother in that their mother was never able to meet the expectations set forth by their belief of what motherhood should be because of their adherence to the DIM.

In line with prior work exploring experiences of children with parents with mental illness, one of the most common themes that ran throughout the data was that of *parentification*. These stories of parentification were voiced by many participants and served as a useful lens through which to understand how daughters communicatively constructed understandings of motherhood via their experiences of providing care. Participants often articulated their need to "step into the role" of motherhood. For participants adhering to the DIM, they described the need to carry out activities traditionally done by mothers through the framing of parentification with participants noting that they felt as though they did not have a mother and were instead parenting themselves. Conversely, daughters who talked about motherhood using the DRM did *not* report an experience of parentification and instead noted that taking care of themselves and their mother was a natural way to grow up. Their mothers, as individuals and not solely their mothers, had their own things to do to get through their days. Rather than describing their work as stepping into motherhood, they described it as stepping up in their role as a daughter. Though parentification is generally understood in scholarship as a role reversal in expectations of parent and child, depending on how the role of motherhood is conceptualized, these results demonstrate that not all families view these responsibilities as a role switch but rather as normative family functioning.

Struggle Two: The Reality of Depression

The second primary struggle in the study surrounded the meaning of depression as a real illness versus a personal trait. Overall, two distinct discourses of depressions emerged in the data. The first discourse, the *Discourse of Depression as Sadness* (hereafter the DDS), is comprised of three primary tenets and defines depression as: (1) concomitant with sadness, (2) a personal trait, and (3) a chosen state. The second discourse was the *Discourse of Depression as Illness* (hereafter the DDI). The DDI is also comprised of three tenets that parallel the three tenets of the DDS in communicating depression as a true illness. In the DDI, depression is defined as: (1) distinct from sadness (2) distinct from one's personhood, and (3) beyond one's control.

The Discourse of Depression as Sadness (DDS)

Daughters speaking about depression utilizing the DDS talked about depression as an emotional state and/or a personal trait of their mothers. Depression was described as negative emotions and sadness (e.g., "I never saw it as a problem. I just saw it as sadness. Like sadness and depression went hand in hand"). Additionally, daughters talking about their mother's depression using this discourse commonly talked about depression more as a pre-established personality trait rather than an illness separate from her (e.g., "[t]hat was a big overarching thing like depression is a weakness ... And I think that changed the dynamics kind of too because people wanted to tiptoe around and nobody should talk with her about it"). In describing depression as both an emotional state and a trait of the individual, the DDS ultimately framed depression as a chosen state that individuals could elect to have or not have (e.g., "Can't you shake it off? Like can't you just pull yourself out of it? And I didn't understand why she couldn't do that."). Overall, the discourse of depression as sadness framed depression more as a part of who someone is rather than an illness that someone has.

The Discourse of Depression as Illness (DDI)

In direct opposition to the DDS is the DDI, which positions depression as a diagnosable illness that originates outside of one's control; it is a part of an individual only in that it is an illness one has. In the DDI, depression is experienced through a myriad of emotions and in some cases as an inability to experience any emotion at all. Daughters voicing the DDI described depression as separate from their mothers' identities (e.g., "It's just like oh it's not really her ... it's her depression"). Daughters voicing the DDI talked about rejecting the idea that depression is a chosen state (e.g., "I wish people would understand, I don't know. It's not something you can just beat") and noting that it often required the help of outside resources to handle.

Overall, daughters in the study voiced difficulty both in separating depression with the experience of sadness and in conflating depression with their mother's personality rather than seeing depression as distinct from their mother. For the majority of daughters in the study, both the DDS and the DDI were voiced with no one discourse consistently occupying the centripetal understanding. In other words, daughters honestly struggled to articulate an understanding of depression that was *only* that of illness or *just* that of a trait or state of their mothers. Subsequently, they had a difficult time articulating the line between their mothers and their mothers' depression. Daughters who did primarily voice the DDS reported less communication about depression arguably because it was not framed as an illness. Conversations centered more around their mother's behavior and less on their depression. Conversely, the few daughters that primarily talked about depression using the DDI noted significant amounts of communication in the family and with their mothers about the illness. Though it is hard to know which comes first, communication about depression leading to a belief in the DDI or adherence to the DDI as leading to communication, understandings of mental illness and communication in the mother-daughter dyad affect and are affected by one another.

WHAT DOES ALL THIS MEAN?

These findings demonstrate the potential impact of understandings of health on perceptions of family roles like motherhood. When articulating meanings of depression, participants voicing the discourse of depression as sadness (DDS) often described viewing their mother in a negative light. In defining depression as an emotional choice or trait of a mother rather than an illness, participants understandably noted frustrations in their mothers' inability to mother them, as they believed she should via the discourse of ideal motherhood (DIM). Conversely, participants who adhered closely to the discourse of depression as illness (DDI) noted that depression was a significant illness out of a mother's control. In framing a mother's inability to mother as a result of an illness rather than a result of a personal choice or character trait, participants talked about motherhood in new and different ways via the discourse of real motherhood (DRM) and accepted their mothers' attempts at mothering.

Clearly, the experience of depression affected participant understandings of the family role of motherhood. Similarly, many participants described the effect of family on perceptions of depression. In situations where a family did not communicate about a mother's depression at all, participants noted understanding depression through the DDS. With no information beyond the witnessed behaviors of their mothers, participants framed depression as an effect of sadness or as a personality trait. In other family contexts, participants noted having frank discussions surrounding depression. This consequently impacted daughters' understandings of depression. Across interviews, it was clear that how a family communicated about depression, or in many cases lacked clear communication, had an impact on how emerging adults constructed their understandings of both mothers and depression.

WHAT DO WE STILL NEED TO KNOW?

- Scholars need to focus on diverse populations. Given the importance of culture on how individuals communicate about mental illness and motherhood, future work should explore cultural discourses beyond the United States. Considering the rich diversity of current U.S. citizens in addition to projected demographic shifts in the U.S. population, communication scholars should understand U.S. culture as heterogeneous when studying mothers and daughters and mental health.
- Scholars might explore mother-daughter communication and mental health across time. Though the capturing of longitudinal data is often more difficult to obtain than traditional one-time interviews, this longitudinal data might capture the complexities of making sense of what is often a chronic health issue in a relationship that can span a lifetime.
- Future work should focus explicitly on potential positive relational and communicative outcomes between mothers and daughters navigating mental illness. This focus would allow for scholars to better identify and understand best practices.

HOW DOES THIS WORK IN REAL LIFE?

- Given that a strong mother-daughter relationship protects against adverse mental health outcomes, striving for a consistent supportive and positive communication climate in the mother-daughter relationship is an excellent way to both strengthen the mother-daughter relationship and ideally soften the harmful effects of mental illness.
- Open communication is key. Knowing that daughters may sometimes have trouble distinguishing a mother's or daughter's identity from her mental illness, consistent communication is likely beneficial for mothers and daughters as they learn how to best provide support and navigate mental illness within the mother-daughter dyad. Indeed, few illnesses rely on communication as much to keep identity and illness separate as mental illnesses.
- Mothers and daughters should communicate about relational expectations and experiences. Understanding that cultural expectations for mothers (or daughters) are cultural constructions and not lived realities may help individuals understand what expectations they are bringing into a relationship

and how those expectations are affecting how they view and behave towards each other.

- Remember that individuals may understand mental illnesses such as depression differently. Through communication, mothers and daughters can create common understandings about the legitimacy of the illness, what it is, what is causing it, and how to be mutually supportive and loving for one another as both navigate the situation.
- Communication about mental illness, on its own, is not sufficient for treating mental illness. Ideally, communication with family members is a positive part of a comprehensive plan for managing one's illness.

CLASSROOM ACTIVITIES

- Discuss: Do you and your mom or the person who has the role of mother in your life ever talk about mental health and/or illness? If yes, what do those conversations generally look like? If no, why do you think you have not had any conversations about mental health and/or illness?
- Discuss: Can you think of instances when you experienced feelings of parentification? How do you think those experiences affected your relationship with your parents?
- Discuss: How do you define motherhood? How do you think this definition affects your expectations for your mother or the person who fills the role of mother for you?
- Activity: Choose two family members or close friends and ask them how they understand each. Do you think that you and your family members have similar or different understandings of terms like depression, motherhood, or even being a daughter? Consider how their answers align with or depart from your own understandings. Do they align with our culture's understanding of these terms? Some possible questions are:
  - What do they think causes depression?
  - What do they think are best practices for treating depression?
  - What do they think a mom is?
  - What do they think a "good" mom or a "good" daughter look like?

REFERENCES

Abraham, K. M., & Stein, C. H. (2012). Emerging adults' perspectives on their relationships with mothers with mental illness: Implications for caregiving. *American Journal of Orthopsychiatry, 82*(4), 542–549. https://doi.org/10.1111/j.1939-0025.2012.01175x

Ainsworth, P. (2000). *Understanding depression*. Jackson, MS: University Press of Mississippi.

Arendell, T. (2000). Conceiving and investigating motherhood: The decade's scholarship. *Journal of Marriage and Family, 62*(4), 1192–1207. https://doi.org/10.1111/j.1741-3737.2000.01192.x

Arroyo, A., Segrin, C., & Curran, T. M. (2018). Maternal care and control as mediators in the relationship between mothers' and adult children's psychosocial problems. *Journal of Family Communication, 16*(3), 216–228. https://doi.org/10.1080/15267431.2016.1170684

Baxter, L. A. (2011). *Voicing relationships: A dialogic perspective*. Los Angeles, CA: Sage.

Champion, J. E., Jaser, S. S., Reeslund, K. L., Simmons, L., Potts, J. E., Shears, A. R., & Compas, B. E. (2009). Caretaking behaviors by adolescent children of mothers with and without a history of depression. *Journal of Family Psychology, 23*(2), 156–166. https://doi.org/10.1037/a0014978

Douglas, S. J., & Michaels, M. W. (2005). *The mommy myth: The idealization of motherhood and how it has undermined all women*. New York, NY: Simon & Schuster.

Hays, S. (1996). *The cultural contradictions of motherhood*. New Haven, CT: Yale University Press.

Hequembourg, A. (2013). *Lesbian motherhood: Stories of becoming*. New York, NY: Routledge.

Hirshbein, L. D. (2009). *American melancholy: Constructions of depression in the twentieth century*. New Brunswick, NJ: Rutgers University Press.

Jones, D. W. (2002). *Myths, madness and the family: The impact of mental illness on families*. New York, NY: Palgrave Publishing.

Kadish, Y. (2016). Five women's recollections and reflections on being raised by a mother with psychosis. *South African Journal of Psychology, 45*(4), 480–494. https://doi.org/10.1177/0081246314481565

Lampard, A. M., Franckle, R. L., & Davison, K. K. (2014). Maternal depression and childhood obesity: A systematic review. *Preventative Medicine, 59*, 60–67. https://doi.org/10.1016/j.ypmed.2013.11.020

Liss, M., Shiffron, H. H., Mackintosh, V. H., Miles-McLean, H., & Eachull, M. J. (2013). Development and validation of a quantitative measure of intensive parenting attitudes. *Journal of Child and Family Studies, 22*(5), 621–636. https://doi.org/10.1007/s10826-012-9616-y

Lovejoy, M. C., Graczyk, P. A., O'Hare, E., & Neuman, G. (2000). Maternal depression and parenting behavior: A meta-analytic review. *Clinical Psychology Review, 20*(5), 561–592. https://doi.org/10.1016/S0272-7358(98)00100-7

Manczak, E. M., Donenberg, G. R., & Emerson, E. (2018). Can mother-daughter communication buffer adolescent risk for mental health problems associated with maternal depressive symptoms? *Journal of Clinical Child & Adolescent Psychology*, 1–11. https://doi.org/10.1080/15374416.2018.1443458

Mesidor, M., & Maru, M. (2015). Mother-daughter relationships in the recovery and rehabilitation of women with major depression. *Women & Therapy, 38*(1–2), 89–113. https://doi.org/10.1089/02703149.2014.978222

Miller, G. A. (2010). Mistreating psychology in the decades of the brain. *Perspectives on Psychological Science, 5*(6), 716–743. https://doi.org/10.117/1745691610388774

Miller-Day, M., Dorros, S. M., & Day, E. (2016). The impact of maternal and paternal communication dominance on offspring's negative self-talk, depression, and suicidality. In L. N. Olson & M. A. Fine (Eds.), *The darker side of family communication* (pp. 27–47). New York, NY: Peter Lang.

NIMH (2018, March 30). *Mental illness*. Retrieved from https://www.nimh.nih.gov/health/statistics/mental-illness.shtml

Petrowski, C. E., & Stein, C. H. (2016). Young women's accounts of caregiving, family relationships, and personal growth when mother has mental illness. *Journal of Child and Family Studies, 25*(9), 2873–2884. https://doi.org/10.1007/s10826-016-0441-6

Prescott, M. E., & Le Poire, B. A. (2009). Eating disorders and mother-daughter communication: A test of inconsistent nurturing as control theory. *Journal of Family Communication, 2*(2), 59–78. https://doi.org/10.1207/S15327698JFC0202_01

Schomerus, G., Matschinger, H., Angermeyer, M. C. (2006). Public beliefs about the causes of mental disorders revisited. *Psychiatry Research, 144*(2–3), 233–236. https://doi.org/10.1016.j.psychres.2006.05.002

Shin, Y. J., Lee, J. K., & Miller-Day, M. (2013). The effects of maternal emotional wellbeing on mother-adolescent communication and youth emotional wellbeing. *Communication Research Reports, 30*(2), 137–147. https://doi.org/10.1080/08824096.2012.763025

Van Parys, H., Smith, J. A., & Rober, P. (2014). Growing up with a mother with depression: An interpretive phenomenological analysis. *The Qualitative Report, 19*(15), 1–18. Retrieved from http://www.nova.edu/ssss/QR/QR19/van_parsy29.pdf

CHAPTER EIGHTEEN

Motherless Daughters
AND THE Communication OF
Grief AND Comfort

MICHELLE MILLER-DAY* AND DANIELLE GRAINGER†

> When a daughter loses a mother, the intervals between grief responses lengthen over time, but her longing never disappears. It always hovers at the edge of her awareness, prepared to surface at any time, in any place, in the least expected ways.
>
> —EDELMAN (2014, P. 27)

In my lifetime I (Michelle) have been a sister, aunt, cousin, student, teacher, wife, and parent, but I never thought I would be a motherless daughter. Intellectually I understood this was inevitable, but I never really thought it would happen to me. My mother was my anchor and I couldn't imagine being adrift without her. But in 2017 she passed away and now I am afloat, left to re-define myself as a daughter. I ask myself, am I still a daughter if I do not have a living mother? Will my longing for her ever disappear?

This sense of not being "anchored" is common among motherless daughters of any age (Edelman, 2014). A mother's death is often a defining moment in a daughter's life because she loses her source of identification and role model for many issues associated with being female (Rowe & Harman, 2014). Rowe and Harman (2014) reported that examinations of the impact of maternal loss on a daughter's identity reveal daughter's increased empathy, wisdom, independence and a stronger appreciation for life. Schultz (2007) discovered that for daughters, maternal

---

* Michelle Miller-Day, Professor, Chapman University, millerda@chapman.edu.
† Danielle Grainger, Chapman University.

loss promoted positive change in their lives and enhanced relationships with other people. In comparison, other research suggests that motherless daughters experience adjustment and interpersonal difficulties, heightening feelings of inferiority, discomfort, and isolation, and feeling less competent and confident in their role of "mother" if they have their own child (Rowe & Harman, 2014). Pill and Zabin (1997) reported that maternal loss has a lifelong impact on a woman's sense of self and on her development. It is difficult to imagine for some women, but I ask you to consider it. What would your life be like without your mother's presence?

Being motherless may not be the result of a mother's death. Indeed, women can "lose" their mother through illness, separation, or estrangement in childhood, adolescence, or adulthood as well as death. A woman who has grown up lacking a "good enough" mother and secure base (due to mental illness or personality disorders) endures the lack of a nurturing, supportive mother. These women may have ongoing trauma from psychological abuse and sometimes physical abuse. Sometimes daughters can be cast into a parentified child role, with role-reversal requiring them to take care of mom, an impossible task and burden for a child (Russell, 2018). Because the mother-daughter relationship is often close and intimate, a bereaved daughter who experiences the loss of her mother through death or absence may have a difficult time accepting this absence (Silverman & Silverman, 1979). Research indicates that daughters both hold onto their absent mothers, while at the same time letting her go (Moss, Moss, Rubinstein, & Resch, 1993). In the case of a mother's death, some daughters hang on to the sadness of her mother's death to keep her alive psychologically (Edelman, 2014), while others acknowledge her death and accept it, but frequently dream of her, are comforted by thoughts and memories of her, communicate with others about her, and feel certain they will be reunited with her again (Silverman, 1987). The focus of this chapter is to increase your understanding of communication that may surround the experience of losing one's mother.

COMMUNICATION, GRIEF, AND COMFORT FOR MOTHERLESS DAUGHTERS

Communicating with others about grief and the experience of loss can be exceptionally challenging, but as Bosticco and Thompson (2005) assert, communicating about grief is central to the healing process, allowing a bereaved daughter to make sense of the finality of her mother's death and obtain necessary support. Despite outlining the need for communication to fight loneliness and confusion after the death of a loved one, Bosticco and Thompson (2005) discuss the concept of a *conspiracy of silence*, which refers to consistent avoidance by self and others to references about loss. Many times, it is too difficult for outsiders to listen to the emotional toll another's death has taken on a bereaved person (Silverman, 1987), but the bereaved are also restricted by their inability to bring up the subject, leaving the bereaved with a lack of support (Bosticco & Thompson, 2005). This is consequential, since the emotional support received from comforting messages and socially sharing grief communication are important ways to achieve emotional recovery from a mother's death (Rack, Burleson, Bodie, Holmstron, & Servaty-Seib, 2009).

Receiving emotional support during times of grief often comes in the form of comforting communication. *Comforting communication* "encompasses the verbal and nonverbal messages that people use when trying to reduce others' emotional anguish. It is a strategic communication activity that has the primary goal of alleviating another's emotional distress, enhancing another's self esteem, facilitating the other's coping, and/or assisting the other's problem-solving in a troublesome situation" (Burleson, 1984, p. 63). Rack et al.'s (2008) study of comforting communication after the loss of a loved one identified messages of support that include shared remembrances and stories that facilitated grief management and emotional recovery. Similarly, grief communication is central to recovery and adjustment after the loss of a loved one. *Grief communication* includes clear, direct communication about the loss, and sharing the meaning of the experience of loss with supportive others (Vandenberg, 2001).

COMFORTING AND GRIEF MESSAGES IN SOCIAL MEDIA

Pennebaker, Zech, and Rimé (2001) describe the power of the writing experience especially when communicating about grief. They report that, when writing, bereaved individuals can uninterruptedly disclose "a remarkable range and depth of traumatic experiences" (p. 530). In response to this written grief communication, Baym (2001) reported that online communities have a propensity to be interpersonally supportive, with social media providing new outlets for grief communication. In fact, given the ubiquity of social media in our lives, there is currently heightened interest in social media as platforms for the expression of grief. *Social media* (n.d.) refers to forms of electronic communication through which users create online communities to share information, ideas, personal messages, and other content (para.1).

Communicating comfort and grief on social media is a functional alternative to face-to-face interactions. First, it allows many people with similar issues to communicate with each other at one time despite geographical constraints (Wright, 2000). Also, the online nature allows for the possibility of anonymity, which may alleviate the shame and stigma that come with expressing emotion or asking for help (Carroll & Landry, 2010; Sanderson & Cheong, 2010). Indeed, there are social media sites dedicated to grief and these include exchanges of hope, validation of grief, resource provision, and psychosocial support (Smartwood, Veach, Kuhne, Lee, & Ji, 2011). Yet, despite this interest in social media and grief, there has been little examination of social discourse surrounding the specific experience of being a motherless daughter.

To address this gap in the research literature, we set out to conduct a study to examine social media discourse pertaining to motherless daughters during a holiday that reminds many of us about the importance of mothers in our lives— Mother's Day. Every spring, people in the United States celebrate a holiday characterized by flowers, balloons, and endless gratitude for our mothers. Social media sites are lit up with Mother's Day cards, happy family photos, and shout-outs to Mom herself, thanking her for all she has given over the years, admiring her for her enduring strength and love that knows no bounds, hoping her eyes will light up with joy when she sees the heartfelt posts that now occupy her timeline. But what do you post when you're motherless on Mother's Day? How do you feel when you scroll through your feed, only to see an endless stream of Tweets from friends who cannot help but express how grateful they are to have their mothers in their lives? How do you cope with such a loss on a day that is devoted to celebrating motherhood? The remainder of the chapter is devoted to describing this study and what we learned.

THE STUDY

What Were We Interested in Learning?

This study attempted to *(a) identify the social discourse surrounding "motherless daughters" on Mother's Day* and *conduct a qualitative content analysis of that discourse to (b) understand the dominant themes within that discourse.*

How Did We Go About Learning This Information?

We sought to examine the "Tweets" of motherless daughters on Mother's Day on the social networking service *Twitter*. This information will increase our understanding of brief comforting and grief communication within the motherless daughter community. Twitter is an online news and social networking service on which users post and interact with 140-character messages known as "tweets" (Twitter.com, n.d.). Twitter was chosen for this study based on its prevalence of use across various age-groups. Every second, on average, around 6,000 Tweets are tweeted on Twitter, which corresponds to over 350,000 Tweets sent per minute, 500 million Tweets per day and around 200 billion Tweets per year (Twitter usage statistics, 2018).

Data Collection

Utilizing NCapture Software we conducted a Twitter search featuring the key-word *motherless* between the dates of May 13 to May 15th, 2017. The Mother's Day holiday was on May 14th. Tweets posted the day prior to and immediately following Mother's Day were included to capture discourse in anticipation of and in reaction to the holiday. The search yielded a total of 2,260 Tweets including 1,220 retweets. All retweets were deleted. Additionally, a total of 13 Tweets were deleted that clearly reflected discourse about/from motherless sons and not motherless daughters. The remaining dataset consisted of 1,027 Tweets that were gender neutral (referencing motherless children in general) or specifically addressing motherless daughters.

Because Tweets are limited to a total of 140 characters (at the time of data collection), several Tweets featured links to outside websites, many of which were blogs that provided a platform for motherless daughters to share their experiences with one another. To achieve our goal of identifying the social discourse surrounding "motherless daughters" on Mother's Day, we included the websites that were linked to most frequently and whose content was specifically tailored toward women coping with being motherless on Mother's Day (N = 24). The resulting dataset for analysis included 24 website blogs and 1027 Tweets.

Data Analysis

All data were analyzed using qualitative content analysis. The first step is to read all content to gain a holistic understanding. The second step is to conduct open-coding by identifying meaningful units of data including individual Tweets and meaningful text from the blogs addressing motherless daughters on Mother's Day. These units of data could be entire Tweets, individual sentences, or a part of a sentence. Each unit was then categorized into codes/nodes using Nvivo software, a qualitative data management software. It can be helpful to think of codes/nodes as small organizing bins that allow researchers collect content with similar features or characteristics. These bins can then be combined into larger bins or *categories* of information, combining codes that are conceptually similar. The final step is to examine the data within and across categories to understand dominant themes. That is, to understand the key patterns of social discourse surrounding "motherless daughters" on Mother's Day.

What Did We Learn?

The data included Tweets and website content were organized into the following categories of messages: *"Happy Mother's Day" to other motherless daughters, acknowledging mothers of motherless children, Grief communication* (including the sub-categories of Seeking support, Loss, Bitter messages, and Gratitude), and *Comforting communication* (including Providing network support, Providing emotional support, and Connection to absent mother). We will discuss these and then the overarching themes that cut across these data, telling a story about experiencing Mother's Day while being motherless.

"Happy Mother's Day" to Other Motherless Daughters

More than 600 Tweets examined in this sample were simple "shout-outs," or acknowledgments, to a person or a group of persons who were motherless on Mother's Day. For example: "Shouts to all the amazing Super Moms, the motherless and the ones still waiting to bear children. Much love! #MothersDay," "To my motherless brothers and sisters out there: know you are loved. I sing for us all tonight," "While celebrating all mothers, remember those who are now motherless #mothersday #missmymom #eternallove #mothersinheaven," "Happy Mother's Day to all the motherless children of the world," and "#Happymothersday motherless unicorns. How are you all feeling today?" These messages bring to the forefront the absence of mother on this day meant to honor her, acknowledging those who are affected by that absence.

Many Tweets included links to other websites, including *TwitLonger—When you talk too much for Twitter. TwitLonger* is a site designed for those who want to post things on Twitter that exceed the 140-character limit. On TwitLonger, users write freely and limitlessly while the site automatically Tweets a link on their corresponding account that coincides with their entry. Tweets in our sample frequently linked to a specific TwitLonger entry featuring a commentary titled *Happy Mother's Day to the Motherless.* The content of this commentary included a deeply descriptive, prosaic account of the experience of a motherless daughter on Mother's Day.

Acknowledging Mothers of Motherless Children

The message in this category acknowledged those who are "mothers to the motherless," the women who may otherwise not be recognized for the maternal roles they serve. Examples of these messages include the following: "Shoutout to moms and anyone who's ever been a mother to a motherless child. #MothersDay" and "#HappyMothersDay to all the Mothers who were there for motherless children or those who just extend their motherly love to you as their own," "Happy Mother's Day to all the mothers and the ones who act like moms to a motherless child, and happy Mother's Day to all the lost ones," "Happy Mother's Day to all the women in my life who have never let me feel motherless. You made me strong and you made me powerful," "Happy Mother's Day to all the women that play the role of a guardian/protector to a motherless child. This is your day as well."

A small percentage of content was religious in nature, such as, "God I ask that you please be a mother to the motherless today, Amen," With a good deal of the messages expressing gratitude, "To be a motherless child, I sure have a lot of mothers to make up for it. I'm so grateful for that" and "PSA! Salute to all the mamas and women stepping in for them and being a mother to the motherless. #Respect." Yet, some of these messages acknowledged those others who mother, while expressing regret. For example, "Happy Mother's Day to all the motherless people (by choice or not). Everyone needs some mom energy even if the one you're born into trash."

Grief Communication

As indicated earlier in the chapter, grief communication includes clear, direct communication about the loss itself, and sharing the meaning of the loss experience with supportive others. In these data, grief communication was comprised of seeking support explicitly, sharing loss, bitter messages, and expressions of gratitude.

Messages coded as *Seeking support explicitly* included explicit requests for support such as, "So, if any motherless children want to spend the holiday smoking with me, please come over" and "As you celebrate Mother's Day today, please keep us motherless kids and kids with abusive/negligent moms in your thoughts. Today is tough." But, these requests for support were not prevalent. Soliciting support tended to be more implicit bids for empathy and emotional support when discussing their loss.

Many messages were focused on *Communicating loss*. These messages expressed sorrow for the loss of a mother. For example, "Being motherless on Mother's Day is the worst feeling you can have in your heart," "Today is my first day as a motherless mom. It's difficult to know I can't stop by mom and dad's and wish her happy Mother's Day anymore," "Not a day passed by without missing Mom. Being motherless is a very painful experience. Like no other," "My first motherless Mother's Day," "Starting grad school and mothering while being widowed and motherless is a brutal blessing this weekend. This paper is STILL due tomorrow though," and "Motherless Mother's Days never get any easier." A link frequently inserted into Tweets included "Letter to the Motherless on Mother's Day" (Rose, 2015). This letter was a longform message written as a special article for the USA Today newspaper in 2015 but posted for Mother's Day in both 2016 and 2017. The letter began with an acknowledgment of the pain involved with loss:

> Today sucks, I know. It's going to be hard. But so is every day since you lost your mother. There is absolutely no love in this world like the love of a mother. There is a void that cannot and will not ever be filled, no matter what anybody tells you. You don't miss her today any more than you will tomorrow, or the next day, or the day after that. Today, Mother's Day, is just another painful reminder that she is no longer physically here … I feel the pain within your heart as another day passes by without her. (para. 1–2)

Messages expressing loss typically began with the expression of loss, but then moved into articulating the various challenges experienced when unable to turn to mothers for guidance or enjoy her company, especially on days devoted to celebrating the bond between mother and child. Several women also pointed to the loss experienced when not able to share mother-daughter turning points such as graduating, getting married, or having children. These messages convey the sense of loss faced by the motherless on Mother's Day and appear to come from a genuine place of sorrow, while other messages seemed to be coming from a place of resentment and anger.

Some expressions of loss took on a frustrated, angry, or even bitter tone. For example, "What makes Mother's Day harder? The 'inclusive' posts that assert it's a day for all of us, even those who are motherless/childless. Vomit" and "I'm a woman who is both childless and motherless on Mother's Day. This should not be an excuse to shit on everyone else's joy today #shutup." Tweeted links to featured articles frequently expressed frustration with the holiday, such as "I'm Not Okay with being a Motherless Mother" (Noll, 2016) and "Why Mother's Day is Now the Toughest Day of My Year" (Nath, 2017). Consider the following excerpt from Nath (2017):

> Most days the memory of my mum is like the hum of my fridge in my apartment; it's constantly there but with time, I've trained myself not to notice it. But each year around Mother's Day, it feels like the world cranks up the volume to the point that it cannot be ignored.
>
> For the entire month of May, we're bombarded with greeting card commercials advertising how nothing quite matches a mother's love. Stores slap labels on stacks of pastel-colored items marking the perfect gift, picked just for her. Flower shops create bouquets designed to show your mum just how much you appreciate her.
>
> I used to be a happy consumer of all these items. I'm an only child, so Mother's Day was my responsibility and I took it seriously. Growing up, this day in May typically entailed a somewhat challenged attempt at making brunch and finding the perfect sweater, item of jewelry or mani-pedi appointment for the occasion.
>
> Now, it is a day of forced remembrance. Mother's Day is a Motherless Day for me and many others, but what about those who have a bad relationship with their mum or who never knew them at all? (para. 5–9)

This type of disclosure may provide a cathartic relief allowing the author to better cope with being motherless on Mother's Day, rather than being paralyzed by grief and resentment. She continues her post, providing background on the historical context that led to the celebration of the first Mother's Day (Nath, 2017):

> I was surprised to learn it was that very feeling of loss that actually sparked the creation of Mother's Day. In the early 1900s, an American woman named Anna Jarvis created the day as a way of showing her appreciation for her mother, who died in 1905. Her Mother's favorite flowers were carnations, so she gave red and pink blooms to mothers and white blooms to people with mothers who had passed away. It was only a matter of time before

greeting card companies and florists began using her day as a marketing opportunity. When that happened, Jarvis denounced the holiday completely. (para.10)

In providing this background, the author implicitly asks readers to consider how retailers capitalize on deceiving their consumers into purchasing nostalgic, holiday-themed products while simultaneously misguiding them away from the true spirit of the holidays. She goes on to voice her frustrations (Nath, 2017):

> I'm all for appreciating moms—or now, for me, my maternal stand-ins—and special days that commemorate the people we love in our lives but greeting card companies need to stop telling us how to feel, who to celebrate and when to mark the occasion. Because at one point, these arbitrary holidays that separate the haves from the have-nots will become daunting for all of us. It took losing my mum for me to realize that. (para. 12)

Another frequently linked to article, "Motherless on Mother's Day" (Kocsis, 2018) also expresses similar frustration:

> I don't quite understand these constant holidays, dedicated to moms and dads and bunnies and love. I see them as marketing scams, a way to boost economy almost every month, by throwing in a Holiday. (para. 1)

Kocsis (2017) proceeds to describe her unconventional, grief-stricken upbringing and the challenges she has faced as a motherless daughter:

> On these days I am reminded of my absent mother. See, not only did she pass away in 2007, her mother's soul was stolen when I was three. Recruited by an ill-intended woman into a sinister cult, my mother was forced to be separated from her children, initially physically starved through food rationing. After years of brutal torture, all of our spirits were broken. Emotionally, I never had a mother. In cult life, I was rarely allowed to express my feelings to anyone. This was considered to be self-centered behavior, a feeding of the flesh and a sin in the eyes of God!
>
> These days feel so distant to me. Social media is filled with flowery and adoring words dedicated to mothers. They are loved and adorned with the flowers of sparkly attention.
>
> I wonder if those mothers are supported every single day as they raise children, work and juggle schedules. I wonder if they have their own mothers to love them. (para. 2–9)

In this message, Kocsis (2017) implies that Mother's Day is often treated as a superficial celebration in which sons and daughters shower their mothers with gifts that fallaciously supersede the value of providing them with more authentic support.

Despite these bitter messages, there were numerous messages that conveyed loss, but also gratitude. For example, "Motherless Mother's Day are always hard, but I cherish every moment I had with you Mom! I miss you every day!" and "Mother's Day is hard when you're motherless. But I'm so blessed to be a mother and to be able to show them the love that I received" and "I thank God for the years and memories I had with my mommy. Lord knows that was truly my best friend. To the motherless child, be strong."

In this study, grief communication on social media was multidimensional, consisting of explicit requests for support and expressions of loss sometimes accompanied by expressions of gratitude, and sometimes by frustrated and bitter messages. Regardless of the length limitation for Tweets, people were able to participate in grief communication as well as share resources for support and comforting communication with others.

Comforting Communication

While many individuals employed social media to participate in grief communication, a great number were able to focus their messages on comforting communication. As defined earlier in the chapter, *comforting communication* includes messages intended to reduce others' emotional distress and enhance esteem and coping (Burleson, 2003). The comforting communication offered in these data included providing network support, providing emotional support, and promoting connection to the absent mother.

While past research suggests that most face-to-face support messages seek to provide emotional support to those experiencing the loss of a loved one, the messages in this study often combined both *network support* with *emotional support*. *Network support* is communication that reminds people that they are not alone in whatever situation they are facing because there is a network of people available to give the needed support. It entails generating feelings of social connection and creating a sense of belonging (Burleson, 2003). *Emotional support* includes communication that meets individual's emotional or affective needs, increasing empathy, connection, and decreases stress, but it doesn't try to fix a person's problems (Sarason, Sarason, & Pierce, 1990).

Network support messages were predominantly from motherless daughters that seemed to facilitate a sense of community and a place for other motherless daughters to connect with one another. For the most part, these messages were positive and suggested that connecting with fellow motherless daughters has a significant therapeutic value because only other motherless daughters can truly offer the empathy, connection, and emotional support needed. To demonstrate, consider the following messages, "Every Mother's Day, my motherless friends all text each other support and love; us all sticking together is powerful" and "Celebrate today, no matter what. Smile, my fellow motherless daughters, she loved you. And to my fellow Childless mothers, you loved them." These supportive messages may be particularly comforting for those who may otherwise feel alone as they face being motherless on Mother's Day. This suggests that connecting with fellow motherless daughters can be an important tool for providing emotional support and coping; sentiments may include "Let's celebrate our motherless-ness together" and "Sending love to my fellow motherless people out there. It's a difficult day (and social media offers no escape) but we'll get through it." These messages emphasized the existence of a network of motherless daughters who are available to give needed emotional support and encouragement to celebrate the day (or at least get through it) together.

Several Tweets included links to different articles providing network support while simultaneously acknowledging grief, providing emotional support, and suggesting solutions to other motherless daughters. Take for instance the following excerpt from "An Open Letter to Motherless Daughters on Mother's Day" (Edelman, 2017):

> Grief is a lonely hunter. And it's cruelest when we try to face it alone. Many of us had no choice in that matter, especially if we were children in families that didn't know how to talk about the death. The most healing experiences I've encountered over the past 36 years have come from meeting those who understand how grief really works. Not those who routinely recite the "stages" of grief, but who understand the true nature of grief, and understand it lasts a lifetime. We never stop missing mothers we were close with. How could we? What would "letting go" even look like? Letting go would be an assault to our nature and need for connection, and an insult to the integrity of the relationship. A collective movement has started to alchemize the prevailing cultural message about grief into something that actually makes sense to those who have actually gone through it. It's high time.
>
> Grief, in my experience, doesn't occur in stages. Instead it's elemental, and it ebbs and flows. The Elements of Grief include ones you probably recognize: Sadness, Longing, Disbelief, Anxiety, Confusion, Disorientation, Depression, Denial, Fear, but others are in there, too, ones that don't always come to mind first, like Appreciation, Certainty, Wisdom, Self-Knowledge, Gratitude, and Grace.
>
> That's not to say we need to appreciate that our mothers are gone. Not at all. But it is to say that we can, over time, come to appreciate who she was and what she gave us, even if our time together was brief. And also that we can come to recognize what she may have appreciated in us, too. Eventually, this appreciation can begin to counterbalance the pain. I promise you. It can.
>
> If you're having a particularly hard time this Mother's Day, you can try the following: Ask yourself, What did my mother see in me that would have helped her know I could get through this Mother's Day without her? What did she know about me that would have made her feel confident I could manage without her? And what helpful qualities do I have that perhaps she didn't? When you can recognize those things about yourself, too,—that, my sisters, is part of the Wisdom and the Grace. (para. 7–10)

Messages like these foster a sense of empathy among fellow motherless daughters. Rather than turning a blind eye to motherlessness and simply trying to get through the day, authors of these messages encourage readers to embrace grief in its entirety—including sadness, confusion, and debilitating fear—but also to embody the healing qualities of wisdom, gratitude, and grace.

Finally, in addition to providing network and emotional support, many Tweets promoted the therapeutic necessity of maintaining a connection with the "lost" mother. For instance, "Here's to the ones motherless on Mother's Day. May we stay strong and keep going on. Their love flows endlessly to us, even without out being here" and "Happy Mother's Day to you too, the childless mother and the motherless child. May their love transcend barriers, so you can feel them today" or "There is no such thing as a motherless child. She is still with you wherever she is. She is still in you wherever you are in your heart." Several Tweets included links to websites/blogs that emphasized maintaining a connection to the missing mother. Here are several examples:

To the Motherless Daughters this Mother's Day,

She's there. She's always right there where ever you are. Nothing this side of Heaven could separate the love your Mother has for you. Give yourself grace today, do the best you can. Your best today won't look like everyone else's. Your best might be simply getting out of bed to face the day and that's okay. I'm thinking of each of you today and wishing I could take away all your grief. Wishing I could get a day pass for all of our Moms from Heaven. Hoping you will remember if they could be here with you today physically, they would move Heaven and Earth to do so. (Pennington, 2017, para. 13 –15)

I feel the pain within your heart as another day passes by without her. She doesn't want you to be sad. She wants you to honor her life in the best way possible, and that way is to live it. Live it for you. Live it for her. I know it is sometimes easier said than done and sometimes words just don't help and I know this because I lost my beautiful 48-year-old mother almost two years ago when I was 24. I have come to find that the best way to heal is to remember. Remember her. Remember the sorrow, remember the love, remember everything. Talk to her, she's always listening. And simply cherish the time you did have with her and the memories you have made. (Rose, 2015, para. 4)

These messages acknowledge the challenges that motherless daughters face, but also suggest a belief that the spirit of a mother never leaves her child, regardless of whether she is physically alive or not, and that this connection can continue throughout the daughter's lifetime.

WHAT DOES ALL THIS MEAN?

In this chapter we have learned that daughters can become motherless through losing a mother physically through death or separation, but also psychologically through separation, estrangement, or mental illness. Communicating with others about grief and the experience of loss can be challenging, but it is essential to the healing process. Unfortunately, there is often a "conspiracy of silence" shutting down any discussion of the loss because it is difficult and uncomfortable, leaving daughters to manage their grief in solitude.

Fortunately, many motherless daughters receive comforting communication from others to reduce their emotional distress and assist with coping with the loss of a mother, as well as participate in grief communication to express their feelings of loss with others. Increasingly, daughters are seeking this release and support on social media. There are websites devoted to grief, there are Facebook memorials, and there are blogs specifically dedicated to offering support to motherless daughters.

To understand more about the experience of motherless daughters on Mother's Day, we conducted a qualitative content analysis of the Tweets and messages posted in social media over the Mother's Day period in 2017. From this study we learned that motherless daughters continue to recognize deceased or missing mothers, they acknowledge other maternal figures for their mothering efforts, and take the opportunity to participate in grief communication and provide comforting communication to fellow motherless daughters. Network support seems to be particularly salient in these messages; that is, letting motherless daughters know that there is a network of people available to give needed support. Moreover, these messages reinforce the importance of maintaining a spiritual connection with the deceased mother for healing and grief management.

As I write this final paragraph, I take stock of this advice and look at a photo of my mother, think of a memory, and am certain that she is with me. Knowing this provides the anchor I have needed, and I am moored to this certainty.

WHAT DO WE STILL NEED TO KNOW?

- Are there best practices for providing support and mothering to motherless daughters? How can we break the "conspiracy of silence" for our friends and relatives?
- In what ways does being motherless impact maternal identity and daughter's mothering behaviors?
- What are the differences in the perceived supportiveness of short form social media messages (e.g., Tweets) and long form social media messages (e.g., motherless daughter blogs)?

HOW DOES THIS WORK IN REAL LIFE?

- If you are grieving a loss, it is important to your health to participate in clear, direct communication about the loss, and share the experience of loss with supportive others.

- Grief communication can occur on social media networks. If you are grieving a loss, seek out dedicated websites, forums, and blogs intended to provide support.
- To grieve the loss of a mother it is suggested that you: accept the reality of the loss, process the pain, learn how to navigate through deep feelings, adjust to the world without her, and find an enduring (spiritual) connection with her even as you embark on your new life without her.
- Avoid contributing to the "conspiracy of silence." Encourage friends and family who are experiencing loss to share their thoughts and feelings. To reduce discomfort, remember that just by listening to them you are helping.
- When providing comforting communication, remember that it can be nonverbal (a hug) as well as verbal ("I can see that you are in pain.")
- When providing comforting communication, try to reduce another's emotional distress by offering concrete assistance instead of a vague offer such as "Call me if you need me." For example (recover-from-grief.com):
  - Sit them down to help pay the bills and balance the checkbook.
  - Help them make a "to-do" list for the coming week.
  - Let them know you are bringing over a spaghetti dinner one night, complete with salad and dessert.
  - Help make a grocery list, then go do the shopping for them.
  - Offer to clean up the place for them … and do it (yes, even the bathroom).
  - Spend an evening playing cards with them, putting together a jigsaw puzzle, or doing an art project.
  - Offer a big hug and let them cry on your shoulder … and don't tell them "everything will be alright."

CLASSROOM ACTIVITIES

- If you have lost a loved one, create a memorial webpage.
- Let's face it, bereavement is simply a sensitive, awkward subject. Yes, you do care, and yes, you want to help … but how? Think about someone who has recently lost a loved one. Brainstorm two different (concrete) things that you can do to help this person out.
- Think about the women and girls that you know who are motherless. What is your sense of the experience of motherless daughters on Mother's Day?
- If you are motherless, what are some ways you can take care of yourself next Mother's Day? If you are not motherless, what are some ways that you can be supportive on the next Mother's Day of someone who is?

REFERENCES

Baym, N. K. (2001). Interpersonal life online. In S. Livingston & L. Lievrouw (Eds.), *The handbook of new media* (pp. 62–76). London, UK: Sage.

Bosticco, C., & Thompson, T. (2005). The role of communication and storytelling in the family grieving system. *Journal of Family Communication, 5*(4), 255–278. https://doi.org10.1207/s15327698jfc0504_2

Burleson, B. R. (1984). Comforting communication. In H. E. Sypher & J. L. Applegate (Eds.), *Communication by children and adults: Social cognitive and strategic processes* (pp. 63–104). Beverly Hills, CA: Sage.

Burleson, B. R. (2003). Emotional support skills. In J. O. Greene & B. R. Burleson (Eds.), *Handbook of communication and social interaction skills* (pp. 551–594). Mahwah, NJ: Lawrence Erlbaum.

Carroll, B., & Landry, K. (2010). Logging on and letting out: Using online social networks to grieve and mourn. *Bulletin of Science, Technology & Society, 30*(5), 341–349. https://doi.org/10.1177/0270467610380006

Edelman, H. (2014). *Motherless daughters: The legacy of loss.* New York, NY: Hachette.

Edelman, H. (2017). *An open letter to motherless daughters on Mother's Day.* Retrieved from http://hopeedelman.com/2017/05/open-letter-motherless-daughters-mothers-day/

Kocsis, V. (2017). *Motherless on Mother's Day.* Retrieved from https://venniekocsis.com/2017/05/14/motherless-on-mothers-day/

Moss, M. S., Moss, S. Z., Rubinstein, R., & Resch, N. (1993). Impact of elderly mother's death on middle age daughters. *International Journal of Aging and Human Development, 37*(1), 1–22. https://doi.org/10.2190/QNA3-F9FY-UTRV-L8GE

Nath, I. (2017). *Why mother's day is now the toughest day of my year: I lost my mum in April, but feel her absence most in May.* Retrieved from http://www.chatelaine.com/living/real-life-stories/mothers-day-toughest-day/

Noll, S. (2016). *I'm not okay with being a motherless mother: Turns out I've been lying to myself.* Retrieved from http://modernloss.com/im-not-ok-with-being-a-motherless-mother/

Pennebaker, J. W., Zech, E., & Rimé, B. (2001). Disclosing and sharing emotion: Psychological, social, and health consequences. In M. S. Stroebe, R. O. Hansson, W. Stroebe, & H. Schut (Eds.), *Handbook of bereavement research* (pp. 517–544). Washington, D.C.: American Psychological Association.

Pennington, N. (2017). *Happy Mother's Day to the motherless daughters.* Retrieved from http://grieftohope.blogspot.com/2017/05/happy-mothers-day-to-motherless.html

Pill, C. J., & Zabin, J. L. (1997). Lifelong legacy of early maternal loss: A women's group. *Clinical Social Work Journal, 25*(2), 179–195. https://doi.org/10.1023/A:1025710525228

Rack, J. J., Burleson, B. R., Bodie, G. D., Holmstron, A. J., & Servaty-Seib, H. (2008). Bereaved adults' evaluations of grief management messages: Effects of message person centeredness, recipient individual differences, and contextual factors. *Death Studies, 32*(5), 399–427. https://doi.org/10.1080/07481180802006711

Recover-from-Grief.com. (n.d.). *Grief loss recovery: Hope and health through creative grieving.* Retrieved from www.Recoverfromgrief.com

Rose, J. (2015). *A letter to the motherless on Mother's Day.* Retrieved from https://www.usatoday.com/story/opinion/2015/05/08/a-letter-to-the-motherless-on-mothers-day/70933756/

Rowe, B., & Harman, B. A. (2014). Motherless mothers: Maternally bereaved women in their everyday roles as mothers. *A Journal of Family Studies, 20*(1), 28–38. https://doi.org/10.5172/jfs.2014.20.1.28

Russell, C. (2018). *Motherless daughters*. Retrieved from https://www.colleenrussellmft.com/Motherless Daughters.en.html

Sanderson, J., & Cheong, P. H. (2010). Tweeting prayers and communicating grief over Michael Jackson online. *Bulletin of Science, Technology & Society, 30*(5), 328–340. https://doi.org/10.1177/0270467610380010

Sarason, B. R., Sarason, I. G., & Pierce, G. R. (1990). *Traditional views of social support and their impact on assessment*. Oxford, England: John Wiley & Sons.

Schultz, L. E. (2007). The influence of maternal loss of young women's experience of identity development in emerging adulthood. *Death studies, 31*(1), 17–43. https://doi.org/10.1080/07481180600925401

Silverman, P. R. (1987). The impact of parental death on college-age women. *Grief and Bereavement, 10*(3), 387–404. https://doi.org/10.1016/S0193-953X(18)30550-1

Silverman, S. M., & Silverman, P. R. (1979). Parent-child communication in widowed families. *American Journal of Psychotherapy, 33*(3), 428–441. https://doi.org/10.1176/appi.psychotherapy.1979.33.3.428

Smartwood, R. M., Veach, P. M., Kuhne, J., Lee, H. K., & Ji, K. (2011). Surviving grief: An analysis of the exchange of hope in online grief communities. *Omega: Journal of Death and Dying, 63*(2), 161–181. https://doi.org/10.2190/OM.63.2.d

Social media. (n.d.). In *Merriam-Webster* dictionary. Retrieved from merriam-webster.com/dictionary/social%20media

Twitter.com. (n.d.). Retrieved from https://help.twitter.com/en/using-twitter

Twitter usage statistics. (2018). Retrieved from http://www.internetlivestats.com/twitter-statistics/

Vandenberg, S. K. B. (2001). Grief communication, grief reactions and marital satisfaction in bereaved parents. *Death Studies, 25*(7), 569–582. https://doi.org/10.1080/07481180126576

Wright, K. (2000). Perceptions of on-line support providers: An examination of perceived homophily, source credibility, communication and social support within on-line support groups. *Communication Quarterly, 48*(1), 44–59. https://doi.org/10.1080/01463370009385579

CHAPTER NINETEEN

Making Difficult Conversations Normal
IN Later Life

Mother-Daughter Communication, Narrative Inheritance, and Planning for Death

MELISSA W. ALEMÁN* AND KATHERINE W. HELFRICH†

> We are storytellers seeking meanings that help us cope with our circumstances. Our stories must be adequate for the situations with which we must deal.
> —BOCHNER, ELLIS, & TILLMAN-HEALY (1997, P. 312)

In our family, there are three major ways that people die, massive heart attack, undiagnosed Stage IV cancer, and dementia-related body failure. In some cases, we have been shocked and blindsided by an unexpected loss, while in others we have had the "long goodbye" with family members who have declined slowly over a decade or more with dementia. Our experiences with family members' deaths are an important part of our family histories that influence how we imagine our own potentialities. Do you have a vision or fear for what yours or your mother's end of life will be like? How do mothers and daughters talk about the meaning of health, illness and projected futures in the context of family stories about dying? What do those stories teach us? We believe these are essential questions to ask and conversations to have as mothers and daughters.

In this chapter, we seek to demonstrate how intentional storytelling between mothers and daughters can open doors to normalizing conversations about end of life. Through sharing our stories with one another and with you, we show how family stories about death and dying provide us with guiding rules for our later

---

* Melissa W. Alemán, Professor, James Madison University, alemanmc@jmu.edu.

† Katherine W. Helfrich, Professor Emeritus, Frederick Community College.

life mother-daughter relationship. We specifically confront two different sets of family stories about dying to examine our *narrative inheritance* (Goodall, 2006) and project expectations about end-of-life mother-daughter relationships in our family. The concept of narrative inheritance helps us to understand the lessons we draw from the lives of our family members who came before us —we have inherited their stories. We retell them, both accept and resist them, and incorporate them into our family's shared legacy of "who we are as a family" and "how we are to be as a family."

For the past 20 years, we have been telling family stories of women with dementia, jointly foreshadowing and sometimes denying the likelihood that we too will spend the last decade of our lives needing care and living with some form of dementia (Alemán & Helfrich, 2010). At the same time, we have been rendering less important another competing yet oft-told family tale of death, that of Katherine's father and Melissa's maternal grandfather Stanley and his siblings. The tale of Stanley's death has most often served as a counter health and illness story for us, gendered masculine, that we have set aside as "not us" as females. Even as a counter story, Stanley's sudden death, has offered up lessons to our family.

In the following pages, we offer our stories, narratives that move back and forth between our voices as a mother (Katherine) and daughter (Melissa) that illuminate the productive character of storytelling around end-of-life issues, reframing the possibility of such communication as "normal," rather than "difficult." Co-constructed narratives (Ellis, 2004) such as ours provide readers with a window into their own possible journeys and shed insight into their own agency as they endeavor to navigate dialogue about end of life issues. We hope that our stories will give you something to consider when talking with your own mothers and daughters about end-of-life. To assist you in following our stories, we offer a chart of the central characters in the Figure 19.1.

A BROKEN HIP STORY

Katherine (*Mother*)

The door to the hospital room was closed, so I knocked, waited, and entered slowly while peeking around the corner. The dimly lit room contrasted with the noon-time sun brightly shining outside the windows. A young woman with a nametag that identified her as a registered nurse was holding Betty's hand in a way that looked more like a wrestling match than a warm and caring gesture.

As I walked in the room, Betty lifted both her head and one foot off the bed, reached out her hand in my direction and asked, "Will you help me get out of here? I've got to get out of here."

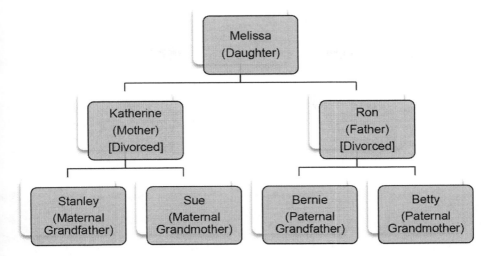

Figure 19.1. Major Characters in the Narratives.
This figure provides a family tree of the central characters in the chapter's stories.
Source: Author.

Not yet responding to Betty's request, I introduced myself to the nurse, "Betty was my mother-in-law many years ago. I'm here to check in on her. Her sons are on route from out west."

"Oh good," replied the nurse, "perhaps since you are familiar to her she will calm down. She has been quite agitated." The nurse had no idea that Betty, diagnosed with probable-Alzheimer's disease a decade ago, recognized few people in her family.

In the short time between walking in the door and introducing myself, Betty continued to try to lift her body out of bed, grimacing with even the slightest move. The nurse stopped her. "Betty, you can't get out of bed."

"Why? I have to go. I really have to go! I have to get to my boys."

"You have a broken hip, so you can't get up yet. Later on, you can."

"No, I have to go now!" Agitated, turning to me, Betty again tried to lift her body off the bed and said, "Will you help me get out of here?" Noticing that her lifted foot had a sock on it, she added, "I don't have shoes on. Do you have any extra pairs of shoes with you?"

I replied, "No I don't, but I'm sure we can get you shoes later."

"I have to get out of here NOW!"

Betty's persistent demands are like déjà vu to my own mother's hospitalization over 15 years ago. I am overwhelmed by the memories of my mother Sue's final weeks. Suddenly my memory takes me back to another room in this same hospital in the year 2002. My mind's eye rests on my mother, Sue, who is in bed insisting that I help her get out. She also had a broken hip. The rails were up on Sue's bed that day, and she tried to throw her body over them. She tugged at her IV and almost succeeded in pulling it out. Vivid flashbacks of that day in the hospital were visceral. My memories of the period of caring for my mother had been muted by time, but spending an afternoon with my mother-in-law Betty brought it all back to the foreground.

Startled by these memories caring for my own mother, I turned to the nurse, "The last time I was in this hospital was 15 years ago. I was here with my own mother who had dementia and also had a broken hip."

She nodded sympathetically. "It happens a lot that way."

Melissa (*Daughter*)

I traveled two hours north to meet my Dad and uncle who were with my grand-mother Betty for her first day in nursing and rehab care. I found my grandmother's room and quietly entered, interrupting the middle of her intake interview. They paused and greeted me with nods, and then the team of caregivers circled her and continued talking about rehabilitation. My grandmother sat awkwardly positioned in a wheelchair staring blankly out a large window appearing to give no mind to those discussing her care. Shortly after I arrived the team dispersed. While my dad and uncle went to address some administrative tasks, I stayed in the room with my grandmother and Karla, who was a new caregiver we hired to spend each day with her in the nursing home.

Moments later an occupational therapist entered the room and introduced herself to my grandmother. She asked, "Betty, can you introduce me to your guests?"

"I don't know who any of these people are," Betty responds, looking confused and irritated by her question.

"I'm her granddaughter, Melissa," I answer. The occupational therapist looks up at me and nods.

"So, your granddaughter's here with you Betty. That's nice," the occupational therapist keeps her focus on my grandmother's gaze and attention.

"I'm Karla. I'll be spending several hours a day with Betty while she's here," her caregiver chimed into the conversation.

"Great," the occupational therapist replied, without the exclamation point I'm accustomed to hearing in the tone of that word. She continued asking Betty questions directly, largely ignoring us. Impressed with the dignity and respect she is showing my grandmother, even as she cannot respond to any of her inquiries, she seemed to be trying to create a relationship with her. Still, trying to be helpful, I occasionally interjected to answer questions about her normal gait and abilities.

After her brief conversation with my grandmother, the therapist determined, "I'd like to get her out of bed and to the dining room for lunch. If that's OK, I'll be back shortly." We nod, and she spins around and tears out the room.

"Your family really cares," Karla points out. "Hiring someone to be their eyes and ears and making sure she is getting good care is important. You wouldn't believe the number of times I've gone into a place and there will be some residents with loads of family with them during the holidays, while others are sitting all by themselves."

I nodded, "My dad and uncle take turns. One of them comes out for several days each month," all the while disagreeing with her assessment of our family in my head. I feel guilty thinking that it should be one of us coming to see her daily. That is what my mom did for my maternal grandmother Sue and my great aunt too. Both were in assisted living and nursing homes near my mom's house, while none of us live close to my grandmother. My sister and I are the closest, both of us living two hours away. My dad will leave home for Minnesota and my uncle for Las Vegas by the end of the weekend. My attempts to persuade them to move my grandmother closer to me have been unsuccessful. *Have I really tried in earnest to make a case that she should live near me? Why am I assuming that feeling of responsibility?*

Three years ago, Betty's husband, my paternal grandfather Bernie, died from inoperable Stage IV lung cancer. Bernie was the primary caregiver for Betty after her sharp decline and diagnosis of probable-Alzheimer's disease. He was adamantly opposed to any long-term or institutional care options for her, despite the apparent fact that he was suffering from caregiver exhaustion and experiencing significant physical deterioration. The time between his cancer diagnosis and death was relatively short, but we had known for months before that something was not right. During his final months, he was hospitalized, spent several weeks in nursing care, and then his last few days in the hospice near my grandmother so she could visit. He reluctantly agreed with his children's decision to move Betty to assisted living near their former home. During one of my final visits with my grandfather before he died, he grabbed my hand tightly as I was leaving to head home for the evening, his watery eyes piercing mine in a pained stare he asserted, "Make sure you take care of your grandmother."

Holding back tears, I assured him, "I will. I love you, Granddad." I kissed him on his head, holding everything back and quickly walked out of the room and into the hallway.

As soon as I left the room my chest was heaving with uncontrollable sobs. My dad put his hand on my shoulder to comfort me, "That was unfair of him. He shouldn't have put that on you." *Why not? I thought.* Betty's care was Bernie's most pressing concern at the end of his life.

Bernie's concern was highlighted during my mother Katherine's final visit with him too. He turned to her and lamented, "I didn't think it was going to turn out like this. I didn't think I'd go first [before Betty]."

Four years after these final conversations with Bernie, and six months after fracturing her hip, Betty entered hospice care. Our family was unsure whether she would be in hospice for weeks or months. I arranged my schedule to drive north every Friday afternoon to spend the time by her side, holding her hand and quietly talking with her. Several days following my first visit to her while in hospice Betty died peacefully in her sleep.

MOTHER-DAUGHTER STORYTELLING ABOUT END OF LIFE

Bernie's memorable message to his daughter-in-law Katherine is an integral part of our more recent family history and has framed how we retell our family stories and make sense of their meaning (see Chapter 18 for a discussion of messages in end-of-life conversations). Unwilling to frankly consider the consequences of predeceasing his wife Betty, Bernie's own end of life and Betty's transition to dementia care in assisted living were rocky, destabilizing, and difficult for the entire family. In fact, none of the oldest generation in our family had living wills, expressed explicit wishes for their final care, nor were willing to have open conversations about end-of-life caregiving preferences with their adult children. This is not unusual in aging families. The topic of potential dependency and end of life of older family members are sources of anxiety for many adult children and their parents (Hummert & Morgan, 2001). For example, one adult daughter in Pecchioni's (2001) study of mother-daughter discussions of later life caregiving reported, "talking about it makes it real," adding that they "want to avoid any unpleasantness" (p. 232). Indeed, it is not surprising that only 22% of adult daughters and their mothers in her study had explicit conversations about future care, instead relying on heavily implicit decision-making processes (Pecchioni, 2001). While Fowler, Fisher and Pitts (2014) argue that there is not a "one-size-fits-all approach" to these conversations, they propose that "normalizing" conversations about eldercare earlier in life might lead to future family communication contexts wherein thoughts and expectations about later life care become part of routine conversations that take place (p. 725). Storytelling is one pathway toward normalizing talk about the end of life.

Family stories are also instructive. Pelias (2011) offers that family stories ultimately serve as "lessons, a pedagogy for living" (p. 186). We further argue that our stories are pedagogies for our ideals of dying. Jointly telling family stories about end-of-life circumstances prepare us to make sense of death, contemplate the possibility of new mother-daughter relationships at the end of life, and give us the opportunity to say "goodbye" if death is sudden or unexpected. Perhaps some would see this premise as morbid. Indeed, some members of our own family engage actively as participants in the telling of stories of our family members' deaths, but immediately tense up and become quiet when we shift the conversation to our possible futures, fears, and wishes.

Joint family storytelling about end-of-life potentialities is one way to *introduce the topic* of future caregiving, end-of-life wishes, and even death itself. Such family storytelling provides one means for families to cope with uncertainty and make sense of end-of-life possibilities. Both the structure (Koenig Kellas & Kanstruber Horstman, 2015) and the telling of the stories themselves (Alemán & Alemán, 2013) becomes a way of making coherent something that is potentially chaotic or complicated, more manageable. In the context of late-life mother-daughter relationships, storytelling also provides a forum to say all the things we want to say, to express fear and uncertainty even when it may be uncomfortable, and to ensure that caregiving and end-of-life wishes are known and often repeated. Thus, our family stories inform how we live in the present moment, while also providing us with lessons on how to care for family members in the future (Alemán & Helfrich, 2010). For us, the act of telling stories of death and dying helps us to live with the ever-present awareness of our mortality, regardless of how and when we ultimately die.

"WE HAVE A TIME BOMB AND IT GOES OFF AT 70": A SUDDEN DEATH STORY

Katherine (Mother)

"Do you have your affairs in order?" *Pregnant pause.*

"Just saying," said my brother Ed as he smiled slyly and joked with me just days before my 70th birthday. Unlike my father Stanley who insisted on a giant birthday celebration for his 70th, I chose a more subdued weekend at the beach with my two adult daughters.

Melissa (Daughter)

My sister and I were both anxious as our mother's 70th birthday approached, especially as we had planned to spend it in the same town where our grandfather Stanley died on his 70th birthday 30 years prior. "70" holds a mysterious and mythic character in our family. It had been easy to joke about. Up until now, at least.

Katherine *(Mother)*

The gentle knock and voice of my brother Ed's voice saying, "Kathie, wake up. Something is the matter with Dad. I think he may be having a heart attack," startled me awake early in the morning hours of Jan 2, 1986. Grabbing a robe and rushing out into the living room of my parents' beach house, I saw my father holding onto the bar countertop between the kitchen and the dining room with his left hand and clutching his chest with his right hand. He was breathing heavily and sweating. The sound from the TV streaming in the background, I gently touched my father's arm and could feel the dampness of his skin under his shirt.

"I'm calling an ambulance," I quickly announced as my mother rushed out of my parent's bedroom scurrying over to Dad.

The emergency line was answered quickly, followed by endless questions from the operator on the line. *Just send an ambulance.* "The reason for my call? I think my Dad may be having a heart attack. Our address is Sunset Drive, Bethany Beach."

"What is your house number?"

"I don't know," I panicked. "There is nobody in our neighborhood. I'll stand on the porch and wave."

My father answered, "It is 630 Sunset Drive." I repeated that into the phone.

The questions continued! "Please just send the paramedics," I answered impatiently. "I'll answer the questions later."

The paramedics arrived shortly after that. Just as Dad was going to sit on the stretcher, he stood up, hugged my mother and looked into her eyes for what seemed like a long time. My panic increased as I watch what looked like a goodbye.

I hear my husband, Ron, talking to our daughters, telling them that we're following the ambulance to the hospital. "We'll be back in a little while," I hear him say. I'm in our adjacent bedroom throwing on jeans and a sweatshirt and grabbing my coat as I head out the door.

As my mother was climbing into the ambulance, she turned and said, "Kathie will you ride with us?"

When I attempt to follow her the paramedic turns, "There's not enough room. You can join your mom in the Emergency Room."

I quickly ran to our car and jumped into the back seat. Ron and my brother were already situated in the front seats and ready to go. We followed the ambulance down Coastal Highway toward Lewes, Delaware. The interior of the ambulance was brightly lit, and Ron and Ed can see the paramedics attending to Dad. "Dad looks scared," Ed reported, his voice shaking.

We arrived at the emergency room waiting room in time to see an attendant squatting in front of my mother as she searched her wallet for insurance information. Mom took the paperwork given to her and looked at me helplessly as if she hasn't a clue what to do. I sat on one side of her, my brother and Ron on the other.

"What are they going to do to Stanley? What do I write on these forms? Do I need to do it now?"

The loudspeaker broke the silence calling for the cardiac team and cart to come to the ER STAT. Ron and I looked at each other over Mom's head locking eyes in a recognition that this call was for Dad. As the loudspeaker stops, Mom's tiny voice inquired, "Do you think they'll let us take Stanley home tonight?"

"I don't know Mom," I answered.

When what seemed like an eternity of questions from my Mom ends, a nurse gently knelt in front of her, "The doctor would like to talk with you now."

Mom turns to me, "Do you think they'll let us take Stanley home now, Kathie?"

"I don't know," I replied.

We were ushered gently into a tiny room where the ER doctor told us that Dad went into cardiac arrest almost immediately upon arrival and that they had been trying to resuscitate him ever since but to no avail. "We weren't able to get his heart beating again. We are so very sorry for your loss. Would you like to see him?"

As we nodded numbingly, we were ushered to his bedside with a warning that his skin was dark from the cardiac arrest. Mom went to him immediately putting her hand on his, which were now folded on his chest, then touched his face with her hands and wept. Except for a purplish hue to his skin, he looked himself. Crying, each of us said goodbye in turn.

Mom seemed to get smaller as I held her shoulder walking out of the ER. She looked lost, asking, "What are we going to do, Kathie?"

We pulled up to the house 45 minutes later to see the lights on and Melissa and her sister Caroline sitting in the living room. The TV was on, and they were looking out the window with anxious questioning faces. Ron walked into the house first and said, "Papa died. His heart stopped beating." As we all quietly fell into chairs, I slipped off my coat to discover that my sweatshirt was on inside out.

After sitting silently together in zombie-like trances, punctuated by occasional questions about next steps, I put on a pot of coffee, and we made the first call.

Melissa (Daughter)

It was my maternal grandfather Stanley's 70th birthday, January 1, 1986. My sister and I were already in bed, but not yet asleep when the commotion started. Our bedroom in my grandparent's home was adjacent to the living room and shared a wall with a built-in daybed. The paneled walls seemed paper-thin. We could hear the muffled sound of worry in the conversations with my grandfather as he sat on the daybed on the other side of our wall. My sister and I exchanged concerned glances across our twin beds. I whispered, "Do you think we should go out and see what is going on?" We tacitly agreed that we better stay in our room.

The activity in the living room only got louder with the thuds of a stretcher and paramedics stomping through the front door. Dad abruptly opened our bedroom door. We were already sitting up in our beds. "We need to take your grandfather to the hospital," he told us. We required no other explanation.

My sister and I left our bedroom as soon as we heard the front door slam shut. We dashed to the front window, moving the heavy curtains aside and watching as they closed the ambulance doors, turned the sirens on, and sped down the street away from the house. I remember very little of the next several hours as we sat and watched TV, no mobile phones to keep us updated. We just waited.

Hours later, we hear the distinct sound of a car pulling into my grandparents' gravel driveway and sluggishly get up to look out the window. My mom had her arm around my grandmother, supporting her as they gingerly walked toward the house. Instinctively, we knew my grandfather was not coming home.

A NEW DIAGNOSIS STORY: DIGGING UP A BURIED INHERITANCE

Katherine *(Mother)*

Just a year ago, I was at my physician's office for a yearly physical. As usual, the nursing assistant had taken my weight, blood pressure and amid doing a resting EKG I said to her, "Does this resting EKG ever really tell you anything? It seems like such a waste."

Distracted, the nurse replied, "Hmm hmm." She pulled the tape out of the machine, took the heart monitors off of me and quickly left the room.

Moments later the doctor walked into the examining room and without so much as a salutation said, "This is an abnormal EKG! I don't know if it is an aberration or if this is a new normal." She waved a paper that had a scribbly pattern over it that was quite unlike my usual tidy "perfect" EKG of past years. "I'd like you to see a cardiologist in the next two weeks." She then calmed down a bit and said, "This is not an emergency, but I'd like us to find out what it means."

Within two weeks I was sitting in a cardiologist's office who said, "Your heart is not supposed to do this. You are intermittently going from a normal heart rhythm into what is called a left bundle branch block. The electrical system on the left side of your heart does not operate correctly. The electrical signal travels more slowly to the left chambers of your heart than the signal traveling to your right chambers. This results in your heart contracting in a way that is uncoordinated."

He continued, "You are young for your heart to do this, and you present even younger than you are. We'll arrange for a full work up to see what the underlying cause might be since there really is no treatment for this. We want to rule out the worst possible causes such as any indications of existing heart disease, as people with left bundle branch are more likely to go into cardiac arrest."

Fortunately, the battery of tests found no underlying heart disease or structural problems in my heart, so at my follow-up appointment, my cardiologist again explained the characteristics of the left bundle branch block and what is next for me. I interrupted, "Given my father and other members on his side of the family had first heart attacks and immediately went into cardiac arrests, is it possible this is genetic?"

Looking at me, eyebrows thoughtfully raised, "I don't know. We don't know enough about the genetic make of this disorder." *Even so, it will now firmly become part of our family's narrative inheritance of illness, if not our genetic inheritance.*

He continued, "We will monitor your heart yearly and then down the road perhaps talk about a pacemaker or other measures to prevent cardiac arrest. As you age, I expect that it will get worse and you will spend more and more time in the left bundle block rhythm." He looked at me as if he were delivering devastating news. "The only thing you can do for now is to eat a heart-healthy diet and exercise regularly."

At that moment, in the face of this news, I felt oddly lighter. I knew that looking calm and happy seemed a rather strange response to hearing that I have a heart condition that can lead to sudden cardiac arrest and death. Then again, my cardiologist didn't know that until this moment I had expected to spend the last decade of my life suffering from dementia. The thought that I might escape a decade with dementia was strangely freeing. *To me at least.* My daughters, who have vivid and traumatic memories of my own father's death, did not receive the news as positively. They weren't too keen on the idea of another sudden death, especially as my own 70th birthday was on the horizon when I shared the news. My dad and both of my dad's siblings died in their 70th year. The distant memories and stories of the mythic "70" painfully resurfaced.

WHAT DOES ALL THIS MEAN?

Our stories about dying, death and end-of-life caregiving are important parts of our narrative inheritance. As discussed earlier, narrative inheritance is a concept that helps us to understand the role of the storied experiences of the generations who preceded us in crafting our understandings of family and who we are in that family. Our family's narratives passed from one generation to the next are not static but live on and change in our routine retellings. As a mother and daughter telling and retelling our layered narrative inheritance of our family members' (and possibly our) deaths, we draw several lessons that highlight how stories offer instructional guides for living and dying:

- Family stories about death and dying provide ground rules for later life mother-daughter relationships and communication.
- Family storytelling about death and dying organize respective locations of mothers and daughters in the lifespan in relationship with one another.
- Family storytelling about death and dying catalyze everyday conversations about caregiving and end-of-life wishes.

First, like all family stories, stories about family member's deaths provide mothers and daughters with ground rules (Stone, 2008) for our later life relationship. Such ground rules inform women about what it means to be a mother and daughter that guide behavior and offer instruction for how they might care for one another in the end. Perhaps more importantly, family stories told between mothers and daughters about dying provide lessons about how to approach their everyday lives. In our case, our stories and our storytelling impact an outlook toward time, both the present and distal future. For example, the telling of Stanley's sudden death and Katherine's recent diagnosis have resulted in a renewed focus on the present, and less of a focus on future-oriented talk. As someone in mid-life, Melissa tends to look ahead to the next chapter in her life, while Katherine focuses less on plans for the distant future. The storytelling does not change Melissa's long-range planning in all contexts but shapes her outlook and actions regarding time in relation to her mother. Our stories about the distant and recent past constitute meanings of the future in the context of our relationship as a mother and daughter.

Katherine's philosophy "treat each day as a gift" emerges from these stories and leads to the coordination of a present-based philosophy when we are together. Still, Melissa's words in her mother's recent birthday card "Looking forward to many more summers together in the future. Yes, I am planning!" point out that this *rule* that we should "remain in the present, rather than plan for the future" is negotiated and up for grabs in mother-daughter interactions. Indeed, conversations are characterized by a proximal future and focus on ensuring more time spent together, such as arranging a mother-daughter trip this year or anticipating the Thanksgiving holiday together. Consequently, the ground rule "stay present" is continually reasserted.

Second, family storytelling about end-of-life possibilities organizes and orders relationships between generations, as mothers and daughters experience storytelling from their developmental place in the lifespan. Thus, as Langellier and Peterson (2006) assert, the practice of storytelling is a way of "doing family." Storytelling between mothers and daughters about end of life, illness, and death constructs who we are in relationship to each other. While both of us serve as storytellers and listeners, the focus of the storytelling positions us in the lifespan by focusing our attention to the anticipation of Katherine's end of life and situate her as the matriarch.

Finally, the act of family storytelling between mothers and daughters catalyzes everyday conversations about caregiving and end-of-life wishes. For mother-daughter relationships in later life, the storytelling is a way of participating in the ongoing negotiation of our relationship, organizing expectations of one another, and even acknowledging the grief of past and anticipated future losses. Family storytelling thus can mobilize more explicit conversations about end of life, emotional experiences of fears, uncertainty, and hopes, as well as practical matters such as wishes for caregiving and living wills. Such storytelling can be a path to calls from scholars to normalize conversations about care prior to dependency and end-of-life wishes (Fowler, Fisher, & Pitts, 2014; Pecchioni & Nussbaum, 2000).

We tell these stories openly and engage in conversation about end-of-life wishes around family members. Not surprisingly, this is met with quite diverse responses. Some express discomfort and anxiety, not wanting to think about Katherine's death. Others have slowly begun to ask questions even while acknowledging how difficult the topic is emotionally. Older family members have brought up issues around practical considerations like medical powers of attorney and living wills, as we talked about topics such as quality of life in relationship to Stanley, Sue and Betty's stories. One breakfast table conversation led a family member to reflect, "Your conversations really unnerved me. I guess I need to be thinking and talking about my own wishes." This observation sparked a more extended discussion and revelation about caregiving wishes, an understanding of who would need to be told about them, and what it would require to ensure they were met. These examples show how the ritual of family storytelling (Alemán & Alemán, 2013) created a fertile context for more explicit conversations about end-of-life care and wishes.

Ultimately, we don't know what our end-of-life circumstances will be. However, we unpack our narrative inheritance as a mother and a daughter to make talking about the myriad possibilities, a more everyday activity. In many ways, this act of storytelling in later life is yet another form of mutual caregiving between mothers and daughters. Storytelling about death and dying provides an opportunity for both mothers' and daughters' fears, wishes, and hopes to be heard and affirmed, acknowledging our inheritance in all its complexity.

WHAT DO WE STILL NEED TO KNOW?

- Our stories of death and dying in the family are told from our social locations as white, middle class, heterosexual women. Our family experiences considerable privilege, including access to resources for end-of-life care that provides us with choices that other families don't have, and our privilege likewise impacts how we view "quality" at the end of life. Thus, we must ask how mother-daughter storytelling is shaped by cultural beliefs and values about aging, dying, and "good deaths" across different families.

- How do institutional forces such as access to health care, racism, and sexism shape the stories of mothers and daughters about death and dying, and their experiences at the end of life?
- How does family storytelling about death and dying ultimately shape the kinds of decisions that family caregivers, particularly daughters, make when facing end-of-life decisions about their mothers?
- Families create different rules for the nature of disclosure and openness in their families. Family stories, for example, may set into motion the expectation that "we don't talk about death" or that a particular family member is to care for aging parents without question. Examining the role of stories of death and dying across families with different orientations toward communication is critical in considering the unique challenges of making conversations about end-of-life wishes normal, rather than stressful.

HOW DOES THIS WORK IN REAL LIFE?

- Family stories of death and dying can serve as catalysts for weaving conversations about end-of-life wishes into every day to make talk about death and dying more normalized and less stressful.
- Whether those conversations are fleeting and abstract, or more involved and focused on details, building this kind of talk into your family's relational repertoire has the potential to lessen the need for decision making during crises and fosters understanding, trust, and intimacy between mothers and daughters.
- When mothers and daughters talk together about memories of death they can begin to experience empathy for one another's experiences. For example, words like "traumatizing" and "sudden" describe our experiences of Stanley's death. The pain associated with talking about our memories of Stanley's death helps Katherine understand why her daughters do not share her relief that she may share his fate. These frames were in stark contrast to our memories of caring for Sue and Betty where words like "endless" and "difficult" instead characterize our talk. This helps Melissa better empathize with her mom's fears of the possibility of a decade-long decline with dementia.
- Invite conversations about specific wishes for end-of-life care. For example, informal conversations allow Katherine to comfortably and openly express her wishes about when to move to palliative care and what interventions she definitely doesn't want. She tells Melissa, "I never want you to put me on ventilators or use feeding tubes—or any extensive life-saving care for that

matter, particularly after I have been diagnosed with any form of dementia. You're going to have to advocate for me with my cardiologist because I want to be taken off statins at that point too."

- Create an environment where other family members are present during these conversations, cultivating a family culture where talk about death, dying, and end-of-life is normal, helping to eliminate taboos for future generation. For example, our conversations often occur in shared spaces such as the living and dining rooms of family homes, allowing others to listen or participate.
- Acknowledge the intimacy of these informal encounters and embrace the complex emotions that you may confront. As we reflect on the spaces we inhabit during conversations about death and dying, we recognize they often feel thoughtful and intimate, and sometimes sad. It is a relief to Katherine to be able to talk about these things. She feels close to Melissa and understood. With each telling and conversation, Melissa feels more at ease with the topic, even as she comes to terms with the reality of the limited time she has left with her mom. Thus, with each conversation, Melissa encourages Katherine to continue talking.
- *Whether a mother or a daughter, we encourage you to initiate these conversations and to continue talking about end-of-life wishes in your family.* It is not easy. Indeed, sometimes it is painful, but talking about family stories of dying can lead to discussions of our own wishes, allowing us to check our assumptions and avoid the kinds of implicit decision-making that often happens in families when it is too late to ask.

CLASSROOM ACTIVITIES

- Visit *The Conversation Project* at https://theconversationproject.org/.
  - Read several stories posted in "Your Stories." With a partner, identify challenges the storytellers experienced in talking with a family member about their end-of-life wishes. Identify the positive outcomes the storytellers expressed as a result of their conversations. How did the storyteller feel after having the conversation?
  - Download the "Conversation Starter Kit" and review the questions and topics in the starter kit. Discuss how a daughter would approach this conversation with her mother. What might be challenges and opportunities for young daughters having this conversation with their middle-aged or older mothers?
- Some mothers may experience daughters who are resistant to having conversations about end-of-life wishes. Discuss some ways that daughters can

prepare to be open to the conversation and ease their own discomfort with their mother's potential death.

- After watching the video "It takes practice" in class (https://theconversationproject.org/practice-makes-perfect-video/), take turns role-playing in which one person is the mother and the other the daughter. Practice one scenario in which the daughter begins the conversation and one in which the mother begins the conversation.

REFERENCES

Alemán, C. G., & Alemán, M. W. (2013). The trouble with family stories. In A. Gonzalez & T. M. Harris (Eds.), *Mediating cultures: Parenting in intercultural contexts* (pp. 31–44). Lanham, MD: Lexington Press.

Alemán, M. W., & Helfrich, K. W. (2010). Inheriting the narratives of dementia: A collaborative tale of a daughter and mother. *Journal of Family Communication, 10*(1), 7–23. https://doi.org/10.1080/15267430903385784

Bochner, A. P., Ellis, C., & Tillmann-Healy, L. M. (1997). Relationships as stories. In S. Duck (Ed.), *Handbook of personal relationships: Theory, research, and interventions* (pp. 308–324). Chichester, UK: John Wiley & Sons.

Ellis, C. (2004). *The ethnographic I: A methodological novel about autoethnography.* Walnut Creek, CA: AltaMira Press.

Goodall, H. L. (2006). *A need to know: The clandestine history of a CIA family.* Walnut Creek, CA: Left Coast Press.

Fowler, C., Fisher, C. L., & Pitts, M. J. (2014). Older adults' evaluation of middle-aged children's attempts to initiate discussion of care needs. *Health Communication, 29*(7), 717–727. https://doi.org/10.1080/10410236.2013.786278

Hummert, M. L., & Morgan, M. (2001). Negotiating decisions in the aging family. In M. L. Hummert & J. F. Nussbaum (Eds.), *Aging, communication, and health: Linking research and practice for successful aging* (pp. 177–201). Mahwah, NJ: Lawrence Erlbaum.

Koenig Kellas, J., & Kanstruber Horstman, H. (2015). Communicated narrative sense-making: Understanding family narratives, storytelling, and the construction of meaning through a communicative lens. In L. H. Turner & R. West (Eds.), *The sage handbook of family communication* (2nd ed., pp. 76–90). Thousand Oaks, CA: Sage.

Langellier, K. M., & Peterson, E. E. (2006). Family storytelling as communication practice. In L. H. Turner & R. West (Ed.), *The family communication sourcebook* (pp. 109–128). Thousand Oaks, CA: Sage.

Pecchioni, L. L. (2001). Implicit decision-making in family caregiving. *Journal of Social and Personal Relationships, 18*(2), 219–237. https://doi.org/10.1177/0265407501182004

Pecchioni, L. L., & Nussbaum, J. F. (2000). The influence of autonomy and paternalism on communicative behaviors in mother-daughter relationships prior to dependency. *Health Communication, 12*(4), 317–338. https://doi.org/10.1207/S15327027HC1204_1

Pelias, R. J. (2011). *Learning: A poetics of personal relationships.* Walnut Creek, CA: Left Coast Press.

Stone, E. (2008). *Black sheep and kissing cousins: How our family stories shape us.* New Brunswick, NJ: Transaction Press.

CHAPTER TWENTY

Mothers' AND Daughters' End-OF-Life Communication

MAUREEN P. KEELEY,* LAUREN LEE,† AND
MARK A. GENEROUS‡

I slept with her nightly before we got the hospital bed and I would frequently awake to her stroking my hair and telling me she loved me. At the moment of her passing, I was ejected out of the bed beside her hearing my name called aloud. She clearly could not speak at the time, and it was then that I discovered she had passed. I feel that this was her voice calling to me as her death had only been moments before. I said my goodbyes and really feel this was my greatest wish, to have been with the person who gave me life when she left this world.

—TERESA

Communicating at the end of life (EOL) can feel overwhelming and intimidating, but as Teresa demonstrates in the story above, it can also be incredibly rewarding and positive. I (Maureen) personally experienced all these reactions almost twenty years ago, while my mom was dying from breast cancer. I didn't know what to say to her and there was practically no information or advice available to me on this topic. The little information that did exist on the topic came from the perspective of the person that was dying. What about those of us struggling to find the right words or actions with our mothers at the EOL? What should we say or do? What does this communication mean to us and do for us? Are there risks associated with communicating at the end of life? Why is

* Maureen P. Keeley, Texas State University, maureen.keeley@txstate.edu.
† Lauren Lee, Texas State University, lauren_lee@txstate.edu.
‡ Mark A. Generous, California State Polytechnic University, Pomona, magenerous@cpp.edu.

communication at the EOL important for all family members? I began looking for answers to these and other questions by asking people to share their stories with me about their communication with a dying loved one. I have found many answers to these questions while conducting research on this topic over the past two decades. Specifically, in this chapter we explore the importance and complexity of the mother-daughter relationship at the EOL, reveal the memorable EOL messages (verbal and nonverbal) shared between mothers and daughters as disclosed from the surviving daughters' perspective, and we also highlight the gifts and challenges of these interactions.

THE MOTHER-DAUGHTER RELATIONSHIP

The mother-daughter dyad maintains a unique bond that begins at birth and is a constant influence in the physical and emotional development of both parties (Fingerman, 2001). Mother-daughter relationships are developed through communication, are transformative, and remain significant across the lifespan (Koenig Kellas, 2010). Women in families (grandmothers, mothers, and daughters) co-write their stories, creating and recreating their identities throughout their lives (Miller-Day, 2004). Accordingly, mothers and daughters have complicated relationships that "reveal an entangled love, a struggle to simultaneously manage separation and connection, stability and change, ideal and real, open and closed, powerful and powerless" (Miller-Day, 2004, p. 222). These relationships are multifaceted and filled with mixed emotions sustained across lifetimes (Fingerman, 2001) and often becoming magnified at the EOL.

Mother-daughter relationships become more complex at the EOL because daughters experience a role-reversal with their mothers, usually becoming responsible for the caregiving duties at the EOL, leading to more time spent together. Flipping caregiving roles changes the dynamics within the mother-daughter relationship, often giving both mothers and daughters new perspectives on and respect for the other and further lessons to learn. Daughters often take-on the cleaning, cooking, and caregiving duties necessary at the EOL. Caring for someone at the EOL is an intimate experience because of the types of care that must be provided (e.g., giving baths and taking them to the bathroom, hand-feeding, walking with, holding or sleeping with their mother to protect them from falling) (Keeley & Yingling, 2007). These caregiving duties are accomplished while dealing with a wide range of raw emotions (e.g., sadness, joy, anger, frustration, fear) that are experienced at the EOL. As the primary caregiver, daughters often get more time with their mother at the EOL than other family members. More time spent together provides additional opportunities for communication at the EOL, for the creation of more memories, and for less regret because of things left unspoken (Keeley, 2007). Thus, it is vitally important to explore the communication at the EOL between mothers and daughters to give insight into this relationship during a significant stage of life.

COMMUNICATION AT THE END OF LIFE: FINAL CONVERSATIONS

Communication at the end of life in a close relationship offers a unique opportunity for mothers and daughters to "turn towards death together" (McQuellon & Cowan, 2000, p. 318) when they take advantage of the chance to find meaning through actions and words during their final conversations as they face an impending death (Keeley, 2007). *Final conversations* (FCs) are any conversations that occur beginning with the diagnosis of a terminal illness until the moment of death between family members or close friends with the person who is dying (Keeley & Yingling, 2007). FCs may be only one conversation, but they often include multiple conversations. Ideally, FCs should begin sooner rather than later following the terminal diagnosis because the person who is dying can fully participate, diminishing in communication abilities as his or her body shuts down and death nears.

The closer individuals perceive their relationship to be, the more frequently individuals participate in FCs (Generous & Keeley, 2014). Both mothers and daughters often consider their mother-daughter relationship to be the closest, most enduring, bond in their lifetime (Fingerman, 2001). Consistent with my past research over the past decade and a half (see Generous & Keeley, 2014; Keeley, 2007; Keeley, Generous, & Baldwin, 2014), six core themes embody most mother and daughter FCs: messages of love, identity, religious/spiritual messages, everyday talk/routine interactions, difficult relationship talk, and instrumental talk. Most mothers and daughters do not talk about all six themes during their FCs, their conversations are co-created and focus on what is most pertinent to their personal relationship. The following section will detail each of these themes and provide examples from real mother-daughter FCs. All examples in this chapter were from consenting but anonymous participants—we assigned pseudonyms instead of numbers to personalize the chapter. All participants completed a national survey (which included open ended questions) and all participants gave consent as part of the on-line national survey. The survey was completed on-line by 29 participants, consent obtained, and included both quantitative measurements and open-ended questions about FCs. Only the answers from the open-ended questions from mother-daughter dyads was included for this chapter.

Themes of Final Conversations

Messages of Love

Love is a common emotion experienced and expressed between mothers and daughters because of their unique bond (Fingerman, 2001). Love becomes the most predominant message conveyed at the EOL because everything else (e.g., money, power, status) has been stripped away and no longer seems important (Keeley, 2004a). Love is more available and indispensable at the EOL, perhaps because "when we let go of everything, only love remains" (Levine, 1984, p. 243). At the end of life, daughters have the opportunity to communicate their love and concern for their mothers through their words, actions, time, and daily caregiving.

The expression of love is often more pressing, available, and essential at the EOL (Keeley & Yingling, 2007). Messages of love often reinforce a sense of connection and affection that is clearly understood and shared. Many of these messages are simple words and/or nonverbal actions. For example, Nadia stated, "The evening before my mother's death, we were cuddling and whispering. She was in immense pain. We kept saying "I love you" [to] each other. It was enough." Love can also be communicated by simply being present when it matters the most to the person that is dying. For instance, Karen shared:

> When it became very clear she was dying, I sat next to her bed and held her hand. I told her it was me, and she asked: "What are you doing here?" (I live out of town). I told her, "I wanted to see you." She said, "I wanted you to come. I knew you would." And then I started crying quietly. She moved her hand in mine and asked me not to leave. I sat holding her hand until she fell asleep.

Love is also clearly communicated and understood through nonverbal actions such as when Danielle's mother "gave [her] a kiss on the cheek and a big hug." For others, the EOL creates the impetus that is needed to finally share messages of love freely. For instance, Danielle expressed:

> [My] mother was not [one to] demonstrate her love for us either verbally or physically when we were growing up because "it would spoil us" (she was a child of the depression). As an adult, she told me she loved me less than 10 times ... After she was diagnosed with cancer, she told me at least once a day she loved me.

Often at the very end, dying loved ones have very limited physical capability as their body is shutting down; therefore, nonverbal communication may be the only way to demonstrate love; through a look, touch, and time spent together up to the end (Keeley & Yingling, 2007). Olivia demonstrated this in the following statement:

> The last "conversation" I had ... was all nonverbal. She had hung on long enough for us to see her again in ICU. She turned her head to me and I caressed her cheek with my hand, kissed her, and then just stayed with her until the end.

These nonverbal messages at the EOL are as precious and powerful as any spoken word (Manusov & Keeley, 2015). When the message of love is completely understood and shared, it can act as a way to complete the relationship.

Identity

Family members are often the most important people who contribute to a person's identity, helping to create, shape, and evaluate individuals' self-concept and self-esteem (Brockmeier & Carbaugh, 2001). FCs messages of identity pertain to individuals' personality, physical attributes, talents, and skills (Keeley, 2007). FCs identity messages are especially strong within the mother-daughter relationship because they spend a lifetime negotiating identity issues and learning who they are in relation to the other. Daughters observe ways that they are like their mothers, while also looking for ways to differentiate themselves, all negotiated through verbal and nonverbal communication within a socially constructed expectation and desire for a close emotional bond (Miller-Day, 2004).

An impending death often creates an identity crisis for individuals (Fletcher, 2002). Questions that can surface at the EOL include: Who am I without you? Have I done enough with my life? Do I like who I am? These questions can lead daughters to reexamine, reevaluate, and redefine who they are and how they want to evolve in the future (Keeley, 2007).

Additionally, messages of identity are especially powerful because they provide a final insight (Keeley, 2007) from one of the most important people in daughters' lives, their mother. Surviving family members often hold strong beliefs that these messages are incredibly honest because the message is given at the cusp of death (Keeley & Yingling, 2007). Identity messages often remain long after their loved ones die because they usually strengthen, validate, and at times even modify individuals' sense of self (Keeley & Koenig Kellas, 2005). We found this to be especially true in the case of mother-daughter relationships because three aspects of identity emerged from this study for daughters upon their reflection of their FCs with their mothers: (1) how do I view my mother and who am I in regard to that perspective; (2) what is my mother telling me about myself; and (3) how does this FCs experience lead me to see myself in a different light. The following examples illustrate the messages that highlight identity via these three questions:

First, regarding the question of "how I view my mother and who am I in regard to that perspective" Wendy shared:

> I am left ... knowing her [personality traits and character], relatives in her past that she took after. [I also learned] what her other family members were like that helped shaped who she became ... she has taught us about life [and] living.

Second, FCs gave mothers opportunities to tell their daughters things about themselves. Zoey shared that the FCs with her mother:

> Was not just one conversation. It was a series of small conversations over a period of about a week. A minute to say something here, she'd wake up and just say a few things and then lay back down. She'd say things like "I want you to go to church" or "you did this well" or "take care of your health."

Third, the EOL journey provided daughters the opportunity to see themselves in a different light because their roles had switched, daughters were now "mothering" and caring for their moms, Danielle revealed:

> I looked at her and asked her how many times did you wipe my butt when I was little? She said she did not keep track; that was her job as my mom. My reply was well I am not keeping track because this was my responsibility as her daughter.

Ultimately, FCs provide a valuable opportunity for daughters to learn about themselves, their mothers, and fortifies the daughters' identities by viewing themselves in new roles or by seeing themselves through their mothers' eyes.

Religion-Spirituality Messages

Messages pertaining to religious and/or spiritual (R/S) beliefs are important at the EOL because, in the face of death, many individuals search for meaning through an examination of their R/S belief systems (Marrone, 1999). R/S messages frequently provide consoling explanations for events that cannot be explained by science or logic and reduce peoples' anxieties surrounding death (Davis & Nolen-Hoeksema, 2001). Through FCs, both participants may grapple with their belief systems, often leading to validation of or an adjustment to their R/S views (Keeley, 2004b). Furthermore, R/S provides messages of comfort and help to create a sense of community in the midst of death. Comfort is given through words that embrace their beliefs and offer hope in an afterlife. For instance, Rachel stated that "it was touching and light-spirited that we knew we would see each other again." Rachel also shared that she was:

> Whispering spiritual matters into her ear and included scripture (John 3:16) that alludes to eternal life so she would be assured (OK, so we would both be assured) that we had eternal life and would live forever even in a spiritual afterlife.

This sense of community comes from the realization that no one should take the death journey alone (Keeley, 2009). Michelle stated, "Our Pastor was sitting beside me holding my hand, and in just a few minutes, I felt this peace and calmness come over me." Messages about R/S are beneficial because they offer a framework for acceptance of the impending death and provide a sense of consolation that the participants will be together again in the afterlife (Keeley, 2004b).

Everyday Talk/Routine Interactions

Life and relationships are made up of a compilation of small moments filled with *everyday talk* that includes discussion of mundane topics such as the weather, shopping, daily events, and even the sharing of personal historical stories (Keeley, 2007; Wood & Duck, 2006). *Routine interactions* are predictable patterns of behavior that become habitual and part of the norm within the family that are repeated, such as playing a favorite game together on a regular basis, giving each other with a hug with every greeting and departure, or sharing favorite meals together (Keeley, 2007). Everyday talk and routine interactions set the tone for EOL interactions, build relational cohesion and a sense of normalcy, and create structure within the family which can be very comforting in the midst of chaos (Duck, Rutt, Hurst, & Strejc, 1991; Keeley & Baldwin, 2012).

Everyday talk between mothers and daughters often includes the sharing of stories and laughter amid routine interaction. For instance, Danielle told a story about FCs that her daughters had with her and their terminally ill grandmother (3 generations of mothers and daughters):

> They asked Gran, we know you had an outhouse growing up but where did you take a bath? At that time they were helping me give her a bath. My mom and I looked at each other and started laughing and I nearly dropped her! I told my mom ok I'll take them to the feed store. Her bathtub was a #3 washtub!

The topics of the conversation don't really matter; it is the act of sharing of ideas, opinions, and actions to live every minute with your loved one as close to the moment of death as possible. For instance, Victoria stated that she and her mother talked about and did things together that they loved such as "We held hands and looked at old pictures, letters, and watched President Obama get inaugurated," and Deborah's conversations focused on talking about their "favorite memories." These examples illustrate that the ordinary can become extraordinary remembrances, as they embody how the two parties have always interacted together. Everyday talk can include everyday hassles and ways to solve them based on the experience of the terminally ill. Laura shared that her mother "described our hard water problem at our house and how it impacted the washing machine; she taught me how to deal with it! I guess that's what happens when you have three months to talk about things."

In addition, the use of shorthand code or brief phrases indicates intimacy and understanding between individuals (Keeley, 2007). For instance, Rachel revealed that minutes before her mother died "[she] held her hand and said, 'I'll see you later, alligator,' and [her mother] laughed and kept saying 'later, gator.'" This was clearly a phrase often used between the pair and was meaningful to Rachel.

Routine interactions are habitual activities that make up most of our day to day lives (Wood & Duck, 2006). Routine interactions can include short outings that were common between mothers and daughters such as the example that Hannah shared about their shopping trip to Kohl's in which the pair "talked about what was cute and what wasn't." Laura highlighted that routine interactions remained until almost the very end, but became an abbreviated version of previous activities. Specifically, "we spent a lot of time playing backgammon, which she always loved, but with her leukemia, couldn't play more than one game at a time." If repeated enough, routine interactions can become a part of family rituals. Family rituals are defined as a "voluntary, recurring, patterned communication event whose jointly enacted performance by family members pay homage to what they regard as sacred, thereby producing and reproducing a family's identity and its web of social relations" (Baxter & Braithwaite, 2006, p. 263). Hence, everyday talk and routine interactions at the EOL help to sustain relationships until the very end by providing continuity of actions through familiar communication events and by doing so create simple, but meaningful family rituals to carry on after the death.

Difficult Relationship Talk

Not all relationships are positive. In fact, some daughters struggle in their relationships with mothers. In the case of historically difficult mother-daughter relationships, FCs often expose relational issues and begin to mend the past. Daughters' may realize they are running out of time to discuss and clean up the mess (Keeley, 2007). Relationships that are framed as being difficult include past interactions with the dying family member that involves criticism, defensiveness, guilt, silence, and negative behaviors (Keeley & Yingling, 2007). In some cases, there may be an admission of past wrong-doing and a request for forgiveness. For instance, Yvonne stated:

> Mom left me a phone call one day on my cell and I still have it. She kept saying that I was right after all, she had made many, many mistakes, enough to last her a whole year, and she was sorry.

The fact that this daughter has kept the message years after it was given is a testament to the importance and value of taking the chance to be vulnerable, open, and forgiving at the EOL. Kelley (2003) states that forgiveness is about "abandoning the negative and fostering the positive" (p. 224). This is especially true at the EOL because not to do so, will often leave the surviving daughter with bitterness, resentment, or disappointment, thereby keeping her stuck and unable to move past the hurt (Keeley & Yingling, 2007). In other cases, it is the surviving family member that is looking for forgiveness and a release from guilt. For instance, in the following story, Zoeyfelt that she had disappointed her mother because she had postponed having children to pursue other things. Through their FCs, Zoey's mother had an opportunity to acknowledge what they had missed, while at the same time, releasing her daughter from guilt and leaving her with a positive affirmation. Zoey shared this account of her FC: "I said through tears, 'I'm sorry if I disappointed you, Mommy.' 'What do you mean? It's just the opposite,' she said, 'I know you'll be a great mama.'"

Difficult relationship talk is often filled with emotion, restraint, and compassion (Keeley, 2007; Waldron & Kelley, 2005). Conversations involving difficult relationship talk are never easy, and some people may choose not to have FCs because they find it too difficult to become vulnerable within their challenging relationship. However, when individuals do engage in difficult relationship talk at the EOL, it may potentially release heartache and allow them to move forward (Keeley & Yingling, 2007). Daughters who shared their FCs concerning difficult relationship talk with us emphasized that this theme was the *most* important topic for them to confront because it allowed them to see their mothers with a new perspective, giving them new understanding and compassion.

Instrumental Talk

Finally, FCs at the EOL also include conversations about the terminal illness as well as death and dying. These conversations may consist of simply talking about dying, treatment options, decisions regarding when it is time to stop medical interventions to sustain life, choices for pain and palliative care treatment, and talk regarding funerals and eulogies (Generous & Keeley, 2014). The ability to have an open and honest conversation about the impending death can be freeing to the participants. For example, Gabrielle stated that her mother: "needed to tell 20 people about what she was going through before it was "normalized" for her ... that stuck with me." Taking death out of the shadows and into the light helps to remove much of the fear, leads to acceptance of the inevitable, and hopefully allows for a death with dignity and ideally less pain (Kubler-Ross, 1997). Discussions of death and dying make it possible for the terminally ill not to feel alone at the EOL because they are able to discuss all aspects of the dying journey. For instance, Gabrielle shared that she and her mother "went through it together and talked about it in open and honest ways." Another woman, Hannah, revealed that her mother had cancer in three areas, with multiple surgeries and removal of the tumors, along with many therapies. It was important for Hannah "to [go to] these [therapies and surgeries] with her ... [and] discuss whether or not they made her feel better." Without open and honest conversations about the illness, treatments, and potential for death, her mother would have been enduring all of her suffering alone.

The decision to begin Hospice care is often a challenging and fear-inducing experience, for instance, Victoria shared the following story:

> I was talking to my mom about how we needed to go ahead and start at home hospice care for her, and she agreed, but she just kept saying she didn't understand why she had to have

it … I explained to her every day that her body was just done and as much as we all wanted her here, it was time for her to just be at peace and allow her body to rest.

Hospice admittance nurses are in the perfect position to assist daughters' in helping their mothers' transition into Hospice (Candrian et al., 2017). If the EOL decisions are not a collective family decision, then the choice of who is appointed decision-maker is often based on a number of factors including: gender (women are primarily the caregivers in families, their role in the family (e.g., eldest adult child, the selfless one, etc.), who in the family has the expertise (e.g., the nurse or medical expert in the family), who in the family has the closeness and trust with the terminally ill person, as well as who has the willingness and strength to make tough decisions (Trees, Ohs, & Murray, 2017). For instance, Danielle shared a conversation concerning how to care for her mother as her terminal illness progressed:

> She did not want to become a burden, but I wanted to keep her with me in my house for as long as I could. When it became apparent [that she was getting much worse] I talked to her about not causing her death, not hastening her death but my mom was tired and was ready to move on. I spoke with her hospice nurse about this and was told that I could take her off her medicine but not her pain medicine. That is what I did and she died 6 months later.

Tough decisions at the EOL are common, but as Danielle highlights, they are best made from a place of knowledge about what her mother wanted and in consultation with the EOL health professionals. At the very end, individuals need to acknowledge the inevitable truth. For example, Jill shared that her mother told her that "she was ready for death and was not afraid." Others, though, seem to need permission to let go and move on to the afterlife as Lisa did for her mother when she "put a hand on her and said, 'It's OK.' … Then she died." Instrumental talk at the EOL is honest, compassionate, and necessary.

Gifts of Final Conversations

One advantage of the diagnosis of a terminal illness is that it gives both the terminally ill and their family members the chance to begin the grieving process prior to death. Specifically, people need "anticipatory time to reflect on and begin to make sense of their loved one's death prior to the moment of death" (Tenzek & Depner, 2017, p. 9); to prepare for the impending death with their loved one and to be ready to let them go (Keeley, 2007). FCs enable dying mothers to help their daughters accept, understand, and prepare for the impending death through their conversations; leading daughters to find realization and acceptance that mothers are at peace with their impending death (Keeley, 2017). Further, a good death has been described as one where there is full engagement in the process by the family members with their dying loved one (Tenzek & Depner, 2017). Knowledge and acceptance at the EOL gives a sense of control, a mutual understanding of what is wanted and needed by the dying loved one and family members, and the commitment to be present until the end (Keeley, 2016). Thus, the three most significant gifts talked about by daughters include the opportunity to be fully present in the moment, saying a heartfelt goodbye, and the ability to see that there was peace at the end.

Being Present and Saying Goodbye

For daughters, presence includes the idea of being physically present with their mother, but also being wholly focused and aware of what was going on throughout the process, especially at the end (Tenzek & Depner, 2017). Acceptance of the impending death gives mothers and daughters the freedom to face the reality of the situation and make the most of the time they have left together (Keeley & Generous, 2017). Acceptance of death does not forego hope at the EOL, instead it shifts the focus away from an unrealistic cure for a terminal disease toward valuing and prioritizing open communication at the EOL. This process of acceptance fosters openness, honesty, and greater closeness (Koenig Kellas, Castle, Johnson, & Cohen, 2017). Communication at the EOL provides daughters an opportunity to accompany their mothers to the very end, resulting in the perception that time is a precious gift. Allison shared that she was grateful that she was able to "quit my job ... and able to spend every day with her. I treasured every moment." Likewise, Lisa stated, "I am so thankful that I was there the moment that she died." It is not easy to be a witness at the death of your mother, but it is better than not being prepared or present when the moment comes. While not everyone can be there at the exact moment of death, the point is to be there as much as possible during the death journey (Keeley & Yingling, 2007).

Peace

Pretending that death can be avoided impedes authentic conversations, but if mothers and daughters choose instead to keep a "sustained gaze" on the truth that death is inescapable, they may discover a newly realized sense of relational closeness that living fully in the knowledge of an illness can bring (Goldsmith & Ragan, 2017, p. 7). It creates a space where compassion is given despite personal suffering because the reality of the impending death can motivate daughters to act with selflessness and focus on the needs and desires of their mothers (Goldsmith & Ragan, 2017). If mothers and daughters have the opportunity to acknowledge death's nearness, they are given the gift of embracing life's remaining opportunities together (Keeley & Yingling, 2007). Acknowledgment and acceptance of the impending death afford mothers and daughters the time to address both participants' emotional, psychological, spiritual, and existential pain, resulting in peace (Goldsmith & Ragan, 2017). Deborah stressed that she was "at peace with it because we got to tell her goodbye and that we loved her." Jill acknowledged that in the end, her mother's death was acceptable because "she died peacefully." Presence and peace are hidden treasures at the EOL and are invaluable for daughters as they cope with their grief. While FCs are an opportunity for many benefits that we have highlighted in this chapter, we don't mean to suggest that FCs are easy or come without challenges.

Challenges of Final Conversations

Challenges at the EOL highlight the constraints of "terminal time" (Keeley & Yingling, 2007), as well as inherent tensions and struggles that accompany communication at the EOL (Keeley & Generous, 2015). *Terminal time* begins with the awareness that a loved one is dying and ends at the moment of death; it highlights constraints regarding the amount of time left to have FCs (Keeley & Yingling, 2007). When time runs out, it is gone, there is no negotiation for more time to communicate at the EOL. "Three specific challenges of FCs include: (1) waiting too long, (2) denial of the impending death, and (3) the concealment of emotion that occurs during the death journey" (Keeley & Generous, 2017, p. 5).

Waiting Too Long

Time is often the underpinning of the challenges characteristic to the EOL because it is the motivation for FCs and it creates the context for conversations at the EOL (Keeley & Generous, 2015). Endings such as that of impending death, offer daughters the permission and justification for prioritizing events in their lives so that they have the chance to increase their bond with their mothers (Carstensen, Isaacowitz, & Charles, 1999).

Simultaneously, there is a great deal of denial and fear surrounding death (Marrone, 1999), so time may run out before the opportunity for communication is engaged at the EOL. Some daughters described falling victim to this fundamental challenge. Zoey shared that "we had waited too long" and Christina acknowledged that she and her mother had waited to the point where "[her mother] couldn't talk." Teresa revealed a number of reasons for limited communication in her relationship with her mother that included "too much pain" and mental degeneration made "conversations were very hard to follow." Michelle revealed that only "short periods of visitation were allowed," whereas Deborah stated that her mother's "eyes were open, [but] she wasn't responding to anyone." These daughters were left disappointed by their inability to have meaningful FCs because, at the very end, the mother's declining body limited verbal communication. At the EOL, time is finite, and individuals never know when two-way conversations will become impossible.

Acceptance-Denial of the Impending Death

The opposition between accepting the approaching death and denying the truth of death is a noticeable challenge at the EOL, especially for family members who may be at different points of acceptance (Keeley & Generous, 2015). For instance, Danielle was the most open and accepting of the diagnosis and what it meant for her mother; specifically, she stated, "Even though 3 of my 4 siblings were in the room, the 4th was on the phone long distance, when the Dr. told us her cancer was terminal, I seemed to be the only one to hear 'terminal.'" The mere fact that Danielle was the only one able to hear the truth about the diagnosis regarding her mother's terminal illness illustrated that there would be challenges regarding most, if not all, aspects of communication at the EOL within her family. In other instances, the denial is based on fear or a lack of acceptance of what they are being told by the doctors, such as in the case of Emily where she stated, "We knew this meant my Mom didn't have long, but we didn't want to believe it." Sometimes the denial is not from the daughter or other members of the family but is from the mother who is dying. Teresa shared that "[her mother] was determined that our doctors had given up on her, and she wasn't ready to give up." This dialectical tension between acceptance and denial must be overcome to achieve open, honest, and authentic communication at the EOL (McQuellon & Cowan, 2000).

Expression-Concealment of Emotions

The dialectical challenge of expressing emotions (i.e., crying, showing fear) or concealing emotions (i.e., avoiding emotional talk or nonverbal expressions of feelings) is complicated because the outcome must be negotiated between the EOL participants and for each EOL interaction. It is important to recognize that the death journey produces a lot of emotions, most of which are distressing and sorrowful for family members (Moller, 1996). Family members disclose that they struggle with how much emotion to reveal, as well as determining the appropriate time and place to share feelings of sadness, fear, and anger (Keeley & Generous, 2015). Lily exemplified this struggle when she had FCs with her mother. Specifically, she shared the following account:

> I felt like I wasn't being totally truthful with her in some things. And I wasn't, I was hiding a lot of things ... my own emotions ... I would try to be really encouraging to her ... my, my biggest fear and ... sadness was knowing that she was going to go. And, and so I did everything I possibly could to see if I could avoid that somehow.

It also seems that the emotion of anger is the most difficult to deal with in the moment and after the fact because it can leave guilt for daughters to deal with after their mother has died. Amanda shared that she was:

Angry with my mother because she went from a vibrant, full-of-life, healthy woman to an overweight lazy person in what seemed like months. I expressed my disappointment and anger that she had allowed herself to get into such poor shape so quickly. I wish that I could have let that go and not be my focus during her last days.

A final example comes from Katherine who came to realize that "you die the way you live" and that this is especially true for how her mother and her whole family displayed emotion at the EOL. Specifically, she stated:

My family had not been very emotionally open and that situation [mother dying] just kinda busted it open … we struggled with it. … It's a difficult emotional place to be … you know, the heaviness of death, which none of us had ever talked about … You have no choice about it. But you can deny it. You know, it's like this huge thing in the room with you which you're just ignoring. … on the one hand, I always thought that she was intentionally being so difficult to make us go to that emotional place … Because we would have days where we talked about the weather, we talked about the food, and we watched TV real surface … then she would throw these fits … it would force the emotionless (sic) to come out, even as ugly as it was.

Katherine draws attention to the internal and familial struggle at the EOL regarding the expression of emotions juxtaposed with the desire to conceal negative emotions. There are many reasons for this struggle including family norms, gender expectations, cultural customs, and individual personalities (Keeley & Generous, 2017). Ultimately, at the EOL, there is not a right or wrong response for daughters and mothers regarding the resolution of these three FCs challenges (time, acceptance or denial of the impending death, and expression or concealment of emotions). There is, however, one fundamental question that should be asked when faced with these challenges: What will leave me with the most regret after the death? The answer, of course, is a personal decision based on the relationship, the circumstances in the moment, and the expected consequences (short and long-term).

WHAT DOES ALL THIS MEAN?

As Teresa shared in the opening quote of this chapter, her "greatest wish, [was] to have been with the person who gave [her] life when she left this world." It is not surprising that other daughters share this desire to be with their mother at the EOL, sharing communication as well as providing their mothers with comfort and care during their last weeks, days and hours. Communication at the EOL is inherently vulnerable, and it is the act of creating meaning through shared communication that evokes some of the most precious and memorable moments in peoples' lives. FCs between mothers and daughters include: love, identity, religion/spirituality, everyday talk, difficult relationship talk, and instrumental talk. FCs remain with daughters long after their mothers have died and provide them with gifts and challenges during their communication at the EOL.

WHAT DO WE STILL NEED TO KNOW?

- How does the role of culture impact how people communicate at the EOL? Are FCs the same or different for African-American, Hispanics, Asians, Middle Eastern cultures? In what ways?
- How does the role (i.e., partner, parent, child, etc.) of each family member impact their FCs? How does the family's relational climate (i.e., happy, conflicted, etc.) impact FCs?
- What kind of communication is going on backstage (i.e., conversations away from the person that is terminally ill amongst various family dyads) at the EOL?
- How do different death circumstances (i.e., sudden death by accident, suicide, murder, death following Alzheimer's, cancer, heart attacks, strokes, etc.) impact FCs?

HOW DOES THIS WORK IN REAL LIFE?

During EOL Communication:

- Give yourself a reason to listen carefully and avoid distractions (i.e., leave your cell phone in the other room).
- Be other-centered. Focus on the other person's needs and what they want to talk about.
- Stop talking. Once the initial pleasantries are over, try a little silence and see what emerges.
- Ask questions, paraphrase, do some perception checks to make sure that you are really understanding.
- Get out of your own head. Are you thinking about what you should say? Are you trying to say just the right thing? There is no one right thing to say, the goal is not perfection, it is connection.
- Pay attention to their nonverbal behaviors, their actions and expressions will tell you how you are doing, how they are feeling, and often what they are thinking.
- Say what you feel. Speak honestly and authentically. Speak with your heart and mind.
- Show up. Spend as much time as possible with your loved one.

CLASSROOM ACTIVITIES

- Interview your parents (or elders) about their thoughts on communication at the end of life.
  - What are their thoughts on death and dying?
  - Do they believe in an after-life?
  - Do they have a living will? Do they have an advance directive?
  - What kind of memorial service or funeral would they like?
- Watch movies about EOL and write up a reflection paper or talk about the movie in small groups. Suggestions for movies include:
  - *How to Die in Oregon*
  - *Bucket List*
  - *What Dreams May Come*
  - *Meet Joe Black*
- Add a service-learning component to your project by visiting a hospice and interviewing the Social Worker, Chaplain, Director, Volunteer Coordinator, etc. and then writing up your observations and interview(s).

REFERENCES

Baxter, L. A., & Braithwaite, D. O. (2006). Family rituals. In L. Turner & R. West (Eds.), *Family communication: A reference for theory and research* (pp. 259–280). Thousand Oaks, CA: Sage.

Brockmeier, J., & Carbaugh, D. (2001). Introduction. In J. Brockmeier & D. Carbaugh (Eds.), *Narrative and identity: Studies in autobiography, self and culture* (pp. 1–22). Amsterdam, Netherlands: John Benjamins Publishing.

Candrian, C., Tate, C., Broadfoot, K., Tsantes, A., Matlock, D., & Kutner, J. (2017). Designing effective interactions for concordance around end-of-life care decisions: Lessons from hospice admission nurses. *Behavioral Sciences, 7*(2), 22, 1–12. https://doi.org/10.3390/bs7020022

Carstensen, L. L., Isaacowitz, D. M., & Charles, S. T. (1999). Taking time seriously: A theory of socioemotional selectivity. *American Psychologist, 54*(3), 165–181. https://doi.org/10.1037/0003-066X.54.3.165

Davis, C. G., & Nolen-Hoeksema, S. (2001). How do people make sense of loss? *American Behavioral Scientist, 44*(5), 726–741. https://doi.org/10.1177/0002764201044005003

Duck, S. W., Rutt, D. J., Hurst, M. H., & Strejc, H. (1991). Some evident truths about conversations in everyday relationships: All communications are not created equal. *Human Communication Research, 18*(2), 228–267. https://doi.org/10.1111/j.1468-2958.1991.tb00545.x

Fingerman, K. A. (2001). *Mothers and their adult daughters: Mixed emotions, enduring bonds.* New York, NY: Springer.

Fletcher, P. N. (2002). Experiences in family bereavement. *Family Community Health, 25*(1), 57–70. https://doi.org/10.1097/00003727-200204000-00009

Generous, M. A., & Keeley, M. P. (2014). Creating the final conversations (FCs) scale: A measure of end-of-life relational communication with terminally ill individuals. *Journal of Social Work in End-of-Life & Palliative Care, 10*(3), 257–281. https://doi.org/10.1080/15524256.2014.938892

Goldsmith, J., & Ragan, S. L. (2017). Palliative care and the family caregiver: Trading mutual pretense (empathy) for a sustained gaze (compassion). *Behavioral Science, 7*(2), 1–8. https://doi.org/10.3390/bs7020019

Keeley, M. P. (2004a). Final conversations: Messages of love. *Qualitative Research Reports in Communication, 5,* 48–57. https://doi.org/0.1177/0265407507075412

Keeley, M. P. (2004b). Final conversations: Survivors' memorable messages, concerning religious faith and spirituality. *Health Communication, 16*(1), 87–104. https://doi.org/10.1207/S15327027HC1601_6

Keeley, M. P. (2007). "Turning toward death together": The functions of messages during final conversations in close relationships. *Journal of Social and Personal Relationships, 24*(2), 225–253. https://doi.org/10.1177/0265407507075412

Keeley, M. P. (2009). Comfort and community: Two emergent communication themes of religious faith and spirituality evident during final conversations. In M. Wills (Ed.), *Speaking of spirituality: Perspectives on health from the religious to the numinous* (pp. 227–248). Cresskill, NJ: Hampton Press Health Communication Series.

Keeley, M. P. (2016). Family communication at the end of life. *Journal of Family Communication, 16*(3), 1–9. https://doi.org/10.1080/15267431.2016.1181070

Keeley, M. P. (2017). Family communication at the end of life. *Behavioral Science, 7*(3), 1–6. https://doi.org/10.3390/bs7030045

Keeley, M. P., & Baldwin, P. (2012). Final conversations phase II: Children and everyday communication. *Journal of Loss and Trauma, 17*(4), 376–387. https://doi.org/10.1080/15325024.2011.650127

Keeley, M. P., Generous, M., & Baldwin, P. (2014). Exploring children/adolescents' final conversations with dying family members. *Journal of Family Communication, 14*(3), 208-229. https://doi.org/10.1080/15267431.2014.908198

Keeley, M. P., & Generous, M. (2015). The challenges of final conversations: Dialectical tensions during end-of-life family communication from survivor's retrospective accounts. *Southern Communication Journal, 80*(5) (Special Issue on Family and Health), 377–387. https://doi.org/101080/1041794X.2015.1081975

Keeley, M. P., & Generous, M. (2017). Final conversations: Overview and practical implications for patients, families, and healthcare workers. *Behavioral Science, 7*(3), 1–9. https://doi.org/10.3390/bs7020017

Keeley, M. P., & Koenig Kellas, J. (2005). Constructing life and death through final conversations narratives. In L. M. Harter, P. M. Japp, & C. S. Beck (Eds.), *Narratives, health, and healing: Communication theory, research, and practice* (pp. 365–390). Mahwah, NJ: Lawrence Erlbaum.

Keeley, M. P., & Yingling, J. (2007). *Final conversations: Helping the living and the dying talk to each other.* Acton, MA: VanderWyk & Burnham.

Kelley, D. (2003). Communicating forgiveness. In K. M. Galvin & P. J. Cooper (Eds.), *Making connections: Readings in relational communication* (3rd ed., pp. 222–232). Los Angeles, CA: Roxbury.

Koenig Kellas, J. (2010). Transmitting relational worldviews: The relationship between mother-daughter memorable messages and adult daughters' romantic relational schemata. *Communication Quarterly, 58*(4), 458–479. https://doi.org/10.1080/01463373.2010.525700

Koenig Kellas, J., Castle, K. M., Johnson, A., & Cohen, M. Z. (2017). Communicatively constructing the bright and dark sides of hope: Family caregivers' experiences during end of life cancer care. *Behavioral Science, 7*(2), 1–12. https://doi.org/10.3390/bs7020033

Kubler-Ross, E. (1997). *Living with death and dying.* New York, NY: Simon & Schuster.

Levine, S. (1984). *Meetings at the edge: Dialogues with the grieving, and the dying, and the healing and the healed.* New York, NY: Doubleday.

Miller-Day, M. A. (2004). *Communication among grandmothers, mothers, and adult daughters: A qualitative study of maternal relationships.* Mahwah, NJ: Lawrence Erlbaum.

Manusov, V., & Keeley, M. P. (2015). When family talk is difficult: Making sense of nonverbal communication at the end of Life. *Journal of Family Communication, 15*(4), 387–409. https://doi.org/10.1080/15267431.2015.1076424

Marrone, R. (1999). Dying, mourning, and spirituality: A psychological perspective. *Death Studies, 23*(6), 495–519. https://doi.org/10.1080/074811899200858

McQuellon, R. P., & Cowan, M. A. (2000). Turning toward death together: Conversation in mortal time. *American Journal of Hospice & Palliative Medicine, 17*(5), 312–318. https://doi.org/10.1177/104990910001700508

Moller, D. W. (1996). *Confronting death: Values, institutions, & human morality.* New York, NY: Oxford University Press.

Tenzek, K., & Depner, R. (2017). Still searching: A meta-synthesis of a good death from the bereaved family member perspective. *Behavioral Science, 7*(3), 1–18. https://doi.org/10.3390/bs7020025

Trees, A., Ohs, M., & Murray, M. (2017). Family communication about end-of-life decisions and the enactment of the decision-maker role. *Behavioral Sciences, 7*(3), 1–1. https://doi.org/10.3390/bs7020036

Waldron, V., & Kelley, D. L. (2005). Forgiving communication as a response to relational transgressions. *Journal of Social and Personal Relationships, 22*(6), 723–742.

Wood, J. T., & Duck, S. (2006). *Composing relationships: Communication in everyday life.* Belmont, CA: Wadsworth.

PART THREE

Moving Forward TO Develop Mother-Daughter Communication Courses

---

Emphasis must be put on learning; there is no substitution to education. It can be briefly formulated in a few words: always, whatever you do in life, think higher and feel deeper.
—WIESEL (2011)

REFERENCE

Wiesel, E. (2011, September 23). *The Elevator Interview.* Retrieved from https://www.algemeiner.com

CHAPTER TWENTY-ONE

A Mother-Daughter Communication Course Guide

MICHELLE MILLER-DAY[*]

What does it mean to be a good daughter or a good mother? How are these ideals constructed? What if I don't have or want a close relationship with my mom? How can we stay connected as I get older and have my own life? What does a good daughter do? What happens when I lose my mom? What are the best ways to connect with my daughter? What is the best way to talk with her about health? These, among many others, are questions that daughters and mothers may ask themselves as they try to create navigate their identities as mom and/or daughter. In some ways, the mother–daughter relationship holds a curious fascination for women because it promises a key to the understanding of self (Walters, 1992). To understand themselves, many women look first to their relationship with their mother, achieving selfhood by contextualizing it with the mother-daughter relationship (Miller-Day, 2004). Since the relational connection between mothers and daughters is characterized, above all, by communication (Jordan, 1993), mother-daughter communication is an increasingly important area of study.

I have taught a mother-daughter communication course for more than fifteen years and it has never been less than fulfilling. It is often one of the more popular courses in our department, with the final class session of the course dedicated to a

* Michelle Miller-Day, Professor of Communication Studies at Chapman University, millerda@chapman.edu.

mother-daughter party. For this party we invite mothers, grandmothers, and other family members to campus to celebrate, to honor, and to serve as an audience for students' storytelling and other class projects.

A mother-daughter communication course provides both teachers and students a challenging, content course with the potential for important personal insight. The course attempts to provide students with an understanding of how communication functions to develop, maintain, enrich, or limit the mother-daughter relationship. This course highlights a constitutive approach to mother-daughter communication; that is, emphasizing that communication in not just a tool for expressing information within relationships, but it serves to constitute the nature of the mother-daughter relationship itself. In this course students learn that it is through interactions with others that we come to learn what is involved in enacting family roles such as mother and daughter. Although the course tends to draw female students, male students often register for the course and all course assignments can be adapted to examine the mother-son relationship.

This chapter will provide a sample course description, sample syllabi for both a 15-week term and 10-week term, ideas for assignments, and a discussion of a final mother-daughter class party featuring student authored narratives.

SAMPLE COURSE DESCRIPTION

The mother-daughter relationship has been explored in the media and examined in the social sciences. This course challenges students to explore the socially constructed nature of the mother-daughter relationship and provides students with an understanding of how communication functions to develop, maintain, enrich, or limit the mother-daughter relationship. For both daughters and sons, this course relies heavily on class discussion and offers several opportunities for personal application and insight.

Sample Syllabi

The following tables provide an approach for covering the material in this book over a 15-week term and a 10-week term. These outlines presume that the class will meet for at least three hours per week. Table 21.1 shows a sample semester schedule for a 15-week term.

Table 21.1. Sample Semester Schedule—15 Weeks.

WEEK	ASSIGNED READING	TOPICS
1	Introduction	• Introduction to the Course • Overview of course and assignments • Opening climate-building exercises
2	Chapters 1, 2 & 3	• Introduction to Social Constructionism • Daughtering, daughter work, and daughterhood • Mothering, mother work, and motherhood • Framework for understanding mother-daughter communication
3	Chapter 4	• Media messages and the social construction of the mother-daughter relationship • Media viewing (see media analysis assignment)
4	View Media	• Media messages and the social construction of the mother-daughter relationship • Media viewing (see media analysis assignment)
5	Chapter 5	• Mother-daughter turning points • Relational dialectics • Social support as a turning point • View *"The Mother-Daughter Story"* documentary (Weimberg & Ryan, 2010)
6	Chapters 6 & 7	• Pregnancy, identity, and disability • Rituals in adoptive families
7	Chapters 8 & 9	• Communication about sex • Communication about health and sex
8	Study for Exam	EXAM
9	Chapters 10, 11 & 12	• Mother-adult daughter relationships • Sustaining the mother-daughter relationship in adulthood • Technology use and relational maintenance • The mother-daughter relationship after daughter's marriage

(Continued)

Table 21.1. (*Continued*)

10	Chapters 13	• Mother-daughter storytelling • The power of family stories • Stories about love and romance
11	Chapters 14 & 15	• Discursive constructions of motherhood and culture • Social expectations: What is a "good" mother? • Mommy wars
12	Chapters 16 & 17	• Health and mother-daughter communication • Mothers, daughters and breast cancer • HPV conversations
13	Chapters 18	• Motherless daughters • Planning for end of life: 5 wishes
14	Chapters 19 & 20	• View *Complaints of a Dutiful Daughter* (Hoffmann, 1995) or *Mum and Me* (Bourne, 2009) documentary • Communicating at the end of life
15	Prepare student narratives or displays for party	Party and Student Narratives

Source: Author.

The 10-week course represents a fast-paced approach to the material. Some sections may have to be condensed or omitted to accommodate student discussion and experiential approaches. No class session is devoted to an exam. Table 21.2 shows a sample quarter schedule for a 10-week term.

Table 21.2. Sample Quarter Schedule—10 Weeks.

WEEK	ASSIGNED READING	TOPICS
1	Introduction	• Introduction to the Course • Overview of course and assignments • Opening climate-building exercises
2	Chapters 1, 2 & 3	• Introduction to Social Constructionism • Daughtering, daughter work, and daughterhood • Mothering, mother work, and motherhood • Framework for understanding mother-daughter communication

WEEK	ASSIGNED READING	TOPICS
3	Chapter 4	• Media messages and the social construction of the mother-daughter relationship • Media viewing (see media analysis assignment/activity)
4	Chapter 5	• Mother-daughter turning points • Relational dialectics • Social support as a turning point • View "*The Mother-Daughter Story*" documentary (Weimberg & Ryan, 2010)
5	Chapters 6, 7, 8 & 9	• Pregnancy, identity, and disability • Rituals in adoptive families • Communication about sex • Communication about health and sex
6	Chapters 10, 11, 12	• Mother-adult daughter relationships • Sustaining the mother-daughter relationship in adulthood • Technology use and relational maintenance • The mother-daughter relationship after daughter's marriage
7	Chapters 13, 14 & 15	• Mother-daughter storytelling • Discursive constructions of motherhood and culture • Social expectations: What is a "good" mother? • Mommy wars
8	Chapters 16 & 17	• Health and mother-daughter communication • Mothers, daughters and breast cancer • HPV conversations
9	Chapters 18, 19, & 20	• Motherless daughters • Planning for end of life: 5 wishes • View *Complaints of a Dutiful Daughter* (Hoffmann, 1995) or *Mum and Me* (Bourne, 2009) documentary • Communicating at the end of life
10	Prepare student narratives or displays for party	Party and Student Narratives

Source: Author.

IDEAS FOR ASSIGNMENTS

I have found that many students' mothers complete course readings along with their daughters, although this is not something that I ever explicitly request. One of the key ideas to keep in mind when implementing a course like this is not all mother-daughter relationships are balanced and healthy. Encouraging self-reflection is important in this course, but application exercises should include alternatives for students not in contact with or estranged from maternal figures.

Classroom Activities and Discussion Questions

Each of the chapters in this book end with ideas for classroom activities including some take-home assignments ("Classroom Activities/Discussion Questions"). I encourage you to review all the suggestions at the end of each chapter. The activities and discussion questions provided here are a sampling of those used in the classroom by the authors in this book. Always select assignments that feel comfortable for you as an instructor and for your students.

What We Still Need to Know

Read the information in the "What Do We Still Need to Know" section at the end of each chapter. Ask advanced students to design a study that could provide us with the information we still need to know.

Media Analysis Assignments

Compare Films Across the Decades

After reading Chapter 4 (this volume), it is useful to demonstrate some of the contrasting media images of mothers and the mother-daughter relationship in film and television over the decades. The chapter recommends several films and television shows as options. It is recommended that you have a film viewing sheet available (with the APA citation for the film) for each film. The viewing sheet can direct students to observe specific aspects of the films that they can then compare and contrast across the decades. For example, students can compare the following concepts across time: Representation of the sacrificial mother, filial comprehending, sexual objectification of mother, mother as best friend, mother to blame for daughter's misfortune, what is a good mother/daughter? what is a bad mother/daughter?

This analysis can be conducted in class, with a viewing of at least two different films during class time (in a 15-week semester) followed by class discussion. If time is short, shorter television episodes can replace the films, or clips from film or television can be used. Alternatively, students can choose at least three preselected films or television episodes to view on their own and discuss their observations during a class session.

Develop Your Own Television Show

Prior to the class, students can be assigned to invent a new television sitcom or drama and write a one-page synopsis of a pilot episode for this show. Students should describe the main characters and the events taking place during the episode. In class, students can break down into groups and analyze each other's synopses. (1) Does the show have a mother/daughter dyad? (2) If so, what are the theoretically meaningful characteristics of mothers and daughters? (3) To what extent these mothers/daughters are consistent or inconsistent with what we see on the screen today? Discuss how students came up with these characteristics and how these student-based ideas are similar to or different from current media representations and why.

"The Story of Mothers and Daughters" (2010)

View the documentary film "The Story of Mothers and Daughters" (Weimberg & Ryan, 2010) as a class and discuss the different chapters in the documentary. The Story of Mothers & Daughters:

> … is an epic story told in intimate detail. Over 50 women share the most pivotal moments of their lives in this documentary weave of mother/daughter experiences. In the diversity of age, race, and experience, the film reveals the universal threads of the bond that endures over a lifetime. This is a story from cradle to grave, about life and death, love and hate—a story about the essence of what we all feel and what we all share. Produced and directed by an Emmy award winning and Academy Award nominated team, this film was originally aired on ABC and PBS. (Weimberg & Ryan, 2010, p. 1)

A "viewing sheet" handout is recommended with questions or statements directing the students to the elements of the film you wish them to focus on for class discussion. This film can nicely set up the "Identify your Turning Points" activity described at the end of Chapter 4.

Storying the Mother-Daughter Relationship

Family stories serve key ongoing functions in the family's development. In some families, stories serve to teach about values, reinforce identity, discipline or inspire, or create new levels of relationships among members (Koenig Kellas & Trees,

2006). The objective of this assignment is to learn more about your mother/grand-mother's life, how your mother/grandmother was mothered, and how all of this impacted how she mothered her children. This assignment requires students to conduct an oral history interview, gather family stories, and then provide an analysis of these accounts. Provide students with the following information:

> As we have been reading and discussing, mothering practices and the expectations of women as mothers, daughters, and family members have changed over the years. To examine some of these changes with more detail, interview your mother or (mother figure) or your maternal grandmother (or grandmother figure) to solicit HER stories of her relationship with her mother.

The Interview

You can provide a primer on basic interviewing techniques such as:

- Be prepared with your questions.
- Don't just print them out and conduct the interview. KNOW the questions you wish to ask so that you can have a conversation with her.
- Don't ask too many questions, she is the expert on her life and so she should do most of the talking.
- Begin with a very broad, open-ended question such as, "For this assignment, I just want to learn more about your life. Can you tell me the story of your birth?" This will get her talking freely about a topic that she probably feels comfortable talking about. From there you can ask your additional questions.
- All questions should be open-ended. That is, questions that cannot be answered with a yes/no and require longer discourse. Instead of asking, "Where were you born?," ask instead, "Tell me the story of your birth." Additionally, you can provide a sample list of questions that students might use when conducting their interviews to (a) learn more about her life growing up (e.g., What is her birth story? How did she get her name? What are key memories she has of her relationship with her mother? What were the turning points she experienced in her relationship?); (b) learn more about how she was mothered, and how all of this impacted how she mothered her children.

The Paper

In section #1 of the paper ask students to write her mother/grandmother's "story." The student can write out the story reporting the story (e.g., "She was born …") or write it in the first person as if the study was the subject of the story (e.g., I was born …). Section #2 is a discussion of the student's reaction to what was learned. Finally, section #3 of the paper requires students to apply course concepts to story to enhance understanding of her mother/grandmother's experience and how it impacted her mothering. Provide students with the following information:

> After you complete the interview, think about what you have read and what we have discussed in this course. What are some of key concepts that help you understand "her story" better? Select 3–4 concepts from our class (e.g., turning points, daughtering, social construction) that might help you explain or understand what you learned from your mother/grandmother. Did you learn anything that nicely illustrates any of the information we are learning in class? Did you learn anything that might contradict what we are learning in class? Make sure to clearly identify and define each concept and provide a clear application of each concept and discussion of your analysis.

The Five Wishes

This assignment can also be combined with the "Storying the Mother-Daughter Relationship" assignment. The five wishes assignment requires students to talk with their mothers about wishes and plans for when she might need to be taken care of in the future. The assignment requires the student to initiate a dialogue with his/her mother or parents, while they are still capable, about future caregiving desires and arrangements. The first part of the assignment asks the student's mother to visit the "Aging with Dignity" website (https://fivewishesonline.agingwithdignity.org/), order and complete her five wishes online ($5 at the time of this writing). Alternately, students can draft questions they want answered about mother's wishes should she become in need of caregiving (e.g., Who in the family would you want to care for you? Do you have a living will and, if so, where can we find it if something happens to you?) Using her answers to these questions, daughters can begin a conversation about how their mothers wish to be treated if they become seriously ill. Some mothers just do not want to have this discussion. Therefore, an alternative assignment may be considered.

Mothers and Daughters in Fiction

Select five concepts from the class and apply them to a film, novel, play to deepen your understanding of the mother-daughter relationship in the work of fiction. Be sure to clearly identify the concepts, define them, and apply them appropriately to provide insight into the function of communication in mother-daughter fictional relationships. The following are some ideas for sources as of 2018.

Film

There are many films about mothers and daughters to choose from: *Stella Dallas, Now Voyager, Imitation of Life, Marnie, Carrie, Terms of Endearment, Autumn*

Sonata, The Joy Luck Club, Wild at Heart, Thirteen, Pin Cushion, Precious, Tumble-weeds, Mothers and Daughters, White Oleander, Freaky Friday, Bad Moms, Lady Bird, Brave, Mother and Child, Stepmom, Because I said so, and *Mamma Mia.* Avoid science fiction, horror, or "way out" spoofs that do not reflect real life situations.

Novel

Students may select a full-length fictional novel such as: *The Joy Luck Club, My Name Is Lucy Barton, One True Thing, White Oleander, Remind Me Who I Am Again, Dumplin', The Poet X, Moxie,* or *I Am Not Your Perfect Mexican Daughter.*

A Full-Length Play

This may be a play that you view live or on television or merely one that you read. If you view the play, you should also refer to the written text afterward to check dialogue, character, relationships, etc. Some ideas are: *Night Mother, The Glass Menagerie, Memory House, Tongue of a Bird, The Beauty Queen of Leenane, My Mother Said I Never Should, August Osage County, Chalk, Too Much, Too Much, Too Many, On Your Feet,* and *Runaway Home.*

Book Reviews

Ask students to select a book from a list of non-fiction books you have already selected. The book report should be approximately five typewritten pages. Included should be a summary of the book; at least 50 percent of the report should contain a discussion of the material in the book, its application or contradiction to the material covered in the course, and examination of the information using the framework of the student's personal experiences.

End-of-Term Family Party

The end-of-the-term family party is a wonderful way to celebrate the end of the semester or quarter, but also an opportunity to students to enhance their mother-daughter relationship. This is a pot luck party and larger room might need to be reserved for the event. There are three recommended activities, but of course all are optional.

Presentation of Mother-Daughter Narratives

After watching "The Story of Mother and Daughters" or reading chapter 13 (this volume), students can be asked to write their own mother-daughter story. Students can be directed to write about a specific topic (e.g., what I have learned about love from my mother), a specific turning point in their relationship, or write a more comprehensive account of their relationship. Students who are comfortable with their story being read aloud will submit their story for the final party presentation. Of those submitted stories, the teacher will script a presentation no more than 15 minutes in length including excerpts from the submitted stories. Some scripting ideas include: (a) highlighting light-hearted or funny stories at the beginning of the presentation, moving into more serious material, providing the most emotionally charged stories near the end of the piece, with commentary, a poem, or story to pull it all together at the end. No staging is necessary other than a row of chairs for student volunteer readers. Students may wish to provide digital mother-daughter photographs to present as a slideshow during the presentation.

Mother-Daughter Poster Collage

Students may create a physical poster presentation with a collage of photos, quotes, terms, sayings, poems reflecting their mother-daughter relationship. Encourage the student to incorporate concepts from the course. The posters can be displayed throughout the classroom during the party.

What I Love About My Daughter Is ...

At each table or desk provide pencils and a few phrases/prompts to be completed by both daughter and mother. During the party, ask mothers and daughters to share what they wrote with each other. Sample prompts might be: What I love about my mother/daughter is ...; What I most admire about my mother/daughter is ...; What I most want to know from my mother/daughter is ...

Gift

A small mother-daughter gift can be purchased by the instructor and a random drawing during the party selects the mother and daughter recipients. A mother does not have to be present to win the gift. Suggests gifts are mother-daughter charm bracelets or necklaces, two books on the topic of mother-daughter communication, two journals, or a mother-daughter figurine.

SUMMARY

Mother-Daughter communication is central to women's lives and as we learned from the preceding chapters, it can have consequences for women's health. Since communication in the mother-daughter relationship is increasingly studied, there is now ample scholarship to include in a mother-daughter communication course. This course can highlight the social and communicative factors that influence our understanding of and behaviors in important personal relationships over the lifespan. Topics in the course may include defining motherhood and daughterhood, maternal identity, the importance of daughtering, social constructionism, turning points and dialectics in mother-daughter relationships, rituals, sex and sexual health communication, storytelling, technology use and relational maintenance, and communicating at the end of life.

Upon completion of this course, students should be able to (1) explain the socially constructed nature of motherhood/mothering and daughterhood/daughtering, (2) analyze the communicative factors affecting one's own personal relationships, (3) critique the influence of media on social understandings of the mother-daughter relationship, (4) analyze, explain and implement communicative practices related to improving the mother-daughter relationship, and (5) recognize future directions for the study of mother-daughter communication. In a perfect world, mother-daughter relationships would be expertly maintained and in constant repair across the life course. But, until that time courses such as these are important at both a personal and societal level.

REFERENCES

Jordan, J. (1993). The relational self: A model of women's development. In J. van Mens-Verhulst, J. Schreurs, & L. Woertman (Eds.), *Daughtering and mothering: Female subjectivity reanalysed* (pp. 135–144). New York, NY: Routledge.

Koenig Kellas, J., & Trees, A. R. (2006). Finding meaning in difficult family experiences: Sensemaking and interaction processes during joint family storytelling. *The Journal of Family Communication, 6*(1), 49–76.

Miller-Day, M. (2004). *Communication among grandmothers, mothers, and adult daughters: A qualitative study of maternal relationships.* Mahwah, NJ: Lawrence Erlbaum.

Ross, S. J. (2002). *Movies and American society.* Malden, MA: Blackwell.

Walters, S. D. (1992). *Lives together/worlds apart: Mothers and daughters in popular culture.* Berkeley, CA: University of California Press.

Weimberg, G. (Director), & Ryan, C. (Director). (2010). *The story of mothers and daughters* [Motion Picture]. Passion River. Available at http://www.passionriver.com/the-story-of-mothers-and-daughters.html

Contributors

EDITORS

Allison M. Alford (Ph.D., The University of Texas at Austin) is a Clinical Assistant Professor teaching Business Communication at Baylor University. She earned her B.A. in International Studies, Journalism, and French from Texas A&M University (2003) and her M.A. (2005) and Ph.D. (2016) in Communication Studies from The University of Texas at Austin. She has been teaching communication courses at the post-secondary level since 2005. Her primary research focus is on the social construction of roles, looking at adult daughters in relation to their mothers, which she studies using qualitative methodology. In her cross-disciplinary work, she is beginning to examine family roles related to business and professional communication. Current projects include messages from parents to adult children about future careers and communication within family businesses.

Michelle Miller-Day (Ph.D., Arizona State University) is a Professor of Communication Studies at Chapman University. She is also the recipient of the 2015 Bernard J. Brommel Career Award for Outstanding Scholarship and Distinguished Service in Family Communication by the National Communication Association and the 2019 Charles Atkin Translational Health Communication Scholar Award. Dr. Miller-Day's research is funded by the National Institutes of Health and the Centers for Disease Control and Prevention. Her work examines the mother-daughter relationship and health outcomes. Her current work is focused on developing and evaluating health promotion and risk prevention programs. Her cross-disciplinary work spans communication, medicine, family studies, and sociology and she has published numerous peer-reviewed articles, books, and chapters in a variety of outlets.

AUTHORS

Melissa W. Alemán (Ph.D., University of Iowa) is Professor of Communication Studies at James Madison University where she teaches courses in family communication, culture and identity, qualitative methodologies, and women and gender studies. Her published work uses a variety of ethnographic and narrative approaches to examine communication in aging relationships, multicultural families, and educational contexts.

Maria Butauski (M.A., Kent State University) researches how individuals communicate to manage diverse identities. Specifically, she investigates how people communicatively regulate the revealing and concealing of vulnerable information and make sense of their identities and relationships, with focus on health outcomes and contexts. Her research in diverse identities primarily draws from communication privacy management (CPM) theory and communicated narrative sense-making (CNSM) theory with aims to produce resilience-focused, translational research. Maria's work has been published in the *Journal of Family Communication, Communication Studies, Western Journal of Communication,* and *Iowa Journal of Communication.* She has presented her work at regional and national conferences.

Colleen Warner Colaner (Ph.D., University of Nebraska-Lincoln) research centers on discourse dependence and identity formation in diverse families. A major focus of her research is communication in adoptive families, specifically examining how parental communication facilitates the formation of an adoptive identity and sustains open adoption relationships with birth families. Colleen's work has been published in *Communication Monographs, Communication Research, Sex Roles, Journal of Family Communication, and Adoption Quarterly.* She has presented her work and received top paper awards at a number of regional and national conferences. With Dr. Haley Horstman, Colleen is founder and co-director of the Institute of Family Diversity and Communication (www.ifdc.missouri.edu).

Huong Duong (B.A., University of California, Irvine) is a doctoral student at the University of California, Irvine in the Department of Population Health & Disease Prevention. Her research has focused on various aspects of communication around the HPV vaccination and cervical cancer. Her interests lie in cancer prevention, developing communication interventions, and addressing health disparities in minority populations, particularly in the Asian American community. Her current research involves understanding intergenerational health communication in Vietnamese families and designing effective cancer communication interventions in the context of social media messaging platforms.

Sandra L. Faulkner (Ph.D., The Pennsylvania State University) is professor of communication and Director of Women's, Gender, and Sexuality Studies at Bowling Green State University where she writes, teaches and researches about close relationships. Her interests include qualitative methodology, poetic inquiry, and the relationships among culture, identities, and sexualities in close relationships. Her latest books are *Real Women Run: Running as Feminist Embodiment* (Routledge) and *Poetic Inquiry: Craft, Method, and Practice* (forthcoming, Routledge). She received the 2013 Knower Outstanding Article Award from the National Communication Association for her narrative work and the 2016 Norman K. Denzin Qualitative Research Award.

Carla L. Fisher (Ph.D., Pennsylvania State University) is an Associate Professor at the University of Florida and Member of UF Health Cancer Center and Center for Arts in Medicine. Her mother-daughter breast cancer research (www.motherdaughterbreastcancer.com) has received national awards, includes collaborations with leading cancer centers (e.g., Mayo, MSKCC), and been federally funded (e.g., NIA, NIEHS). In 2014 she published *Coping Together Side by Side*, the only evidence-based book using narratives to illustrate healthy communication practice for mothers and daughters when coping with breast cancer or addressing risk across the life span. Her research focuses on building communication resources for families and clinicians to promote better health outcomes and is published in outlets like *Psycho-oncology; Journal of Genetic Counseling; Families, Systems, and Health;* and *Family Medicine.*

Elizabeth Flood-Grady (Ph.D., University of Nebraska-Lincoln) is a Postdoctoral Associate in the STEM Translational Communication Center, College of Journalism and Communications, at the University of Florida. Her research examines interpersonal and family communication processes and outcomes associated with navigating complex health contexts and strategies for developing, promoting, implementing, and evaluating health and science communication interventions, particularly for underserved populations. Her work has been grant-funded and published in several communication and interdisciplinary peer-reviewed journals.

Samantha Garcia (M.P.H., California State University, Northridge) is a doctoral student at the University of California, Irvine in the Department of Population Health & Disease Prevention. Samantha's research focuses on developing, implementing, and testing community-based interventions informed by qualitative data. Recent research projects have included in-depth qualitative interviews investigating HPV decision making among parents of adolescents. Samantha's research focus is on advancing the understanding of health communication among Latina women and its role in cancer disparities.

Mark A. Generous (Ph.D., Arizona State University) is an Assistant Professor in the Department of Communication at California State Polytechnic University, Pomona. His research focuses on challenging, taboo conversations in interpersonal relationships, including: end-of-life communication, sexual communication, and swearing/profanity. He has published in *Health Communication, Southern Communication Journal, Communication Reports, Death Studies*, and other peer-reviewed journals.

Danielle Grainger is a graduate student pursuing an M.S. in Health and Strategic Communication at Chapman University where she teaches Public Speaking in a Diverse Society. She became interested in qualitative communication research when she began working with faculty mentor Dr. Michelle Miller day during her undergraduate studies. Her current research focuses on nature relatedness, self-determination, and substance abuse treatment among emerging adults.

Meredith Marko Harrigan (Ph.D., University of Nebraska-Lincoln) is an Associate Professor in the Department of Communication at the State University of New York College at Geneseo. Her research centers on the intersection of communication, family, and identity and seeks to understand how members of discourse-dependent or nontraditional families communicatively construct and negotiate personal and relational identities. She teaches courses in Interpersonal, Family, Intercultural, Organizational, and Small Group Communication and has published research in a variety of journals, including the *Journal of Family Communication, Social and Personal Relationships*, and *Applied Communication Research*.

Katherine W. Helfrich (M.A., Hood College; M.S.W., Catholic University of America) is Professor Emeritus at Frederick Community College where she taught courses in human relations, psychology, social work and coordinated the Human Services Concentration. She is a licensed social worker and prior to her retirement practiced systems and narrative therapy in family contexts.

Amanda Holman (Ph.D., University of Nebraska-Lincoln) is an Assistant Professor in the Department of Communication Studies at Creighton University. Her research focuses on challenging family and peer relationships to better understand how communication shapes individuals' identity, attitudes, and behaviors. Her work includes understanding communication in emerging adulthood, parent-adolescent relationships, and intimate couples. Dr. Holman has most recently developed a community-based campaign that stems from her work on high school adolescents' perspectives surrounding how parents talk to their children about sexual relationships and health. She has been published in outlets including *Communication Monographs, Health Communication*, and *Journal of Family Communication*.

Suellen Hopfer (Ph.D., The Pennsylvania State University) is an Assistant Professor in the Department of Population Health & Disease Prevention at the University of California, Irvine. Her educational training is in human genetics and health communication. She teaches health and risk communication, and qualitative methods courses. Her research around HPV vaccination includes modeling family and peer communication behaviors, and, designing culturally targeted communication interventions. She has developed a national cancer institute (NCI) recognized research tested intervention program (RTIP) encouraging informed decision-making around HPV vaccination. Other areas of research include modeling family communication in genetic health decision-making and communicating the health impacts of climate change. Two methodologies she often uses in her research involve eliciting decision narratives and latent class modeling to identify subgroups of the population.

Haley Kranstuber Horstman (Ph.D., University of Nebraska-Lincoln) researches communicated sense-making in the context of family diversity and difficulty. She grounds much of her work in narrative theorizing, and often studies diverse families as a context ripe with sense-making. Haley's work has been grant-funded and published in top-ranked peer-reviewed journals such as *Communication Monographs, Health Communication, Journal of Applied Communication Research, Journal of Social and Personal Relationships*, and *Personal Relationships*, Haley has been awarded more than a dozen Top Paper Awards for her work at international, national, and regional communication association conferences. Along with Dr. Colleen Colaner, Haley is a founder and co-director of the Institute of Family Diversity and Communication (www.ifdc.missouri.edu).

Angela M. Hosek (Ph.D., University of Nebraska-Lincoln) is an Associate Professor and Basic Course Director in the School of Communication Studies at Ohio University. Her research interests focus on investigating the extent to which social group categorization impacts relational functioning as people communicate to create, negotiated and express their identities. Overall, her research and teaching interests bring together the content areas of instructional communication, communication education, intergroup communication, interpersonal/family communication, and training and development. Her current research examines student resilience, memorable messages about math education between parents and child and their association to math learning, anxiety and efficacy, hate messages, and the ways in which teachers and students manage their social identities and privacy during interactions whether they are facilitated by face-to-face, out of class or through mediated forms of communication. Her teaching interests focus on intergroup communication, interpersonal communication, family communication, pedagogy, instructional communication, research methods, and training and development. Dr. Hosek has published in *Sage Handbook of Family Communication, Communication Education, Communication Quarterly, Journal of Social and Personal Relationships, Journal of Social Media in Society, Basic Communication Course Annual, Communication Teacher*, and is a co-author of *Human Communication* (McGraw Hill).

Sydney Jacobs (B.A., Chapman University). Since earning her B.A. (2017) in communication studies with a minor in psychology, Sydney has continued her work at a startup music management company, The Artist Group, in Los Angeles, in which she was the first employee at its inception in 2016. While at Chapman, she conducted studies on deceptive communication within dating apps and other interpersonal communication fields including mother-daughter communication.

Maureen P. Keeley (Ph.D., University of Iowa) is a Professor at Texas State University where she conducts research and teaches classes on Interpersonal, Family, Nonverbal, Relational, and Health Communication. Her primary program of research focuses on communication at the end-of-life (EOL) focusing on encouraging and improving communication between family members and their loved ones who are terminally ill. She is considered the preeminent expert on "final conversations" and is at the forefront of EOL communication research. Her published scholarship includes: 1 book, 1 edited journal issue on *EOL Family Communication* for an International Journal, 35 articles, book chapters, and encyclopedia entries in International/National academic journals/edited books. She has won numerous National awards for her scholarship, including 3 "Book of the Year" awards for her co-authored, popular press book. Her work has been covered by media outlets such as *The Washington Post, The Wall Street Journal, and National Public Radio.*

Jody Koenig Kellas (Ph.D., University of Washington) is a Professor at the University of Nebraska-Lincoln and conducts research and teaches classes on interpersonal, family, and health communication. The overarching purpose of her research program is to study the ways in which people communicate to make sense of relationships, difficulty, and health. With this focus, much of her research focuses on how narratives, storytelling, and related forms of communicated sense-making can help individuals and families understand, negotiate, and improve communication and coping within the context of difficulty and illness. Her research lab—NARRATIVE NEBRASKA—seeks to implement interdisciplinary, narrative-based interventions to improve caregiving, communication, and psychosocial well-being for families and care providers. She has published over 50 articles, books, and book chapters and received national awards for her scholarship, including the *Journal of Family*

Communication Article of the Year Award and *National Communication Association Family Communication Division's Distinguished Article Award.*

Lynne Kelly (Ph.D., Pennsylvania State University) is Professor of Communication at the University of Hartford in Connecticut where she teaches a variety of courses including interpersonal communication, computer-mediated communication, organizational communication, and research methods. Her current research interests include communication technologies and relationships, and the impact of communication anxiety and avoidance problems on technology usage. A primary focus of her recent research is on how people manage cell phone usage by co-present friends and romantic partners. She is the recipient of the 2015 Distinguished Teaching Fellow and 2008 Distinguished Research Fellow awards by the Eastern Communication Association.

Denise Lawler (Ph.D., Trinity College Dublin) is Head of Midwifery, Director of Midwifery Programmes and Assistant Professor of Midwifery in School of Nursing and Midwifery at Trinity College Dublin, Ireland where her work centers on pregnancy and disability. Denise is also a member and co-founder of the Meta-synthesis in Midwifery group (MMSG) and a member of the board of the Nursing and Midwifery Board of Ireland. Clinical practice remains a priority as she co-facilitates a midwife-led antenatal clinic in the Coombe Women and Infants University Hospital, one of three large tertiary referral hospitals in Dublin, Ireland.

Lauren Lee (M.A., Texas State University) earned her B.A. (2017) and M.A. (2019) in Communication Studies from Texas State University while also working as a HASTAC Scholar. Her research focuses on the intersection of interpersonal, relational, family, and health communication in a variety of contexts including invisible illness. Lauren is passionate about translational communication research and believes that this approach has the potential to help people make sense of their life experiences and foster meaningful interpersonal relationships.

Megan Meadows (B.A., State University of NY at Geneseo) became interested in the topic of Mother-Daughter relationships while doing research her senior year of undergraduate studies. She is particularly interested in emerging adulthood and how Mother-Daughter relationships change as daughters mature into adults. She and was able to present her research at the James C. McCroskey and Virginia P. Richmond Undergraduate Scholars Conference.

Aimee E. Miller-Ott (Ph.D., University of Nebraska-Lincoln) is an Associate Professor in the School of Communication at Illinois State University. Her research interest centers on how romantic partners and family members manage information and identity with each other. She has examined this dynamic in parent-child and women's relationships, and most recently in foster families and in families with parents with Alzheimer's disease. She also examines the role of cell phones in romantic and family relationships. In this research, she is interested in understanding cell phone rules that relational partners develop and follow and how relational partners manage expectations to give full attention to co-present partners but also to people with whom they are connected through cell phones. She teaches graduate and undergraduate courses in interpersonal communication, family communication, research methods, communication and aging, and the dark side of interpersonal communication.

Kelly G. Odenweller (Ph.D., West Virginia University) is an Assistant Teaching Professor in the Communication Studies program at Iowa State University. She received her B.A. in Communication from the University of Pittsburgh at Johnstown (2004) and her M.A. (2011) and Ph.D. (2015) in Communication Studies from West Virginia University. She teaches courses on interpersonal relationships, gendered issues, and professional communication skills. She researches communication within and about families, with an emphasis on gender socialization, mothers' and fathers' gendered roles and relationships, and social change for men and women. Her research has been published in *Journal of Family Communication, Communication Studies*, and *Southern Communication Journal*.

Christine E. Rittenour (Ph.D., University of Nebraska-Lincoln) researches intergroup and family communication dynamics within the family, including how differences within the family (e.g., in-laws, intergenerational, gender, values) link to communication, and also how family socializes its members about difference (e.g., prejudice, feminism, generativity). She received her B.A. at Pennsylvania State University, M.A. at West Virginia University, and PhD at the University of Nebraska-Lincoln. She is an Associate Professor in the Department of Communication Studies at West Virginia University.

Leah M. Seurer (Ph.D., University of Denver) is an Assistant Professor in the Department of Communication Studies at The University of South Dakota. Her work takes a critical approach to intersections of family and health communication by examining how relational and cultural discourses circulating within the family construct meanings for familial relationships and illness within the family. Her work has been published in journals such as *Communication Monographs* and *Journal of Family Communication*.

Riva Tukachinsky (Ph.D., University of Arizona). Her research lies in the realm of media psychology, examining media representations of various social issues and their possible impact on media consumers. Specifically, she conducts qualitative and quantitative analysis of entertainment media, advertising and news, and examines affective and cognitive mechanisms underlying the effect of these media on audiences' well-being, self, and social identity. Her research has been published in outlets such as *Journal of Communication, Communication Yearbook*, and *Journal of Social Issues*.

Wendy K. Watson (Ph.D., Texas Tech University) is an Associate Professor of Gerontology at Bowling Green State University. She is the program coordinator of both the undergraduate and graduate programs in Gerontology at BGSU. Her research interests include women's experiences with new, intimate relationships in mid and later life with a focus on dating, remarriage, sexuality, and sexual decision-making. She is also interested in identity development for women as they negotiate these new relationships, as well as other life course transitions throughout adulthood and later life.

Bianca M. Wolf (Ph.D., University of Iowa) is an Associate Professor in Communication Studies at the University of Puget Sound. Her research intersects family and health communication. Prior to receiving her Ph.D., she worked in health care as a practice management, software, and billing expert and later a product and software expert in the insurance field. She has studied and taught health communication in a variety of contexts including cancer communication among family members (i.e., mother-daughter), patient-provider communication, and persuasion and influence in interpersonal and media health risk messages. She has co-authored an empirically based communication skills textbook for dental professionals. She has presented her work at national and international health forums and been published in revered journals like Psycho-Oncology and Qualitative Health Research. Her work is largely translational and interdisciplinary.

Seungji Yang (B.A., SUNY Geneseo) was born in Daegu, South Korea. She graduated with a bachelor's degree in Personal and Professional Communication in 2016 from the State University of New York College at Geneseo. She is mostly interested in studying Family Communication and Interpersonal Communication. Previously, she participated in the research of work-life conflicts experienced by working parents. She plans to pursue her Master's and Ph.D. in Communication Studies and is in the process of preparing for a graduate program.

Subject Index

A

Addams Family, The, 60
adolescence, 9, 60, 78, 135, 149, 152, 164, 168, 172, 179, 200, 296
adoption, 8, 111–126
    adoption rituals, 8, 112–126
agency, 21, 26, 31, 38, 47, 51
asynchronous technology, 168
autonomy. *See* relational dialectics

B

bad mom, 7, 47, 63, 79
    see also expectations
    see also good enough mothering
Bad Moms, 63, 261, 356
birth, 7, 8, 26–27, 30, 39, 50, 52, 76, 81, 89, 102–107, 111–124, 217, 260, 354
blame, 3, 45, 61–62, 77–78, 352
boundaries, 8, 22, 27, 52, 67, 80, 130–131, 133, 166, 168, 192–193, 276
    metaphoric boundaries, 8, 131

see also Communication Privacy Management Theory
breast cancer, 10, 265–277, 327, 350–351

C

caregiving, 4, 7, 20–21, 33, 39, 48, 82, 89, 136, 139, 212, 219, 226, 253, 256, 258–259, 268, 284, 314–317, 321–324, 328–330, 336, 355
Carrie, 71
Cheers, 60
childhood, 8, 37, 75–76, 99, 105–106, 124, 135, 200, 228, 296
Communicated Narrative Sense-Making Theory, 218–219
Communication Privacy Management Theory, 130–131, 166, 182, 201
conflict, 9, 12, 23, 26, 77–78, 80, 89, 104, 171–172, 200, 201, 212, 228, 252, 267
connectedness, mother-daughter, 4, 5, 8–10, 22–23, 27, 49, 51, 69, 77, 80, 84, 89, 165, 168–169, 171–175, 181, 189, 191, 199–211, 247, 265–266, 304–308, 328, 330, 347

LIFESPAN
COMMUNICATION
Children, Families, and Aging

Thomas J. Socha, *General Editor*

From first words to final conversations, communication plays an integral and significant role in all aspects of human development and everyday living. The Lifespan Communication: Children, Families, and Aging series seeks to publish authored and edited scholarly volumes that focus on relational and group communication as they develop over the lifespan (infancy through later life). The series will include volumes on the communication development of children and adolescents, family communication, peer-group communication (among age cohorts), intergenerational communication, and later-life communication, as well as longitudinal studies of lifespan communication development, communication during lifespan transitions, and lifespan communication research methods. The series includes college textbooks as well as books for use in upper-level undergraduate and graduate courses.

Thomas J. Socha, Series Editor | *tsocha@odu.edu*
Kathryn Harrison, Acquisitions Editor | *kathryn.harrison@plang.com*

To order other books in this series, please contact our Customer Service Department at:

(800) 770-LANG (within the U.S.)
(212) 647-7706 (outside the U.S.)
(212) 647-7707 FAX

Or browse online by series at www.peterlang.com

Made in the USA
Las Vegas, NV
09 January 2024

84150897R00216